THE HMONG
IN TRANSITION

THE HMONG IN TRANSITION

edited by

Glenn L. Hendricks
Bruce T. Downing
Amos S. Deinard

1986
Center for Migration Studies of New York, Inc.
The Southeast Asian Refugee Studies of the University of Minnesota

THE HMONG IN TRANSITION

A joint publication of the
Center for Migration Studies
of New York, Inc. and the
Southeast Asian Refugee
Studies Project of the
University of Minnesota

First Edition
Copyright © 1986 by

The Center for Migration Studies of New York, Inc.

Center for Migration Studies
209 Flagg Place
Staten Island, New York 10304

ISBN 0-913256-94-3 (hardcover)
ISBN 0-913256-95-1 (paperback)
Library of Congress Catalog Card No. 85-47918
Printed in the USA

TABLE OF CONTENTS

* Indicates invited Conference keynote speaker

PREFACE

The second Hmong Research Conference, held at the University of Minnesota on November 17-19, 1983, drew four hundred people. While this number was far beyond our expectations, perhaps we shouldn't have been surprised. The presence of more than sixty thousand Hmong in the United States--all engaged in the struggle to exist in a culture whose social, political and economic structures are so different from their own--has attracted attention from many groups. Among them are educators, academic researchers, shop owners, social workers, church congregations, appreciators of the arts, health care providers, landlords and neighbors. Their interests range from seeking solutions for immediate resettlement problems such as providing medical care to theoretical considerations of the structure of the Hmong language.

The conference, entitled "The Hmong in Transition," had as its focus the formal presentation of the research papers collected in this volume. It also encouraged informal exchanges between those involved in helping the Hmong resettle in all parts of the country. How much help is too much help, they asked of each other. Can the Hmong adapt to a new culture and also preserve their traditions? What will become of Hmong children who are being taught one set of values at home and another at school? Will the Hmong be caught in the vicious cycle of poverty that afflicts some other minority groups in this country?

When this book is published, it will be almost ten years since the first mass exodus of Hmong from Laos, precipitated by the communist Pathet Lao takeover of the Laotian government. Scholars have now had almost a decade to study the effects of this upheaval on the Hmong not only in the United States but also in other places of their exile around the world. This volume includes information about Hmong in France, Australia and Thailand as well as the United States. Particularly noteworthy is that the Hmong, whose history was borne for centuries only in the hearts and minds and spoken words of its people, have now been surrounded by the written word. The papers prepared for this conference are but one example of their incorporation into mankind's written records.

The international scope of the Hmong dispersion was reflected in the backgrounds of the three invited speakers to the conference: Jacques Lemoine is associated with the School of Advanced Studies in the Social Sciences of the University of Paris; Robert Cooper is a British citizen working for the United Nations High Commissioner for Refugees in Geneva; and Gary Yia Lee, a Hmong trained as anthropologist, is a leader of the Hmong community in Australia.

The conference was sponsored by the Southeast Asian Refugee Studies Project, a research oriented group of academics, established to encourage, coordinate, and support research related to refugees from Southeast Asia who have been resettled in the United States. It is funded primarily by the Center for Urban and Regional Affairs at the University of Minnesota. Additional support for the conference came from the College of Liberal Arts. A generous grant from the National Endowment for the Humanities enabled us to bring the three invited speakers to the United States.

The editors are particularly indebted to the editorial assistance of Ruth Hammond, who helped to bring consistency and readability to the twenty-five papers included in this volume. They were written by individuals trained in a variety of disciplines, each accustomed to using widely varying writing formats and language in the presentation of their research. Since we were aware that a large number of readers of this book would not be academics, one of our chief aims in editing was to make readable the sometimes esoteric, if not idiosyncratic, language some consider the hallmark of academia. Ruth Hammond's considerable experience as a writer and journalist has been instrumental in helping us to achieve our goal of readability.

This volume, a joint production of the Center for Migration Studies and the Southeast Asian Refugee Studies Project is also a departure from usual production methods in publishing a book. SARS not only provided the edited version of the papers but also prepared the papers in camera-ready format. This demanded more than typical typist skills and we are indebted to Pamela Anderson, without whose abilities we could not have given this

type-set appearance to the book. In addition, Douglas
Olney provided a great deal of the technical knowledge of
computers and word processing which allowed us to attempt
this format. The cartographic skills of Carol Gersmehl
provided us with the map indicating areas of Hmong settlement in Southeast Asia and the location of the major
refugee camps in Thailand in which Hmong have been
housed.

For those seeking more background information about
the Hmong other easily available sources include the proceedings of the First Hmong Research Conference, published as The Hmong in the West (1982), published by the
Center for Urban and Regional Affairs, University of
Minnesota, 301 19th Avenue South, Minneapolis, Minnesota
55455, plus these additional publications:

Barney, G. Linwood. 1967. "The Meo of Xieng Khouang
    Province, Laos." In Southeast Asian Tribes, Minor-
    ities, and Nations, edited by Peter Kunstadter, pp.
    271-294. Princeton: Princeton University Press.

Center for Applied Linguistics. 1979. "Glimpses of Hmong
    History and Culture." Indochinese Refugee Education
    Guides, General Information Series #16. National In-
    dochinese Clearinghouse. Washington, D.C.: Center
    for Applied Linguistics.

Dunnigan, Timothy. 1982. "Segmentary Kinship in an Ur-
    ban Society: The Hmong of St. Paul-Minneapolis. An-
    thropological Quarterly, Vol. 55(3), pp. 126-136.

Geddes, William. 1976. Migrants of the Mountains: The
    Cultural Ecology of the Blue Miao (Hmong Njua) of
    Thailand. Oxford: Clarendon Press.

Also, a discussion on Hmong orthography can be found in
Part Three, Language and Literacy, on pages 217-218.

                                   - Glenn L. Hendricks
                                   Minneapolis, Minnesota
                                   August 1985

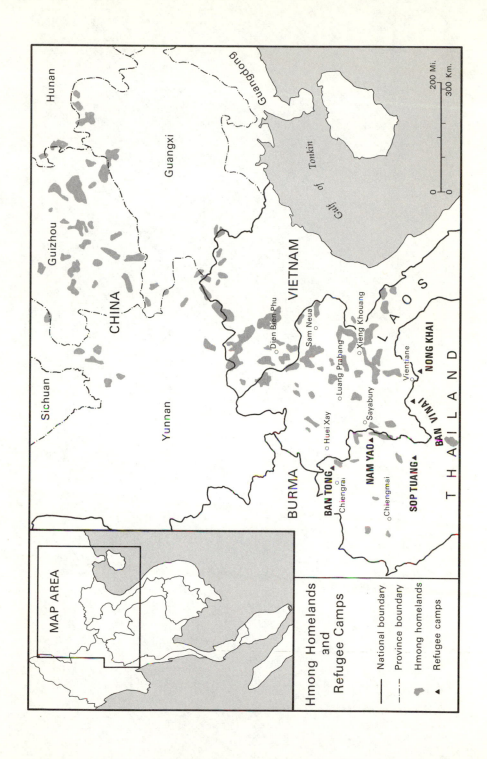

Hunan

Guizhou

Sichuan

CHINA

Yunnan

Guangxi

Guangdong

Gulf of Tonkin

VIETNAM

Dien Bien Phu

Sam Neua

Xieng Khouang

Luang Prabang

L A O S

NONG KHAI

Vientiane

Sayabury

BAN VINAI

Huei Xay

NAM YAO

SOP TUANG

THAILAND

BURMA

BAN TONG

Chiengrai

Chiengmai

200 Mi.

300 Km.

MAP AREA

Hmong Homelands
and
Refugee Camps

National boundary

Province boundary

Hmong homelands

Refugee camps

PART ONE

Hmong Culture and Change

INTRODUCTION

GLENN L. HENDRICKS

A common theme that emerged throughout the conference in both the papers and subsequent discussions was that of the identification of what is representative of Hmong culture and how it has changed in the period of the diaspora. Too frequently some observers and commentators of the Hmong have failed to understand that the concept of culture implicitly assumes it is dynamic and that over time varying degrees of change will take place in any society. The rate that the change takes place is a function of the historical situation as well as attributes of the culture itself. The failure to understand this leads some to think in terms of before and after, that there was a traditional almost unchanging way of Hmong living that has been severely altered by the events of the period of flight and subsequent resettlement. That Hmong life has been radically altered cannot be disputed but the change must be seen as a matter of degree. The papers in this section provide a needed corrective in assisting us to gain a longer perspective of Hmong society, particularly in the nineteenth and twentieth centuries.

It should be noted that these papers, while focusing on aspects of Hmong society and culture, touch on some basic issues in the social sciences. Namely, what is the nature of culture? What constitutes cultural change? What is the relationship between culture and ethnic identity? Can change be directed in such fashion that it becomes disruptive of neither culture nor ethnic identity? We need not discuss these issues here but the careful reader will discern distinct, if not opposing, viewpoints among the authors of the papers that follow. But the issue of change is not necessarily the exclusive arena of the academic. A central question asked by most of those who are involved in the resettlement of Hmong refugees has been how to accomplish the process while allowing them to maintain their distinctive identity as Hmong. These papers provide food for thought for those responsible for making decisions about the immediate issues

3

such as providing housing or deciding who can speak for the Hmong.

William Smalley, a linguist who first became involved with the Hmong over thirty years ago while working on a project to provide a written form of the Hmong language, sketches out a series of stages that he sees as part of the transformation of that part of the Hmong society that migrated to the West. He points out that changes had begun to evolve long before the ultimate flight from Laos. Varying forms of individual and group behavior in the new setting can be understood, at least partially, as a function of events in the past. Contrasting patterns of community leadership that have emerged in various areas of resettlement around the United States can be traced to both the introduction of education in Laos and the way in which refugee camps in Thailand were organized.

Robert Cooper, a British anthropologist who has worked among the Hmong in both Thailand and Laos, presents data arguing that in addition to the commonly understood political reasons for the Hmong flight from Laos there were also economic motivations for the move. His thesis is that in examining historical, empirical and observational data there are grounds for concluding that conditions in Laos were such that the land could no longer support the traditional agricultural economic basis of Hmong life. This paper proved to be the most widely discussed presentation of the Conference, with many of the Hmong present disputing his interpretation of the facts and events cited.

Timothy Dunnigan, an anthropologist who has been keenly interested in the Hmong since they first arrived in the Twin Cities in 1975, carries our discussion of the impact of resettlement on Hmong culture further. He discusses the process by which they are maintaining their ethnic identity even while some of the attributes which are said to be markers of being traditional Hmong are in the process of change. In some cases what appear to be significant changes in group organization, for example, he identifies as latent attributes of Hmong culture which have manifested themselves in previous situations of Hmong history when their ethnic identity was threatened.

Gary Yia Lee, part of the small Hmong group that migrated to Australia, was educated there and earned his

doctorate in anthropology at the University of Sydney.
Subsequently he has been a leader of the Hmong community
of Australia. In both his presentation and his comments
on others' papers he was able to give a valuable insider/
outsider's perspective to our discussions. He argues
that, in the Australian case at least, there are indeed
significant changes in the economic basis of Hmong life,
social structure and religious beliefs. However, this
need not portend a destruction of their identity as
Hmong, but rather must be seen as an adaptation to
changing circumstances.

A particularly valuable contribution to the participants of this Conference was the presentation by Louisa
Schein about the Miao (Hmong) in contemporary China. It
was from this group, or at least parts of this group,
that the Hmong of Laos, Thailand and Vietnam migrated
during the eighteenth and early nineteenth century.

Nicholas Tapp, another British-trained anthropologist, who has worked for several years studying Hmong in
northern Thailand, examines geomancy, the practice of
divination based upon geographical and spatial features,
and its historical place as an attribute of Hmong culture. He points out that while the practice has its roots
in China, it is but one of many factors to be taken into
account in any discussion which assume a "ideal" or traditional Hmong culture against which any change might be
measured.

STAGES OF HMONG CULTURAL ADAPTATION

William A. Smalley

Americans who have had contact with Hmong in the United States are often aware that massive change has come to these new immigrants as they have settled here. However, many of these same Americans are unaware of the changes in Hmong life and culture which took place in Laos and in the Thailand camps over the last generation, and before.

I, for example, had had some minimal contact with Hmong in Laos in the early 1950s, but was puzzled at what seemed to be very different leadership patterns exhibited in Lao Family Community and its layers of Hmong organization in the Twin Cities. I was slow to realize how much the Hmong learned during the years of military action, wartime migration and resettlement in Laos and camp life in Thailand. On the other hand, I occasionally see the opposite extreme of this limited understanding in other Americans who write about aspects of Hmong life that developed in the disruptions of the sixties or seventies as though they were "traditional."

THE STAGES

In what follows I would like to suggest several rather self-evident stages in the modern historical changes which are part of Hmong experience. Each stage manifests certain typical innovations, some of which will be pointed out later.[1]

1. Laos penetration stage: The time when the Hmong were moving into Laos, when they were oriented more to China and/or North Vietnam, when there were relatively small numbers, when they had to begin to learn to cope with new ethnic groups and new power structures around them, notably those of the Lao and the French.

2. Laos traditional stage: The period when the Hmong
    had become a significantly large ethnic group in
    Laos, but when they kept to their mountains as much
    as possible, and largely avoided contact with more
    powerful groups.

3. Laos adaptive stage: The period when a somewhat
    stable relationship had been estabished between the
    Hmong and other ethnic groups, when they had learned
    ways of coping with such groups, and when they were
    seeking more aggressively to take a significant place
    in the larger life of the Lao state.

4. Laos resettlement stage: The period when increasing
    percentages of the Hmong population were forced out
    of their villages into resettlement conglomerations
    where they typically were mingled with peoples from
    other ethnic groups, where the exercise of some tra-
    ditional cultural patterns was curtailed, and where
    new cultural forces were brought to bear on them with
    great suddenness and intensity.

5. Thailand camp stage.

6. United States resettlement stage.

     I have deliberately not set dates for these stages.
They are not discrete periods of time, nor did they take
place at exactly the same time for all Hmong in all parts
of Laos.   Some Hmong people, some villages, some families
were in the Laos adaptive stage when other families, other villages, other people were still in the Laos penetration stage.   In 1974, when he was an official in the Lao
coalition ministry of planning, Yang Dao (personal communication) found Hmong in border areas of Laos who still
knew Chinese but not Lao.   He discovered this case of the
Laos penetration stage at the same time that many Hmong
elsewhere were in the Laos resettlement stage.
     Most Hmong who have reached the United States be-
long, or did belong, to groups which went through all or
most of these stages.   Presumably, very few of these individuals remember when their community was in the Laos
penetration stage, but all the other stages have been
experienced by the older people, and all Hmong in the

United States are products of this history, with some individuals and groups having been more strongly influenced by developments in one stage or another.

THE PEOPLE OF MOOS PLAIS

In the early 1950s there was a cluster of four Hmong villages two days travel (but only sixty miles direct flight) north of Luang Prabang, the Royal Capital of Laos. This cluster is usually called Moos Plais[2] by its former inhabitants now in the Twin Cities. The villages at Moos Plais were relatively stable and prosperous. There was enough land so that people did not have to migrate. They had a surplus rice crop, raised animals and grew opium. I would like to illustrate briefly the stages of adaptation by reciting a few bits of these people's experience.

At least three developments epitomized the transition of Moos Plais from the Laos traditional stage to the Laos adaptive stage. The earliest to develop was regular and frequent trade relations with the Lao. The traditional Laos period included extensive trade, of course. But in the Laos adaptive stage, Hmong did not depend so exclusively on traders coming to them; they also went to Lao towns in very much larger numbers and with greater frequency.

Next was cooperation with the French/Lao military effort. Initially it was simply a matter of Hmong men patrolling under the leadership of their own headmen to ambush occasional bands of Pathet Lao and to defend their villages, but during the early 1950s the French/Lao forces set up a multi-ethnic garrison at Moos Plais, with ten French officers led by a colonel. Lao officers and technicians were also stationed there, as were troops from other mountain peoples in addition to Hmong. Helicopters began to come with increasing frequency. An airstrip was built, shortening the trip from Luang Prabang to a few minutes. Eventually the Lao and French officers at Moos Plais were replaced by Hmong under the command of General Vang Pao, and the garrison was supplied by American pilots.

The third major indication of the Laos adaptive stage was in the establishment of a Lao school in Moos

Plais.   This provided only two years of education, but
for the first time almost all of the boys and many of the
girls began to learn the rudiments of reading and writing
Lao, together with a little arithmetic and Lao civics.   A
small number of boys who showed aptitude and were otherwise suitable then went to live with Lao contacts or
friends in nearby Lao towns to continue their education.

The Laos Resettlement Stage

    Some of the older men from Moos Plais now living in
the Twin Cities look back on the late period of the Laos
traditional stage and the Laos adaptive stage as their
golden age.   They were prosperous; they sensed progress
and change, but they were able to cope; they had a sense
of accomplishment and of power.
    But by about 1967[3] the military garrison at Moos
Plais was forced to withdraw, and most of the villagers
(about 160 people) went with them.   They left everything
they could not carry or lead.   After a day's walk they
reached Mom Phuv, a large Hmong village south of Moos
Plais, which also had a military garrison and an airstrip.   Their military garrison from Moos Plais joined
that of Mom Phuv, and the civilians camped in tents supplied by the military.   They were completely dependent;
all of their food was airlifted in.
    Thus began, on a small scale for these Hmong from
Moos Plais, the Laos resettlement stage.   Other refugees
from nearby areas joined them, fleeing their own villages.   Their settlement was a small example of what
Ajchenbaum and Hassoun (1979) have called an "agglomera-
tion de guerre," and what I will call a conglomeration.
It was characterized by the intermingling of Hmong groups
who themselves did not know each other, in the same community with still other different ethnic groups (Khmu',
Mien, Thai Dam, Lao).   The military provided what overall
organization there was.   In this particular case the
rainy season, the uncertainty about the future and the
danger made farming and other normal economic activity
impossible, so that all food and other supplies were
flown in.
    In scarcely two months the whole Mom Phuv conglomer-
ation had to move on again as the military situation once
more became impossible and the combined garrison with-

drew. Their move formed a new conglomeration at Toos Tub, another Hmong village with a garrison strategically located in the mountains above the confluence of the Nam Ou (Lao: Ou River) with the Mekong, only twenty miles north of Luang Prabang. This conglomeration lasted six months, during which time it was regularly surrounded by heavy fighting and suffered many casualties. Its numbers continued to be swelled by more diverse groups which joined as they fled their earlier settlements and con-glomerations.

Finally, the civilians were flown out of Toos Tub to a safer destination, leaving the military forces to help defend Luang Prabang. They settled along the Nam Poui (Lao: Poui River), in an area that was across the Mekong River from Moos Plais, toward the Thai border and about thirty miles southwest of the provincial capital of Sayaboury.[4] The people flown in from Toos Tub joined a small population of Lao and Hmong already in the area, which had not been appreciably affected by the war. Through further influx of displaced people, the popula-tion in this new conglomeration eventually increased to eight thousand or nine thousand.

Nam Poui was more systematically and more permanent-ly built than the previous conglomerations in which its new residents had settled. Lao and United States aid of-ficials laid out the town in blocks.[5] People from dif-ferent ethnic groups lived in different parts of town. Within the Hmong section, the people originally from Moos Plais lived together and preserved the social structures they brought with them, under the same family and village leaders.

United States aid provided some animals for breeding and seed to plant both irrigated and mountain rice fields. Within a few months the people were growing their own food and were beginning to develop cash pro-duce, primarily in pigs. The government and the American aid program extended a road into the community, helped in the development of irrigated lands and built public buildings, including a school. Lao, Chinese and Indian merchants built stores and moved in.

In many important ways the conglomeration at Nam Poui was very different from the constricted and badly overpopulated larger conglomerations such as Long Cheng, in the heart of the war zone. Nam Poui had a similar mixture of population (without the resident Americans) and a similar dominant military umbrella, but stress levels were lower, and it became economically self-suffi- cient.   Ultimately it did not have to be supplied with food by the government, and it began to prosper.

In terms of adaptation, Nam Poui shared with the other semipermanent conglomerations an increased exposure to nontraditional technology and material goods, greater opportunity for Lao education of the children, signifi- cant interaction with non-Hmong, and an overarching poli- tical structure which was supplied by the military, but which allowed traditional village and family structures (when they were still intact) to operate on a lower lev- el.   In this mixed environment, spurred by the needs cre- ated through displacement, many Hmong rapidly learned things and became used to conditions they had never known before.

Nam Poui was settled about 1968.   In 1975, some weeks after General Vang Pao left Laos, most of the con- glomeration of Nam Poui left en masse for Thailand.   The caravan of several thousand people crossed the border, was disarmed by the Thai, and was resettled in a location that became the camp called Sop Tuang.

The Thailand Camp Stage

At Sop Tuang, life was in some respects a continua- tion of the Nam Poui conglomeration.   Most of the origi- nal refugees moved in together, and as they built Sop Tuang, they followed the organizational patterns they had been using at Nam Poui.   The same Hmong major who had been in charge of the garrison at Nam Poui and who had been the overall leader of the conglomeration was also the Hmong person in charge here under the Thai authori- ties.   The same settlement by ethnic groups took place. These ethnic groups continued to be organized under the leadership each had brought with it.   New refugee groups were added from time to time, as had happened in Nam Poui.   They came as villages or other sizable, previously existing groups--not as individuals, small family groups or parts of families.

What was different about Sop Tuang, as compared to Nam Poui, was that now the groups had constraints result- ing from their status as refugees in a different country.

Placed above the social structure imported from Nam Poui was a level of authority responsible to the Thai government. A Thai military officer presided over the camp, and Thai soldiers were stationed there.

Furthermore, in Nam Poui the Lao and United States governments had provided money, goods and personnel to help lay out and build the community and get the people started. But the people of the conglomeration had been able to outgrow the need for extensive economic help. At Sop Tuang, after an initial period of inaction, the Thai government, the United Nations High Commissioner for Refugees, and numerous religious and charitable agencies gathered to provide food, medical care, education, sanitation, opportunities for economic development and essential supplies of material goods. Here was a loosely-knit group of organizations, sometimes cooperating, often competing, which the refugees had to learn to depend on for survival.

The most significant difference from Nam Poui, so far as the people were concerned, was that there was insufficient economic opportunity for them. Some men were able to take advantage of the limited opportunities for employment within and outside of camp, and women could sell their handiwork to some extent,[6] but neither endeavor was adequate to solve financial needs.

The experience of the villagers from Moos Plais at Camp Sop Tuang was in several important ways different also from that of Hmong in the much larger, more densely settled and more important camp of Ban Vinai. Refugees who arrived at Ban Vinai tended to come in small clusters, accompanied by only fragments of their social groupings. Unlike those at Sop Tuang, they often had to travel through Pathet Lao areas, had to hide out in the jungle for long periods, started out malnourished and arrived starving. They had to break up into small groups to avoid detection, and many groups and individuals who headed for that part of Thailand never did arrive. When people did reach Ban Vinai there may have been members of their social groups already there, but the newcomers had to take whatever housing location was available, and could not live in groupings to which they were accustomed.

So the lower rungs of leadership that existed under the top levels of Thai control and the formal organization of Ban Vinai, were set up somewhat differently from those at Sop Tuang. Both camps were divided into sectors. In Sop Tuang the sectors were natural ones (in terms of preexistent groupings) with people clustered in somewhat familiar ways.[7] In Ban Vinai people belonged to whatever sector they happened to be assigned housing in.[8] As families or villages were reunited at Ban Vinai, they did, of course, reestablish older relationships, and a considerable part of the informal structure of the camp was made up of such groups in spite of their scattered residence. The formal structure, however, did not match the informal structure as well as they matched at Sop Tuang. An important related difference between Sop Tuang and Ban Vinai was in the part played by the educated youth at Ban Vinai. In the years immediately preceding the initial evacuation of 1975, there had been about six hundred Hmong students in Vientiane. They had formed a student association as a mutual assistance group. As they evacuated to Thailand and eventually ended up in Ban Vinai they were very important in organizing and running some of the necessary functions of camp life. They assisted in food distribution, camp cleanup and sanitation, and they took over education of the children, as well as English classes for everyone.

It seems that they were in a strategic place for two reasons: their education better prepared them for some aspects of this new situation, and the shredded social structures perhaps left a vacuum in leadership and potential for action on some levels of camp life. In Ban Vinai, as at Sop Tuang, the Hmong military provided the leadership at the top. Below that, in Ban Vinai, the functions served by the youth group were eventually absorbed into the more formal structure of the camp or, in the case of education, were taken over by the Thai. Furthermore, the contribution was temporary because the educated youth often went on to other countries sooner than many others. But for a while they were critical to the functioning of the camp.[9]

At Sop Tuang, on the other hand, the youth as a group were of little importance in the operation of the camp. They occupied a much more traditional relationship to the community, I am suggesting, because community patterns had not been shredded in the migration, and also because there was not as large a nucleus of students more acculturated than their elders as there was at Ban Vinai.

The United States Resettlement Stage

The only aspect of the United States resettlement stage on which I'll take time to comment is one regarding the evolution of the role of the youth at Ban Vinai. It is the difference in Hmong leadership and social organization between Dallas-Fort Worth, Texas, and Minneapolis-St. Paul, Minnesota, reported by Mason and Downing (Mason 1983; Downing 1983). In Dallas-Fort Worth, a strong youth group operating under young leadership performs adaptive and supportive functions somewhat parallel to those carried out by the youth groups of Vientiane, Nam Phong and Ban Vinai. There is no mutual assistance association controlled by elders. In the Twin Cities of Minneapolis-St. Paul, however, although some of the leaders of the same group which was active in the camp are present, there is no significant youth leadership for the Hmong community. Instead, the primary leadership comes from a variety of older types, including the former military and former people of influence in Laos, as well as people emerging in the American situation.

As for the people of Moos Plais who are now in the Twin Cities, certain aspects of the social structure which they maintained throughout moves to Mom Phuv, Toos Tub, Nam Poui and Sop Tuang still govern their relationships here. This is supplemented by tenuous ties to the Lao Family Community and its network of relationships, all under the umbrella of an American system about which the people of Moos Plais are learning, but still understand very little.

TYPICAL INNOVATIONS OF THE STAGES

Here follows, then, a sketchy list of the innovations which I see as being characteristic of the stages. I do not know much about the Laos penetration stage, but presumably those Hmong who knew an outside language spoke a Chinese language or Vietnamese, depending on where they came from. They were small in number, kept much to themselves, and had infrequent contacts with the Lao or French.[10]

In the Laos traditional stage Hmong had established trade patterns with Haw, Lao and Chinese traders who came to their villages, but there was minimal travel to Lao towns, minimal learning of the Lao language, and minimal contact with the Lao/French military and government. The contact they did have included paying tribute that consisted of mountain and jungle products (Yang 1975:45). Yang Dao reports that the first low-level district officer (tasseng) was appointed as early as 1896, although it was not until much later that this practice became widespread. Hmong numbers, however, were increasing rapidly, and some Hmong did experience some severe conflicts with the French/Lao, notably the revolt of 1919 to 1921. Hmong cultivation of the poppy for the opium trade became economically very important in the country.

In the Laos adaptive stage, major changes, which significantly began to alter the position and role of at least some Hmong in Laos, took place. The Hmong presence now became very noticeable as they traveled in groups to Lao provincial centers to trade, becoming regular vendors in the markets (Yang 1975:122-127), and as some of them began to live closer to these Lao towns. The provincial capital of Xieng Khouang became an important Hmong center. The establishment of Lao schools in Hmong villages[11] and the practice of sending a few Hmong students to Lao towns to study, began in this period. Virtually all Hmong men now spoke some Lao, and Lao vocabulary borrowings laced Hmong discourse. A few Hmong went to France to study, and a tiny educated Hmong elite began to emerge.

A national Hmong leadership was epitomized at first with Touby Lyfoung, who became officially recognized as leader of the Hmong by the French/Lao goverment in 1947 (Yang 1975:51), and by his rival Faydang Lobliayao, who led the communist faction (Yang 1975:54). Later there were Vang Pao and others. During this period the cooperation with the French/Lao military and civilian authorities became strong among some of the noncommunist Hmong, and a sense of participation in the Lao state began to emerge. Hmong district heads (tasseng) were now frequently appointed.

Christianity, both in Roman Catholic and in Protestant forms, made solid headway for the first time among the Hmong in Laos during this stage. Missionary efforts had existed long before that, but for some Hmong, conversion to Christianity now became a desirable option

(Barney 1957a,b).

Some Hmong also began to make use of Western medicine as administered in Lao hospitals to a much greater degree than before, although Western medical treatment still tended to be a solution of last resort, and the quality of the medical treatment available was not good (Dooley 1958:192ff; Halpern 1961).

In the Laos resettlement stage, modern war came to a large percentage of the Hmong population in Laos with cruel force and disruption. The Hmong participation in the war became intense. Hmong suffered terrible casualties, many villages being uprooted, some several times; and large parts of the population were resettled in refugee conglomerations, often around military centers.[12] Normal agricultural and economic activity were often impossible on any adequate scale, and in many of the centers Hmong were forced to live by external aid plus whatever new economic skills they could learn. Traditional sewing skills were adapted to make items directly salable to Westerners.[13]

For many Hmong, war and conglomerate life brought participation in some forms of modern technology. Instruments of war--and in some areas, those of transportation and agriculture--became more widely known. Military participation and life in the conglomerations brought new social structures that overlaid the traditional ones still in place. Many military learned an English-based code for communication with American officers and civilian pilots, while some Hmong learned to communicate in everyday English.

Westernization and adaptation to Lao culture was intensified for some Hmong as they participated with Lao and Americans in the war effort, lived in the same conglomerations with Lao and other ethnic groups, and in a few cases became more educated in Lao.

Hmong literacy increased slightly. In addition to the romanized orthography, two Lao-based writing systems were in use during the period. One was developed by the Hmong who sided with the Pathet Lao and the other by parts of the Protestant church (Smalley 1976; Lemoine 1972a). As economic and cultural deprivation and military stress increased, there developed the Chao Fa (Lao: "Lord of the Sky") Messianic movement, an attempt to recreate a golden past mixed with elements of the changing present, something which was uniquely Hmong. With it was invented a writing system unlike any of the others in use for the language (Lemoine 1972a:142-146).

The Thailand camp stage was in many ways an extension of the conglomerate life of the resettlement areas in Laos. There were some important differences, of course. Camp life brought contact with a different government and numerous foreign agencies. It brought artificial restriction on movement, and even more limited possibilities for economic self-help. It also brought some relief from war pressures, although the pressure continued for those Hmong who slipped back across the border to continue fighting or who had relatives in danger in Laos.

The degree to which traditional social structures were shredded in camp life depended on the family history of disaster. Some camps preserved the spatial proximity of traditional relationships from earlier village settlement. Ban Vinai in particular did not. For many Hmong the camps brought the trauma of family separation of a new kind. Parts of extended families would leave to travel unimaginable distances to fearful and legendary destinations in other parts of the world.

The camps brought Thai education for children, and intensified desire and opportunity for Hmong literacy. It also brought high motivation and increased opportunity for learning English. Yang Dao (personal communication) states that at Nam Phong, the Thai camp to which the first Hmong refugees were taken, there was an English class taught by the few who knew some English "under every tree." Eventually some of this adult education was taken over by social agencies from outside the camp.

The Hmong who came to the United States, then, came with a far more varied and complex experience than a reading of Lemoine (1972b), set in the Lao adaptive stage, or Geddes (1976), set in an analogous stage in Thailand, would lead us to expect. Some people had been swept along by the changing events, without learning to do much more than minimal coping for survival. Others had responded to the new situations by learning new skills and adapting creatively to new opportunities.

The innovations of the United States resettlement stage are beyond the scope of this paper, even if they were to be presented only in the sketchy form with which I approached the other stages. But for many Hmong this has been the most traumatic stage of all. This is the stage, of course, in which many Americans have come to know the Hmong. The attempt to understand something of what is behind the adaptations emerging in the United States requires us to look at the innovations which took place in the camps and, before that, in the resettlement conglomerations, in addition to examining traditional life. Adaptation to life in America continues the process which has been going on through the lifetimes of the Hmong who are here.

ACKNOWLEDGEMENTS

This work was aided by National Endowment for the Humanities grant #RO-20310-82 to the Southeast Asian Refugee Studies program of the University of Minnesota. I have profited by comments on an earlier draft from Bruce Downing, Lysao Lyfoung, Vang Vang and Yang Dao.

NOTES

[1] I am here concerned only with modern history of the Hmong, and only with developments which took place in Laos and among Hmong who were dispersed from Laos since 1975. The centuries-long experience of the Hmong in China is not included.

[2] This is probably a Hmong pronunciation of the Lao Muong Plai. The Hmong name is Zos Kev Xov Hlau. The villages were located about one third of the way between Muong Sai and Muong Ngoi. Principal informant on the experience of the Moos Plais people was Vam Ntxhais Xyooj (Vas Say Xiong), headman of one of the villages throughout the total experienced described. His information was supplemented by that provided by other members of the group.

[3] This date is estimated by working back from Vam Ntxhais Xyooj's memory of approximate times spent in subsequent locations.

[4] A move of about one hundred direct-line miles.

[5]Note that rectangular blocks and houses oriented to them are not in keeping with traditional Hmong house-orientation patterns.

[6]Doris Whitelock reported (personal communication) that at nearby camp Ban Nam Yao, men sometimes worked with women at the embroidery and became fairly good at it.

[7]"The constraint of space, so common in the other refugee camps, is not a problem in Sop Tuang. The camp is spread over approximately 1,000 acres .... [This has] allowed the residents to group themselves into natural village communities." (Committee for Coordination 1982:52).

[8]I have not had time to find out how conglomerations like Long Cheng were organized, and whether (as I suspect) some of that organization carried over into the camps.

[9]Information about Ban Vinai and the youth group there is primarily from Vang Vang, who was one of the youths involved.

[10]For a map of nineteenth century Hmong migration into Laos, see Yang 1975:10.

[11]Yang Dao reports that the first such school in Xieng Khouang Province was established in 1939 (1975:134).

[12]For an indication of the distribution of Hmong resettlement areas in southern Xieng Khouang Province in 1974, see Yang 1975:144.

[13]The square or oblong paj ntaub decorative pieces sold by Hmong women in the United States date back to 1964, during the resettlement stage in Vientiane. The sewing skills are very much older, of course, as are most of the designs typically to be seen in examples of this craft. However, the square form was adapted for sale to tourists out of the traditional baby carrier shaped to hold the baby on the mother's back, and with straps attached (Lemoine, personal communication).

REFERENCES

Ajchenbaum, Yves, and Jean-Pierre Hassoun. 1979. Histoires d'insertion de groupes familiaux Hmong réfugiés en France. Association pour le Développement de la Recherche et l'Experimentation en Sciences Humaines.

Barney, G. Linwood. 1957a. "The Meo--An Incipient Church." Practical Anthropology 4.2:31-50.

_____. 1957b. "Christianity: Innovation in Meo Culture." Unpublished MA Thesis, University of Minnesota.

Committee for Coordination of Services to Displaced Persons in Thailand. 1982. The CCSDPT Handbook: Refugee Services in Thailand. Bangkok: du Maurier Associates.

Dooley, Tom. 1958. The Edge of Tomorrow. New York: Farrar, Straus and Cudahy.

Downing, Bruce (assisted by Bruce Thowpaou Bliatout). 1983. "The Hmong Resettlement Study Site Report: Dallas-Fort Worth, Texas." (Draft prepared in the Southeast Asian Refugee Studies Program of the University of Minnesota.)

Geddes, William R. 1976. Migrants of the Mountains: The Cultural Ecology of the Blue Miao (Hmong Njua) of Thailand. Oxford: Clarendon Press.

Halpern, Joel. 1961. "Laotian Health Statistics." Laos Project Paper No. 10. Mimeographed.

Lemoine, Jacques. 1972a. "Les ecritures des Hmong." Bulletin des Amis du Royaume Lao 7-8:123-165.

_____. 1972b. Un village Hmong vert du haut Laos. Paris: Centre National de la Recherche Scientifique.

Mason, Sarah. 1983. "The Hmong Student Association of Dallas and Fort Worth". In "The Hmong Resettlement

Study Site Report," edited by Bruce Downing (see above).

Smalley, William A. 1976. "The Problems of Consonants and Tone: Hmong (Meo, Miao)." In Phonemes and Orthography: Language Planning in Ten Minority Languages of Thailand, edited by William A. Smalley, pp. 85-123. Canberra, Australia: Lingustic Circle of Canberra.

Yang Dao. 1975 Les Hmong du Laos face au dévelloppement. Vientiane, Laos: Edition Siaosavath.

THE HMONG OF LAOS:
ECONOMIC FACTORS IN REFUGEE EXODUS AND RETURN

Robert Cooper*

INTRODUCTORY NOTE

This paper is concerned only with the economic aspects of Hmong exodus from and repatriation to Laos. It is not suggested that economic motives for fleeing an intolerable situation preclude or dominate other motives. That the great majority of Hmong refugees fled because of a genuinely-felt fear of reprisal or persecution from the new regime is not called into question. I suggest only that there were additional economic reasons for the Hmong to leave Laos, and to leave when they did. These economic factors in the Hmong exodus are important (or are likely to become important) to any discussion of future return to Laos, however and under whatever political or military conditions that return is envisaged.

I am fully aware that the suggestion that economic factors played a role in the Hmong refugee exodus, albeit a subordinate role, will transgress some Hmong sensitivities. I hope that my Hmong friends, on both sides of the frontier, will understand that my intention in making this suggestion is only to contribute to the debate on the future welfare of all Hmong, particularly those currently caught up in the no man's land of refugee camps.

Naively, I ask the Hmong reader to set aside the intolerance and suspicion bred through years of tragedy and uncertainty and to approach this paper with as much as he or she can muster of the tolerance and sincerity that characterizes traditional, peaceful, village Hmong society.

THE THESIS

So far, 190 Hmong have repatriated voluntarily to Laos since the United Nations High Commissioner for Refugees (UNHCR) began a voluntary repatriation programme in 1980 (see Table 1; all figures are correct as of end of 1983).

Table 1

VOLUNTARY REPATRIATION TO LAOS

Year	Lao	Hmong	Yao
1980	193		
1981	276	130	133
1982	802	59	208
1983	526	1	80
	1,797	190	421	TOTAL: 2,408

Not very many. But the importance of the programme cannot be judged simply by the numbers involved. A great many more Hmong are at this moment (January 1984) sitting it out in refugee camps in Thailand, waiting to see what happens to the 190 before deciding which way to go: on to America or back to Laos.

One-hundred-ninety people is, if you put them all together, only the size of one Hmong village, and not a very big one at that. One-hundred-ninety returnees compared to more than 60,000 Hmong who have chosen resettlement in third countries; 190 returnees compared to more than 40,000 Hmong currently in the camps; 190 returnees compared to more than 100,000 Hmong who have fled the Lao Peoples Democratic Republic. And 190 returnees compared to an estimated 200,000 Hmong remaining in the country.

The number of Hmong who have decided to turn around and go back home is tiny, yet the movement back to Laos has a significance far greater that its size. Their decision to return poses questions which must be answered.

Why did Hmong leave Laos? Why did the exodus take the apparently erratic form evident in the annual and monthly statistics? (Tables 2 and 3). Why are there such remarkable differences between departure patterns of lowland Lao and highland Hmong (Table 2, 3 and 4). Why did the majority of Hmong remain in Laos? Why did some Hmong, having left, decide to return to Laos?

Reference to _political_ factors alone cannot fully answer these questions or fully explain patterns of behaviour. I am going to suggest that by adding an _economic_ theory to the well-known political facts, we can come nearer to an explanation.

In this paper, I shall argue that the environment that supported traditional Hmong swidden (slash-and-burn) cultivation in Laos had changed significantly _before_ the great exodus of 1975, and that because of this change many of those who fled at that time might have died of hunger had they remained in Laos. I shall also consider the possibility that the very magnitude of the exodus re-established something of an ecological equilibrium, further reducing the urgency of the exodus rate and raising the possibility that resources in Laos could support a movement of Hmong refugee farmers back to the mountains of Laos.

I am also going to suggest that Hmong who chose to leave Laos early in the year probably had sound economic motives, in addition to any other motives, for going at just that time.

I find it convenient to arrange evidence and arguments to test the following thesis:

In Laos, a direct correlation exists between the Hmong population/resources ratio and the rate of exodus and return.

I shall consider evidence to support this thesis within three categories: historical, observational and empirical.

Table 2

ARRIVALS IN THAILAND BY YEAR

	1975	1976	1977	1978	1979	1980	1981	1982	1983
LAO	10,195	19,499	18,065	48,786	22,045	28,967	16,428	3,203	4,521
HILL-TRIBE	44,659	7,266	3,873	8,013	23,943	14,901	4,305	1,816	2,870

Table 3

ARRIVALS IN THAILAND BY MONTH

A. HILL-TRIBE*

Year	Jan	Feb	Mar	Apr	May	Jun	Jul	Aug	Sep	Oct	Nov	Dec	TOTAL
1981	651	403	1,221	662	358	228	56	284	151	142	4	145	4,305
1982	182	171	371	319	191	0	4	162	164	127	108	17	816
1983	235	593	239	540	178	9	354	206	0	112	184	220	2,870

B. LOWLAND LAO

Year	Jan	Feb	Mar	Apr	May	Jun	Jul	Aug	Sep	Oct	Nov	Dec	TOTAL
1981	651	403	1,221	662	358	228	56	284	151	142	4	145	4,305
1982	643	612	428	196	189	227	215	250	79	120	96	148	3,203

THE HISTORICAL EVIDENCE

During the years 1850 to 1880, the Hmong in China fought a series of wars against the Manchu Government, which was at the time committed to a policy of heavy taxation in order to pay off the heavy indemnities demanded by the British after the Opium War and was looking for ways of making money. Opium had caused these indemnities and it seems likely that the Manchus saw opium as a way of paying off these indemnities. Certainly the Chinese policy of banning opium cultivation was now reversed and production seems to have been encouraged. With the Hmong sitting on some of the best opium land in the world, it is logical to assume that the Chinese authorities of the time wanted control over it and revenue from it. It seems reasonable therefore to say that the Hmong-Manchu wars were predominantly economic in character.

To say that the wars had economic motives does not, of course, deny that there was repression by the Manchu authorities or that many thousands of Hmong fled across the border. For all we know, the nineteenth century Hmong exodus from China could have been every bit as great as the twentieth century exodus from Laos. Perhaps even greater. Of course, repression was not absolute and in spite of the great number of refugees who fled the country, the majority of Hmong remained in nineteenth century China, as the majority of Hmong remained in twentieth century Laos.

Thus, the history of the Hmong is seen to contain at least one precedent of large-scale refugee exodus. The Hmong, unable to continue their way of life without interference from the Chinese authorities, fled in large numbers from one nation state to re-establish themselves successfully in another nation state.

This nineteenth century refugee movement slowed down once persecution, or the fear of persecution, ceased to exist. However, the movement did not stop. Still less did it reverse. Significantly, it continued. Why?

I can see only one reason to explain the persistent movement from China, through the northern part of Vietnam and into Laos: the economic certainty that resources were much better in the new location than in China.

It seems likely that a situation of environmental imbalance or, to call it by another name, "resource scarcity," existed in some of the Hmong areas of nineteenth century southern China and that the Hmong solved this problem by relocating a large number of their people into an area of fresh resources. Once an environmental balance was reestablished in China, or once the imbalance became less acute, the exodus slowed down.

As far as can be guessed, the migration from China seems to have taken two forms: a large-scale refugee exodus and a small-scale calculated relocation of individual families or groups of families.

Exactly the same forms of migration are evident in the post-1975 Hmong exodus from Laos. This fact in itself suggests a likely similarity of causes, which I would summarize as fear of persecution plus the need to escape a situation of resource scarcity.

By suggesting the existence of historical precedent, I do not wish to imply that the Hmong collectively or individually copied actions which had proven effective responses to problems encountered in the past. I am only saying that the Hmong have demonstrated an ability to face economic and political problems in a certain way, that way being large-scale migration.

After the exodus from China into Vietnam and Laos, a further movement of Hmong took place from Laos into Thailand. This gradual migration took the form of household relocation. It seems to have begun soon after the Hmong left China and to have led to a sizable Hmong presence in Thailand by the early twentieth century. Why did this movement take place?

A political motive seems to have been absent. Although the Hmong in Laos did get into some skirmishes with the French, this was only after the migration was under way. Anyway, the Hmong in Laos probably extracted from the French a much greater degree of political autonomy than they could hope to obtain in Thailand.

I would suggest, therefore, the likelihood that the swidden use of mountain sides for opium cultivation (which progressively reduces soil fertility until land ceases to be productive) created a resources/population imbalance in certain Hmong areas of Laos throughout the first half of the twentieth century and that the Hmong responded to that situation in exactly the same way they had responded to the same problem in China: by moving a proportion of the population--not all of the population-- into a situation of resource plenty.

Thus, it can be argued that two historical precedents of Hmong economic migration across national frontiers predated the beginnings of the Laotian civil war in the 1950s.

The thirty-year-long civil war was undoubtedly responsible for removing further portions of land in Hmong areas of Laos from the possibility of exploitation. Many mountain areas, previously open to cultivation, were stripped of vegetation by the effects of bombing and chemicals.

During the fighting of the 1960s and early 1970s, the Hmong tended to group in certain safe villages, in displaced person camps in the lowlands and in the "secret army" mountain town of Long Cheng, which had been established as early as 1961. Such large population groupings could not hope to supply all subsistence needs by traditional swidden cultivation, and a great many Hmong families came to rely increasingly on food drops by aircraft, handouts in the population centres or the soldier's pay earned by adult males. Most estimates of the number of Hmong on some form of "welfare" during this period total over one hundred thousand.

In addition to these one hundred thousand we should remember that there were also Hmong in uniform on the Pathet Lao side. They earned little money but it is true to say that they also gained at least part of their basic subsistence by nonagricultural means.

The picture of Hmong areas of Laos in 1975 is one in which the pinch of resource scarcity had long promoted a steady movement of Hmong migrants into Thailand; this situation of resource scarcity was compounded by a civil war which had many of the effects of the industrial revolution in Europe, driving farmers from their lands whilst at the same time offering alternative means of livelihood in centres of population.

It is also worth noting that as far as we know comparatively few Hmong fled war-torn Laos in the decade before 1975. This is surprising--even amazing--considering that the Hmong were the principal casualties of the war. This low level of refugee outflow during the war suggests one or both of two things: either that the Hmong stayed in Laos to fight against communism or that the provision of aid and paid employment acted as an economic incentive to remain, even when remaining was not only dangerous but required adaptation or abandonment of traditional lifestyle. (Similar economic incentives induced many thousand Thais to leave the safety of Thailand and fight as mercenaries in Laos.)

When, in 1975, the alternative means of livelihood came to an abrupt end, tens of thousands of Hmong found themselves abruptly face to face not only with the fear of the enemy's revenge but also with a situation of accumulated resource scarcity.

I do not doubt that the Hmong who fled Laos at that time did so from a genuine fear of persecution following the change in regime. However, I feel it is worth making the point that they also had an economic motive for fleeing when they did. Had they remained in Laos, it is difficult to see how they could have avoided large-scale famine. Certainly the Pathet Lao government, had it been inclined to do so, could not have offered any assistance, since the rice harvests in the years following the change of regimes were insufficient to feed the lowland population.

Thus, whatever the political reasons for leaving (which are not in doubt), the convulsive exodus from Laos could be said to have served economic functions, both for the leavers and the stayers. The leavers were removed from a situation of resource scarcity and potential famine whilst the stayers had far less competition for available resources.

THE OBSERVATIONAL EVIDENCE

My argument that the Hmong of Laos suffered from a very adverse population/resources imbalance is supported by my personal observations made over the period of December 1980 to March 1983. During this time, I lived in Vientiane and travelled very widely by aeroplane, helicopter, truck, jeep and boat, and on foot. During these travels around the country I was able to visit Sayaboury, Xieng Khouang, Luang Prabang, Vientiane, Savannakhet, Pakse and Attopeu provinces and got to see a number of Hmong villages.

I was particularly interested in Xieng Khouang for four reasons:

1. The majority of Hmong refugees in Ban Vinai Camp (the Hmong refugee camp in Thailand) seem to come from that province.

2. Only one of the 190 Hmong repatriates to Laos returned to Xieng Khouang. A few others had originated from that province but chose not to return there.

3. Many of some fifteen hundred Hmong who live in the large settlement at KM 52 north of the town of Vientiane said they had left Xieng Khouang because of the difficulty of finding enough land to farm in that province.

4. Several thousand Hmong from Xieng Khouang had resettled in several groups around Vang Viang. Some had arrived there before 1975, but most had come since the change in regimes. All of those I met stated that it was very difficult to make a living in Xieng Khouang.

I was able to fly extensively by helicopter throughout Xieng Khouang Province. Everywhere, the mountains were covered with grass--not trees. And it was the kind of tough grass known technically as imperata, a grass that grows where little else can and puts down long roots which make cultivation by hand hoe extremely difficult if not impossible.

I had flown around northern Thailand ten years previously and seen much the same kind of thing in areas of known resource scarcity. However, even in the worst areas of northern Thailand, it had still been possible to see some trees and some secondary growth on the mountainsides and there was the feeling that resources recovery was at least possible. Throughout most of Xieng Khouang, however, I could find trees only in the folds between mountains, where the slope was usually too steep to permit cultivation.

I did see Hmong villages and fields but far fewer than I had expected to see. There were, by contrast, many Hmong in Phone Savane, the capital of Xieng Khouang Province, including the president of the province. I was able to speak with them without restriction and all gave a rather gloomy picture of the province's economy. Their accounts suggest that it is still possible for some villages to get by by growing opium, and Xieng Khouang remains the major opium-producing province of Laos, but "getting by" means living next to poverty and, as things stand, there is no reason to assume that agricultural prospects in the province will improve very much in the future.

The situation in Luang Prabang, Sayaboury, and Vientiane provinces was less severe than in Xieng Khouang. Several villages I visited seemed to be getting by reasonably well in terms of fields cultivated, food stocks held, household livestock and standard of housing, dress and so on. However, there is certainly no cause for complacency. Even in the best of areas it would be very difficult to find a single location containing adequate resources to support installation of a village-sized group of, say, two hundred Hmong wishing to follow only traditional techniques of cultivation.

Many other foreigners travelling to various parts of Laos have confirmed my impression that the mountain areas of Laos, in spite of very low population ratios, suffer from a situation of resource scarcity that could best be described as varying between serious and chronic. It is, I feel, most likely that the roots of this situation extend back far beyond the great divide of 1975.

THE EMPIRICAL EVIDENCE

The empirical evidence to support the thesis of direct correlation between resource availability and the rate of exodus is, I must admit, not 100 percent convincing. This is mostly because of the difficulties involved in doing any really objective research in Laos and in the camps of Thailand. I have therefore had to rely on statistics collected for various official reasons, none of them collected specifically to test the thesis. It must also be borne in mind that these figures represent only movement in and out of <u>camps</u>. It is most likely that thousands more Hmong than get into the statistics have moved across the border into Thailand without passing through a camp and equally likely that several thousand have "spontaneously repatriated" to Laos.

The figures I am giving here do not conclusively prove my thesis. On the other hand, they certainly do not disprove it. To play it safe, I would say that a reasonable interpretation of available statistics tends to support the thesis.

First, annual arrivals of Hmong refugees in Thailand since 1975, as set out in Table 2, invite analysis against an economic background. (Figures are actually for <u>hill-tribe</u> arrivals and include a few thousand Yao and some members of other minority groups, but the great majority are Hmong.)

Two peaks are evident: 1975 and 1979. The reasons for the 1975 exodus are obvious enough: fear of retaliation against the Hmong by the victorious Pathet Lao and the very sound economic reasons for leaving that I have already gone into. But why should figures peak again in 1979? If fear of such factors as "yellow rain" were the only reason for leaving, why did 23,943 flee the country in 1979 and only 1,816 in 1982? The real answer, I feel, has a lot to do with economics and the economic history of the Hmong.

For a long, long time Hmong have lived near larger, more dominant ethnic groups. Speaking as we must in generalizations: the majority ethnic groups--Chinese, Vietnamese, Lao and Northern Thai--were firmly entrenched in the lowlands where they practiced irrigation methods to grow rice and lived in communities typified by permanent economies, permanent villages, permanent authority structures and so on. The Hmong, on the other hand, were hopping around from mountaintop to mountaintop, practicing shifting cultivation in communities typified by shifting economies, temporary villages and temporary authority structures. During thousands of years of quiet subsistence farming, the Hmong lived near a majority cul-

ture but had little reason to interact with that culture
and experienced no real competition for available resources. Then, along came cash-crop opium.

Starting sometime in the nineteenth century, the
Hmong began to specialize in opium. They continued to
practice economic specialization even when this meant
that sufficient rice or other foods could not be grown to
meet all domestic needs. It was more profitable to sell
the opium and buy the extra food required, or to exchange
opium directly for food.

A situation developed in which, although very few
Hmong actually owned irrigated rice fields, a great many
Hmong--perhaps most Hmong--were dependent for at least a
part of their basic food supply on lowland fields in Lao
hands. The Lao were, in turn, dependent on Hmong (and
some other hill-tribe groups) for opium. But it is possible to live without opium, whereas it is much more difficult to live without rice, as was clearly evident in
Laos in 1977 and 1978.

In 1977, Laos experienced a disastrous drought.
This was followed in 1978 by an even more disastrous
flooding at harvest time. In both years Laos was forced
to appeal for international assistance to prevent famine.
There was, of course, very little rice from any source
available to sell to the Hmong.

The effects of this economic situation on the exodus
pattern of ethnic Lao is seen very clearly in Table 2.
More left in 1978 than in any other year. For the Hmong,
the effect was a little delayed for two reasons. Firstly, the Hmong upland rice crop, insufficient for all
needs as it was, was relatively unaffected by the floods.
The October harvest therefore was enough to keep everybody going until after the January opium harvest of 1979.
By that time, however, it would have been clear that supplementary rice would not be available and it seems reasonable to assume that this has something to do with the
1979 Hmong exodus peak.

The years 1981, 1982 and 1983 have seen the best
rice harvests in Laos for many years. (Laos can now be
considered self-sufficient in rice cultivation.) These
good harvests, like the bad, seem to be reflected in the
annual exodus rate for both Hmong and Lao in 1982 and
1983, which are the lowest recorded since 1975.

A second economic reason for the delayed effect on Hmong exodus patterns is suggested by the <u>monthly</u> figures for Hmong refugee arrivals in Thailand over the years 1981, 1982 and 1983, which are set out in Table 3. (Monthly statistics are not available before January 1981.)

Figures for the first four months of each year are much higher than for the other months of each year and peak around March in all three years.   Why should this pattern emerge and what does it suggest?

A facile explanation often heard and credited, is that the Mekong River, which most Hmong must cross before arriving in Thailand, is low during the first half of the year and at its height towards year's end.   If this fact is to be used to explain the least number of hill-tribe refugee crossings (only four) in November 1981, it cannot explain the high figure of 1,413 lowland Lao who crossed the same river in the same month of the same year.   It certainly cannot explain why no Hmong crossed in June 1982, when the river was at its lowest.

Thus, whilst it is recognized that the Mekong in flood presents a fearsome obstacle to mountain people unused to water travel, we must look beyond the river theory for an explanation of the monthly patterns of exodus evident in Table 3.   I suggest that these patterns are less a result of river level than they are evidence of the dictates of the agricultural year.

Hmong harvest rice around October, sometimes into November.   This harvest is followed by Hmong New Year celebrations, which in turn are followed by the opium harvest.

The opium harvest usually takes a single family three to four weeks to complete.   The precise date it begins varies between localities and depends on soil conditions, type of seeds used and weather conditions in any particular year.   At the very earliest, it begins in early December and at the very latest it is completed in the first days of February.   The two months following the opium harvest, February and March, are used to cut new fields, repair the house and do various tasks to prepare for the coming agricultural year.   <u>Families intending to move to a new location do so at this time of year</u>.   They use the revenue from post-harvest opium sales to help them move and to tide them over in the new location until they become reestablished.

The hill-tribe refugee statistics of Table 3, in showing a significant increase in Hmong arriving in Thailand around March are, to an extent, simply reflecting traditional patterns of movement (movement in these cases being across a national boundary). This suggests that, at least since 1981, economics has played a big part in the decision to leave at a certain time. The main reason for leaving might be fear of persecution, but I can think of no reason why that fear should be greater in the early months of the year. If fear of persecution were the only reason for fleeing the country, we would not expect quite so many to wait around for the opium harvest.

There is a further economic reason for Hmong in Laos to leave the country as soon as the opium is harvested, especially those in Xieng Khouang. If they get out quickly enough, they can avoid having to sell a large part of the harvest to the government. The Laotian government now operates the same kind of opium monopoly that has always caused problems for the Hmong under the Chinese, French and Thai. The main problem involves fixing an appropriate price for the year's supply. Opium is a crop which varies dramatically in supply and price between years. A few days' poor weather can greatly reduce the size of the harvest. When this happens in a free-market situation, the price rises to compensate somewhat for the shortfall. However, when the only buyer is the government, and the price is fixed by the state, small bureaucratic adjustments in the official price (usually made months after the crop has been sold) cannot provide the same level of compensation.

Also relevant are the facts that the government buys in kip, the national currency of Laos, which can be relied upon to devalue as the year progresses, and pays a price which is much lower than the free market within Laos, where payment is made in silver, dollars or Thai baht. And the Laotian free market price is in turn much lower than the price obtainable across the border in Thailand.

The dictates of the agricultural year together with the marketing procedures currently in force in Laos might have very little to do with the total availability of agricultural resources and the total annual rate of exodus, but statistics certainly suggest a link between resource exploitation patterns and patterns of monthly exodus. They also suggest that at least a proportion of Hmong refugees are sensitive to economic factors when selecting a time to flee the country.

SUMMARY

Supporting evidence for the thesis that a direct correlation exists between availability of agricultural resources and rate of exodus follows:

1. Historical precedents exist. The Hmong have behaved in the same way before, moving across national boundaries in very large numbers when threatened by resource scarcity.

2. The Hmong exodus from Laos existed prior to the beginnings of civil war in 1950.

3. The civil war disguised the population/resources imbalance by providing alternative means of livelihood.

4. The civil war promoted large-scale settlement and dependency. Economic survival required large-scale settlements to disperse rapidly in 1975. Thousands faced famine; thousands fled Laos.

5. The drought of 1977 and floods of 1978 meant the traditional supplement of rice could not be purchased from the lowlands in 1979.

6. Vast areas of Hmong lands have become unsuitable for cultivation by traditional methods. This is particularly true in the former Hmong stronghold of Xieng Khouang.

7. The majority of Hmong refugees in the camps in Thailand are from Xieng Khouang.

8.   Departure rate figures suggest that Hmong respond to
     economic factors when deciding a particular time to
     leave the country, in many cases completing an agri-
     cultural cycle before departure.

CONCLUSION

At this moment many a Hmong is sitting in Ban Vinai
refugee camp wondering whether to go back to Laos, go to
America or remain sitting in Ban Vinai.

In the camp, or in America, this Hmong person can be
fairly sure his family will get enough to eat. His family is also likely to benefit from the kind of medical
and educational facilities which would be almost unavailable in Laos.

If he goes back to Laos, he will receive a certain
amount of assistance in the form of rice and salt to help
him over the first year. But even providing this very
basic assistance causes tremendous problems. There is no
budget for the kind of grand-slam air drops of rice that
took place before 1975, and that kind of blanket assistance is not appropriate for programmes aimed at achiev-
ing self-sufficiency within the minimum time period.

Rice in the 1980s is delivered by trucks, boats,
horseback and man-back. Delays in delivery occur and are
normal in the more remote areas. And there is a Catch-22
aspect in the provision of rice assistance to Hmong: rice
can only be delivered to the location to which a Hmong
chooses to return, yet the Hmong person in question is
most likely to move around looking for a piece of land to
support his family. If he stays put in one place he will
probably receive rice but may not become self-sufficient;
if he moves around he stands a better chance of becoming
self-sufficient but he is likely to miss out on the rice
assistance.

Apart from rice assistance, a Hmong returnee family
gets a one-time present of a "resettlement kit." This
contains clothing and black cloth to make Hmong clothing
and the basic items of domestic assistance: pots and
pans, bowls, spoons, blankets, mats, water buckets, soap,
etc. It also contains a set of tools to assist in clearing the ground and building a house: an axe, machete,
hoe, hammer and so on. With this kit and a first in-

stallment of rice, the family is taken to a point as near to home or the chosen area of return as it is possible to reach with available transport; then off they go on foot. Back where they started from. The rest is up to them.

One of the most pleasant parts of my job in Laos was visiting returnees (Hmong, Yao and Lao) several months after they had returned home. I was always impressed with the Hmong ability to take up the old life again-- usually with the help of relatives or clansmen. It was also very nice to see how quickly most camp refugees re- covered their pride once back in the mountains in a newly-built Hmong house, wearing Hmong dress, sitting on a little stool by a big fire, smoking a ying-tong or doing some embroidery.

These impressions of the Hmong returnee at home have little to do with economics. They are of course subjec- tive and are no doubt coloured by the fact that I am both a romantic Westerner and an anthropologist. But, the last thing I would wish to do is romance about a Hmong return to Laos. I would much prefer such a movement to be based on sound economic facts, and some of these facts I have tried to present in this paper.

As things stand at the moment, I would say that the (economic) utilitarian balance swings against the return of Hmong to Laos in large numbers.

Most certainly, Hmong can go back to the mountains and live in Hmong houses in Hmong villages. However, they won't be able to gain much of a livelihood if they go back to Xieng Khouang and start to grow opium, and this I feel is one of the major factors preventing a larger movement back to Laos.

For the economic balance to swing in favour of re- turn to Laos, some form of agricultural change and devel- opment is required. Alternative uses of available re- sources would need to be promoted.

A start has already been made on this development. As yet, a very small start. Some pilot projects have been established in Hmong areas by UNHCR and by the United Nations Development Programme (UNDP). These proj- ects centre on some form of permanent cultivation and residence but are unlikely to require great changes in the Hmong way of life. Mostly they involve creating new irrigated rice fields and rehabilitating old ones, pro-

viding livestock and introducing or improving basic educational and medical facilities. All of these projects
are geared to assisting the local population, i.e. those
who never left the country, whilst creating opportunities
which will be reserved for returnees.

Even if all the projects currently being undertaken
by UNHCR and UNDP in Laos are successful, conditions will
have been created for the return of, at best, two or
three thousand Hmong. Clearly much more needs to be done
before anybody can realistically talk about having laid
the groundwork to support return to Laos as a real economic alternative to resettlement in and assimilation into
a non-Hmong world.

The economic conditions to support a large-scale return to Laos will not suddenly appear tomorrow. They can
only be created by money and hard work. And the availability of money from international sources depends on
political rather than economic factors. It depends on
precisely those factors that I have not mentioned in this
paper.

*NOTE

The author was Programme Officer for the United Nations High Commissioner for Refugees in Laos between
December 1980 and March 1983, and is currently Geneva-
based Resettlement Officer concerned with Indochinese
refugees. He wishes to make it quite clear that, while
observations made during his residence in Laos helped
form the ideas this paper contains, he is writing in a
purely personal capacity. His views do not necessarily
reflect those of UNHCR and he should not be quoted in his
capacity as a UNHCR official.

PROCESSES OF IDENTITY MAINTENANCE
IN HMONG SOCIETY

Timothy Dunnigan

INTRODUCTION

The long-term survival of an ethnic minority does not
depend upon the retention of specific cultural characteristics. Edward Spicer (1980) points out that the Yaqui
Indians of northwestern Mexico have endured as a people
despite more than 350 years of dramatic change. In 1617,
Catholic priests began establishing missions extensively
among the Yaqui. European-derived economic institutions
greatly affected Yaqui subsistence and settlement patterns through the colonial and post-independence periods
(1617-1910). After losing a protracted and nearly geno-
cidal war to the Mexican government in the nineteenth
century, many Yaquis were deported to southern Mexico.
Others became refugees in the United States. Political
and economic pressures of the twentieth century reduced
the indigenous communities almost to extinction. Increased government support of Indian economic rights over
the last several decades has encouraged Yaquis to resettle in their original territories, and a number of Yaqui
towns are beginning to thrive once again.
Considering all the changes that have occurred in the
Yaqui way of life, it is difficult to say in what sense
the contemporary Yaqui can claim continuity with the
past. According to Spicer, Yaqui history reveals the persistence of a collective identity system, a unique set of
symbols that embody group beliefs and sentiments.

> An identity system...develops independently of
> those processes by which a total culture pattern,
> a set of particular customs and beliefs consti-
> tuting a way of life, is maintained. The contin-
> uity of a people is a phenomenon distinct from
> the persistence of a particular set of culture
> traits. (Spicer 1971:798)

The Hmong have survived challenges to their existence similar to those faced by the Yaqui. In both cases,

41

there have been long periods of adjustment to unstable environments. Although each group has remained socially and culturally distinct, popular conceptions of the Hmong and Yaqui as being very traditional distort reality. "Tradition" usually implies a lack of change in respect to some vague preindustrial baseline. In this sense, the term is not useful in describing the ways in which ethnic minorities endure while undergoing culture change for centuries. The issue is not whether the Hmong refugees in America can remain culturally conservative or must accept assimilation. More to the point are questions regarding the future form and meaning of Hmong identity symbols and the evolving structure of social relations through which these symbols will be expressed. Rather than attempting to analyze the extremely complex Hmong identity system as it exists and is being created in America, I will discuss some of the processes of identity maintenance that will affect relations between the Hmong and other groups for some time to come. My purpose is to describe how dynamic identity elements such as ethnic politics, religion, language and kinship reinforce Hmong social boundaries as adaptations are made to changing circumstances.[1]

THE OPPOSITIONAL PROCESS

Group identity presupposes social boundaries defined by "we vs. they" criteria. Whatever the nature of these criteria, they are brought into sharper focus by the opposition of outsiders. In his essay on persistent peoples in North America and Europe, Spicer (1971:797) characterizes such opposition as a "continued conflict between these peoples and the controllers of the surrounding state apparatus." As an enclaved minority, the Hmong have had to contend with the opposing interests of various nationalities. The movement of Hmong from China into Southeast Asia was to some extent impelled by pressure from other ethnic groups (Savina 1924; Weins 1967; Larteguy 1979). Under conditions of extreme threat, revitalization movements led by Hmong prophets have resulted in armed conflict. A more typical Hmong reaction to external political authority has been accommodation. In sixteenth century Kweichow, China, the Hmong constituted a distinct but fully integrated segment of a broader political order.

> Tribal chieftains, including Miao [Hmong] chieftains, were appointed to hereditary administrative positions, adopting Chinese surnames and entering into a kind of feudatory arrangement with the imperial government on behalf of the tribesmen within their jurisdiction (LeBar et al. 1964: 70).

In Laos, the Hmong sought similar arrangements with French colonial authorities and various Lao political factions. They tried to maximize their autonomy by becoming valued supporters of the established government or an emerging power.

Hmong external relations in Laos before the collapse of the Constitutional Monarchy in 1975 and during the recent period of refugee resettlement, suggest the following general assumptions and principles. Accommodation and compromise usually accomplish more than direct confrontation. The interests of the Hmong will not be dependably served by any dominant majority, and it is necessary to maintain the positions of leaders capable of rallying the Hmong in times of crisis. Since a Hmong political leader achieves and holds his position by continuously demonstrating an ability to obtain help for others, he must have access to resources not only within Hmong society, but also within the broader political order than that which encompasses the Hmong. Persons of influence belonging to the dominant majority should be cultivated as potential allies who will understand and sympathetically respond to Hmong needs. The insertion of Hmong personnel into majority-controlled institutions that affect the Hmong begins with the establishment of such alliances.

The Hmong were relatively unknown to the American public when they began arriving in the United States from Thailand refugee camps during the spring of 1976. Hmong leaders who spoke English moved quickly to establish contacts with American citizens willing to publicize how the Hmong had supported United States interests in Laos. The resulting media coverage helped to identify the Hmong as a special group of refugees to whom the United States owed a considerable debt. Exceptionally able Hmong were

promoted by the group as candidates for jobs offered
through resettlement agencies. Although relatively young,
most of the Hmong hired by the agencies to do casework
had already held responsible positions in Laos.

Despite the hiring of Hmong by organizations serving
refugees, misunderstandings occurred between Hmong leaders and some agencies over control of government funds
allocated for resettlement programs. Experience had
taught the Hmong that security depended upon solidarity,
and the refugees were unlikely to remain united if their
only choice was to turn to outsiders for help. The Hmong
wanted to be primary providers of some services to refugee families. They hoped to negotiate arrangements similar to those that had been obtained in Laos, i.e., the
distribution of resources through Hmong political structures. Largely due to Hmong persuasion, Hmong mutual assistance associations were given limited public and private funding to carry out educational, legal service,
housing and job development programs.

Participation in mutual assistance associations increased rapidly during the early years of resettlement,
and some of the local self-help groups formed a loosely
structured national organization. Families looked to association officers and board members for guidance. The
larger, more intact kinship groups were expected to be
the most active in establishing policy. Dissenting groups
were co-opted in the interests of unity. Persons advantaged by education and training felt obligated to contribute considerable time to association affairs.

As the threat of living in a strange country gradually lessened, the number of families regularly participating in association functions declined somewhat. The need
to support a protective alliance that overarched all of
Hmong society no longer seemed imperative. As a result,
many Hmong cut back on community involvement in order to
concentrate on matters of direct consequence to their kin
groups. This has not signaled a breakdown in ethnic group
solidarity. The Hmong appear to be in a new phase of a
cycle wherein reduced hostile opposition allows for a reduction in political hierarchical organization.

The history of Hmong politics indicates that refugee
organizations like the mutual assistance associations and
other supra-kinship modalities, such as athletic and social clubs, student associations, women's support groups,

etc., are unlikely to disappear even If assimilation pressures are minimal and outside financial assistance is unobtainable. These groups will continue to be supported because they are needed to exert leverage when it becomes necessary to influence majority policy toward the Hmong. These organizations also have a number of other important functions relating to the maintenance of ethnic group identity.

THE HOMELAND

Community self-help organizations do much more than deal with local problems. They serve as clearinghouses for political news from Thailand and Laos. Members contribute money to help finance the efforts of their national leaders to lobby government officials in Thailand and the United States on policy matters affecting the Laotian government. The continued interest in Laos is understandable. The concept of a homeland remains central to the symbol system of a people even after control over a territory has been lost (Spicer 1971). The Laotian Hmong trace their roots back to China, but recognize Laos as the place where they attained a special political identity. Refugees raised in Laos feel particularly close to those who come from the same province, district or village. Regional loyalties are de-emphasized by most refugee political leaders, who prefer to focus on the special role that the entire Hmong population played in the emergence of Laos as an independent nation.

Most refugees intend to stay in America, even if a reversal of the present political situation eventually allows the Hmong to resettle in Laos. The unifying power of Laos as a symbolic homeland will likely remain strong because of Hmong historical awareness. As Spicer (1980: 360) so elegantly states,

> In their sense of identity every people molds a vessel into which they pour from generation to generation the meanings of their historical experiences. Each such creation is for every enduring people a summation of their customs; in such a listing the vital dimension is not present. This dimension is the people's feeling

about the way they have performed and the values
they have stood for in the course of their life
history as a people. Such associations with real
events in which people have suffered and tri-
umphed are poured into the mold of identity and
so come to have significance.

Knowledge of Hmong sacrifices in the context of the
real events of Laotian history will be perpetuated in the
general accounts known to the entire refugee community,
and in the more detailed and specific oral histories of
individual lineages.

LANGUAGE

The concentration of Hmong from many areas of Laos
into refugee settlements during and after the recent conflict in Southeast Asia greatly increased interdialectic
contacts. Over the past several decades there has probably been some leveling, but the two major dialects of
Laos known as Hmoob Dawb ("White Hmong") and Hmoob
Ntsuab[2] ("Blue Hmong") remain distinct, and each includes
a number of regional variants. Refugees often switch dialects depending upon the situation. Some young adults,
for instance, speak to their parents in one dialect, and
use other dialect forms when communicating with friends.
Hmong leaders support the idea of continued dialectal
variety, even at the risk of reinforcing political divisions within the ethnic group. It is in regard to written Hmong that political leaders have encouraged attempts
to establish a single standard. Working under the aegis
of the Hmong Association in St. Paul-Minneapolis, respected members from influential kin groups representing
different dialects were able to produce a consensus Hmong
translation of junior high school curricular materials
(Dunnigan and Vang 1980a). All participants agreed to
use an orthography that had been developed in the early
1950s for Hmoob Dawb. Subsequent attempts to modify this
orthography in ways acceptable to some Hmoob Ntsuab crit-
ics, who understandably want equal status for their dialect, have dissatisfied speakers of both dialects. I see
little prospect for a resolution of this problem, but the
political consequences should not be very great.

Research on factors affecting language survival has been inconclusive. Fishman (1974) notes that there are exceptions to even the best documented generalizations about linguistic acculturation. Notwithstanding the many difficulties associated with predicting the future status of any immigrant language, Dunnigan and Vang (1980b) asserted that language shift in the American Hmong community could be expected to reach the stage of stabilized bilingualism due to the persistence of certain kinship structures that will provide the necessary separation of domain use between English and Hmong.

> More important for the maintenance of the Hmong language is its function as an essential part of ritual processes by which social relations are established and intensified. This is particularly true of the extended family (Dunnigan and Vang 1980b:44).

The most elaborate expressions of ritual language called paj lug or "flowery speech" will probably be lost through interregional leveling. The death of many senior leaders of kin groups during the war seems to have accelerated this process. The younger Hmong generally wish to avoid the ritual language contests that were an important part of making social contracts in Laos (Dunnigan and Vang 1980b). Special ritual language will still be needed to negotiate and formalize crucial kin group alliances.

RELIGION

Religious belief and ritual observance, like language, has the potential both to reinforce and to dissolve Hmong social cohesion. A majority of the Hmong in Laos practiced a form of animism.[3] Others were converted by Catholic and Protestant missionaries. Approximately half of the Hmong refugees in the United States identify themselves as Christians. A Hmong revitalization movement called Chao Fa, a Lao term meaning "Lord of the Sky," began in the last years of the Laotian war, and continues to be a force in Laos and in Thailand refugee camps. Hmong political and military leaders were always careful to honor Buddhism as the state religion.

Buddhist symbols are still used to express nationalistic sentiments.

Hmong religious beliefs and practices are diverse, but there is a strong tendency toward uniformity within the patrilineal kin group. This occurs for several reasons. The membership must make collective decisions about sharing resources, and divided loyalties of any kind could undermine cooperation. The group's charter is its history of descent. Religious beliefs define relationships between living members and their ancestors. Sacred rituals provide a means of memorializing these relationships and strengthening group bonds. For the non-Christian Hmong, knowledge of lineage ceremonies helps determine who qualifies as a member. It is not surprising that reconstituted refugee kin groups have been known to reduce internal heterodoxy by pressuring members to switch their allegiance from Christian back to animism. Conversion has also occurred in the opposite direction for the sake of group unity.

A much debated subject in the Hmong refugee community has been the effects of Christian missionary work on kin group relations. One concern is that Hmong solidarity has been weakened because some fundamentalists shun non-Christians. According to my observations, the increase in Hmong religious diversity over the past three and a half decades has not seriously impeded the formation of crucial kin group alliances. Some Christian groups object to members marrying outside of their faith, but such marriages do take place frequently. Because the couple normally lives with the husband's parents, the wife usually adopts her husband's religion. Thus the capacity of refugee Hmong to form suprakinship political structures has not been reduced by religious sectarianism.

Rather than forcing the Hmong to assimilate, Christian affiliation has helped them to maintain their cultural and social distinctiveness. Even when they are officially part of a larger, heterogenous church congregation, most Hmong prefer to meet separately, use their native language during services and worship under the direction of Hmong ministers and deacons. Christianity, as well as animism, has a special ethnic significance for the Hmong.

KINSHIP

Most studies of Hmong kinship[4] describe a set of nested structures defined by patrilineal descent. The emphasis on descent sometimes obscures important differences between what Keesing (1975:9-10) calls cultural categories and social groups. An example of the former is the xeem or "patri-clan." Hmong who have the same clan classification may choose to recognize reciprocal obligations and form a group, but this is not required simply because a clan relationship exists. Those who trace their descent back to a known ancestor are of one caj ces, i.e., lineage or branch. This connection provides a much stronger justification for common group membership. Patrilineal descent, however, is only one of a number of factors that determine the composition of Hmong kin groups.

A common adaptive unit of the Hmong is an association of closely related extended families. There is no Hmong term that refers exclusively to this kind of association, but the expression pawg neeg or "close group" applies in certain contexts. Brothers and lineage cousins, uncles and nephews readily form such groups. Their families constitute a perdurable core to which are added more distant lineage and clan relatives. Occasionally, a married male prefers to join the pawg neeg of his more successful and/or more congenial in-laws. The willingness of the Hmong to recognize even the most distant ties of consanguinity and affinity has been crucial in reestablishing family mutual assistance groups that were decimated and scattered due to war, refugee flight and resettlement.

The assumptions and principles mentioned earlier in regard to external political relations apply in modified form to Hmong kinship organization. Every family group tries to expand the range of its alliance network by accommodating the needs of other groups who will reciprocate when asked. Some kinds of help, e.g., sharing income and housing, can only come from within the family group. A family group will be in a better position to help and protect members if it has capable leaders who unselfishly promote the advancement of the entire group. A unified association of families is the most effective social arrangement for adapting to a changing and sometimes hostile environment.

American Hmong worry that the young are becoming more independent and less committed. to group interests. As resettlement problems abate, and Hmong grow up exposed to values that elevate personal achievement over social duty, reliance on and devotion to the kin group may weaken.   I anticipate that any reduction in the size and influence of Hmong kin groups will be interpreted by non-Hmong observers as a late stage of assimilation.   The expansion and intensification of internal coalitions historically have varied in direct relation to external threat.   A less intensive oppositional process in America will result in smaller corporate kin groups, but large networks of groups related by descent and marriage will be maintained as security against an uncertain future.

IDENTITY MAINTENANCE

Studies of Hmong refugee adaptation must present more than "before" and "after" pictures that show the Hmong suddenly crossing the threshold from a stable, traditional existence to a situation of rapid development in a modern society where ethnic differences are reduced to trivial proportions.   Extensive culture modification and replacement are certainly taking place, just as occurred in China, Laos and Thailand during earlier periods of Hmong history.   It is important to understand these changes by analyzing their causes.   We should also be focusing on how the Hmong are using their acculturation experiences in America to reinforce Hmong social and cultural identity.

Political standing, gender, kinship and other kinds of social roles are being redefined to fit circumstances totally new to the Hmong.   Borrowed elements are being added to symbols of ethnicity and kinship.   Constraints imposed by majority society are forcing the Hmong to revise important social rituals. It is also true that Hmong adjustment strategies in the United States replicate approaches followed in Southeast Asia for managing cross-cultural contacts and preserving Hmong ethnic integrity. The processes of Hmong culture change appear to be both linear and cyclical.

I began by presenting a brief overview of Yaqui history as an illustration of the difference between the retention of cultural traits and the maintenance of an identity system. The Hmong, like the Yaqui, have survived extremely difficult times by changing without suffering identity loss. This kind of resilience teaches some very important lessons. I again quote Edward Spicer (1980:362).

> Perhaps a people which endures, whether for only a century or for millennia, embodies the most important kind of social unit which men create. The persistent identity systems which characterize such social units are living, cumulative interpretations of the significance of human life. Each is unique and unrepeatable. Each is not only the summation of one people's accumulated understanding of their purpose and destiny; it may also be a window for other peoples on the general human purpose. When peoples of different identities learn to cross one another's ethnic boundaries, they come closer to the fullest possible appreciation of the meaning of human existence (1980:362).

NOTES

[1] Linnekin (1983:241) observes that:

> ... tradition is a conscious model of past life ways that people use in the contruction of their identity. The inheritance of an authentic tradition and the naivete of the folk are illusory. The use of a defining tradition exemplifies the objectification ... and the invention ... of a symbolic construct. As a self-conscious category, tradition is inevitably "invented" ... the selection of what constitutes tradition is always made in the present; the context of the past is modified and redefined according to a modern significance.

A bibliography relevant to the issue of ethnic definition is provided by Linnekin.

[2]The preferred self-designation in the Laotian province of Sam Neua is <u>Hmoob Leeg</u>.

[3]Animism refers to a belief in spirits that reside in nature and sometimes interact with people.

[4]See Olney (1983) for a complete list of references on Hmong kinship.

REFERENCES

Dunnigan, Timothy. 1982. "Segmentary Kinship in an Urban Society: The Hmong of St. Paul-Minneapolis." <u>Anthropological Quarterly</u> 55:126-134.

Dunnigan, Timothy, and Chia Vang. 1980a. "Hmong Attitudes Toward Language Maintenance: A Community Sponsored Translation Project." Paper given at the 40th Annual Meeting of the Society for Applied Anthropology. Denver.

Dunnigan, Timothy, and Tou Fu Vang. 1980b. "Negotiating Marriage in Hmong Society, An Example of the Effect of Social Ritual on Language Maintenance." <u>Minnesota Papers in Linguistics and the Philosophy of Language</u> 6:28-47.

Fishman, Joshua A. 1974. "The Sociology of Language: An Interdisciplinary Social Science Approach to Language in Society." In <u>Current Trends in Linguistics and Adjacent Arts and Sciences</u>, edited by Thomas A. Sebeok, 12:1627-1784.

Keesing, Roger M. 1975. <u>Kin Groups and Social Structure</u>. New York: Holt, Rinehart, and Winston.

Le Bar, Frank M., Gerald C. Hickey, and John K. Musgrave, 1964. <u>Ethnic Groups of Mainland Southeast Asia</u>. New Haven: The Human Relations Area Files Press.

Larteguy, Jean, avec la collaboration de Yang Dao. 1979. <u>La fabuleuse aventure du peuple de l'opium</u>. Paris: Presses de la cité.

Linnekin, Jocelyn S.   1983.   "Defining Tradition: Variations on the Hawaiian Identity."   American Ethnolo-
gist 10(2):241-252.

Olney, Douglas P.   1983. A Bibliography of the Hmong
(Miao) of Southeast Asia and the Hmong Refugees in
the United States, 2nd ed.   Minneapolis: Center for
Urban and Regional Affairs.   Southeast Asian Refugee
Studies Occasional Papers, No. 1.

Savina, F. M.   1924.   Histoire des Miao.   Hong Kong:
Imprimerie de la Société des Missions-Etrangerès.

Spicer, Edward H.   1971.   "Persistent Cultural Systems: A
Comparative Study of Identity Systems that Can Adapt
to Contrasting Environments." Science 174:795-800.

_____.   1980.   The Yaquis: A Cultural History.   Tucson:
University of Arizona Press.

Weins, Herold J.   1967.   China.   New   Haven: The Shoe
String Press.

CULTURE AND ADAPTATION:
HMONG REFUGEES IN AUSTRALIA

Gary Yia Lee

In an article on Hmong refugees in San Diego, California, Scott reports that they respond to external adversity "by becoming more Hmong rather than less so" (1982a:154). This is manifested by their preference to settle in the same geographical area and to interact mostly with members of their own ethnic group. The result is a heightened sense of ethnicity which, although reinforced by environmental factors, bases itself on strong primordial sentiments such as "a tradition of political autonomy and social self-reliance" and a "strong homogeneous community" with no major differences in language, religion or customs.

These attributes, whatever their relevance to the refugees, tell a casual reader very little about what is "being Hmong" or, particularly, what is "being more Hmong." To a Hmong, what distinguishes the Hmong from other people is their Hmong way of life. This way of life is centered around shifting agriculture, a language with mutually intelligible dialects, a strong belief in ancestor worship and animism, a division of labour according to family membership and sex, a social structure based on kinship ties through the patrilineage and clan systems, a patrivirilocal pattern of residence, a history of migration from southern China and a long tradition of being stateless.

Let me elaborate on some of these components of Hmong society. Here I will focus on economic productivity, social structure and religion. This will allow us a better evaluation of Hmong cultural articulation in Australia, and may help in determining whether or not the refugees can become more Hmong in the West or whether they have to change in order to accommodate to the new environment.

THE TRADITIONAL PRODUCTIVITY BASE

No Hmong lifestyle is possible without subsistence farming, supplemented by foraging, hunting, some fishing and handicrafts. Agriculture is the dominant form of economic production; it is closely related to the Hmong's religion through such practices as ritual offerings to appease field spirits and "first fruit" ceremonies for the dead members of one's lineage in order to seek their spiritual protection. The "prestige sphere" identified by Dalton (1971:14-16) in another context is also evident in that the more agricultural goods a person can produce and display, the more his position in the community is enhanced. Agriculture, thus, gives rise not only to rituals but also to the ways in which social roles and the division of labour within the household are observed. To some extent, the Hmong come close to the Marxist contention that the economy determines the structures and institutions of society (Marx 1965:121).

The role of family members, for instance, is defined by their order of birth as well as by their abilities to contribute to the survival of the family as a whole. Thus, a husband's duties are to act as head of his household and to provide for its members' physical and spiritual welfare. He is responsible for the selection of farming sites and the felling of trees when clearing new swiddens (farmland prepared by the slash-and-burn method) but is rarely concerned with domestic chores, apart from perhaps getting firewood. A wife, on the other hand, is given the tasks of caring for children, preparing meals, feeding chickens and pigs owned by the family, sharing in all agricultural activities with her husband and consulting him on family needs or major decisions.

In addition to the division of labour, the socialization of children is also affected when farming keeps family members close to one another with little or no outside contacts and influences. Grandparents, parents and children are together at nearly all times, whether in the home or in the field. The norms of primary group cooperation and mutual assistance are thus instilled early in life through the labour requirements imposed by the economic base. Furthermore, agricultural traditions affect the allocation and consumption of goods. While every able-bodied person participates in the growing of crops, these commodities are for the consumption of the whole household. Individual allocation of goods occurs only with jewelry, some domestic animals, clothing, opium or money.

It is obvious that subsistence cultivation plays a most significant part in shaping social roles and relations within the household.[1] In order to achieve their economic ends, the Hmong have evolved their own rules of family behaviour with rights and obligations that must be adhered to. As stated by Cohen (1968:2), in trying to satisfy their needs, people are brought into relationship with one another in an institutionalized framework with common challenges and socially prescribed expectations. This is true of Hmong, as of other human groups.

RELIGION AND SOCIAL STRUCTURE

Two other dominant features of Hmong society are its social structure and religion. Hmong social groupings are generally the product of kinship organization and its manifestations through the rituals of ancestor worship, two aspects of Hmong culture which are intricately inter-related. The fortune of an individual or family depends on close observation of ancestral reverence, geomancy and kinship networks. A Hmong's religion cannot be separated from his social groupings, and his relations with other Hmong are meaningful only in terms of whether or not they share similar ancestral rites. Therefore, he cannot do without his kinsmen and a good knowledge of their rituals in order to carry on his Hmong existence.

When two Hmong meet for the first time, their immediate concern is to establish their clan identities so that they can relate to each other. It is simple to discover one's clan through one's surname. If they belong to the same clan, the next question will be which subclan they originate from. This is done by inquiring whether they perform similar rituals in relation to funerals, the "door ceremony" and the "ox ceremony"; whether the graves of their dead are of the same construction. If these common factors are established, membership to a subclan is confirmed. From this point, they may try to learn whether they descend from the same ancestor and, thus, belong to the same lineage. A lineage is known as a "cluster of brothers" (<u>ib</u> <u>cuab</u> <u>kwv</u> <u>tij</u>) or "one ceremonial household" (<u>ib</u> <u>tus</u> <u>dab</u> <u>qhuas</u>). Members of a "ceremonial household" can die and have funerals in one another's houses, as they would share similar ancestral rituals. People merely belonging to a clan or subclan cannot be granted this ceremonial privilege.

What this means is that the social structure divides Hmong into different groupings united under clans, subclans and lineages. For a man, the clan makes it possible to know which group to identify with and which woman he can or cannot marry. After marriage, he is expected to observe the residential prescription laid down by his kinship system and reinforced by his ancestral cult. Patrivirilocality is preferred, at least until the couple has two or three children and can establish its own nuclear household away from the extended family. This does not prevent the man from maintaining close relationships with relatives of his wife. With the exception of material support, there are no ritual bonds between a married man and his affinal relatives because religious ceremonies are reserved for agnatic ancestors.

The Hmong do not have elaborate ceremonies for birth or during various stages of life. Explanations for the meaning of life are to be found in funeral rites, the meeting point between the living and the dead. This relationship between ancestors and their descendants, between religion and social structure, gives the Hmong a clearly defined way of life. As postulated by Radcliffe-Brown (1941:40), such a belief system gives incentives to those taking part in them to have a sense of dependence on their ancestors and to commemorate them for having given them their life, while they are spurred on to bring up their descendants to whom they will one day also become revered ancestors. It is this sense of duty that creates a direct association between a Hmong's religion and his social structure, particularly his lineage.

In their world view and ceremonial practices, the Hmong see an explanation for their social groupings; in their kinship ties, they find reason to maintain their religion. Religious ceremonies renew group sentiment, strengthen lineage solidarity, and inspire members to carry out their obligations to the living, the dead and those yet to be born. These factors, in Geertz's phrasing, form the group's ethos, and are "rendered intellectually reasonable by being shown to represent a way of life ideally adapted to the actual state of affairs the world view described[,] while the world view is rendered emotionally convincing by being presented as image of an actual state of affairs peculiarly well arranged to accommodate such a way of life" (Geertz 1966:3).

IMPACT OF RESETTLEMENT

Having discussed what I consider to be the most salient aspects of Hmong culture, let us now see how they have been maintained or adapted to respond to the demands and needs of a Western environment. To do this, we will need to examine first the major factors which make Hmong cultural adaptation necessary. Here I will use the Australian experience of the Hmong refugees as illustration of the issues involved. Let me add that the Hmong situation in Australia is by no means typical of other Hmong groups, although some common features may be shared by them.

In contrast to their subsistence farming in Laos, where family members all work together, the complex wage economy of Australia only accepts skilled adults into its work force. For the refugees, this involves those who have some degree of training and who can speak basic English. The division of labour is no longer based on family membership, but on outsiders' decisions as to who is chosen for work and who to be made idle. This means that for the 344 Hmong in Australia, only 50 are gainfully employed, representing 44.6 percent of the total employable population of 112. Thus, a total of 62 adults are not employed. There are 208 Hmong children in Australia, of whom 61.5 percent, or 128, are in primary and high schools.

The old tradition of joint economic productivity by all household members is seriously disrupted with those who work going their separate ways each morning while the elderly and the unemployed remain home with or without children to attend to. The wage-earners are often away from their families for eight to twelve hours a day, five to six days a week, spending only weekends and evenings at home. Children of school age are left to find company with Mickey Mouse or Bullwinkle on television in the morning, and return from school to watch Sesame Street or the Brady Bunch in the afternoon. While at school, they read Walt Disney books or Shakespeare, interact with English-speaking children, and learn from Anglo-European teachers using a curriculum which makes no mention of their culture. The parents often actively support this acculturation process, so that the children quickly identify with the new society due to their ease in acquiring English.

This almost daily fragmentation of the family by school and work has eroded the cherished idea of a cooperative household united by common interests and economic participation. With 35 of the 67 family heads without work, many parents are no longer productive. They often do not speak English and have to depend on their children for simple tasks involving contacts with non-Hmong outsiders. This reversal of roles and the consequent loss of self-esteem on the part of the older family members have made many of them feel despondent. The demands of the West have precluded them from fulfilling their traditional roles as providers and decision-makers for their families. Thus, social values regarding parental authority, filial respect, clan obligations and reverence of ancestors become gradually irrelevant or unenforceable.

This erosion of Hmong social values and norms within the family is also felt in the area of interpersonal relationships between members of the Hmong community. The social structure, as I have discussed previously, is already greatly weakened by the fact that many families share only clan membership but no other kinship features, and a few families are the sole representative of their clan in the new country. This means that there is little or no similarity in rituals between them, since the sharing of rituals is restricted to lineage and subclan members.

Of all the clans in Australia, the Lee has nineteen families with five lineages, the Yang sixteen families with four lineages, the Vang thirteen families and three lineages, the Thao ten families and three lineages, the Xiong and Vue three families and one lineage each, the Moua two families from one lineage, and the Chang one family from one lineage. Families belonging to the same lineage are often young and number no more than five to six, because only households with at least one skilled or educated member are admitted by the Australian Government for resettlement.   Furthermore, not all members of a lineage were able to escape from Laos or to resettle in the West, thereby significantly reducing the traditional networks of kinship and mutual assistance.

The young and skilled families preferred by Australia are generally ignorant of religious beliefs and practices.   Most do not have with them older members who are well experienced in Hmong customs.   Unless they are related to those who have such older members, they do not know where to turn in time of spiritual need.   They exist in a religious limbo, neither as Hmong with knowledge and observance of ancestor worship, nor as Australians with faith in Christianity.[2]   Some appear to be content with this state of affairs, filling the voids of their lives with material objects.   Sooner or later, however, they have to turn to other Hmong, because cultural and language barriers prevent them from reaching out to members of the host society.

CULTURAL CONSCIOUSNESS AND ADAPTATION

In the face of this constant intrusion on their traditions by incompatible external forces, the Hmong obviously feel their very identity threatened.   This is especially true when their unity as a household, lineage or clan is adversely affected by conflicting claims of the new country.   Like any human groups in a state of uncertainty, most of those in Australia have reacted by trying to regain direction by improving themselves with education and economic productivity, or by joining force as a group in order to forge for themselves a new identity.

At the individual level, the cultural value of self-sufficiency is still strongly followed, despite many hurdles to overcome.   The Hmong are now given the chance to stand on their own feet, following years of surviving on handouts in refugee camps in Laos and Thailand. They know that the material comfort enjoyed by members of the new country can be theirs if they strive hard enough for it. Many of those who are able to find factory work see even this as a big step forward compared to the farming they were used to in Laos, for they are no longer at the mercy of nature and war.   As a measure of their adaptability, forty-two of the fifty-six households now own cars, and eighteen have bought their own houses. Two families are in the process of buying land for market gardening. All this has been achieved within the space of four to six years of resettlement.

The formal group, for its part, also encourages members towards self-reliance and towards articulation of their culture--but in a manner acceptable to a Western society. I am referring to the Hmong-Australia Society, which was first set up in the State of Victoria in 1978. At present, it has branches in New South Wales, the Australian Capital Territory and Tasmania, with a federal body to make policies and to coordinate the activities of the state branches. Since I am more familiar with the situation in New South Wales, I will discuss mainly the society's activities in that state, which has 204 of the total Australian Hmong population of 344, in contrast to Victoria, which has 113, and Tasmania with 27.[3]

In a similar vein to other ethnic-based organizations, the Hmong-Australia Society has as its main objectives: (1) to assist Hmong refugees in their resettlement in Australia, (2) to foster mutual acceptance between Hmong and other ethnic groups, (3) to uphold Hmong cultural traditions, and (4) to safeguard Hmong interest in general. Membership is not restricted to Hmong and is entirely voluntary. Nevertheless, nearly all the Hmong in the country are financial members, except for two families.

To achieve its objectives, the society works through committees covering such areas as welfare assistance, financial loans and donations, hospital and home visiting, education, public relations, sports and recreation, women's affairs, culture and religion, and fund-raising. It is clear that most of these concerns reflect a conscious attempt to put Hmong cultural values into practice in a new environment where the kinship networks which traditionally oversee these activities are virtually absent. The society thus replaces the social structure by being a focal point for members to fall back on in time of celebration or crisis.

One of the first tasks undertaken was to get members to understand the Australian government's policies on multiculturalism and to steer the group's activities to be in line with these policies. For example, ethnic groups are now encouraged to maintain their cultures "without prejudice or disadvantage" and "to embrace other cultures" (Galbally Report 1978:4). This is so long as there is acknowledgement of "common values which give all citizens a sense of being Australian," with importance given to the English language (Commonwealth Schools Commission 1983:31). Hmong are, therefore, urged to consider themselves as Australian Hmong with a unique cultural contribution to make to their country of resettlement and with an obligation to identify with it.

Faced with only a residual social structure among its members, the society tries to promote mutual support across clan boundaries by insisting that Hmong refugees assist each other on the basis of their common ethnic background rather than membership to a lineage or clan. Overall, the majority of members have shown a genuine desire to help lessen clan and lineage consciousness by devoting time and energy for the common benefit of the group without regard to kinship ties. There are, of course, a few families which are still reluctant to take part in a common New Year celebration because of their religious beliefs, but this is a minor problem.

A good example of the society's involvement in cultural adaptation is its Ethnic School. Formed in 1980, it was designed to conduct weekend classes on Hmong language and culture for Hmong children who are growing up in Australia and who are not exposed enough to their own mother tongue and their parents' culture. The aim is to enable the students to read and write Hmong, and to appreciate the customs of their older family members so that they may understand and assist the latter in their settlement. With operation costs met from federal government funding, the school has a current enrollment of forty-three, with an attendance rate of about thirty-two in two classes. Two Hmong teachers alternate in the teaching of each class.

After using an old primer from Laos for a year, the teachers found it to be too difficult, since many of the words refer to traditional objects no longer found in Australia, and therefore convey little meaning to the refugee children. This difficulty was compounded by the lack of suitable texts on Hmong culture. With a grant from the state government, the society has attempted to fill this gap by developing its own teaching materials with more relevance to the Australian context. Two books for learning Hmong--one for young children and one for older students--have been completed, along with a book of traditional songs (for learning old forms of poetry), a collection of modern songs (for learning new poetry), a book of proverbs and a collection of folk tales. A Hmong grammar and a text on the changing way of life of Hmong refugees (for social studies) are being completed. The new books, in very simple form, have been used experimentally in class during 1983, and have drawn much enthusiastic response from children and parents.

Cultural materials are taught not only through the use of these texts, but also through simulated performances of simple ceremonies, colour slides, recordings and samples of relevant artifacts. Many young men have successfully learned the mechanics of common rituals through role-playing. The learning of more complex rituals has been offered to older individuals according to their personal interest, with the elders in the Hmong community acting as teachers.

Realising that the teaching of Hmong language and culture may offer the refugees a sense of cultural continuity but will not be sufficient to help them integrate in the Australian setting, the society also teaches them English, or arranges to have English and simple skills courses provided on a short term basis by government instrumentalities. This applies in particular to the adult Hmong, many of whom were illiterate. There have been classes on sewing and dressmaking, Australian laws and society, basic mathematics, general health education and homemaking. The primary aim is the learning of English, but these language skills are acquired through other subjects deemed useful to the social adjustment of the Hmong. Similar orientation information is also published in both Hmong and English in the society's newsletter.

Initially, most of the Hmong were reluctant to carry out any religious ceremonies in Australia, but they have now gained enough confidence to perform readily such rituals as "soul-calling," "wrist-stringing" and shamanic trances. Cultural expression outside the home or at public functions is limited to the display of handicrafts, the playing of reed-pipe music and flute, and traditional singing. Simplified versions of the New Year Celebration and funeral proceedings have been adopted, mainly from lack of time and manpower rather than the fear of being found objectionable.

Unlike some of those in the United States of America (Scott 1982b:63-85), the Hmong in Australia have never questioned the relevance of traditional beliefs to their new life, even when rituals are restricted to those not involving killing of animals. Several explanations for this disparity between the two groups could be suggested. Firstly, the Australian Government's refugee program does not depend entirely on church and community sponsorship. Most of the Hmong were admitted under this official program which provides all necessary support services, with minor assistance from voluntary agencies. They do not, therefore, come into early contacts with people who may influence them to doubt their traditional religion and to embrace a new one.

Secondly, the Australian Government actively supports the idea of a multicultural nation, as mentioned previously, and has made funds available to various groups to test out the concept, especially in the fields of culture, arts and education. The Hmong happen to be in Australia at a time when this experiment is only at its beginning stage. By joining in, they are thus encouraged to carry on with their changing traditions while learning to adapt to the host community.

Thirdly, and most importantly, the leadership and the very small size of the Hmong population have been crucial factors in this process of cultural adjustment. The informal decision-makers, whether of a traditional or Western orientation, have been most accommodating to each other, with decisions based on the democratic process instead of the dictates of a few individuals. The old leadership acknowledges the need for change, and the younger leaders know that change has to be gradual, with cultural elements acting as both an impetus and a buffer. These leaders and their followers have equal roles in guiding this change towards the common good of the Hmong and their new country.

This is, of course, easier said than done, for many problems have to be faced both within and outside the Hmong community. Overall, however, I do believe that 97.7 percent of them share in this long-term vision. With mutual support between themselves and the continuing assistance of such organizations as the Lao Community Advancement Co-operative, local welfare agencies and various levels of government, the Hmong may yet achieve this adaptation through the use of their culture as a means and an anchor.   After all, they are a universal minority group, and the adage of "home is where you make it" has always applied to their situation, even if home will take a bit longer to make in the West.

HMONG RESEARCH AND SOCIAL CHANGE

Lest I am taken to task for being too optimistic and for talking about hopes rather than reality, let me now briefly justify my arguments.

As I have read literature on the Hmong in Thai, Lao, Hmong, French and English, I have been struck by a lack of perspective in many of these works. Too often, sweeping negative statements or generalizations are made from information obtained on the basis of single encounters or interviews.   This is true especially of politically motivated newspaper reporters, travellers and arm-chair writers who often base their comments on second- or third-hand sources of information.   Even government officials and serious scholars have not escaped this tendency to refer to old, outdated accounts of the Hmong, and to make further sweeping statements after a few short visits to them.

Let me illustrate what I mean.   Geddes (1970), following a few years of field work among a group of Green Hmong in northern Thailand, came to the conclusion that the Hmong economy is a cash economy based on opium, with their whole migration pattern and way of life affected by the need to search for opium fields.   He (1976) explained Hmong polygamy on the grounds that the men marry more than one wife in order to obtain more labour for their opium growing.   Geddes did not take enough account of the fact that thousands of other Hmong in other places do not grow opium; and that polygamy is strongly condemned in Hmong society, whether or not opium is produced.

Recently, Cooper (1978) speculated that "almost every Hmong family will have some experience of patri-uxorilocality at some time."   This is because five of the eighty-seven households he studied in northern Thailand exhibit this residential pattern.   How valid is this interpretation when only 5.7 percent of the Hmong in the sample live with relatives of the wives? Again, other factors such as the rules of the ancestral cult and the kinship system have not been given adequate consideration, for the Hmong hold patriuxorilocality as being socially and religiously unacceptable.

More relevant to our concern here are statements by Scott I referred to earlier. In his conference paper two years ago (Scott 1982b:66-67, 81), he discussed in detail how "the relocation of the traditional Hmong religious system into an incompatible environment ... has entailed (1) the questioning of belief, much of which now seems painfully inappropriate in an environment with which it is no longer resonant, and (2) the abandonment of ritual in all but a few of the most conservative families ...." The annual New Year Celebration is the only occasion these rituals are taken out of their closets to be displayed out of context as a reminder of a "rapidly receding past." In an article on ethnic solidarity among the same group of Hmong in San Diego a few months later, Scott wrote that they have become "more Hmong" and interact "less and less with outsiders, even with those whose task it is to help them" (1982a:154). Could the "rapidly receding past" have come reeling back in such a short time, like strips of a movie film being pulled backward?

It is true that more of the San Diego Hmong have now joined in formal meetings or formed ethnic-based organizations, but this does not mean that they have become more Hmong. It is only that they have changed and have learned the value of formal organizations in Western societies. The formalized approach to the requirements of life is in itself un-Hmong, a Western ritual quickly seized upon by the refugees. The traditions based on subsistence agriculture, as I discussed at the beginning of this paper, are mostly now inapplicable or unavailable, and many of them have to be abandoned or changed. If the Hmong react to an alien environment by turning to each other or by migrating, we would not have five million Hmong in China today, but only a few thousand in neighbouring countries where they were supposed to seek refuge from Chinese oppression. If they cannot be assimilated in Laos, why do so many Hmong women in the West still wear Lao skirts while nearly all the men use Lao words that have been integrated into the Hmong language whenever they speak Hmong?

I would argue that, given time and opportunities, the Hmong cannot help but adapt themselves to a new society, change their way of life, and make inroads into various social strata and employment structures. The key factors, however, are time and open doors. This change cannot be achieved quickly. It has to be slow and gradual, from the physical to the abstract, from the tangible to the intangible, beginning now perhaps with cars, housing and clothes, but eventually ending with the adoption of Western values and languages. Despite opinions to the contrary, the Hmong objectively are not the autonomous people some of us like to make them out to be: they are usually accommodating, keen to become acceptable to other groups.

The above comments are not designed to discourage. On the contrary, I would like to see more research and debates on Hmong adaptation in the West. May I urge that in our search for knowledge, we should be more conscious of what is hidden from us, what is not revealed but should be known before useful generalizations can be made. The United Nations Crop Replacement Project for opium farmers in Thailand failed, because there is more, much more to the Hmong economy than the need for cash.

To avoid such pitfalls in social science research, I believe it would be more fruitful to take both the "emic" and "etic" approaches in which the researcher's observations and perceptions are combined with those of the research subjects, with information checked and cross-checked before it is used. This was well stated by Goodenough (1970:104) when he said that: (1) whenever we wish to know what people are doing and why, or what they are likely to do, we must know what kind of things they see and respond to, and (2) we must know what they believe to be the relations between these things and what they see as the possible course of action for dealing with them. As we try to unravel the complexity of the Hmong resettlement experience in the West, I hope that these premises will help yield information, interpretations and ideas on the Hmong in a much wider perspective.

CONCLUSION

I have tried to compare the new Hmong experience in the West with their traditional existence in the hills of Laos in order to see whether or not they can maintain their former way of life in the new social environment. I have used the case of the Hmong in Australia as illustration of the fact that no matter how hard an uprooted ethnic group tries to hold onto its links with the past, those links will gradually be severed and forgotten unless the group's culture can be adapted to fit into the present. Culture is not an impediment, but an instrument of social change. Carefully guided, its transformation may lead to a new form of cultural adjustment. Neglected, it will be doomed to extinction. It is argued here that the active articulation of their culture will help the refugees maintain their personal identity in the face of perplexing external demands, while they attempt to adjust to these demands and to acquire new cultural elements to give themselves a new identity befitting life in a Western society. The cultural past can act as a buffer to the upheavals of the current social change, and can give direction to the uncertainties of the future. Given some patience and the opportunities, this adjustment will certainly be achieved, because most Hmong want to adapt, to become self-sufficient and to enjoy peace and the comfort of life. Where else can they get all of that, but in the West?

ACKNOWLEDGEMENT

I wish to thank the "The Hmong in Transition" conference organizers for financial assistance to present this paper, and the Lao Community Advancement (N.S.W.) Co-operative in Sydney, Australia, for allowing me time off work to attend the conference and to visit Hmong refugees in the United States.

NOTES

[1]Hmong economic cooperation rarely goes beyond the household level. Inter-household or village relations are based on kinship ties and other factors rather than the necessity for economic productivity.

[2]There has been no conversion into Christianity so far because of the group's cohesion.

[3]No Hmong live in the states of South Australia, Western Australia, Queensland or the Northern Territory.

REFERENCES

Cohen, Y., ed. 1968. Man in Adaptation: the Cultural Present. Chicago: Aldine. Commonwealth Schools Commission, Australia.

_____. 1983. Report on the Ethnic Schools Programme. Canberra: Australian Government Printing Service.

Cooper, R.G. 1978. "Unity and Division in Hmong Social Categories in Thailand." Studies in ASEAN Sociology, edited by P.S.J. Chen and H.D. Evers. Singapore: Chopmen.

Dalton, G. 1971. Traditional Tribal and Peasant Economies. McCaleb Module in Anthropology. Reading, Mass.: Addison-Wesley.

Geddes, W.R. 1970. "Opium and the Miao." Oceania, XLI(1): 1-11.

_____. 1976. Migrants of the Mountains. Oxford: Clarendon Press.

Geertz, C. 1966. "Religion as Cultural System." In Anthropological Approaches to the Study of Religion, edited by M. Banton, pp. 1-46. London: Tavistock.

Goodenough, W. 1970. Description and Comparison in Cultural Anthropology. Chicago: Aldine.

Marx, K. 1965. Precapitalist Economic Formations, edited by E.J. Hobsbaum. New York: International Publishers.

Radcliffe-Brown, A.R. 1941. "The Study of Kinship Systems." Journal of the Royal Anthropological Institute of Great Britain and Ireland 71:1-18.

Report of the Review of Post-arrival Programmes and Services for Migrants (known as the Galbally Report).
1978. Migrant Services. Canberra: Australian Government Printing Service.

Scott, G.M. 1982a. "The Hmong Refugee Community in San
Diego: Theoretical and Practical Implications of its
Continuing Ethnic Solidarity." Anthropological
Quarterly 55 (3):146-160.

_____. 1982b. "A New Year in a New Land: Religious
Change Among the Lao Hmong Refugees in San Diego."
In The Hmong in the West: Observations and Reports,
Papers of the 1981 Hmong Research Conference, edited
by Bruce T. Downing and Douglas P. Olney, pp. 63-85.
Minneapolis: Center for Urban and Regional Affairs,
University of Minnesota.

THE MIAO IN CONTEMPORARY CHINA:
A PRELIMINARY OVERVIEW

Louisa Schein

INTRODUCTION

Of the more than five million Hmong and Miao scattered around the world today, the vast majority still live in south and southwest China, the land they have occupied for centuries. From the perspective of Hmong in other parts of the world, this region has been regarded as a remote ancestral homeland, a repository of archaic cultural forms. The result has been a tendency to overlook the fact that development and political changes have been a reality for ethnic groups in China just as they have been in Southeast Asia. Although many Miao in China are still living in the mountains and engaged in agriculture, there have been dramatic changes in their lives over the course of the twentieth century and especially since 1949. It is thus both important and illuminating to update and put into context our present knowledge of China's Miao.

To begin, this paper will describe some characteristics of the Miao group in China, with examples to illustrate that a thorough ethnographic understanding entails an examination of change as well as "tradition."[1] The paper will review relevant aspects of minority policy to provide a background of recent developments affecting all ethnic groups in the People's Republic of China. It will discuss the classification of the Miao as a nationality and the region they occupy. Some features of language and custom will be described along with recent innovations as a result of education. The paper will attempt to show some aspects of unity in an ethnic group that exhibits a great deal of apparent diversity both in language and in cultural traits.

The information presented here is a result of ongoing work among Lao Hmong refugees in the United States and a year-long comparative study of the Hmong/Miao group in France, Thailand and the People's Republic of China.[2] Research in China was conducted over a seven-month period from March to October 1982. Work was primarily under the

auspices   of   the   Central   Nationalities   Institute   in
Beijing where I resided as visiting scholar for a total
of three and a half months.   The remainder of the time
was spent traveling, with short-term research in Nationalities Institutes in the southwest provinces.

Information   was   collected   through   interviews   with
Miao and Han Chinese scholars and researchers, and with
Miao who were students or otherwise members of Nationalities Institutes.   Regular meetings were held at which an
individual or a group of scholars presented relevant material followed by questions and discussion.   In the case
of "cultural exchange" meetings I, in turn, made presentations concerning the Hmong of Southeast Asia or the
United States.   In addition, published material in Chinese was collected and translated.   This paper relies
primarily on these Chinese sources, leaving treatment of
the extensive body of Western literature for future work.
Where there are no specific citations, the information
given is cumulative, based on personal communications and
interviews in China.

ETHNIC CLASSIFICATION IN CHINA

The   population   of   China   surpassed   one   billion   in
1982.   Of that population, 6.7 percent are the officially
recognized   "minority   nationalities."   These   include   the
Mongolians and Tibetans, the many Islamic peoples, and
numerous   smaller   groups   concentrated   especially   in   the
south and west.   In contemporary China, the term "minzu"[3]
or "nationality" is used for ethnic groups, including Han
Chinese, of all sizes and socioeconomic "stages of development."   This usage differs significantly from the Western European connotations of the term "nation-state" (Fei
1980:97-98).   Since 1949, the People's Republic of China
has carried out a systematic effort at identification and
classification of minority groups for the purpose of de-
vising   appropriate   policy,   delimiting   areas   of   "autonomous" government (Weng 1950:7), and allocating seats for
representation   in   provincial   and   national   government.
This effort has undergone several phases and continues to
the present day.

Between 1949 and 1953, a process of formal self-
identification   took   place,   resulting   in   the   registration

of more than 400 minority groups. Chinese ethnologists considered this number misleading and, as a result, active research began in 1953 with the aim of discerning which names were actually local variants or designations of subgroups (Fei 1980:94). At the outset of this project, experts estimated that there were probably about sixty groups that could accurately be classed as distinct nationalities (Tsung 1954:17; Wang 1955:5). Using language, religion, customs, dress style and other aesthetic criteria (De Vos 1982:15), researchers gradually identified discrete groups for official recognition, arriving at the present-day figure of fifty-five minority nationalities. Of these, the Tujia, initially thought to be a branch of the Miao group, received separate nationality status in the 1950s, and the Jinuo, the most recently recognized nationality, received status only in 1979. There are still more than sixteen groups under consideration for nationality recognition (Fei 1980:102).

THE SETTING

The southwest provinces of China occupied by the Miao are varied in topography, with altitudes ranging from four hundred to twenty-five hundred meters (Nationalities 1981). The Yunnan-Guizhou plateau, characterized by precipitous mountain slopes and deep ravines, has peaks of two thousand to twenty-five hundred meters in elevation. Where river valleys or plains exist, they are fertile agricultural areas due in part to the temperate climate and high level of precipitation. A very large proportion of the area is rugged and steeply sloped, with significant mineral deposits of coal, mercury and tin (Nationalities 1981:445). But this proportion is suitable only for the cultivation of such grains as buckwheat, millet and maize (Nationalities 1981:446). Even though the region has valuable and untapped natural resources, survival has been a constant struggle for its indigenous inhabitants. Early estimates (Cressey 1934:369) suggest that as little as 5 percent of the total area of the Yunnan-Guizhou plateau is arable, a figure that has likely been outdated by improvements in agricultural technology (Modern 1977:91; Peng 1983:57). Miao and other mountain dwellers have become known for their utilization of even the apparently inaccessible mountain slopes by means of skillful terracing and irrigation.

In addition to the Han Chinese in these areas, Miao have had neighbors from different ethnic groups depending on their location. In Guizhou, initial surveys after 1949 estimated that 30 to 40 percent of the total population of the province comprised as many as thirty non-Han minority groups (Fei 1951:289). These groups have been reclassified, as described above, but the number illustrates the context of ethnic diversity in which the variety of Miao groups developed. Some of the most important nationalities in the area, for whom a significant degree of coresidence and contact with Miao can be assumed, include the Tujia in Hunan; the Yi, Buyi and Dong in Guizhou; the Yao in Guangxi, and the Zhuang and Hani in Yunnan. Division by province, however, is misleading since ethnic distribution in these areas is in the form of a complex mosaic which, until recently, had no specific correspondence to administrative districts nor any particular constancy over time. With the establishment of regions of autonomous government and the gradual sedentation of formerly semi-nomadic peoples, increasing stabilization of interethnic relations will undoubtedly be the trend.

Since 1949, policy for regional autonomy has been implemented on the basis of minority concentration in what are called "compact communities." Where minority populations are of certain density, regardless of their population in proportion to Han and other nationalities, they have a right to autonomous government (Liu 1954:11; Yin 1977:24-25). In some areas, where more than one minority is represented in compact communities, the region is jointly administered, as in the Xiang Xi Miaozu-Tujiazu Autonomous Prefecture in western Hunan. In all cases, the minorities involved have the right to determine the form of government, to have majority representation in government organs, and to run the affairs of the region in their own language (Liu 1954:11-12).

THE MIAO AS A NATIONALITY

The designation "Miao" has had many different connotations throughout the history of its usage (Ma 1876:

102; Lin 1940:328-329), and thus the classification of
the group to which it refers has been somewhat ambiguous.
In the first half of this century, attempts at comprehensive counts of Miao subgroups arrived at totals of seventy to eighty group names, figures which undoubtedly represented some overlap or subcategorization.   It is likely
that some of the groups then referred to as Miao are now
classified as separate nationalities.

Based on primarily linguistic criteria, the Chinese
survey teams of the 1950s determined that the huge variety of self-identified Miao subgroups were appropriately
classed as one ethnic group, with one language.   Although
a striking degree of cultural diversity obtains within
this group, the subgroups are now said to recognize one
another as coethnics, undoubtedly in part a result of recent improvements in communication, transportation and
education.

Although the name "Miao" had formerly been derogatory, used mostly by Han and other outsiders, the decision was made to adopt it without its original connotations.   It was considered the only appropriate term to
embrace the various subgroups that had been found to be
linguistically similar enough to be considered coethnics.
Thus, unlike any previous era in Chinese history, the
name "Miao" is now widely used for self-identification by
members of that nationality and there is significant evidence that negative connotations have indeed been dis-
pelled. When asked to identify their nationality in their
own language, several Miao, speaking various dialects,
used the Chinese term "Miaozu" first, giving their subgroup name only when prompted.   Given these indications
it is probable that, increasingly, subgroup names will be
used only for internal identification among Miao groups.
This represents a remarkable shift, one that will undoubtedly have far-reaching consequences for the Miao
sense   of group affiliation, particulary if it takes root
in remote villages as well as among the highly educated.

The Miao, numbering 5.03 million as of the 1982 census (Renmin Ribao), are the sixth largest nationality in
China, composing 7.5 percent of the total minority population.   They are widely distributed over the south and
southwest provinces but their largest numbers and greatest densities are in Guizhou province where 54 percent
are located.   Hunan and Yunnan provinces also have rela-

tively large populations, each with 15 percent of the total.   Smaller groupings are scattered over the provinces of Sichuan, Guangxi, Hubei, Guangdong, Fujian, Anhui and Jiangxi, and in the cities of Beijing and Shanghai.

The degree to which geographic isolation has influenced cultural diversification, sometimes for centuries, must be stressed at this point (Barth 1969:12-13).   Miao are commonly characterized as seminomadic hill peoples, swidden (slash-and-burn) cultivators of maize and upland rice.   However, even within what is referred to as south and southwest China, the groups called "Miao" have been widely scattered into varying ecological contexts with different neighbors and particular local histories.   For instance, some of the Miao of southeast Guizhou, formerly referred to as the "Hei" or "Black" Miao, live along the Qingshui River and have developed an elaborate river culture which informs not only their folklore and their customs, but also their economic activities.   The availability of water and fertile valleys has allowed many to engage in lowland cultivation.   Paddy rice is their primary crop and staple food.   This group, accounting for a large proportion of the total number of Miao in Guizhou, cannot necessarily be considered any less "Miao" for its divergence from common stereotypes of Miao ethnic identity (Leach 1954:29-41).

LANGUAGE AND EDUCATION

According to contemporary classification, the Miao language can be divided into three major dialects and one major subdialect.   There are also several regional subdialects and vernaculars (Miao 1962:2-3; Lemoine 1972: 17).   To the untrained ear the major dialects are mutually unintelligible.   This was demonstrated by the observed use of Mandarin Chinese between Nationalities Institute students of different Miao dialect groups.   Linguists specializing in Miao language, however, maintain that, although the dialects differ in vocabulary as well as pronunciation, 40 percent of the vocabulary is shared among the three and that the names used by the Miao for themselves are cognates, or variations of a single word. The dialects, named for the regions in which they are spoken, break down as follows:

Chuan Qian Dian

Spoken primarily in Sichuan, Guizhou and Yunnan by nearly half the total Miao speakers, the "Western" dialect is thought to have retained the most elements of what is considered to be the "ancient" Miao language. Chuan Qian Dian speakers call themselves "Hmoob" (Barney-Smalley romanization), and their speech is clearly intelligible to a speaker of the Hmoob Dawb (White Hmong) or Hmoob Ntsuab (Blue Hmong) dialects of Southeast Asia. The Dian Dong Bei subdialect of Chuan Qian Dian, spoken in northeast Yunnan, bears less resemblance to Southeast Asian Hmong dialect.

Qian Dong

Most speakers of the "Central" dialect are in Guizhou Province, although they are also found in the neighboring areas of Hunan and Guangxi. Qian Dong speakers make up about one third of the total Miao speakers and pronounce their names as variations of "Hmu" or "Hmo."

Xiang Xi

Less than a quarter of the total Miao speakers use the "Eastern" dialect of western Hunan and eastern Guizhou. This dialect differs from the previous two in that it has six tones instead of eight. Xiang Xi speakers call themselves variations of "Qhov Xyooj" (Barney-Smalley romanization).

In addition to speakers of the three major dialects, there are at present more than two hundred thousand Miao who don't speak their own language. The majority of these are Han speakers, but some are also speakers of the Yao and Dong languages. This point raises some questions about ethnic classification.

No evidence has been found of ancient scripts for the Miao language. However, the legend that there was once such a script is widespread among all groups of Miao, as among many other ethnic groups of this region. Before 1949, some writing systems had been created by missionaries working in Miao areas. In Panghai, East

Guizhou, a romanized script was devised for Qian Dong speakers, and in the Zhaotong-Weining district on the Yunnan-Guizhou border, Samuel Pollard developed a script which was learned by an estimated twenty thousand to thirty thousand Dian Dong Bei speakers.

During the 1950s, Chinese policy for development work in minority areas placed a high premium on the creation of written languages for all minorities that had no script of their own. The Institute of Linguistics and Philology of the Chinese Academy of Sciences sent field teams to the southwest provinces to investigate minority languages (Fu 1957:28). Scripts were developed for each of the three major dialects and for the Dian Dong Bei subdialect of Miao. All are romanizations. While the scripts were intended for use in schools and in the affairs of autonomous regions, they have not been as widely employed as was first expected. This is largely attributed to the desire on the part of many nationalities to study and work in Chinese so as to be able to communicate with members of other nationalities.

In addition to development of minority written languages, education for all nationalities has been extensively supported. Primary and secondary schools in minority areas were established at a remarkable rate after 1949 (Yin 1977:74-5). In mountainous regions or where inhabitants were nomadic, boarding schools were set up with students' living expenses absorbed by the State (Huang 1982:7). Ten Institutes for Nationalities, including the Central Institute in Beijing, now operate in addition to local higher education institutions in minority areas. Students receive an education closely comparable to the standard college curriculum in Chinese universities. One can major in such fields as math and science, history and politics, language or arts, with remedial education available where necessary, especially in the case of students for whom Chinese was not a first language. Preferential admissions policies exist in the form of lower qualifying scores required on entrance examinations and priority over Han Chinese with comparable qualifications (Huang 1982:5). After completing their college education, most minority students return to their home provinces to occupy teaching or government positions.

SOME ASPECTS OF TRADITION AND CHANGE

Certain traits and orientations were regularly identified by Miao and Han Chinese in such a way as to be
considered "symbols" in the identity system of the Miao
in China (Spicer 1971).   For instance, members of both
groups noted the historic Miao reputation for opposing
external domination and fighting fiercely for autonomy
(Castile 1981:xix).   Miao are said to differ from Han in
the extent of "respect" accorded to women in their society.   As with most of the minority nationalities, women
never had bound feet and customarily worked alongside men
in the fields.   With regard to dress, there are as many
variations in style as there are Miao localities, but as
a whole the Miao are known for their intricate needlework
(Tsung 1954:18), their wax-resistant dyeing techniques
and the characteristic pleated skirts worn by the women.
Men are renowned for their skill in crafting elaborate
silver ornaments (Peng 1983:60).

Certain forms of music and dance are considered distinctive elements of Miao culture.   A great number of annual festivals and ceremonial occasions require specific
performances which differ by subgroup.   Important instruments include gongs, drums and leaf-blowing, depending on
region.   All Miao groups are renowned for their skill and
versatility in singing.   The improvised dialogue style of
song is quite widespread.   Dance styles are also characteristic—especially courtship dances performed by unmarried youth at festival times. One dance common among Miao
of southeast Guizhou involves a delicately embroidered
ribbon of cloth which the unmarried girl uses as a symbol
of her affection, and the lusheng or qeej (kheng), a
mouth organ of bamboo pipes.   A suitor, playing the
lusheng, asks the girl for her love by asking for the
embroidered ribbon.   She dances, coyly withholding it
until he has pursued her enough to persuade her of his
sincerity.   Then, if she accepts his offer, she ties the
ribbon on his lusheng and they dance together in celebration.

A carefully choreographed performance of this dance
was observed at the annual pan-Miao festival held on the
campus of the Nationalities Institute.   Every spring, on
or about April 8 of the lunar calendar, Miao in the
Beijing area gather for a festival in honor of a Miao

hero from central Guizhou who died defending his people
from conquest by another tribe. Among the songs and dances performed in 1982 was the one described above.

The festival gives some insight into the types of
nontraditional vocations in which Miao are engaged and
into the kind of attention paid to minority customs in
the People's Republic of China. The dancers, both of the
Miao nationality, were professionals who had been trained
in several genres of dance. One is a member of a Beijing-
based nationalities song and dance troupe; the other was
in Beijing for a year of additional training before returning to the home province to work either as a teacher
or a performer. Choreography for this type of performance
is a result of research in minority provinces. Instructors at the Nationalities Institute spend some months out
of each year traveling to minority areas both to recruit
students and to study indigenous music and dance. These
instructors, often minorities themselves, use the results
of their research to design dances which students of all
nationalities will then study and perform.

The bamboo pipe organ, called lusheng (the Chinese
term meaning reed pipe) by many of the Miao in China, is
also considered a symbol of the Miao nationality. There
is an extraordinary range of variation both in the style
of the instrument itself and in the traditions for its
use. In the more easterly locations in Guizhou and northern Guangxi, the bamboo tubes are arranged vertically and
are sometimes as tall as twelve to fourteen feet. Different varieties of the instrument are used for different
festival and ceremonial occasions, sometimes accompanied
by elaborate, almost acrobatic dancing. In the past the
lusheng was also said to have a martial function, used to
call members of neighboring villages to battle, to boost
the morale of the soldiers and to frighten the enemy.

In western Guizhou, Sichuan and Yunnan provinces,
lusheng tubes are horizontally arranged. They are shorter
and are used for fewer purposes than is standard farther
east. In some of the western areas, the use of the instrument is restricted for the most part to funerals.
Again, great differences in style and usage have not
changed the importance of the lusheng as a symbolic instrument of all Miao.

CONCLUSION

I have attempted here to give a brief introduction to the Miao of contemporary China. Diversity is one of the most salient characteristics of the group that is presently classified as Miao in the People's Republic. In language and agriculture, as well as in dress and festival styles, a great variety of cultural traits among Miao subgroups appears to have resulted from geographic separation and from differences in context. Further, directed change, in such efforts as development and education, has had a far-reaching impact on the lives of all China's nationalities, especially since 1949. These points are intended to indicate the importance of investigating the group studied in the context of the times and milieu which inform their daily lives. Toward this end a great deal of work remains to be done.

What I have presented here is some basic data and preliminary conclusions to suggest possibilities for further research. There is a significant and growing literature in both Chinese and Western languages which can provide insight into the contemporary situations of Hmong and Miao in various parts of the world, as well as into their role in the history of China and Southeast Asia. In addition, primary ethnographic research can continue to be a rich source of new information. It is my hope that ongoing work will give us more perspective on the Hmong and Miao, not in terms of static cultural forms, but rather, according to varying contexts, in terms of a dynamically emerging identity.

NOTES

[1]"Tradition" is used here to refer to a concept the Hmong themselves have of their cultural origins. Although it is a problematic construct in the context of ongoing change, it is a powerful image for Hmong who have migrated far from their Chinese homeland.

[2]This latter study was made possible by a Samuel T. Arnold Fellowship from Brown University.

[3]The "Hanyu Pinyin" system of romanization is used here for Chinese terms and the Barney-Smalley orthography for

Hmong terms (cf. Ernest Heimbach, White Hmong-English Dictionary, Ithaca, New York: Cornell University, 1969).

REFERENCES

Barth, Fredrik.   1969.   Ethnic Groups and Boundaries. Boston: Little Brown and Company.

Castile, George Pierre, and Gilbert Kushner, eds.   1981. Persistent Peoples: Cultural Enclaves in Perspective. Tucson: University of Arizona Press.

Cressey, George Babcock. 1934. China's Geographic Foundations. New York: McGraw-Hill Book Co.

De Vos, George, and Lola Romanucci-Ross. 1982. Ethnic Identity: Cultural Continuities and Change. Chicago: University of Chicago Press.

Fei Hsiao-tung.   1980.   "Ethnic Identification in China." Social Sciences in China 1:94-107.

_____. 1951. "The Minority People in Kweichow." China Monthly Review 121, 12:289-94.

Fu Mao-chi.   1957.   "Written Languages for China's Minorities." People's China 3:25-31.

Huang-ying.   1982.   "A Brief Introduction to China's Minority Education." Beijing: Cultural Palace of Nationalities (unpublished).

Leach, Edmund R.   1964.   Political Systems of Highland Burma.   Boston: Beacon Press (first published, 1954).

Lemoine, Jacques.   1972.   Un Village Hmong Vert du Haut Laos.   Paris: Centre National de la Recherche Scientifique.

Lin Yueh-Hwa. 1940. "The Miao-Man Peoples of Kweichow." Harvard Journal of Asiatic Studies 5, 3-4:261-345.

Liu Chun. 1954. "National Minorities Enjoy Regional Autonomy." People's China 1, 1:9-14.

Ma Touan-Lin d'Hervey de Saint-Denys, trans. 1876. Peuples Etrangères à la Chine. Geneva: H. Georg. (1972 by Gregg International Publishers, England).

Miao Language Team, Chinese Academy of Social Sciences. 1962. "A Brief Description of the Miao Language." In Miao and Yao Linguistic Studies, edited by Herbert C. Purnell. Ithaca, New York: Cornell University, Southeast Asia Program, Data Paper Number 88, 1972, p. 1026.

Modern China Series. 1977. China's Minority Nationalities: Selected Articles From Chinese Sources. San Francisco: Red Sun Publishers.

Nationalities Affairs Commission, Editing Committee of the Publishing Series for Five Kinds of Nationalities Problems, "China's Minority Nationalities" Editing Group. 1981. China's Minority Nationalities (in Chinese). Beijing: People's Press.

Peng Jianqun. 1983. "A Miao Nationality Village." China Reconstructs 32 (3):57-63.

Renmin Ribao. 1982. People's Daily. (in Chinese). 29 October 1982.

Spicer, Edward H. 1971. "Persistent Cultural Systems." Science 74, 4011:795-800.

Tsung Yun. 1954. "China's National Minorities." People's China 11: 17-23.

Wang Shu-tang. 1955. China: Land of Many Nationalities. Peking: Foreign Languages Press.

Weng Tu-chien. 1950. "China's Policy on National Minorities." People's China 1, 7:6-7.

Yin Ming. 1977. United and Equal: The Progress of China's Minority Nationalities. Peking: Foreign Languages Press.

GEOMANCY AS AN ASPECT
OF UPLAND-LOWLAND RELATIONSHIPS

Nicholas Tapp

The remarkable practice of geomancy by the Hmong is the focus of this paper. Geomancy literally means a system of divination by reference to the forms of the earth. This is a system for the siting of villages and the graves of ancestors and relatives according to the contours of the mountains and watercourses formed in their valleys. Feuchtwang (1974) has provided the most comprehensive account of this system as it is practiced by the Chinese, and Lemoine (1972) was the first to note its practice among the Hmong. Geomancy, or loojmem, as the Hmong call it, provides a very complete and articulate idiom for the metaphorical expression of social change and conflict. It has much in common with landscape painting and the arts of gardening, which also orginated in China. Unfortunately, I do not have space in this paper to go into the details of the system as practiced by the Hmoob Dawb with whom I worked in the north of Thailand. Instead I have concentrated on the strange anomaly of the practice of this system, which has always been seen as a peculiarly Chinese one, by the Hmong who constitute an ethnic minority within China.

Feng-shui, as the Chinese call loojmem, is most widely practiced in the hilly, mountainous regions of south and southwest China, where the Hmong and certain other minority nationalities have settled. While most of the imagery and directions for the selection of a site assume the presence of a mountainous landscape, feng-shui is practiced in many nonmountainous areas, where trees, rocks and other natural phenomena must suffice to symbolise the great mountains and watercourses which the system properly demands. According to Feuchtwang, feng-shui's concentration on mountains has never been adequately explained. Since expressions of mountainous imagery are far more common in the classification systems of upland-dwelling minorities such as the Hmong[1] than they are in the classification systems of the great wet-rice cultivating mass of the Chinese population, and since the Hmong practice feng-shui with no apparent awareness that it may be of non-Hmong origins, the system can be interpreted as being at least as much a Hmong one as it is a Chinese one.

Some historical confirmation of my point comes from theories which hold that feng-shui itself did not originate in China, but rather came up from the south, together with iron-working and other practices which resulted in the "distinctly Chinese" custom of double burial. But this sort of evidence is not what I wish to base my argument upon. I base it rather upon the very extensive anthropological work on the theory of ethnic boundaries that has been conducted in the region (by which I include the mountainous area of Burma, Laos, Vietnam and Thailand as well as southwestern China).

Very often it has been found that whole communities may be ambiguous about their ethnic status, and consider themselves, for example, as both Shan and Kachin (Leach 1954), or both Lahu and Lisu. (Durrenberger 1970). Very many cases of individuals changing ethnic status to be in accord with changing economic, marital or other situations, have been noted over the years. Lehman (1979) has remarked that an ethnic category must never be confused with the various genetic-linguistic groups with which it may be identified at different times. The ethnic term "Miao" is a prime example of this, since at different times (and particularly before the thirteenth century [Ruey-Yih-Fu 1962]) it has been applied to widely differing groups. (And today again in China since the Revolution it has taken on a different context.) The real issue, as Lehman emphasises, is whether an ethnic label such as "Miao" or "Karen" has remained constant over time, since it is likely to have retained a constant meaning (as opposed to usage). This is the case with the Chin people, where "Chin" was originally a Burmese term for "allies." So it becomes irrelevant, from a historical perspective, whether the term "Miao" in the past included the actual ancestors of the present-day Hmong. What is important is that it conveyed certain connotations (of rebelliousness, for example) and that it is still widely used in this derogatory sense, at least in Thailand, to refer to the Hmong today.

Even the ethnic label "Han Chinese" is notoriously vague in the genetic-linguistic sense, particularly in the southern parts of China where the history of the Hmong extends. Many of the present-day population of southern China who call themselves "Chinese" are the descendants of people who did not call themselves "Chinese" at all, but were the members of quite different groups such as the Norsu.[2] Francis L.K. Hsu studied a whole village of this type (1949). They have "become" Chinese, and--dating back to Leach's work on the Kachin--there are many examples of people "becoming" members of other ethnic categories. So I am arguing that the real issue is not whether feng-shui, or loojmem, is Hmong or Chinese. Rather, I wish to demonstrate that the system has evolved out of the context of interethnic relations in south China. Members of the expanding Chinese state came into contact with the members of other genetic-linguistic groups only gradually, over a period of some two thousand years, often becoming members of those groups themselves, or adopting members of those groups as "Chinese." Thus, the practice of feng-shui as a distinctly Chinese system arose out of an accommodation with the members of many different groups.

From this point of view I would also argue against the common tendency to view the Hmong as an isolated, autonomous group which traditionally lacked relations with other groups (Hinton 1969). On the contrary, it is clear from all their stories and many of their rituals and customs, that they have had long and sustained contacts with the members of other cultures throughout their history. The myth of the self-sufficient tribe has been fostered by colonialists and early anthropologists as a useful administrative tool and a pretext for exploiting the people so categorised (Helm 1968). But such a view does not do justice to the extensive interdependency which in the past, before the nineteenth-century advent of European colonialism, characterised the relations between the uplands and lowlands. In many cases the people of the mountains and the remote regions were dependent on the people of the lowlands for rice, which grows best in the lowlands. The mountains and their forests, in turn, were full of valuable products which could be exchanged for the rice of the lowlands. From this point of view another controversy--over whether the Hmong were origi-

---

nally wet-rice cultivators settled in the lowlands, or have always been shifting cultivators based in the mountains—also becomes irrelevant. Very probably different groups, communities, even families, of the ancestors of the Hmong did both at different times and in different regions. The question of the "original ecology" of the Hmong becomes senseless once one realises the danger of over-reifying ethnic categories, as well as the risks of assuming that the ethnic labels "Miao" or "Chinese" always referred to culturally distinct groups over the past (or that ecological distinctions such as the one between "shifting" and "permanent" agriculturalists were always isomorphic with ethnic distinctions). Also senseless is the related question of who preceded whom in the actual lands of China. What one wants to emphasize, therefore, is the adaptability of the Hmong and groups like them, their capacity to adjust to different ecological situations and the relations they have always held with the members of many other different ethnic groups. These factors are, of course, of some relevance to their current situation as refugees.

The geomantic system which the Hmong practice is truly a remarkable one. On the welfare of the ancestors depends the fortunes of their descendants. There are many accounts of the most ideal burial site, specifying that mountains must be arranged in a particular way around the site, with the rivers flowing in a certain direction down to a dragon's pool where rebirth begins. The deceased must be buried at a certain time, along the loojmem or veins of the dragon, which run through the mountains. (The recurrent image of the mountains is that of the dragon, which has connotations of natural strength and energy and is associated with underwater creatures, royalty and the ancestors.) If a person were buried in such a place, it is said, he would "catch" the loojmem rather as one catches a train, and ride it as one rides an ox, to the place where he enters the otherworld, where he would become a king. And when the father is king in heaven, as was once graphically told me, the son will become king on earth. This is because the ancestor watches over the welfare of his or her descendants in this world of yang, and thus it is in the interests of descendants to assure their parents and other ancestors of the best possible burial places. The Hmong in Thailand assume that one can never find the absolutely perfect burial place, since if someone had, he would be a king and rule the land, and it is not the Hmong who rule the land of Thailand.   Such places might exist in China, they said, but usually one does the best one can, and tries to avoid the more inauspicious conjunctions of natural features.

While I was seeking the origins of loojmem, I collected a most remarkable story that illustrates the precise contours required for the best, the absolutely ideal burial site.   The story is about two brothers who separately requested their respective descendants to bury them very close together, in the same, ideal spot.   The elder brother was buried with gold beneath his head for a pillow, the younger had only a stone pillow.   But when the sons of the elder brother came to pay their respects at the grave three years later, they found that flowers--a sign of the decay necessary for reincarnation--had sprouted first on the grave of their uncle, the younger brother.   So they dug up the stone and gold pillows and exchanged them.   The elder brother was thus enabled to be reincarnated first, traveling along the lines of the dragon's veins to the pool which is the entrance to the otherworld, before his younger brother.   When the sons of the younger brother turned up and discovered what had happened, they realised how wicked their cousins were, and the story concludes that "since that time we Hmong have never got on well together with the Chinese.   We Hmong moved away and refused to speak the same language."

Now clearly this refers to a time in the Hmong imagination, when the ethnic categories of Hmong and Chinese were not clearly demarcated, and this alone is some justification of the historical viewpoint I have adopted. But more important is that here the Hmong are using the geomantic idiom itself, the idiom of feng-shui, which has always been seen as a peculiarly Chinese one, to explicate their own differences from the Chinese.   And this is not the only case where this is done.   A Lolo story employs a similar idiom in a similar context.[3]   Similar themes occur often in the Hmong stories of the various incarnations of Tswb Tchoj, the culture hero who periodically arises to unify the clans and establish hegemony over the land. In these stories, contests take place between the Hmong and the Chinese for the ideal site in which to bury their respective ancestors.   The usual result is that the Hmong lose out, owing to the trickery and deception of the Chinese. Very often the Chinese bury some form of metal in the grave of the Hmong. Because it does not putrefy, the metal prevents the decay which must take place if effective reincarnation is to occur. Often, too, in the stories, the Chinese desecrate Hmong graves in other ways; just as the Imperial dynasties desecrated the graves of ancestors of pretenders to the throne. The imagery is clearly one of <u>sovereignty and rebellion</u> (Feuchtwang, personal communication). It is highly improbable that the Hmong merely adopted the ideology of a conquering people and used it to explain how they lost control of the land to those same conquering people, the Chinese. As a result of these stories, I much prefer to see geomancy as being as distinctively Hmong as it is Chinese. I would also suggest that geomancy evolved (as did the Chinese state itself in the south) out of southern China's complex ever-changing political situation in which interethnic relations were forged around such ideal terms as "Han," "Miao" and "Lolo." This seems truer to both the historical and the ethnographical evidence.

A similiar case can be made for the patrilineal clan-based kinship system of the Hmong, which some authorities believe the Hmong borrowed from the invading Chinese. It is far more likely that what seem to be "Chinese" surnames, but which in fact are shared by many other peoples of the region (such as the Lisu, Yao, Kachin and Shan), actually form part of a <u>common system</u> which such people share with the "Chinese." We are right to consider geomancy, the patrilineal kinship system and the burial system together, since geomancy is above all a system for the siting of ancestral graves, while Hmong surname groups may be differentiated internally as "Hmong" or "Chinese" according to the way each group aligns graves to the slant of the mountain, and whether stones or biodegradable materials such as branches are used to mark the site. Indeed, other stories account for Chinese mastery over the land by their demarcation of their territory by stones, in contrast to the grasses and twigs used by the Hmong, which were blown away by the wind. It is particularly interesting that geomancy itself should be above all a system concerned with acquisition of certain types of territory which assure the prosperity and welfare of one's descendants, and that it should be this very system which has been chosen by the Hmong to express their ethnic rivalries with the Chinese and other peoples. We know that throughout the recorded history of southwest China fierce conflicts took place between the expanding Chinese state--which was attracted by the mineral resources, salt wells and forest products of the mountainous regions--and the people who lived there. The written accounts provide a very clear record of the long historical struggle for control of material resources. It may even be that metal is felt to be particularly unlucky because it was through knowledge of the principles of ironworking, at about 600 B.C., during the mid-Chou period, that the early Chinese states began to establish their hegemony. This point is speculative, but leads me to my conclusion.

Apart from contributing my findings to some of the controversies about the origins of the Hmong, their kinship system and technology, this paper makes a more important point. This is that history is not always to be read in books or written documents, or even archaeological remains, and that the oral legends of the Hmong about their past have much to teach us about real history; that is, a history which is being lived and felt now. What I hope to have emphasised is the continuing power of the Hmong oral tradition to encapsulate and deal with changing conditions through the use of traditional symbols, even in the context of what McLuhan called a post-literate society. Memories of the past are always selective, and can never be accurate or comprehensive in every detail. Thus one is looking for a new kind of history, not one divided into "true" or "false," but one arising from a more phenomenological concern with historical consciousness as it affects current behaviour. Real history is what is remembered.

NOTES

[1]In the Hmong language, this mountainous imagery is found in such upslope/downslope dichotomies as _pem_ (uphill from) and _nram_ (downhill from); _sab hnub tawm_ (the east, the side the sun leaves) and _sab hnub poob_ (the west, the side the sun falls), and _ib nrab_ (one half of a horizontal measurement) and _ib ntav_ (one half of a vertical measurement).

[2]There is even some evidence to suggest that the Hmong term _Suav_, used to distinguish the Chinese, referred more to social than ethnic differences, being also applied for example to their "Lolo" (Norsu) landlords.

[3]See Graham (1955).

REFERENCES

Durrenberger, E.P. 1970. Lisu Project: A Socio-Medical Study of the Lisu of North Thailand. Tribal Research Centre, Chiangmai.

Feuchtwang, S. 1974. Chinese Geomancy, An Anthropological Analysis of. Vientiane, Laos: Vithagna.

Graham, D.C. 1955. "A Lolo Story: 'The Great God of O-Li-Bi-Zih' by Lin Kuang-Tien." Journal of American Folklore 68.

Helm. J., ed. 1968. Essays on the Problem of Tribe. Proceedings of the 1967 Annual Spring Meeting of the American Ethnological Society, Seattle, University of Washington.

Hinton, P., ed. 1969. Tribesmen and Peasants in North Thailand: Proceedings of the First Symposium of the Tribal Research Centre, Chiangmai 1967. Tribal Research Centre, Chiangmai.

Hsu, Francis L.K. 1949. Under the Ancestors' Shadow: Chinese Culture and Personality. London: Routledge & Kegan Paul.

Leach, E.R. 1954. Political Systems of Highland Burma.

Lehman, F.K. 1979. "Who Are The Karen, and If So, Why? Karen Ethnohistory and a Formal Theory of Ethnicity." In Ethnic Adaptation and Identity: The Karen on the Thai Frontier with Burma, edited by C. Keyes. Institute for the Study of Human Issues, Philadephia.

Lemoine, Jacques. 1972. Un Village Hmong Vert du Haut Laos.   Paris: Centre National de la Recherche Scientifique.

Ruey, Yih-Fu. 1962. "The Miao: Their Origins and Southwards Migrations."   Proceedings of the International Association of Historians of Asia. Taipei, Taiwan.

PART TWO

Adapting to a New Society

INTRODUCTION

Glenn L. Hendricks

In the previous section the papers focused on some global issues of Hmong history, culture and the process of change and adaptation over time. In Part Two the papers provide concrete cases of these processes at work.

Hmong women are faced with possibilities for establishing new roles in the United States. But their lack of education has made the search for employment opportunities quite difficult. Sarah Mason examines training programs that have been designed for Hmong women and finds many of them lacking in their ability to provide adequate economic mobility for the future. Rather she sees them as slotting the women participants into marginal low-wage backwaters of the employment market.

William Meredith and George Rowe report on a study of shifts in Hmong attitudes towards aspects of marriage as a consequence of their contact with western ideas and experiences. Echoing some of the authors of Part One they suggest caution in generalizing about cultural commonalities in such practices as polygyny, bride price and clan endogamy of the Hmong in their Lao homeland. They suggest that in some cases changes were already underway long before their arrival in the United States. However, their data indicates that in certain areas, particularly for the educated and female, under the influences of the new environment, changes are reported in attitudes toward gender equality in family decision-making and the acceptability of polyandrous relationships.

Beth Goldstein's study of a case of sexual assault details the social implications when American values and their legal expression conflict with Hmong values and traditional forms of dispute adjudication. She points out that in the American view such cases are seen as conflict between individuals and consequently resolution pits one against the other. From the Hmong standpoint the emphasis is upon the effect the assault has upon the family and clan system and therefore settlements represent negotiations that heal the breach in group relations.

Catherine Stompus Gross provides a case study of the adaptation of Hmong to a specific community, Isla Vista,

California. She outlines what she finds to be both inhibiting and facilitating factors in the adjustment of this
group of Hmong to the community.

Nancy Donnelly's description of a Hmong needlecraft
sales cooperative provides a sociological analysis of the
tenuous relationships that exist in a joint American-
Hmong economic venture. More importantly she provides
those individuals and groups who have an interest in similar endeavors with a framework by which they might examine aspects of their own activities. As she points out,
the very nature of the refugee situation places the Hmong
in the subordinate role of client to others, typically
Americans, who assume the super-ordinate roles of broker
or patron.

The final item in this section is a report introduced by Stephen Reder of a symposium organized to discuss major issues that emerged in a government funded
study of Hmong resettlement in the United States. Doug
Olney reviews available demographic information. John
Finck discusses the significance of the large migration
of Hmong to the Central Valley of California. Bruce
Downing outlines some issues relating to the acquisition
of English. Shur Vang Vangyi reviews the employment situation and the related problem of welfare dependency,
while Mary Cohen offers a hopeful view for the future as
Hmong have come to view education as a key to their eventual accommodation to life in the United States. Finally
Simon Fass takes an economist's viewpoint in a report on
the various efforts that have been made to assist the
Hmong in gaining economic self-sufficiency.

TRAINING HMONG WOMEN: FOR MARGINAL WORK OR ENTRY INTO THE MAINSTREAM

Sarah R. Mason

INTRODUCTION

Since the American withdrawal from Southeast Asia in 1975, approximately 650,000 refugees from Vietnam, Cambodia and Laos have resettled in the United States. While this refugee population as a whole has adjusted well to American life, serious problems remain unresolved for subgroups such as the elderly, older youth, preliterate people and women. Recently the situation of refugee women has become a focus of serious concern among resettlement officials, service providers, volunteers and women's advocacy groups. The problems of Indochinese and other refugee women have also been addressed by several international conferences, including the United Nations Decade for Women (Copenhagen, July 1980), the Intergovernmental Committee for Migration Seminar on Adaptation and Integration of Permanent Immigrants (Geneva, April 1981), and the United Nations High Commissioner for Refugees Workshop on Integration of Refugees from Indochina in Countries of Resettlement (Geneva, October 1980).

A major issue at these international meetings has been the low economic status of refugee women, a disproportionate number of whom are household heads with large family responsibilities. In the United States, a study conducted in 1980 (Walter 1981:17) of 347 Indochinese refugee women sponsored by Lutheran Immigration and Refugee Service, showed that one-third of the 238 households were headed by women. Despite the stipulation of the 1980 Refugee Act that women must have the same employment training opportunities as men, training programs accessible to women have been inadequate and inequitable. Generally job training programs targeted for male heads of households are designed to prepare them for employment in the economic mainstream, while women are channeled into programs leading to marginal work such as housecleaning and cottage industry sewing. Income-generating projects for refugee women have also focused on piecework sewing, craft production, crop picking and other low-paid, exploitative labor. Although this type of employment provides refugee women with much-needed income, it tends to stabilize their economic status at a low level without providing them with the skills necessary for economic mobility. Recent research (Fass 1983: Table 1) indicates that sewing projects organized in the United States as employment training and income-generating programs for refugee women, for example, have provided an average annual income per participant of only $117 in projects with minimal external funding and $303 in those with substantial external funding.

The purpose of the present study is to survey the employment training programs available to Hmong women since 1975 in Minneapolis-St. Paul, Minnesota--which has one of the largest urban concentrations of Hmong in the United States--and to evaluate the effectiveness of these programs in resolving the problem of low economic status among refugee women. The focus of the study is on the types of training provided, accessibility of the programs and economic outcome for the women trained.

The method of the study is, first, the collection of statistical data, annual reports and other printed materials available from program administrators. The second step is the interviewing of administrators, instructors and Southeast Asian counselors and interpreters involved in refugee employment training to gain additional information not included in printed materials. This includes data on support services provided (including child care and transportation), location of training sites, tuition costs, priorities in enrollment and tuition assistance, educational prerequisites and potential for economic advancement in various areas of employment. The third step is the evaluation of the training programs available to Hmong women within the larger framework of training programs provided for Southeast Asian refugees.

The author views this as an exploratory study that will provide preliminary data for a more comprehensive study of employment training programs for Southeast Asian women throughout the United States. The larger study will include interviews with Southeast Asian women who have participated in these programs, thus providing individualized data on refugee women's work experience. This type of data has not been available for the present study.

The conceptual framework of the study is based on recent research in the growing field of Third World women's education. New studies in this field have developed fresh perspectives on the effect of educational programs on Third World women's lives as workers, citizens, mothers and wives, whereas earlier research focused on women's education as a means of advancing the economic development of Third World countries. Basic issues include accessibility of educational programs, type of education provided, content, quality of instruction and the social, political or economic outcome of the training. The author views these issues as basic to the study of educational programs for Third World women moving into new socioeconomic orders, whether in developing countries or in immigrant/refugee communities in the United States.

FEDERAL ASSISTANCE TO REFUGEE JOB TRAINING

Federal educational assistance for refugees in the United States has been available since the influx of Cuban refugees following Fidel Castro's rise to power in 1959, but until 1980 these benefits have varied widely among nationality groups. The Cuban Refugee Program, authorized under the Migration and Refugee Assistance Act of 1962, provided for adult education and employment training, as well as refresher courses for medical professionals to assist them in meeting certification requirements. The 1962 act remained in effect for over twenty years, with no time limit on eligibility for the approximately 800,000 Cuban refugees who arrived in the United States during that period.

The Indochina Migration and Refugee Assistance Act of 1975 extended these benefits to Southeast Asian refugees but imposed a limit of three years on eligibility (reduced to eighteen months in 1982). The 1975 act expired on 30 September 1977, and nearly a month elapsed before new legislation authorized the continuation of educational programs and other forms of assistance. From October 1977 to March 1978 an interruption of five months occurred, causing confusion in the refugee community and frustration among administrators of refugee training programs. It was not until the enactment of the Refugee Act of 1980 that permanent, comprehensive refugee legislation became effective. By early 1981, retrenchment in federal spending on social programs caused drastic cuts in refugee educational programs, despite the provisions of the 1980 act. These discontinuities have had a devastating effect on refugee women's programs, looked upon by many administrators as secondary in importance to other refugee programs.

DEVELOPMENT OF INDOCHINESE WOMEN'S PROGRAMS

Indochinese refugee women's programs have evolved as a complex network of English and cross-cultural orientation classes, support groups and employment training programs. Funded by various combinations of public and private funds, they have been sponsored by voluntary agencies, adult education centers, technical and vocational schools and Indochinese mutual assistance associations (MAAs). While many publicly funded women's programs have ceased to exist since 1981, employment training programs have in some cases continued to receive federal and state funding and others have continued with the help of private resources. Some income-generating projects for refugee women have also developed training components.

EMPLOYMENT TRAINING FOR SOUTHEAST ASIAN REFUGEE IN THE ST. PAUL-MINNEAPOLIS AREA

Minnesota has been a major area of Southeast Asian refugee resettlement since the late 1970s. In the fall of 1981 the refugee population reached a peak of twenty six thousand, 85 percent of whom lived in the St. Paul-Minneapolis metropolitan area. The largest group were the Hmong, who numbered nearly twelve thousand and--with the exception of a small settlement in Duluth--virtually all of this group resided in the metropolitan area. During the winter of 1982, which was a period of unusually harsh weather and increasing unemployment in Minnesota, several thousand Hmong left the state in hopes of finding jobs and a warmer climate elsewhere. With the return of warmer weather and an upturn in the state's economy, the Hmong population stabilized in mid-1983 at approximately

eighty-five hundred out of a total of twenty-three thousand Southeast Asian refugees in Minnesota. About twenty
thousand Southeast Asians continued to live in the metropolitan area.

Employment training for Southeast Asian refugees in
the St. Paul-Minneapolis metropolitan area has included a
broad range of programs, the majority supported by state
and federal refugee assistance funds. At one end of the
spectrum is the University of Minnesota's degree and certification program for bilingual teachers. Only the most
educationally advantaged Southeast Asians have qualified
for this program. Employment training for refugees at
six metropolitan-area technical and vocational institutes
has also been provided but, due to the sheer number of
refugee applicants, only on a selective basis. Vocational schools with large Southeast Asian enrollments have
established special bilingual preparatory classes for
those lacking English proficiency.

At the other end of the spectrum is the publicly
funded Refugee Homemaker Program, where large numbers of
Southeast Asian refugee women--particularly Hmong women--
are enrolled in prevocational programs. There are no
prerequisites for these classes, and bilingual interpreters are employed to assist in conducting the classes.
Some classes have long waiting lists.

Several small-scale employment training programs
have been supported by both public and private funds.
While these programs--many of which are sewing projects--
train a relatively small number of women, some have developed innovative training programs that may prove useful in generating new ideas.

Two agricultural projects for Hmong families--one
privately funded and the other supported by public and
private funds--have provided English classes and training
for adult members of participating families. One of the
projects, sponsored by a voluntary agency, has thus far
provided training for the men only, although many of the
women are enrolled in Refugee Homemaker classes and may
be trained in record keeping. The other project has provided winter classes for men and women together, although
the men have far outnumbered the women during their first
season.

Hmong women have participated in training programs organized for refugees and nonrefugees, programs initiated specifically for Hmong refugees and programs that enroll predominantly Hmong women.

EMPLOYMENT TRAINING FOR HMONG WOMEN IN THE METROPOLITAN AREA: AN ASSESSMENT

While Hmong women in the metropolitan area have participated in a broad range of employment training programs, most of these programs have trained them for industrial or cottage-industry sewing, housecleaning or food service, labor that is generally low-paid and seasonal or part-time. Despite the initial availability of federal funds for training refugee women on an equitable basis, these programs have tended to channel Hmong women into conventional sex-typed labor that represents a direct extension of household activities. This policy can only reinforce the traditional pattern of exploitation of immigrant women's work that has prevailed since the turn of the century. Programs departing from this convention have generally trained only a few women but have played an important role in the development of a core of leaders among Hmong women in the metropolitan area. A handful of these had prior education in Laos, but most did not. A crucial factor in gaining admission to all but the lowest levels of training has been access to English as a Second Language (ESL) classes. Adequate time for ESL has not been available to all Hmong women on an equitable basis due to priority lists favoring heads of households, and lack of support services such as child care and transportation.

At the post-secondary level, the University of Minnesota's bilingual teacher training program included fourteen Southeast Asian refugees, among them three Hmong men and one Hmong woman, during its first academic year, 1982 to 1983. Although only one Hmong woman participated during the first year, more may be trained in the future as increasing numbers of Hmong students graduate from high schools in Minnesota. The first Hmong woman enrolled may also serve as a role model for female Hmong high school students, providing an example of a Hmong woman who completed high school and continued her education at the university level.

This program is administered by the University of Minnesota's College of Education and is funded by bilingual teacher education grants from the United States Department of Education. Participants receive financial assistance for tuition, insurance and books. To qualify for admission, applicants are required to pass the Minnesota Battery Test, designed for students who did not graduate from high school in Minnesota and have lived in the United States for less than three years. Students admitted to the College of Education or College of Liberal Arts are also eligible.

Most of the participants during the first year of the program were already employed as bilingual teachers in the St. Paul and Minneapolis public schools; by special arrangement they were paid at the same rate as teachers with B.A. degrees and certification. However, a degree and teacher certification will enable the bilingual teachers to attain higher pay levels or move into other areas of employment such as administration or research.

At the six metropolitan area vocational schools, approximately eight hundred fifty Southeast Asian refugees enrolled in employment training programs (including remedial and prevo-cational classes) during the fall term of 1983. Of the total eight hundred fifty about three hundred (35 percent) were Hmong, but only sixty (7 percent) were Hmong women. Most of the Hmong women enrolled in either the St. Paul Technical Vocational Institute (TVI) or the Minneapolis Technical Institute (MTI). Nine enrolled in a part-time prevocational program administered by the Special Intermediate District 916 Vocational Technical Institute (916 Vo-Tech) at the Galt School in White Bear Lake, an eastern suburb of St. Paul.

Southeast Asian refugees applying for employment training at these three schools are required to take the Structured Tests in English Language (STEL). Those with satisfactory scores are admitted to regular vocational classes, and a limited number with lower scores are placed in remedial or prevocational classes.

In many ways vocational training for Southeast Asian refugees at these three schools is reasonably accessible. All have Southeast Asian counselors, and two have bilingual assistants in some of the classes in which Hmong students are enrolled. Most Southeast Asian students are eligible for Pell grants and guaranteed student loans, and some are eligible for public assistance while enrolled in employment training courses.   All three schools can be reached by public transportation.

For many Hmong women with preschool children, however, a major obstacle is the lack of adequate child-care facilities.   Although some have a mother-in-law in the home who can care for the children while the younger woman attends school, in many instances this is not the case.   MTI students may use the child care services at the adjacent Minneapolis Community College (MCC), but the cost—up to $65 per week for a full-time student with one child—is prohibitive for most Hmong women.   Neither 916 Vo-Tech nor TVI provides child-care facilities.

The largest number of Hmong women have enrolled in training programs at TVI.   About thirty-two enrolled during the fall term of 1983.   The convenience of TVI's location in the Summit-University area—an area of concentrated Hmong resettlement—has made it a popular choice among Hmong women. More important, TVI is the only vocational school in the metropolitan area that has developed a full-fledged bilingual program.   Because Hmong women generally received less education than men in Laos, and have often had lower priority for enrollment in ESL classes in Minnesota,[1] this is an important factor in making vocational training more accessible to this group of women.

The Bilingual Program of TVI is the outgrowth of an earlier program initiated for Hispanic students in 1975. The latter program was established after the AFL-CIO and affirmative action groups urged the Minnesota Legislature to provide employment training for Hispanics who arrive each year as migrant farm workers and often remained to look for work in the winter.   When the Southeast Asian refugees arrived in the state soon after the program was initiated, the program was extended to meet the needs of both groups.   Bilingual services for Southeast Asian students at TVI include bilingual counseling, bilingual assistants in classes as needed, and bilingual support services, including tutoring, for students in all vocational programs.   In addition, some bilingual courses are offered each term for students with a low level of

English proficiency. These prepare them for jobs that also require little English, such as wall painting or apparel arts.

While a few Hmong women who have graduated from Minnesota high schools achieve a high enough level of English proficiency to enter programs in such subjects as office skills or bookkeeping, the majority of Hmong women at TVI have enrolled in apparel arts, a class in industrial sewing that requires an English proficiency level of only 200 (the minimum for regular vocational classes) as measured by the STEL tests. Often there is a waiting list of Hmong women for this class. At the end of each term recruiters from the garment industry and other manufacturing companies come directly to the school to sign up Hmong women who have completed the training. These recruiters usually offer the women about $3.70 per hour, or just over minimum wage, and also offer them piecework. The hourly wage Hmong women can eventually earn in this industry may reach $5 or $6, but layoffs are frequent during the winter months, and while some companies offer benefits, others do not. Several companies have hired as many as forty Hmong women to work under a Hmong foreman. With this arrangement the women need only a minimum level of English proficiency.

A much smaller number of Hmong women have enrolled in special programs in commercial foods that also require only a minimum of English proficiency. During the early 1980s eighteen Hmong women were trained in food service for work in a restaurant at the Twin Cities International Airport. Twelve of the eighteen women were hired by the restaurant manager as salad makers at minimum wage. In early 1984 a bilingual class for Southeast Asian students with English proficiency levels as low as 100 was initiated to train kitchen assistants for restaurant work. Four Hmong women and four men signed up for the course which will prepare them for work at just over minimum wage.

A housecleaning class for refugees with low English proficiency, which was offered in the summer of 1983, also enrolled a majority of Hmong women (although most Hmong women training for the workplace seem to prefer to enter sewing programs). Only about 40 percent of the students got jobs after completing the course, and for that reason the class was not repeated. Women who did find employment earned $4.50 or slightly more per hour, but worked part-time without benefits. After a number of men joined the class, however, instruction in janitorial work was added for them, while the women received training in cleaning homes. Some of the men got janitorial jobs at $5.50 to $7.50 per hour, although they too worked on a part-time basis.

A comparison of the types of training and economic outcome for Hmong men and women at TVI illustrates the inequities of Hmong women's training opportunities in vocational schools generally. If a woman trained in food service works full-time year around in a minimum wage job at $3.35 per hour, she can earn $6,968 per year. A woman trained in industrial sewing can earn $4 per hour or $8,320 per year if she works full-time year around in a garment factory (most are laid off during the winter months). If her pay reaches $5 per hour she can earn $10,400 if she is not laid off. Women trained in housecleaning earn far less in part-time work. All the above incomes are well below the poverty level for a family of six, the average size of Hmong families in St. Paul and Minneapolis.[2]

In contrast, Hmong men at TVI, many of whom also lacked formal education when they arrived in the United States, have been channeled into fields such as auto mechanics, welding and machinists' training. Welders make from $8 to $15 an hour or more and machinists earn from $6 to $9 an hour. Wages for auto mechanics vary according to the number of skills mastered, and range from just over minimum wage to $12 an hour. The economic benefits increase if an individual opens his own shop.

While much of the training of Hmong women at TVI and other vocational schools has been conventional, sex-typed job training, it should be pointed out that other types of training for Hmong women have existed in the past and still occur from time to time. For example, from 1980 to 1982, TVI staff developed one of the most innovative refugee programs in the metro area, the Health Interpreters Training Program. About half the forty-five interpreters trained in this program were Hmong women. Supported by federal and foundation funding, the primary goal of the program was to train Southeast Asian health interpreters to provide effective communication between local health care providers and refugee patients.

Initiated by the Ramsey County Child Health Consortium (comprising public and private health, education, welfare and social service agencies), the Health Interpreters Training Program served both the East and West Metro Refugee Health Projects. The projects were organized in 1980 in response to the growing recognition by local health care providers of the need to expand their services to the large number of Southeast Asian refugees arriving in St. Paul and Minneapolis in 1979 and 1980.

With the guidance of the Refugee Program Office, TVI staff members developed curriculum and teaching materials for a short-term certificate training course for health interpreters that included both health education and ESL. The two main criteria for acceptance into the program were prior health care experience, either in Southeast Asian or the United States, and sufficient proficiency in English (tested at TVI). Trainees for the first class were recruited through CETA and contacts in resettlement agencies and refugee mutual assistance associations. After the first class was trained, recruitment was no longer necessary as refugees applied for admission after hearing about the program, or were sent by resettlement agencies in Minnesota and neighboring states.

More than half the trainees were Hmong, due to the large size of the Hmong communities in St. Paul and Minneapolis as compared to other refugee settlements. Only three or four Hmong men were accepted for the program. About twenty-two Hmong women were accepted and completed the health interpreters training course.

Health interpreters were generally placed in metropolitan area clinics or nutrition programs, or returned to agencies in other states immediately after certification. Initially their pay at the entry level was $5 an hour, but those employed by city or county agencies became civil servants and usually received substantial raises after their jobs were evaluated by the civil service system. Those employed by voluntary agencies also received raises, and most were eventually earning between $8 and $10 per hour by the time the program ended in 1983. While most health interpreter positions became permanent, those who lost their jobs after the program ended had no difficulty finding other jobs in the health care field.

MTI and 916 Vo-Tech have enrolled fewer Southeast Asian students than TVI. However, the pattern of employment training for Hmong women is the same at MTI, and 916 Vo-Tech enrolled only one woman in regular vocation classes in the fall of 1983. In 1983 approximately 200 Southeast Asian students enrolled at MTI each term. About 60 of these were Hmong, but only 18 were Hmong women. The majority of the women enrolled in apparel arts services, a class in industrial sewing. There was no Hmong counselor--the only bilingual counselor was Vietnamese--and remedial and prevocational classes were no longer available at the school. At 916 Vo-Tech approximately 154 Southeast Asians enrolled in the fall of 1983. About 90 were Hmong (including those in remedial and prevocation classes). Only 10 of these were Hmong women, and only one attended regular vocational classes. Nine were enrolled in a prevocational clas. A Hmong counselor, who assists in classes when needed, and his Hmong assistant provided support services to Hmong students.

The Refugee Homemaker Program in St. Paul and Minneapolis, supported by state and federal funding, enrolls the largest number of Hmong women of any refugee education program in the metropolitan area. While the homemaker program has been described as prevocational, it is far less formal in format than prevocational classes at vocational schools. While the latter require testing for admission and are concerned mainly with improving the students' English and math, homemaker classes have no prerequisites, and bilingual interpreters are available for all sessions. Tuition is free. Classes meet for two hours, once or twice a week.

In St. Paul, classes are located in public housing projects, and Hmong women living in the projects are within easy walking distance of the class sites. Child care is provided without charge. In Minneapolis, classes are held in schools, churches and community centers. While they are generally located near refugee residential areas, the women must provide their own transportation. Only one site provides child care.

The St. Paul homemaker program dates back to 1964, when the residents of public housing projects were largely immigrants or migrants from the South. The initial goal was to enable low-income, homebound women to conserve their resources by efficient home management. Curriculum included food and nutrition, family sewing, child development, consumer education and home management. The first Hmong enrolled in homemaker classes in St. Paul in 1977. As the number increased, special sections were set aside for them because of language problems, and interpreters were provided for these sections. Very quickly the classes became predominantly Hmong. Because the Hmong women wanted to learn employment skills, an attempt was made to provide prevocational training in classes like home sewing and housecleaning. Other classes like coat relining and knitting--skills for cottage industry projects--have been added more recently. Nearly four hundred Hmong women were enrolled in homemaker programs in St. Paul in the fall of 1983.

An innovative spin-off of the St. Paul program has been the Training for Hmong Liaisons, a project initiated in the fall of 1983. Initially liaisons were selected from women in the classes and trained informally by the instructors to serve as intermediaries between American teachers and Hmong women students. The main criteria in their selection was proficiency in English and knowledge of the subject, although most were women with no prior education in Laos. Formal training in professional interpreting and general work skills will enable these women to find comparable jobs if funding for their present positions is cut off, or to seek full-time, year-round work from which they can earn more than in their present part-time, seasonal work (no classes are held in the summer). Ten liaisons were enrolled in the Training for Hmong Liaisons program, which included ESL as well as professional training. Initial training sessions were held at TVI with the help of TVI staff. These were followed by classes in homemaker classrooms with instructors from the homemaker program. While pay for liaisons has varied according to length of experience, trained liaisons will earn up to $7 per hour. They may be able to find higher pay outside the homemaker program.

The Minneapolis Refugee Homemaker Program was initiated in January 1983. While the St. Paul program served as a model, the Minneapolis classes have been more obviously shaped by the need of Southeast Asian refugee women to learn a skill for employment. One of the Minneapolis programs, the Regina Project, which began as a community education class before the Minneapolis home-maker program was established, is a full-fledged employment training course in industrial sewing and housecleaning. The Regina Project, begun in the fall of 1982, enrolls forty Hmong women per semester in two eighteen-week terms, beginning in September and ending in May. From Tuesday to Friday, two groups of twenty women each attend one hour of English and two hours of sewing (including instruction in the use of industrial machines). On Mondays, all students attend two hours of housecleaning instruction (four hours each Monday during the last six weeks of the class), taught by an employee of a professional cleaning service.

Women enrolled in the program are allowed to use both the industrial and home sewing machines after hours and on Saturday to do piecework on commission from local businesses. This provides the women a means of earning supplementary income. By working very quickly, a few can make up to $5 an hour, but most earn just over the minimum wage of $3.35 an hour.

While Hmong women trained at TVI have had little difficulty finding employment in the garment industry, Regina graduates often have not found work in industrial sewing, particularly in winter. A few have found sewing jobs elsewhere at $3.50-an-hour entry wages. Many have continued to do piecework at home if they own a sewing machine. Apparently employers are looking for Hmong women with a higher level of English and sewing skills, such as those trained at TVI.

Cleaning jobs have been available at $4 an hour, part-time, with no benefits. Many women trained in the Regina Project have found such jobs, although most prefer piecework sewing. Training at Regina has not included hotel or janitorial work thus far. Hmong women could get full-time hotel jobs at minimum wage, or part-time janitorial work in the evening at $5 to $10 an hour. The latter includes no benefits, although full-time hotel work may include them.

Although no child care or. transportation is provided by the Regina Project, it has drawn Hmong women from all over the metropolitan area and 100 are on the waiting list. A survey of women in the English class indicated that most were able to leave their children with unemployed spouses or other relatives, and that many had formed car pools from St. Paul or north Minneapolis to reach the Regina Project in south Minneapolis. While this shows the resourcefulness of Hmong women and their need for employment training, it may also mean that women at Regina are a self-selected group that has greater resources and more relatives to turn to than many other Hmong women may have available.

Other Minneapolis homemaker classes besides the Regina Project have included instruction in family planning, consumer education, foods and nutrition, use of community services, home management, office skills and orientation to employment. Most of the classes have interpreters available. About 250 Hmong women, as well as other refugee women, were enrolled in these programs in the fall of 1983.

An experimental program was also initiated in 1983 by the coordinator of the Refugee Homemaker Program. While still in its earliest stage, and already threatened by cuts in federal funding, the program provides state vocational part-time teaching licenses for Southeast Asian instructors in health and nutrition. The instructors are employed as interpreters by metropolitan area health agencies, but are paid for their part-time teaching by the homemakers program. Eventually classes will be taught by Southeast Asian instructors in other homemaker subject areas as well.

Three Southeast Asian instructors--all Hmong women-- have been licensed thus far. Licensing is obtained through MTI, and job training is provided by sponsoring agencies. The three already licensed were trained in the Health Interpreters Training Program at TVI, and then employed by the Ramsey County Nursing Service, the St. Paul Public Health Department and the federal food program for Women, Infants and Children (WIC). They teach weekly classes in health and nutrition at McDonough Homes in St. Paul and were paid $14.23 an hour in 1984.

While the main purpose of the Refugee Homemakers Program has not been to provide vocational or prevocational training to refugee women, several innovative projects in interpreter and teacher training that have emerged from the Homemaker Program provide evidence of the possibilities for Hmong women's employment training beyond the conventional areas of industrial sewing and domestic housecleaning.

Five small training projects for Hmong women in the metropolitan area have been sponsored by a private agency, an MAA, a church organization and two enterprising individuals. Three are sewing projects that are primarily income-generating, but have added a training component. In two of these the women work for minimum wage or less while receiving training in handwork or machine sewing. Some earn just over minimum wage on piecework, if they work very quickly. In the third, three women who were trained in the shop earned $4.50 per hour in the fall of 1983, and continued to learn other business skills in the course of their work. In two projects the women work part-time only, while one provides full-time work for four or five women a year. None of these projects provide child care or transportation, and none receive public funds.

Family Service of St. Paul, a private agency supported largely by United Way funding, has provided bilingual instruction for Hmong women interested in licensing their homes for day care as a means of supplementing their income. Since early 1981 more than 100 Hmong women have participated in the agency's Family Day Care Training Program. This training includes twelve to fifteen hours of training in application procedures, county regulations on health and safety, nutrition, first aid and children's activities such as crafts and games. There is no charge for the training. No child care or transportation is provided.

Although many Hmong women have participated in the program, a large number have not completed the program for a variety of reasons. Often their homes did not pass fire inspection or they could not afford the required equipment. In early 1984, twenty-seven Hmong homes were licensed for day care.

Many of the clients of Hmong day-care homes are Southeast Asian refugees attending ESL or employment training classes. If they are on public assistance the Minnesota Department of Public Welfare pays for day care while they attend classes. The Department of Welfare makes day-care payments directly to the care provider at the rate of $1.40 per hour or a maximum of $9.75 per day per child. No more than five children, including a maximum of two infants, can be cared for by one woman. However, the majority of clients leave their children only a few hours each day, and in the summer far fewer children are brought to day-care homes, with the result that most care providers' incomes vary considerably according to the season.   If a Hmong woman cares for three children for four hours a day, five days a week, she can earn $336 a month, from which she must subtract any expenses involved in providing the care.

Often Hmong women who provide day care are themselves on public assistance, and welfare regulations require that 40 percent of the earnings of self-employed recipients (providing day care) must be deducted from their welfare grants.   If they live in public housing, their rent will be raised proportionately to the amount earned.

Training for family day-care licensing does not qualify an individual for work in a day-care center, and jobs in such centers are often difficult to obtain.   Thus while Hmong women may gain some knowledge of American expectations in caring for children, the training they receive does not provide directly transferable skills or qualifications.

In the fall of 1983 a housecleaning training program for Southeast Asian men and women was initiated by a publicly funded refugee employment service.   Of the seven who completed the ten-week course in December, three were Hmong women.   All are working for $4 an hour on a part-time basis with no benefits.   Because they are welfare recipients they must work under twenty hours a week to avoid jeopardizing their benefits.   No support services are provided by the training program; those receiving welfare may be eligible for child-care and transportation assistance.

All four of the small-scale projects described have provided training in traditional areas of women's work, leading to low-paid, part-time or seasonal work.   Business skills learned in one project could be transferable to another job or used for self-employment in a business or cooperative enterprise.   Neither child care nor transportation has been provided by these projects.

In the spring of 1983 the Agricultural Extension Service of the University of Minnesota launched a training program for thirty Hmong families as part of the Minnesota Agriculture Enterprise for New Americans, known as the Hmong Farm Project.   Participating Hmong families have remained on public assistance during the training period, but eventually will be owner-members of a Hmong cooperative. While no households headed by women have thus far been included in the project, Hmong women have participated in winter training classes on an equal basis with their husbands during the first year of operation. Training has included ESL and agriculture courses. Women have participated in machine maintenance, woodworking and other work traditionally performed by men. During the winter of 1983-1984, these classes comprised thirty-two men and seven women. The number of women participating is expected to increase after the first year. The project pays transportation and child-care allowances for participating families. The economic outcome cannot yet be determined.

CONCLUSION

The data from the present study indicates that most training programs for Hmong women in the St. Paul-Minneapolis metropolitan area have reflected a conventional notion of immigrant women as needleworkers and house-cleaners, a notion more relevant to an era that is long past in the American economy than to the 1970s and 1980s. While such labor provided immigrant women with a stable but meager income at the turn of the century, current policies of training Hmong women in the same areas of marginal, low-paid work can only create a permanently disadvantaged group of women.

On the other hand, several innovative training projects that have emerged in the fields of teaching, interpreting and health care suggest that, given the opportunity for adequate preparation in ESL and employment training, Hmong women can successfully enter the economic mainstream of American society. A program still in the planning stage proposes retraining health interpreters, and others with health-care backgrounds in Laos or the United States, as health professionals. This might include training as nurses, nurses' aides, medical technicians and dental assistants. Other areas not fully explored include training Hmong women in administrative skills, business management and organization of cooperatives.

Data from this study also indicates that the lack of support services--particularly day care and transportation--has been a serious obstacle for many Hmong women who want to study ESL and attend employment training courses. The lack of these services in some cases has brought about a process of self-selection whereby only those women with relatives they can turn to for child-care assistance can attend classes.

The question raised by this study is how resettlement policy can be restructured to provide more innovation in training programs for Hmong women, and to assure the availability of support services necessary to give them a fair chance to participate in the employment opportunities in the United States.

ACKNOWLEDGEMENTS

I owe a great debt of gratitude to all the administrators, teachers, bilingual counselors and students who patiently answered my questions about Hmong women's training programs in the St. Paul-Minneapolis metropolitan area. Among them are May Beecham, Sandra Becker, Father Cherian, Gloria Congdon, Joyce Dewey, Sandra Duvander, Sharon Washburn-Dreyer, Karen Gensemer, Patricia Hattiberg, Lucy Hartwell, Colleen Holverson, Shirley Hume, Laurel Janssen, Kathleen Johnson, Sister Marie Lee, Herbert Murphey, Janice Pederson, Ninh Phan, Naida Reda, Darlene Ross, Rebecca Storlie, Richard Teachout, Francisco Trejo, Blang Vang, Constance Walker, Kia Moua Yaj, Blang Yang, Gaoly Yang and Hoa Young.

NOTES

[1] In the early years of resettlement, heads of households in the metropolitan area were often given priority in attending ESL and employment training classes. This was discontinued following a lawsuit. (Patricia Hattiberg, interview with author, St. Paul, Minnesota, 26 January 1984.)

[2]Douglas Olney's Hmong Community Survey, Center for Urban and Regional Affairs, University of Minnesota, unpublished, 1983, indicates the average size of Hmong families in St. Paul is 5.9, and in Minneapolis 5.7; 1981 Bureau of Labor Statistics.

REFERENCES

Fass, Simon M. 1983. "Development Dynamics: Hmong Refugees in America." Unpublished.

Walter, Ingrid. 1981. One Year After Arrival: The Adjustment of Indochinese Women in the United States, 1979-1980. Lutheran Immigration and Refugee Service, New York, N.Y. (Available at no charge from Lutheran Center, 360 Park Ave. S., New York, N.Y. 10010.)

CHANGES IN HMONG REFUGEE MARITAL ATTITUDES IN AMERICA

William H. Meredith and George P. Rowe

Hmong refugees from Laos have been tossed from an isolated, simple environment into a technologically modern society with customs and language very strange to them. The Hmong are known for their strong, highly cohesive, extended families. How have their family, and marriage practices in particular, been able to adjust to such dramatic changes? What traditions have they maintained in this strange land? Which have they been forced or chosen to drop?

This article will examine the impact a new culture had on the institution of marriage for one ethnic group of refugees that began entering this country in 1975. It will also review marriage customs the Hmong practiced when they lived in Laos. The adaptation of their marital relationship in the United States will then be examined based on the results of a research study of 134 Lao Hmong adults.

MARRIAGE IN LAOS

Hmong society was a patrilineal clan system. The society was divided into social groups, or clans, and a child at birth was automatically placed into the clan to which the father belonged (Clarke 1973; Barney 1967). Therefore, a modified brother-sister taboo was observed. It was not proper for a young man to express interest in a girl bearing his clan name. However, the child of a man could marry the offspring of that man's sister because--in the eyes of the Hmong--they would not have been of the same clan.

After puberty, a young man attempted to gain the attention of a girl of his liking. This was generally done during the New Year's Festival season when different villages join each other for feasting. Girls proudly wore their colorful skirts as a display of their ability to sew and embroider. Young men demonstrated their prowess with horses and in contests. They also serenaded the girls with various musical instruments (Barney 1967).

If a relationship between a boy and a girl developed into a serious mutual interest the boy found excuses to visit the girl's village. Girls who had attained puberty slept apart from the rest of the family so young men might be expected to visit during the night when the rest of the family was asleep. Premarital sex, however, was closely controlled and disliked by parents. A girl who became pregnant was considered a disgrace to her family (Barney 1967). Men married between eighteen and thirty, while women married between fourteen and eighteen.

Marriage could only be realized after considerable maneuvering and bargaining. The young man secured a "go-between," usually a relative, to carry on negotiations with the girl's parents (Clarke 1973; Barney 1967).

When the negotiations between the go-between and the girl's parents resulted in consent to the marriage, a written agreement was signed. (Hmong informants told us that every village had at least two or three people who could write, and most marriage contracts were put in writing from 1972 on. Prior to that time, contracts were about evenly split between oral and written. If oral, the leaders of the clan and the go-betweens were the contract witnesses as long as they lived.) As part of the marriage agreement the man would pay the prospective wife's parents a bride price of at least four fifteen-ounce silver bars. Under recent silver prices that would be the e-quivalent of $600 in the United States. The agreement would also include provisions concerning the possible eventualities such as divorce. In addition, the husband generally agreed not to say bad things about the girl's clan of origin. Prior to any use of physical force, the man would also agree to take his wife back to her family for "counseling and assistance" if she did not prove to be a good wife. To be a good wife, the woman must listen to her husband and know her responsibility to him. She must accept his decisions although she need not agree with them. She also was expected to be active in farm production and to open her house to guests.

A feast with a roasted pig was then held over two days as the official announcement of marriage. It also served to provide a bond between different clans. Sometimes, for political reasons, young men and women were forced by their families to marry mates they did not wish to marry.

If a settlement could not be reached, the couple might resort to an elopement. In such cases settlements were made afterwards by a panel of neutrals. Before the 1960s, elopement was not possible because of tight parental control. However, young people gradually started learning about customs in other countries. Occasionally a girl would not wish to marry a boy. While the parents would act upset, it was considered acceptable for the boy, with the help of his friends, to kidnap the girl. Generally the threat of kidnap was enough to encourage the parents to negotiate an agreement.

Marriage had very important effects on the girl's relationship with her parents (Barney 1967). In theory, when she left her father's family, household and clan, she became fully identified with her husband's family. Should he die, she would become responsible to his family. However, she could visit her family of origin frequently.

Sometimes an additional wife was secured to add to the family work force. In some cases, the first wife would request her husband to marry an additional woman. Having more than one wife was a common custom but was usually the result of the levirate, which is the practice whereby a man's widow automatically becomes the wife of his brother (Barney 1967). This practice increased rapidly in the 1960s as the result of the war. Wealthy men were able to have several wives. This was a sign of their wealth. Hmong leaders would also take more than one wife to gain political support from rival clans. One of them was considered to be the more important "big wife" and directed the others in terms of household duties. All wives usually shared the same sleeping area. Divorce was possible, but was avoided at all costs (Barney 1967). Disagreements between couples were heard by clan leaders and strong words of advice were given. If a woman left her husband she would lose all rights to whichever of their children the husband's family wished to keep. The husband's family would generally choose to keep all able-bodied males and girls who could be expected to bring a good marriage price. In earlier times the wife's family had to return the bride's price to the forsaken husband.

In more recent times, the wife had to pay the husband
what he had given for her. Unhappy wives were left with
the choice of fleeing the village or, in rare cases, com-
mitting suicide, at which time the husband would have to
pay damage to the wife's parents.

The family structure after marriage was patriarchal
(Barney 1967). The father was head of the family and was
in strict control of the family. The mother was in charge
of housework. The father made all final decisions and
would not tolerate strong disagreement. Women's influence was more subtle and indirect and they generally held
an inferior position to men. Although families varied,
the ideal role of the wife was to have devotion and respect for the husband (Vang 1979). If a wife came from a
family of power or wealth she would expect more influence
in decision-making. Because of the husband's pleasure in
being connected to her family he would usually give her a
greater role in family decisions. In other cases where
the wife was clearly more intelligent than her husband or
in those few cases where she earned more money than he,
her power was increased. Others in the village, though,
generally disapproved of the man who could not "control"
his wife.

METHOD

In order to determine changes in marital and family
life attitudes, twenty-six statements were selected that
included both values commonly held by the Hmong in Laos
and values commonly held by Americans in the United
States. The statements were selected with the help of
four Lao Hmong consultants who also conducted the interviews. The interviews were handled in small groups. After hearing the question each respondent marked his or
her own answers on an answer sheet. The questionnaires
were administered orally to the refugees because the majority were illiterate. The language used for the oral
delivery was Hmong.

With the exception of the first four questions concerning the respondents sex, age, education level and
length of time in the United States, the remaining thirty-one

statements all involved the same response format. This was done to make the questionnaire easier for a population not acquainted with surveys to understand.

Two response formats were included as one: the Likert scale and the Faces scale (Andrews and Withey 1976). Each of the categories of the Faces scale corresponded to a rating level on the Likert scale. The interviewers read the titles of the faces to the respondents several times. After that point, the illiterate Hmong, in particular, basically answered to the Faces scale. As many of the illiterate Hmong do not know numbers, it would have been unrealistic to expect them to follow an answer sheet where questions were labeled with numbers. therefore, a picture was substituted for each statement number. The interviewer read each question and told the illiterate refugee to answer on the line labeled by a certain picture. The Faces scale and this numbering method allowed illiterate respondents to answer in a confidential manner.

In order to better understand changes in attitude toward marriage over time and culture changes, a retrospective method was used. Respondents recorded both what they remembered their attitude toward the statement to have been in Laos and their attitude at the time of the survey.

Data were analyzed in terms of percentages and in terms of significant differences (based on the Chi-square test) between the retrospective and present view. Also, significant differences for the present view were correlated with demographic data. Significance was set at .05 or lower.

POPULATION

The population studied consisted of every Lao Hmong refugee, age sixteen and above, living in Omaha, Nebraska. One hundred thirty four persons fell in this age range. Most were young adults between sixteen and thirty. In terms of education, the formal educational level attained was limited. Forty percent of the 134 participants had no formal education while another 23 percent had some grade school education only. High school graduates and those with some college background or specialized training accounted for 18 percent of the refugee adults. Nearly one-quarter of the Lao Hmong refugee adults had lived in the United States for between five and six years. Fewer than 19 percent had resided in this country less than two years.

There were seventy females in this study and sixty-four males. Since the total population was studied, all the married participants in the population were married to another participant.

RESULTS

The results of the marriage attitude survey with 134 Lao Hmong refugee adults will be discussed under four topical areas: mate selection, marriage preparation, marriage roles and divorce. Significant differences in responses based on demographic data between the retrospective and present views will be indicated when present. See Appendix 1 for the present attitude responses for the total group of Hmong refugees only.

Mate Selection

With the exception of the attitude toward polygynous marriage, past attitudes concerning mate selection have generally been maintained. Slightly more than half of the respondents felt it was not proper for a Hmong person to marry someone who was not also Hmong. Most of the remaining adults were unsure. Only 7 percent supported remarrying someone from the same clan, although a significant difference was found based on education (p=<.05). Marriage within the clan was seen as more acceptable by those with greater education. Women held more traditional views than did men. Marrying for greater family power was viewed as a good reason for marriage by 79 percent; only 5 percent disagreed. While marrying for family power appeared to be an important consideration, nearly all the refugees felt love should also be present. Many of the Hmong thought that young adults should make their own choices in terms of marriage partners after a period of courtship. Younger persons were significantly more likely to agree with this attitude, however (p=<.001). While couple choice was important, only 38 percent would approve of a boy taking a girl for marriage when the parents disapproved. Nearly half reported they had thought that was proper in Laos.

In terms of age of marriage, 87 percent stated that it is best if a woman waits until she is eighteen to marry. This was significantly higher than the reported retrospective view of attitudes in Laos (p=<.001). The greatest increase was among women (p=<.01).

One of the few areas that showed a great change in attitude concerned the Hmong's cultural tradition of polygynous marriage. If it were legal in their new country, only 21 percent would maintain that custom. While the change was significant for the total group (p=<.01), it was particularly striking for the women (p=<.01). Only 7 percent currently agreed with that custom as compared to 31 percent in Laos. Men's attitude had changed as well, although not as dramatically. At present, 38 percent believe they should have the freedom to have more than one wife. More than half stated they felt that way in Laos. Many men and women were obviously in disagreement on this issue. Surprisingly, those with higher levels of education were significantly more likely to favor polygyny if it were legal (p=<.05).

Marriage Preparation

Two-thirds presently believe that it is best to have matchmakers who make the final negotiations for the marriage rather than leaving it up to the boy and girl alone. A similar proportion believed that a marriage works best if a written contract between the families is agreed upon in advance. Significant decreases in agreement with these statements occurred with increasing education (p=<.05) and time in residence in this country. Women were more likely to agree than men (p=<.01). The number who agreed that payment of a bride price is proper significantly decreased from the number who held that view in Laos (p=<.05), although 58 percent still favored the bride price. Again, more women than men approved of this custom. However, a significant change has occurred among women: 89 percent approved in Laos compared to 65 percent in this country (p=<.01).

Marriage Roles

While greater agreement with the idea of equality as a general principle exists now as opposed to these adults' perceptions of their past view, still clearly the husband holds the dominant role. In fact, 83 percent of the respondents agreed with the statement, "A good wife should do what her husband tells her to do." However, those who were educated were significantly less likely to agree with the statement (p=<.05). The Hmong also agreed that the man and not the woman should make the decision in the family. While none of the demographic variables proved significant, more women agreed with the decision-making statement than did men. The husband's decision-making power does have its limits in the view of women, however. Women were less likely than men to believe that the man should determine the limits of the wife's education. Women's views on this subject had changed greatly in this regard from their attitude when they lived in Laos.

More than 80 percent of the refugee adults believed that husbands should help care for their children and assist their wives with housework. Although the father should assist, nearly three-quarters of the refugees viewed it as the mother's job to take care of the children. While not to a significant degree, more women agreed with these statements than did men. Education was the only significant variable. The man's involvement in the home was more accepted with increased education (p=<.05).

Women were significantly less likely to feel they should work outside the home when they had small children than did their husband (p= <.05). In fact, one half of the men, compared to only one-quarter of the women, felt it to be acceptable for the young mother to work.

Divorce

While divorce among the Lao Hmong is not common, the issues surrounding divorce showed considerable confusion. In fact, "not sure" was the most commonly picked response. This was only true with the statements concerning divorce. Such statements included issues concerning the custody of the children and the division of possessions.   In spite of the confusion present, both men and women were significantly less likely to believe presently that the children belong with the father's family than they did in Laos (p=<.01).   Even at that, 47 percent of the men agreed with that custody arrangement to 26 percent of the women.   In Laos 73 percent of the men recall feeling that way.

CONCLUSION AND DISCUSSION

The results seem to indicate that the Lao Hmong have experienced some change in terms of marriage attitudes as a result of their dramatic cultural transformation.   Several aspects have experienced significant change, namely attitudes concerning polygynous marriage, the bride price, age of marriage and general views on equality within marriage.   These changes have departed from the culturally prevalent views held by the Hmong in Laos toward views more accepted in this country.

In other areas such as the means and motivations of selecting a spouse, the use of go-betweens to negotiate the marriage settlement and use of written contracts in marriage, little change had occurred from Laos to this country.   And while general views on equality in marriage had changed, responses to specific statements reflected a strongly male-dominated society. Attitudes on the proper roles of husbands and wives had changed little.

Women, in general, were more traditional and also gave greater support to male authority than did men. And in terms of women working outside the home, men were significantly more agreeable to that prospect than were their wives.

Faced with the greater acceptability of divorce in our society, the Hmong experience considerable conflict concerning the dissolution of marriage.   Men were unsure in their attitudes.

With the exception that the more educated responded more favorably to the custom of polygyny, increased levels of education appeared to facilitate changes toward Western ideas.   Education allowed greater exposure to new ideas and new ways of thinking.   The greater acceptance of polygyny, if it were legal, presents somewhat of a contradiction.   In Laos, the number of wives was an indication of wealth and influence. Those who were educated would more likely be in positions of power and wealth. They would more likely feel robbed of a badge of influence by our laws on marriage. Polygyny found very little support from the Lao Hmong women.

Past material concerning the Hmong has been of a historical, anthropological or journalistic nature. Some writings suggest a strongly cohesive culture. Marriage customs are discussed as being held by all Hmong. Such discussions do not include the differences of opinion and variability in attitude that this study shows to exist. Past writings appear to have problems with generalization.

The present paper has examined the current attitudes toward marriage of Lao Hmong refugees in the United States. Retrospective views were also examined as were the influences of various demographics. The paper has also shown the differences of opinion that exist within this population.

The Lao Hmong can anticipate further change in attitudes towards marriage as their residence in the United States lengthens and they come under increasing Western influence through the educational system, the media and personal relationships with those of the new culture. Increasing financial independence will also create greater freedom from the Lao Hmong community. Such factors will allow many Hmong the ability to closely examine their past customs, as well as the new dominant culture's attitudes. Many will choose to blend the new with the older customs to meet their specific needs.

REFERENCES

Andrews, Frank M., and S.B. Withey. 1976. Social Indicators of Well-being. New York: Ptenum Press.

Barney, G.L. 1967. "The Meo of Xieng Khouang Province." In Southeast Asian Tribes, Minorities, and Nations, edited by P. Kunstadter, pp. 271-294. Princeton: Princeton University Press.

Clarke, R.   1973.   Peoples of the Earth.   Verona: Danbury Press.

Vang, Tou Fu.   1979.   "The Hmong in Laos."   In Introduction to Indochinese History, Culture, Language and Life, edited by J. Whitmore, pp. 93-192.   Ann Arbor: Center for South and Southeast Asian Studies, University of Michigan.

Appendix I

Present Attitude Responses to the Hmong Marriage Inventory
for the Total Group of Hmong Refugees in Omaha, Nebraska
(in rounded-off percentages)
N=134

		Strongly Agree	Mostly Agree	Not Sure	Mostly Disagree	Strongly Disagree
	Mate Selection					
1.	It is not right for a Hmong person to marry someone who is not also Hmong.	33%	39%	13%	6%	1%
2.	It is all right to marry someone from the same clan.	7%	0%	9%	14%	69%
3.	Marrying for greater family power is a good reason for marriage.	51%	28%	16%	4%	1%
4.	The husband and wife should love each other in marriage.	76%	13%	6%	1%	4%
5.	If a boy wants to marry a girl and her parents disapprove, it is all right for him to take her anyway.	21%	17%	19%	26%	17%
6.	A woman should have the final say on whom she wants to marry.	51%	29%	10%	4%	4%
7.	Young people should meet or date several people before deciding whom they want to marry.	33%	31%	18%	10%	6%
8.	A girl should not have to get married until she wants to.	49%	24%	9%	8%	7%
9.	Women should wait until they are at least eighteen years old to marry.	64%	23%	5%	2%	5%
10.	If it were legal, I believe that a man should have the freedom to marry more than one wife if he wants to.	14%	7%	21%	11%	44%
	Marriage Preparation					
11.	It is proper for a man to pay a bride price for his wife.	34%	24%	21%	11%	10%
12.	A marriage works best if a contract between the families is agreed upon in advance.	42%	28%	19%	6%	5%
13.	It is best to have go-betweens arrange the marriage, rather than the boy and the girl themselves.	47%	20%	15%	11%	5%
	Marriage Roles					
14.	It is the mother's job to take care of the children.	33%	39%	13%	6%	10%

		Strongly Agree	Mostly Agree	Not Sure	Mostly Disagree	Strongly Disagree
15.	The husband and wife should be equal in power in marriage.	53%	20%	13%	6%	10%
16.	The man, not the woman, should make the major decisions in the family.	24%	38%	23%	11%	3%
17.	A mother with small children should not work at a job outside of the home.	38%	24%	15%	11%	12%
18.	A good wife should do what her husband tells her to do.	53%	30%	7%	4%	6%
19.	Husbands should help their wives with housework.	54%	27%	10%	7%	1%
20.	A father should help take care of his children.	63%	22%	7%	2%	4%
21.	The man should make the decision as to whether his wife continues her education.	27%	21%	24%	21%	5%
22.	It is all right for a woman to work outside of the home once her children are grown.	57%	29%	2%	1%	8%

Divorce

		Strongly Agree	Mostly Agree	Not Sure	Mostly Disagree	Strongly Disagree
23.	In case of divorce, possessions should be divided in half between the husband and wife, regardless of whose fault it is.	16%	16%	35%	18%	16%
24.	In case of divorce, the children belong with the father's family.	23%	13%	36%	16%	13%
25.	If the father dies, the father's family should decide what happens to the children.	30%	22%	27%	8%	13%

RESOLVING SEXUAL ASSAULT:
HMONG AND THE AMERICAN LEGAL SYSTEM

Beth L. Goldstein

Much of the research on sexual assault in the United States either focuses on the person, seeing sexual assault as an act of violence of one individual against another, or focuses on power relations between genders and how they are acted out in our jural and social systems. The American legal system itself emphasizes the protection of individual rights and punishes individuals for violation of others' rights. Institutionalized assistance to both victims and assailants also centers on the individual. Men and women participate in the private and public negotiations which take place.

Hmong mores about gender, male-female interaction, and family and social control contrast sharply with American ones. Within Hmong society, sexual assault is a matter involving the family, kinship group and intergroup relations, rather than centering on individuals and gender relations. Hmong emphasis on the group over the individual assigns responsibility for actions, including individual ones, to the group. In the private, home-centered sphere, women participate in decision-making, but the public sphere is dominated by men. Therefore, Hmong values and actions are often at odds with the way the American system assists in resolving sexual assault. When assault of a Hmong occurs in the United States, the differences between American and Hmong social structures, conceptions of personhood and approaches to conflict resolution become critical.

The situation is further complicated by the current period of acculturation to life in the United States. As has been documented for various immigrant ethnic groups, individual members of the group go through a process of selective acculturation during which their behavior is modified by and for the majority culture, based on patterns of interaction and conflict (Clark, Kaufman and Pierce 1976; Melville 1980). The Hmong adolescents and young adults typically involved in sexual assault cases have been exposed to both Hmong and American attitudes. Their emerging adult identities are a composite of Hmong and American values, perspectives and expectations. As the following case study illustrates, their attempts to cope with the emotional, jural and social aspects of an assault are entangled by personal internal conflicts as well as public external ones between the two sociocultural systems. As DeVos and Romanucci-Ross (1982) suggest, to understand continuity and change in ethnic identity, we must study people in social settings and examine how the subjective experience of an ethnic identity is related to adaptive behavior.

This paper presents a case study of a Hmong girl assaulted by a Hmong man to examine how different cultural lenses influence the resolution of an assault. One afternoon after school, a fourteen-year-old Hmong high school girl was offered a ride home by two Hmong boys who were fellow students. Although she usually rode the bus, she accepted a ride on this occasion because one of the two was her cousin. The first person to be dropped off was the cousin. Then the driver turned onto an unfamiliar route, over the protests of the girl, stopped in an isolated wooded area and assaulted the girl. She eventually escaped from the car and began to walk home. Police on routine patrol passed her, noticed the torn clothing and bruises and picked her up. Soon after, the assailant was located and arrested, and a statement was taken. The victim was brought to the hospital for a gynecological exam, at which time a counselor from a rape counseling center and members of her family were brought in. The assailant was booked for first-degree sexual assault of a minor and later released on bail. The case was handed over for prosecution to the district attorney's office, and a public defender was assigned to the assailant. Eighteen months later, following a plea bargain, the assailant was sentenced to probation.

The assault victim, a tenth grade girl whom we shall call Joua, had lived in the United States for three years. Born in Laos, she spent two years in a Thai refugee camp before being resettled together with her mother and older brother in the United States. She was sponsored by her brother-in-law, who had arrived two years previously. She lives with her mother, an older woman who speaks no English and seldom leaves home without another family member as escort.

The assailant, whom we shall call Pao, was a nineteen-year-old high school junior. He had lived in town with elderly parents for more than four years. Because his English is quite fluent, while his parents are illiterate and speak only Hmong, Pao has become their primary interpreter of American society. Pao has no other family in the immediate vicinity. As a legal adult, Pao receives welfare assistance payments independently of his parents and is therefore more financially mobile than many of his classmates.

Joua's and Pao's mothers were acquainted with each other in Laos. However, the two children had had no contact with each other until they coincidentally enrolled at the same high school in the United States. Until the day of the assault, Pao and Joua were never alone together. He had repeatedly offered rides to her, which she always refused. In Hmong traditions, unrelated males and females have no contact with each other after puberty unless in the company of other people. Married couples do not touch each other in public, and teenage boys do not touch even the women in their immediate family. It was only because of her cousin's presence that Joua agreed to accept a ride on this one occasion.

Cultural conflicts arose in the days immediately after the assault. The girl's adult male relatives gathered at her home to await a personal call from the assailant's family. The culturally appropriate Hmong response to assault would be for Pao to publicly acknowledge responsibility and for his family to pay restitution to Joua's family in lieu of the bride price that could have been expected from a marriage. As became clear later, the money was most important as a symbol of the re-establishment of balance between the two clans and thus as a public peacemaking gesture. However, the assailant and his family did not contact the girl's family. Through the community grapevine, her family was informed that because she went to the police and sought the intervention of an external authority, his family felt they were no longer bound to follow Hmong tradition. Instead, the assailant went to a state-level Hmong employee to request that the government worker extricate him from the charge on the grounds that a marriage was pending. This request was denied on the basis that they lived in the United States now and that, since the police were already involved, American legal procedure must be respected. Only if satisfactory settlement was not reached within the court would a Hmong council of elders be willing to become involved.

Among the issues raised in this incident is that of ethnic boundary maintenance (Barth 1969). At stake for the Hmong is how to balance their desire to re-establish Hmong social organization and control through clan networks, with the fact that they must simultaneously live within American structures and controls. Whereas the girl's family expected Hmong procedure to be followed, the assailant's family argued that the boundary between Hmong and American tradition had already been crossed. But then, when Pao violated Hmong protocol, Joua's family decided to use the American court system to achieve its desired ends. While the senior members of the two families advocated settling within the Hmong community, the younger members, all of whom interacted daily with both Hmong and American communities, vacillated as to which system could best settle the dispute. Hmong marriage custom calls for courting during public celebrations, such as the New Year. Marriage arrangements are subsequently made by the two families or a form of "elopement" occurs. "Elopement" is normally preceded by mutual consent of the couple, with the girl leaving her home to join her suitor. Within days of the "elopement," public acknowledgement of the marriage is made, and the bride price is settled between the families. When Pao went to the Hmong government employee, he changed his account of the incident from the admission of assault given to the police, to overtures of marriage. By claiming that Joua had consented to accompany him, he reframed the incident in terms of traditional marriage--"elopement"--procedures.

Before the preliminary hearings, Joua's senior male relatives gathered to have a representative of the rape counseling center explain the legal proceedings to them. She explained the court system and prosecution process, the presumption of innocence until proof of guilt, the court delays that could be expected in reaching a resolution and the difficulties that Joua could expect giving testimony. She tried to explain why Joua was considered a victim and not a guilty party by American law and by the counseling center. According to American social norms, Joua would be able to lead a normal life as a girl and later as a woman. The counselor perceived Joua's most pressing need at the moment to be for psychological and emotional support from family members. The men responded that the assault may be of little long-term consequence in American society but that while marriage was still possible, no self-respecting Hmong man would marry Joua now. And the family certainly did not want her to marry a non-Hmong. The meeting allowed the men to understand the options available to the family in the American court system and to decide on their action. This entire conversation took place in English and Lao, languages that the women standing on the periphery of the group could not understand. When it was requested that the men translate it into Hmong for the women, the three-hour discussion was summed up in one sentence. What might later have been conveyed to the women is not known.

Through this process, Joua became increasingly confused about her identity and self-worth. At this early stage in her selective acculturation to American society, Joua had assumed many of the material-culture characteristics of American teenagers. For example, her physical appearance was that of a typical high school girl. She had acquired commercialized teen notions of romance and marriage. These superficial characteristics led the American lawyers and counselors to a false expectation of her sexual attitudes and ethnic values. School had become very important to her. She had come to judge her personal value according to accomplishments in school (a new and still uncommon phenomenon for Hmong women). But, following the assault, particularly given the presence of the assailant in the same school building, she could not concentrate on her schoolwork and her grades dropped. Thus, at the same time as her family's estimation of her declined, her own self-image was falling.

Because of her strong bonds with family members, Joua wanted support from them. She said she had nobody within the family to talk to, since her mother did not understand what was happening and she could not discuss such personal topics with her male relatives. In Laos, a network of kin women would have lent the girl personal

support.   She would have been able to talk to them, ask
them about how the incident might affect her future and
discuss the physical pain she'd endured.   However, this
network of support had been scattered by war and resettlement.   Joua became confused by the contradictory messages she was receiving from male relatives and from
American counselors.   She took to heart family criticism
of her behavior and attempted to suppress her anger over
the assault and the slowness with which the courts were
handling it.   She became increasingly concerned that the
family be satisfied with the court decision, since that
would relieve her of family pressure.

Pao was also suffering from cultural disorientation
and misunderstanding of American sexual mores.   His interpretation of what he saw and heard of American high
school males' behavior initially led him to expect le-
niency, if not support, from Americans for his own behavior.   He perceived his sexual aggressiveness as a permissible blend of American and Hmong actions.   He was taking
advantage of the context of the weakened Hmong social
controls and experimenting with his own version of a
"liberated" American male.

At the preliminary hearing many of these issues came
to the fore.   All the officials present were male, which
intimidated the girl.   Testimony was arranged through a
translator, which proved difficult for several reasons.
It was impossible to find an available translator competent in Hmong and English who was unrelated to either of
the two parties.   Therefore, a Hmong social worker who
was related to both was used.   But he was concerned that
his neutral position in the community would be destroyed
by his participation in the hearing.   Only with the consent of community elders did he agree to translate.   However, the translation itself proved hard because of its
sexual content.   It was inappropriate for him to be discussing such topics with the girl; verbatim testimony and
translation were therefore hampered.

It became clear that Joua's family did not want to
be held responsible for any greater disruption of Hmong
and kin networks than necessary.   They tried to use the
court to achieve the desired ends of public punishment of
the youth and financial settlement.   They wanted it to
appear that the decisions were the court's and not their
own since they knew the financial burden on Pao's family

would be severe and therefore potentially divisive. Because financial settlement is not usual in assault cases, the court would have required a public statement from Joua's family that it would be appropriate according to Hmong custom. Since her family did not want to publicly acknowledge this claim, the issue was dropped. Joua's family decided it would instead be satisfied with a jail sentence to be served in the local community so all would see justice achieved.

This single incident has raised many of the culturally distinct conceptions of gender and interpersonal relations. The American perspective was represented by two different approaches: the rape counseling center and the court system. The center is oriented toward treating rape victims as individuals through one-to-one and peer counseling in groups. The woman is seen as victim and the damage understood to be her emotional and psychological disruption. Healing occurs through the support of other women who think women should be independent, in control of their own destiny and able to move around freely. With minors, this counseling includes work with the parents. It is the decision of the rape victim to determine the extent of the counseling to be provided.

Because Joua was a minor, the court automatically entered a charge of first degree sexual assault, the premise being that a minor cannot consent to sex. The court system also views assault from an individualistic perspective. Though it will bring charges for a minor, the burden of proof still rests with the victim. Though attempting to be culturally sensitive, the court must operate within its mandate designated by local law. The assailant is free until proven guilty. Testimony relies on accuracy of translation. Family and Hmong community concerns must be excluded until a verdict is reached.

In contrast, the Hmong view rape as a family and community problem. The girl is the site of the trouble; she symbolizes her family position and honor. Although concern about and love for the girl were evident throughout, family actions centered on kin group balances, reestablishment of which would also heal the victim. Little attention is given to the immediate personal or psychological needs of the woman. Once she is past puberty, the girl is no longer a minor by Hmong standards and is considered responsible for her actions. Concern is pri-

marily with kin group honor, symbolic financial settlement and male public control of individual behavior in
the community. Although women provide emotional support
for each other, they are not in authority positions within the Hmong social structure. Decision-making and actions are controlled by groups of men. Individual identity is formed as a member of a specific family group,
with females' positions formally represented by the male
head of their households. Intervention of the police and
law is viewed as interference that can impede justice.

The case also illustrates the clash between external
public and internal private means of settlement. American court systems operate in a public sphere, whereas the
Hmong turn to private resolution between kin groups before resorting to public assistance from a council of
elders. The American court isolates individuals and pits
them against each other in public, instead of allowing
family units to negotiate appropriate settlement and punishment in private. In the process, not only does the
American system isolate individuals and bring outsiders
(police, lawyers, counselors) into a dispute between kin
groups, it also violates gender roles as they divide between the public and private domains. Hmong women's networks have traditionally operated in the private sphere
of action and influence, but the American court demands
that Hmong women take individualized public action.

ACKNOWLEDGEMENTS

I wish to thank the Hmong who permitted and encouraged this discussion of a personal, painful event.
Thanks also to Susan Bolyard Millar for her comments on
an earlier version of the paper.

REFERENCES

Barth, Fredrik, ed. 1969. "Introduction". In Ethnic
    Groups and Boundaries, pp. 9-38. Boston: Little,
Brown and Company.

Clark, Margaret, S. Kaufman, and R. Pierce. 1976. "Explorations of Acculturation: Toward a Model of Ethnic Identity." Human Organization 35(3): 231-258.

De Vos, George, and Lola Romanucci-Ross, eds. 1982. Introduction. In Ethnic Identity: Cultural Continuities and Change. Chicago: The University of Chicago Press.

Melville, Margarita B., ed. 1980. "Selective Acculturation of Female Mexican Migrants." In Twice a Minority. St. Louis: The C. V. Mosby Company.

THE HMONG IN ISLA VISTA:
OBSTACLES AND ENHANCEMENTS TO ADJUSTMENT

Catherine Stoumpos Gross

INTRODUCTION

Within the college community of Isla Vista, California, exists an enclave of approximately eight hundred Indochinese refugees.[1] Comprising half of this group are the Hmong of Xieng Khouang Province in northern Laos. A number of articles about the Isla Vista Hmong have appeared in both the local and national press, almost invariably referring to them as an illiterate, animistic, independent mountain tribal society, whose men were outstanding guerrilla fighters and whose people in general had never seen an electric switch or door lock, or lifted a pencil prior to their arrival here. Other than this press image, little is known about the Hmong, even by their Isla Vista neighbors.

The information in this paper arises from an analysis of the findings of an ethnographic study of the Hmong of Isla Vista, which was undertaken in 1982 (see Gross 1983). One purpose of this study was to record some of the Isla Vista Hmong people's recollections of their specific historical and cultural background. The study also attempted to investigate to what degree these cultural traits have changed or continued since flight from Laos, and to explore the effects of cultural change on Hmong youth, adults and the elderly, and on family relationships.

METHODOLOGY

Focused, open-ended interviews were conducted between January and October 1982, of eleven English-speaking Hmong representing approximately 13 percent of the Isla Vista Hmong families and 20 to 25 percent of the households. Informants varied in age (from sixteen to thirty-eight), sex, education, marital and parental status (see Appendix), and included two community leaders. While no elderly were interviewed, most informants referred repeatedly to the problems and feelings of the elderly. The interviewer posed more than fifty questions referring to specfic aspects of life, including housing, employment, diet, dress, daily life, leisure activities, education, ceremonies, and religious and traditional practices, both as they existed in northern Laos and as they occur presently. Interviews also explored the degree of interaction with Americans and others, specific advantages and difficulties in adjusting to life in the United States, Hmong thoughts regarding actions Americans could take to ease their difficulties, and individual and community mechanisms for adjustment and accommodation. Also investigated were changes in parent-child relationships as children assume some roles normally reserved for adults, such as translating for elders and representing the family in dealings with the larger community. Among those consulted were social service and welfare workers, high school and English as a Second Language (ESL) teachers and administrators, and volunteer organization representatives concerned with the Indochinese community.

What emerged from the data is an illumination of some of the obstacles which inhibit the adjustment of the Hmong, as well as an illumination of the factors--particularly those in the Isla Vista environment--which enhance adjustment and encourage greater interaction with American society.

OBSTACLES TO ADJUSTMENT

The Hmong in Isla Vista feel that their greatest barrier to adjustment is language; they are certain that mastery of the English language will lead to better jobs, higher income and improved housing. Language, however, is only one of the obstacles facing the Hmong. Without some awareness of the anxieties and apprehensions that besiege the Hmong, one cannot begin to understand their difficulties in adjustment. Almost everything that alarms the Hmong can be considered an obstacle to their adjustment.

A chief anxiety of the elderly is their concern over differences in burial practices. Most elderly Hmong in Laos traveled from mountain to mountain, carefully selecting a burial site "high on the slopes and with a good view." The bodies were never buried side by side.   The subject of burial is of considerable interest to the Hmong.   When a local mortuary representative came to talk to the community, he drew the largest turnout of Isla Vista Hmong ever seen up to that time.   Despite his explanations, confusion and concern continue.   One informant, for example, asked me if the grave location is now decided by the church, and many old people are reported to "feel sad" at the prospect of adjacent burials, as well as the possibility of bodies being placed on top of one another and of bodies disinterred to make room for others.   In addition, while it is permissible to cut a person when alive, it is objectionable to do so after death.   This objection apparently refers to both embalming practices and autopsies.

The elderly are aware of their high vulnerability to crime.   Fearing robbery and rape, they will not go out alone.   Crime was much lower in Laos and, in any case, informants report, the elderly feel unable to call for help in the English language.   Many are not eligible for ESL instruction, which is officially limited to employable adults between ages eighteen and fifty-five.   The few elderly receiving such instruction are finding greater difficulty than other age groups in learning and in retaining what they learn.

Still another area of concern for the elderly is the impending changes in Hmong culture, which they see as adversely affecting existing family structure.   Among other concerns, they fear an escalated divorce rate as the result of increased education and freedom for Hmong females.   Such apprehensions are not without foundation. Some student teenage brides are finding it difficult to manipulate both school homework and duties traditionally relegated to the youngest married woman in a household. In addition to learning about alternative lifestyles in sociology classes, these brides often receive sympathetic moral support from classmates.   A few such teenage brides are leaving their husbands and returning to their families.

These areas are more a matter of concern for the elderly than for younger people.   Nevertheless, in view of the continuing strong   tradition of respect and concern for the well-being of elders, the unhappiness of the elderly affects the entire community.   In fact, every person who answered my questions about what Americans can do to help more, replied that we should help the old people to learn English or to find a job. The elderly need to be useful, the informants said.

Isolation brought on by cultural and language differences is a principal factor inhibiting adjustment. Despite the advantages of such a support system, which I will address later, the cohesiveness of the Hmong community effectively retards acquisition of the English language and limits interaction with the larger society.

High on the list of obstacles are economic difficulties. With welfare assistance essentially phased out, many Hmong are having trouble supporting large families and finding housing they can afford on their meager salaries. The little-known requirement to repay the Intergovernmental Committee on Migration (ICM), for transportation costs from Thailand to the United States, imposes one further economic and psychological burden upon the Hmong. Families receive a bill each month for the entire amount, and have been advised to send a monthly payment to "show their good faith," according to an Indochinese Community Project (ICP) representative.

Hmong sensitivity to misrepresentations and inaccuracies about them in the press also serves to inhibit interaction with the outside community. Contrary to the myth perpetuated in the press, some Isla Vista Hmong did attend school in Laos and are literate in Laotian. A few informants are also literate in French and one informant reads Chinese. Most Isla Vista Hmong speak Lao and some Thai in addition to two Hmong dialects. Neither is the persistent report that the Hmong have no written language accurate, since the Hmong language was endowed with a Romanized script by missionaries in Indochina. This script is being read in some of the Hmong households in Isla Vista. A Hmong elder concerned with the preservation of Hmong culture and language has been conducting reading classes for mothers in this script.

Not only is such misinformation and underestimation dangerous in terms of the direction of official policy, but such irresponsible reporting further inhibits interaction with the outside community. For example, a leader who was at first very responsive avoided a further interview with me, mentioning the negative press about the Hmong. This occurred shortly after the publication of one such poorly researched article in the Los Angeles Times (Japenga 1982).

The desire of some Hmong to return to Laos appears to reflect a combination of anxiety and loneliness for those left behind and a sense of despair over the seemingly insurmountable obstacles to successful survival in the new society. Reunification with family and friends was the most common reason given for the desire to return. One informant cited the problems of the elderly as another reason.

While a number of refugees hope to return to Laos someday, many fear being sent back by a president who may at any time decide that Laos is now safe and cancel their refugee status. The abrupt reduction and termination of welfare benefits--perhaps seen as reflecting a change in policy toward refugees--probably caused anxiety that reached beyond monetary concerns. Various cases of Hmong reluctance to call upon the police may stem from similar underlying apprehensions. In one instance, an informant received three visits from an intoxicated male who used the family shower, made long-distance calls from its telephone, and gave orders to family members. Yet neither the informant nor anyone in her family tried to contact the police. After the third such visit, family members called a leader, also a relative, who contacted the apartment manager, who then notified the police.

An unwillingness by most Isla Vista Hmong to remember former non-Christian religious practices may be seen as yet another manifestation of what they feel is their tenuous position in this society. Even recent converts to Christianity appear sincerely not to remember any former traditional religious practices. A question that must be raised, therefore, is to what extent the concept of Christianity is considered by the Hmong in a nonreligious context; that is, how many convert as a matter of faith and how many because they believe it's a necessary step in adjustment? Additionally, the danger exists that this reluctance to remember may adversely affect the oral transmission of cultural information and folk history to offspring and, hence, to succeeding generations.

Also revealed in the interviews is the custom of conferring a different, or "old" name upon a male when he becomes a father for the first time or soon after his twenty-fifth birthday. His original first name is con-

sidered his child name, which is usually erased thereafter. His mature name, given to him by his father-in-
law, becomes his given name. Most Hmong do not legally
change their names, both because of the difficulties
involved and the confusion it might create in the workplace, at school and elsewhere. More and more men,
therefore, are known by one first name within the Hmong
community and by another--their child name--in the larger
society. While some men are reported to feel badly about
this, others says that it is "no problem." Nevertheless,
the difficulties encountered in retaining this custom
forge another link in the chain of obstacles separating
Hmong and Americans.

In addition to concerns expressed in interviews and
through other sources, the Hmong in the United States undoubtedly experience anxieties which they can never discuss with outsiders, ranging from horrifying war experiences to the forbidden existence of a second wife who has
managed to enter the United States. Such wives and their
children are obliged to live a lie in their dealings with
the American community throughout their lifetimes. They
possess one identity within the Hmong community and
another outside of it.

Finally, family heads have experienced the loss of
some authority, prestige, self-esteem and self-confidence
as the result of forced dependence on outside support and
of shifting roles within the family. Being corrected or
criticized by offspring, however gently, is a source of
embarrassment and sadness. One informant reports a suicide by a Hmong father in another community as the result
of such loss of authority. It is to be expected that,
especially among older people, some depression exists as
a result of these factors.

FACTORS ENHANCING ADJUSTMENT

One factor easing the Hmong through the adjustment
process is a number of similarities between Hmong and
Americans in important cultural values--among these the
hard work ethic, an emphasis on the importance of education, a strong desire for upward mobility and economic
advancement, an independent spirit, high self-esteem and
an emphasis on money. These values are held for somewhat

different reasons. While Americans value the material aspects that money can provide, the Hmong have traditionally used money--in the form of both bride-price and fines--to solidify marriages and maintain social order.

Further, the historic Hmong qualities of flexibility, adaptability and resourcefulness, which were amply exhibited throughout this study, have undoubtedly helped the Hmong cope with their new surroundings. Flexibility has been the keynote in most facets of Hmong life, from dress and division of labor to courtship, marriage and naming practices. Change and adaptation to different environments and peoples are not new to the Hmong but have long been a part of their way of life. Secondary and tertiary migrations within the United States to improve housing and income may not be seen by the Hmong as particularly disruptive, in view of their historical tradition of migration. It should be remembered that the Hmong have not come from a point of stability directly to the United States, but have endured warfare, upheaval and family separations since about 1960.

One example of Hmong resourcefulness that was brought out in the study is the organization in the United States of neighborhood or clan lending pools, to which each member contributes a small amount monthly and from which he is able in return to draw out large amounts in order to purchase expensive items, such as a refrigerator or car. No interest is charged, and the borrower repays when he can. In Isla Vista, however, very few Hmong belong to such an organization.

Expectations of the welcome and assistance to be received in America appear to be low. This is predictable, considering that, even in good times, the Hmong have been tolerated rather than welcomed in the areas through which they have migrated. Historically, minority status has been their lot, so their present situation is not so very unfamiliar.

Although the Hmong people's organization as a community could be considered a disadvantage in terms of the extent to which it retards acculturation, the presence of the Hmong community provides a substantive vein of continuity and stability during a period of great disruption and change, and probably ranks as the foremost factor enhancing the Hmong people's adjustment. This finding is supported by other studies and surveys which suggest that

Indochinese refugees be settled only in clusters (Trillin 1980; Bureau of Research 1979).

Despite some shifts in family power relationships, a degree of filial rebellion is expected, and parents are confident that they remain in control of their children. Young informants report a continued desire and obligation to care for parents "until the end of their days."

Finally, the socioeconomic climate of Isla Vista itself appears influential in easing adjustment and promoting friendly relations between Hmong and Americans. Competition for factory employment is minimal; neither the student community nor the adjacent affluent community of Santa Barbara seeks factory employment. As a result, 75 percent of the employable Indochinese in the area are employed. This compares favorably with larger urban communities, such as the Twin Cities area, where only 20 percent of Hmong adults are employed (Southeast Asian Refugee Studies Newsletter 1983). Competition for housing is limited to university students, who realize they have no permanent stake in the community and generally react with indifference to the Indochinese presence. The Hmong in Isla Vista, therefore, are not subjected to the degree or intensity of hostility from other segments of the community that is being experienced by Hmong in some larger, problem-ridden communities such as Long Beach and Minneapolis (Calderon 1982; Kershaw 1982).

On the contrary, in their contacts with Americans, the Isla Vista Hmong are exposed primarily to sentiments of concern, sympathy, admiration and friendliness. These come from teachers, welfare workers, students and other American community volunteers.

In addition to ESL and vocational programs, a number of other forms of American community assistance are being extended to refugees. An American woman organized a "Mama's Class," at which children are welcome, for those refugees who were unable to attend regular ESL classes because of child-care problems. Most of the students are Hmong; their numbers include elderly women ineligible for regular ESL classes. This informal Mama's Class, taught five days a week by volunteers, emphasizes practical English for home management. A university student organized student volunteer tutors in a program funded by the university. The Isla Vista Youth Project, frequented by Hmong and other refugee children, is also staffed by volunteers and provides tutorial services as well as an after-school activities center for children of working parents. The Indochinese have found such private lessons helpful, and there are not enough volunteers to provide the hours of tutoring sought by the Hmong. Some American women have attempted to initiate a cottage industry by combining Hmong embroidery and Western dress, and two other American women are active in exhibiting and selling Hmong handicrafts at local fairs and craft shows. A small plot in community gardens has been made available to each Hmong family in Isla Vista.

A nutritional program called the "Let Isla Vista Eat (LIVE)" Project was initiated recently. It provides free cold breakfasts five mornings a week and distributes bulk foods three mornings a week. A large percentage of those taking advantage of the breakfasts and food distribution are Hmong children and Hmong women, respectively.

Recently, the school district jointly sponsored a workshop for Indochinese parents, emphasizing (1) differences between Indochinese and American educational systems and the roles of parents in each, (2) what children learn and how parents can assist and encourage them, and (3) career awareness. Educators stimulated a dialogue to help themselves discover what particular questions and frustrations these parents might have. While another sizable Indochinese group was absent, the Hmong attended the workshop in large numbers.

The favorable employment rate is not the only indication that the Isla Vista Hmong have had a comparatively easier adjustment experience than Hmong resettled in other communities. While Hmong mutual assistance associations have sprung up around the country, Isla Vista Hmong seem to have found it unnecessary to form or belong to one. Neither is there significant membership in clan associations, as there is in other Hmong communities. By 1982, at least seven Hmong out of this small community had entered college. This compares favorably with other communities, such as the one at Long Beach, which had approximately ten times the Hmong population but still had no Hmong students in college.

Another likely indication is the increasing degree of Hmong participation in community activities. For example, in 1982, Hmong men and women in traditional dress participated for the first time in Santa Barbara's Summer

Solstice parade.   No other Indochinese group was represented.   In addition, Hmong handicrafts are displayed and
sold from a booth operated by Hmong women at numerous
local art and craft exhibits.

It is not the intention of this paper to minimize
the overwhelming obstacles faced by the Hmong in Isla
Vista or to imply that the forms of external assistance
described above are in any way sufficient to meet the
economic needs of the Hmong in this high-cost area.
However, the obvious desire of Americans in this community to help, and the expressions of warmth and welcome
which are transmitted by Americans with whom the Hmong
are in direct contact, are undoubtedly instrumental in
easing the adjustment difficulties of the Isla Vista
Hmong.

OUTLOOK

The Hmong are survivors.   While they miss their
former way of life even more than their homeland, most
feel their new home is the United States, and they are
striving to accommodate and adapt to American society as
quickly as possible.   They are least concerned about
their children, who seem to have no adjustment problems.
Neither do the Hmong seem concerned with retention of
authority over their children, in spite of the way relationships within the family have shifted as children
learn English more rapidly than their parents.   Nevertheless, change in the desirable age for marriage and in
existing extended family structure can be predicted.

While their resourcefulness, flexibility and adaptability support them in this latest challenge for survival, the Hmong people's internal community network is
unable to dispel negative rumors or allay fears and misunderstandings which arise concerning American motives,
values and bureaucratic regulations.   The rigidity and
impersonality that now characterize management of the
refugee problem are in need of re-evaluation.   Clearly, a
meaningful, continuing dialogue with the Hmong, on both
a community and governmental level, is needed to deal
with sometimes easily solved but frustrating issues which
plague the Hmong.   The recent education workshop for
Indochinese parents was a step in the right direction.

Other such dialogues should be implemented. Police representatives could address the Indochinese community to explain the people's rights as well as their obligations. Another discussion might investigate the feasibility of changing Hmong men's first names without lengthy legal proceedings, perhaps by changing them on a collective basis each year. If small garden plots were made available to refugees in other communities as they are in Isla Vista, it would provide a degree of self-reliance by means of a familiar form of labor and would bring a small measure of economic assistance. Such continuing efforts can ease the adjustment of the refugees and, in the process, serve to reduce the social distance between Americans and Hmong.

ACKNOWLEDGEMENTS

This study was supported by a President's Undergraduate Fellowship from the University of California, Santa Barbara. I am grateful to the following for their advice and support: Dr. Ruth L. Moore and Debreana McGrath of the University of California, Santa Barbara, and R. Greet Kershaw of the University of Long Beach. I am also indebted to the Hmong people of Isla Vista who graciously received me into their homes or came to mine, and tolerated the multitude of questions.

The ethnographic study on which this paper is based was conducted in the Isla Vista community between January and October, 1982. While some information has been included or clarified as the result of continued research through October 1983, the ethnographic present of this paper remains the time within the original study period.

NOTE

[1] Refugee population figures were provided by an Indochinese Community Project (ICP) representative during the study period and supported by a Hmong leader, also connected with ICP at the time. These figures, I discovered recently, were underestimated to the public in an attempt to minimize the Indochinese presence in the community--an example of fear once again, the time on

the part of non-Hmong personnel concerned with the refugee community. This underestimation resulted in reduced refugee assistance efforts. A year-end 1983 estimate is approximately one thousand Hmong and Laotian refugees combined in the Isla Vista area. This higher figure also reflects the recent one-way flow of Hmong refugees into the area. Only one Hmong family has left Isla Vista since April 1983.

REFERENCES

Bureau of Research and Training. 1979. National Mental Health Needs Assessment of Indochinese Refugee Populations. Prepared by Office of Mental Health, Pennsylvania Department of Public Welfare. July 1979.

Calderon, Eddie. 1982. "The Impact of Indochinese Resettlement on the Phillips and Elliot Park Neighborhoods in South Minneapolis." In The Hmong in the West: Observations and Reports, Papers from the 1981 Hmong Research Conference, edited by Bruce T. Downing and Douglas P. Olney, pp. 367-386. Minneapolis: Center for Urban and Regional Affairs, University of Minnesota.

Gross, Catherine Stoumpos. 1983. "Transition in Perspective: A Study of the Hmong of Isla Vista." DISCOVERY, UCSB Journal of Undergraduate Research, Spring 1983. University of California, Santa Barbara. Vol. 6, pp. 1-34.

Japenga, A. 1982. "A Meeting of Young Minds in 24 Languages." Los Angeles Times, Part V. 13 October 1982.

Kershaw, Greet. 1982. "Hmong Families in Long Beach 1978-1982: Between Incorporation and Rejection." Paper at Southwestern Anthropological Association Conference Meetings. Sacramento. April 1982.

SARS (Southeast Asian Refugee Studies) Newsletter. 1983. Minneapolis: Southeast Asian Refugee Studies Project, University of Minnesota. January 1983, Vol. 3, 2, p. 1.

Trillin, Calvin. 1980. "U.S. Journal: Fairfield, Iowa. Resettling the Yangs." The New Yorker. 24 March 1980, pp. 83-100.

APPENDIX

INFORMANT DATA

Yrs. in Refugee Camp	Arrived in U.S.	Approx. Age	Sex	Marital Status	No. of Children	IN ISLA VISTA			IN LAOS		
						No. in House-hold	No. of Families in HH	No. of Bed-rooms	No. in House-hold	No. of Bed-rooms*	Subtribe of Family or Couple
3	1976	24	F	Widowed	1	5	2	2	5	2	Unknown
4	1978	35	M	Married	5	8'	1	***	8	***	Blue
3-4	1978	33	M	Married	4	14**	2**	2	5	3	Blue
4	1978	24	M	Married	1	3	1	***	3	***	Blue/White
3	1978	38	F	Married	7	9	1	3	15	4	White
3-4	1978	32	F	Married	4	14**	2**	2	5	3	Black/Blue
2 months	1976	36	M	Married	2	8	3	4	12	4	Blue/White
3	1978	16	M	Married	0	10	2	4	9	5 or 6	Blue/White
3	1978	19	F	Single	0	6	1	3 + 2 baths	6	1	White
1	1976	25	M	Married	2	9	2	3	22	6	Blue
3	1978	32	F	Married	4	11	2	3 + 2 baths	6	3	Blue/White

* In addition, the living room was often used as a bedroom for single family members.

** Two members of same household inadvertently interviewed. Household size normally 6, but swelled temporarily with migration of 8 relatives to Isla Vista from another state.

*** Information not obtained.

NOTE: Two informants, both leaders, live outside of the physical boundaries of Isla Vista.

FACTORS CONTRIBUTING TO A SPLIT WITHIN A CLIENTELISTIC NEEDLEWORK COOPERATIVE ENGAGED IN REFUGEE RESETTLEMENT

Nancy D. Donnelly

Refugees who resettle in countries very different from their land of origin face difficult problems of adjustment. Not only must they cope with physical illness attributable to changes in diet and climate, and with painful memories of loss, but they may also be expected to find a productive niche in a society whose economy, political structure, language and customs of social interaction are unfamiliar to them. Researchers who have studied refugee responses to their new situations often have drawn on concepts from the literature of psychological adjustment. For instance, Bar-Yosef (1968) describes a process that she calls "dematuration" undergone by immigrants (some of them refugees) to Israel; even in Israel, where newcomers were very welcome, immigrants floundered for a time in their new setting because they had lost the underpinnings of their former identity--their jobs, material possessions and familiar round of daily activities. Bar-Yosef presents a model in which the Israeli bureaucracy assumes a parental role, while the immigrants perforce occupy the status of children until they remature by one means or another.

For Hmong in the United States, Bar-Yosef's model may seem to describe a situation analogous to their own, arriving as sponsored refugees only to find a society they did not expect, so that they must depend on others to teach them how to live. This paper seeks to understand the process by which some Hmong have tried to reassume control of their own lives. Thus it describes a particular instance of what Bar-Yosef terms a "coping mechanism" (1968:27). Instead of drawing on the concepts of the psychological literature, however, the process is described here in terms of patron/client interactions. The patron/client model permits delineation of the dialectical nature of resettlement; the actual situation described in the paper is presented in a simplified and diagrammatic manner, in order to clarify relationships that may have been experienced by many Hmong who have been re-settled in the United States.

BACKGROUND

In 1980, Hmong and Mien refugee women in an American city asked their American teachers to help them sell their needlework. The American women began to arrange entry into street fairs and other markets, eventually organizing a nonprofit cooperative with themselves as officers, the many refugee women as members, and other American volunteers as a sort of auxiliary. In fall 1981 they incorporated as Asian Needlecrafters (AN).[1] Soon they moved into a small shop (Harris 1982). By the fall of 1982, more than 100 women had sold pa ndau and other handmade needlework through AN at one time or another. Sales in 1982 exceeded $40,000.

When the store opened in the spring of 1982, there was rhetoric about putting the refugee women in charge of sales, and in articles and public statements the refugee members were clearly implied to be running the operation. Officially, AN was under the control of a board which included refugee women. But in fact, AN continued through the summer of 1982 to be run by a core of American volunteers, who made such decisions as: (1) whether to accept particular pieces made by refugees, (2) how large an inventory to retain undisplayed, (3) which fairs to enter, (4) which pieces to take to what fair, (5) what materials and thread to order, (6) how to display merchandise, (7) how the shop would be staffed, (8) what hours the shop would be open, (9) what sorts of new products to try, (10) whether to attempt wholesaling, (11) what kinds of publicity to seek, (12) how to set up the bookkeeping, (13) what sort of receipts, price tags and brochures to use, and (14) what nonprofit grant funding to pursue.[2] The American volunteers decided that the general goals of the organization should be: "cultural preservation and supplemental income" (E. Thomas 1982). To facilitate these two goals they would engage in "production and sale of handcrafted art and needlework by Indochinese refugees living in [this city]" (Hafey 1982; emphasis mine). This position, that all the work was done locally, differentiated AN from other groups that, frankly, imported needlework. It appealed to buyers with charitable interests, permitted higher prices, and was also connected to the goal of cultural preservation.

The American managers made an effort to promote the sense that AN was a cooperative venture, that everyone was helping in her own way to make a success out of it, and simultaneously, that everyone was helping each other. The American women made home visits and redistributed used clothing. Relationships between the American women and the refugees were characterized by amity. Personal income generated by AN's sales accrued only to the refugee women.

Hmong members of Asian Needlecrafters were also making some decisions during the summer of 1982. These included (1) whether or not to sell through AN, (2) color and style of the products they made (out of a range of possibilities suggested by the Americans), (3) how many hours to spend sewing at home, (4) when to "donate" two half-days per month in "volunteer" work at the store (this was required), and (5) what price they wanted for their work (Americans often recommended that they raise their prices).

If these lists are compared, it is clear that there was some discrepancy between the public stance of AN as an enterprise operated by refugees and the actual operational structure. Notably, decisions made by American women affected the overall operation and deeply affected the income levels of individual refugee members, while decisions made by refugee women affected themselves almost exclusively. Refugees selling through AN were basically in the position of pieceworkers producing on consignment. This said, it is important to add that one decision during this period had been made jointly by American and refugee women. The amount of the store markup (20 percent) was the outcome of negotiation. Refugees would have preferred no markup at all, and Americans began by suggesting a range from 10 percent to 40 percent. In discussion the compromise figure was finally reached.

The negotiation over markup demonstrates what everyone who has worked with nonliterate refugee women already understands: there were compelling reasons for the division of responsibility that existed in AN during 1982, since the refugee women did not know ordinary American business practices. They lacked skill in English, as well as in salesmanship and in knowledge of their market. They were unable to plan for their own futures because of their inexperience with life in the United States, and they could not have continued selling their needlework, especially through a retail outlet, without the help of American women.

There were also other reasons for the division of responsibility stemming from the personal goals of the American volunteers. By the summer of 1982, volunteers consisted almost entirely of committed Christian women. None of them had had prior business experience. They were oriented instead toward service. Perhaps they were giving the refugee women religious instruction. (This was not discussed with me, however.) Besides the novel experience they were gaining in running a business, the American women developed friendships among themselves and received positive attention from members of the local community working in refugee resettlement and from the local media. They were happy to receive the expressed appreciation and good will of the Hmong and Mien women and their families, and they felt they achieved a sense of greater closeness to God. They felt that Asian Needlecrafters was what I will call a nursery of democracy, and that they were demonstrating Christian love. Since all these goals were accomplished by the status quo of Asian Needlecrafters, the American volunteers--who remained in control of AN's structure--had little incentive to push actively for greater autonomy among their refugee members.

PATRON/CLIENT RELATIONSHIPS

The relationships outlined above are very similar to classic patron/client relationships, as described in the anthropological literature. Much has been written about patronage structures (see Eisenstadt and Roniger 1980 for a thorough review). Most anthropological work has concentrated on Mediterranean and Latin American societies, but recently there has been increasing recognition of clientelism as part of the formal governmental structures in Southeast Asian societies (Hanks 1977). Informal patronage networks have been noted within Euro-American society; for instance, inside corporate structures (see Lande 1977). Patron/client relationships have also been noticed growing up between people from different societies that have economic interaction and great disparities in wealth. In this case, individuals called "brokers" may find profit in mediating between the two, when there are communication difficulties between them (Hendriksen 1971).

The schematic and somewhat simplified drawings in Figure 1 will help clarify patron/client ties. "Patrons" are defined as persons in possession of material resources or favors, who distribute them to other people in return for loyalty and praise (and ultimately for profit, since a sizable following generally facilitates the aggregation of resources in various ways). "Clients," who have fewer material resources, nevertheless can offer the patron an intangible good--loyalty--needed by the patron to continue in this superordinate position. Clients gain directly from the patron through the patron's disbursement of goods or favors. Thus both patron and client provide each other with something of value which is less useful to them than what the other can provide to them.

Friendship (or at least cordiality) is an important element of patron/client relationships. Still, it is easy to distinguish these relationships from true friendship, and to distinguish the patron from the client: which goods are transferred and when they are transferred, is in the hands of only one party, the patron. The patron takes a position of leadership, while the client accepts a position of followership. These are actually relations of exchange. In Lande's (1977) view, the counters of loyalty have less value than the counters of material benefits, so that the clients are at a disadvantage, and have to even the score by giving the patron an added increment of obedience when necessary to the patron.

Figure 1

EXCHANGE MODEL IN PATRON/CLIENT SITUATION

material goods, access to advancement, favors	The Patron's Fund

PATRON   STRONG VERTICAL
                                ASSOCIATION, AMITY

CLIENT CLIENT CLIENT   weak horizontal ties
                                between clients

loyalty, praise, support	The Client's Fund

(obedience)   (the increment)

--- --- --- --- --- --- --- --- --- --- --- --- --- --- -

EXCHANGE MODEL IN PATRON/BROKER/CLIENT SITUATION

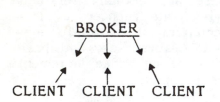

PATRON

BROKER

CLIENT CLIENT CLIENT

Broker commonly translates, interprets and/or manipulates the intention, meaning or implication of the Patron's largesse to the Clients and the Clients' responses to the Patron. Usually has own personal goals. Often retains some goods and some support/obedience for own use.

Brokerage can commonly arise when a Patron cannot or will not contact Clients directly because of physical or social distance.

--- --- --- --- --- --- --- --- --- --- --- --- --- --- -

Where a broker intervenes between patron and client, there is probably a social or physical distance between the patron and the clients. But a broker is not simply a transmitter of social and economic goods. Very likely, a broker has his own agenda and goals that are facilitated by this intermediary role, and the broker commonly retains for his own use some of the goods that pass through him from patron to client, as well as some of the loyalty offered by the clients. Nontangible goods like loyalty and demands for obedience are likely to be reinterpreted by a broker to suit his own purposes (see Paine 1971).

Hmong society in Laos did not include the clientelism seen in Southeast Asian societies with more vertical levels (for instance, the Thai monarchy; see Hanks 1977). This is probably because each extended family (sublineage) formed an independent economic unit that could fill its own needs by farming or by trading, using connections formed along family lines (Lemoine 1972:158-9). Though these family networks might depend on one central family member for success, they could not be considered clienteles surrounding a patron, because each member household was self-sufficient. They did not display the chronic neediness and insufficiency associated with dependency that seem to be prerequisite for the emergence of patron/ client structures.

IMPLICATIONS

But obviously most refugees enter the United States in a condition, however temporary, of dependency. Clientelism is a fact in the heart and essence of refugee resettlement. Clearly the largest patron is the federal government, and there are doubtless many smaller clientelistic networks. I don't think clientelism in a setting of resettlement is a negative thing, because I don't know how else resettlement could be pursued. How to bring these relationships to a close, however, may not be readily apparent, especially to the patron and the broker, whose social power depends on the presence of a clientele, and who may like the rewards of being a patron (or broker).

In the case of Asian Needlecrafters, I would say the American women were unaware of any difference between mu-

tuality of enterprise and the operation of their business.   The Mien members' attitudes are not known to me.
The Hmong members to whom I spoke in the summer of 1982
seemed to be exclusively interested in the organization's
potential for providing income.   To me, AN looked (struc-
turally speaking) like Figure 2.   Here, money rewards
move downward while needlecrafts and "volunteer" time
move upward.   Though the vertical associations between
the American volunteers and the refugee members were
characterized by friendship, horizontal ties between refugee members were much weaker (another characteristic of
patron/client arrangements), and charged with competition
and hostility, especially between some Hmong women and
some Mien women.   Volunteers arranging fairs needed to
call a dozen or more women in small networks.   Once at a
fair, certain refugee women were likely to bury other
work beneath their own, and hostile scenes occasionally
occurred.   I think it would not be entirely far-fetched
to add God as the ultimate Patron of AN.   Without bela-
boring the point, Christianity provides a parallel model,
with believers in the position of clients, the pastor as
broker, and the exchanges taking place with counters
called "Love" (Paine 1971:15).

Despite these various viewpoints, AN might have continued unchanged for a while, except for a crisis precipitated by an outside force, the federal funding cuts of
May 1982.   Any refugee who had been inside the United
States longer than eighteen months lost federal support
payments at that time.   Nearly all the Hmong members of
AN experienced great financial difficulty.   This sudden
loss of income was combined with a deepening recession,
so that jobs were scarce.   Families began to leave for
states with more generous welfare programs or for states
with jobs.   Suddenly the remaining Hmong women had to
take farm labor and house-cleaning jobs.   Suddenly, they
noticed the value of their time.   Before the funding cut,
an embroidered pant leg panel that took two months to
complete might sell for $50 (Harris 1982).   Afterward, a
woman saw that she could not retrieve the value of her
labor.

Figure 2

STRUCTURE OF ASIAN NEEDLECRAFTERS,
SUMMER 1982

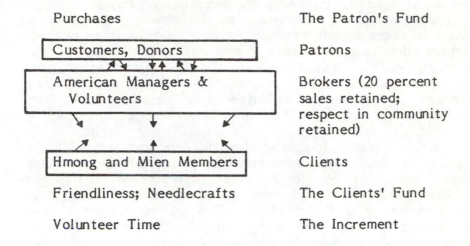

Purchases	The Patron's Fund
Customers, Donors	Patrons
American Managers & Volunteers	Brokers (20 percent sales retained; respect in community retained)
Hmong and Mien Members	Clients
Friendliness; Needlecrafts	The Clients' Fund
Volunteer Time	The Increment

--- --- --- --- --- --- --- --- --- --- --- --- --- --- --

The Hmong women solved this problem by starting to import the time-consuming centers of appliques and embroideries from their relatives in refugee camps; they expected to remit part of the profit from the sale of a piece to the person in the camp. But they discovered that AN would not accept these imports, for AN was differentiating itself in the local market by selling only locally-produced needlework. The American women felt that they could not accept foreign-made work because of their previously announced goal of cultural preservation. The Hmong women could not get the American leadership to agree that cultural preservation was identical with earning more money.

Faced with this dilemma, some Hmong women quit. Others began to present the imported work as their own, perhaps adding a border first. Thus a conspiracy grew to deceive the American women. It seems that out of this dispute about the origin of pieces, the Hmong women arrived at the conviction that in spite of appearances and rhetoric, the Americans "owned" Asian Needlecrafters and were ignoring the needs of the Hmong women in favor of themselves.

Some became quite assertive, even offering to meet customers in private to avoid the 20 percent markup. Disputes arose as various refugee women accused the Americans of favoritism (these accusations came from Mien as well as Hmong women). Nobody could get enough money to live on, it seemed. Everyone appeared desperate.

Mien members, in contrast to the Hmong, behaved in a generally more pliant, noncompetitive and passive manner. Perhaps they perceived the Americans to be truly acting in their behalf. The treasurer of AN had sponsored several Mien families. The coordinator had learned the Mien language. One central volunteer told me that "the Mien are so cute," and that "whatever the Hmong are, they're not cute."

When federal Impact Aid funds became available in August of 1982, AN successfully applied for a training grant that provided for twelve part-time clerk-trainees to staff the store and two part-time translator/organizers, one Hmong and one Mien. The primary candidate for the Hmong position was a woman who had never been a member of AN and who did not produce needlework. She had good business skills, but her main qualification was her position as wife of a Hmong leader. In October 1982, in an Asian Needlecrafters meeting attended by about sixty people, this leader (who had never come to an AN meeting before), announced that the Hmong women had formed a new organization, the Hmong Artwork Association (HAA).[3] The members of this new organization included nearly all the Hmong women currently in AN; the president of the new organization was the leader's own wife. Presenting himself as spokesperson for the Hmong women, who were too shy to speak for themselves, the leader said that the Hmong women demanded as a bloc that his wife should be hired as AN's Hmong translator/organizer.

The American women of AN felt that the leader's wife would try to sabotage the success of any other candidate so they hired her. But after this meeting they were convinced that the leader, through his wife, intended to take control of AN, eject the Mien and convert AN into a vehicle for reinforcing his own position in the local community.

In this assessment they were partly correct. In November 1982, the leader was indeed speculating on tactics for taking over AN. But the American women failed to consider how much his actions were permitted and invited by the women themselves. They were unaware of the Hmong women's anger regarding the AN policy on imported pieces (among other things), because the refugee women in their clientage position had felt unable to express this openly. They were ignorant of the traditional cohesion of Hmong society, with its processes of consensus. They saw the leader as an independent force bearing down from above on the hapless and bedeviled Hmong women. They paid little attention to the fact that the leader's wife relied on her own charisma and strength to unify the Hmong women, instead preferring to think of her as a mere agent of her husband. Having little experience with refugee women who were already competent to survive fairly independently in American society, the American women of AN underestimated the ability of the leader's wife to supplant them, in her role as broker, as the principal mediator between Hmong women who wanted to sell needlecraft and American buyers. Above all, they could not see that the way into their organization was open to her because of their own policies, which no longer met the suddenly increased financial needs of the Hmong women, and which they would not alter to accommodate their members.

The winter of 1983 is a story of struggle between the American women and their new Hmong translator/organizer, full of jockeying and distrust. She appears in my notes as a wedge driving an ever-widening gap of misunderstandings between the Americans and the Hmong women. The grant specified that classes should be conducted in math; soon the teacher realized that during translation the translator was providing the answers. The American women refused to tell her most financial information relating to the operation of the store, and they would not let her distribute fabric in case she gave it away. The scope of her job became a point of contention--she called herself a "management trainee" while they called her an "employee." She asserted that she should be taught to operate the store and should take it over. It was indeed one of the grant's goals to turn operations over to the refugee women. But the American women did little to facilitate this goal, and the point was not discussed at AN meetings. Hostility between Hmong and Mien members increased during this period. Hmong complaints directed through the translator/organizer did not reach the Hmong women.

By February 1983, the rift between factions had become unbreachable to all the women. The catalyst for action proved to be very trivial: a Hmong baby hat that the Americans would not hang in the store because it had not been made locally. Early in March, amid acrimonious debate, almost all of the twenty-six actively selling Hmong women followed their translator/organizer out of AN into an independent Hmong Artwork Association.

Patron/client ties are by their nature rather fragile, according to Eisenstadt and Roniger (1980), since they are subject to constant reappraisal and may be terminated by either party if found wanting, especially if a more promising situation is available. Wells (1979), for instance, describes a Mexican-American community in a midwestern American city, which found a willing broker (Wells says "patron") in a local foundry's Mexican-American assistant personnel manager. This individual could provide jobs as long as workers were "uncomplaining." As happened in Asian Needlecrafters, it was during a conflict (over job-related injuries) that the clients eventually perceived that their broker did not always act in their behalf, but instead had been using their loyalty as a basis for pursuing his own goal (incorporation into Anglo-American society). This discovery, combined with hard economic times and lay-offs, increased strain between clients and broker, at the same time that new brokers (Chicano representatives of La Raza, an ethnic organization) appeared on the scene. In the following crisis, the foundry workers shifted allegiance to the new brokers, who more closely shared their own cultural goals, and who could also deal effectively with the larger non-Mexican community.

The Hmong defection from AN obviously displays similar dynamics. In both cases an easily marked minority sought more sympathetic linkages between itself and the dominant society during a financial crisis. What could be (and was) described as a retreat into "enclavement" actually constituted a tactic to maximize effective interaction with the dominant group. In neither case were clients unaware of their options. In fact, whether the Hmong leader's wife has used her followers more or less than they have used her to achieve their own ongoing goal of financial adjustment to American life, is an interesting question that might be pursued. During its first nine months of operation, HAA produced an impressive total in sales, of which nearly three-quarters went to members while none went to HAA's manager (the Hmong leader's wife); she, however, retained her superordinate position.

Many anthropologists writing on the topic of clientage have noted that the short-term material rewards may go predominantly to the clients themselves, while the rewards of patrons and brokers (which a following of clients cannot provide but can only facilitate) may exist in primarily disembodied form as social opportunity and influence. Patron/client relationships from the client's viewpoint are worthless without immediate rewards, while the patron/broker may intend long-term gains that can be easily frustrated if clients melt away during times of slender returns. Thus the risk of such relationships seems to accrue primarily to the patron/broker, at least where the clients have other options, as is demonstrable in the cases of Asian Needlecrafters and also the Hmong Artwork Association, whose true "winners" so far are the clients. Thus the goals of refugee resettlement (improvements in the social and economic position of refugees) have been successfully attained so far by both organizations, the major costs being in the realm of disappointed expectations for some of the brokers. In an American setting, it seems, patrons and brokers should seek short-term as well as long-term rewards to justify establishing relationships that might tend to be expensive and full of potential disappointment. What these rewards may be, when they are not financial, is another topic of interest.

ACKNOWLEDGEMENTS

I want to express my appreciation to the members and volunteers of both Asian Needlecrafters and the Hmong Artwork Association for their great patience in answering questions and for accepting me as a mere watcher in their organizations. My thanks are also due to Dr. Marshall G. Hurlich of the Department of Anthropology, University of Washington, for his continuing encouragement.

NOTES

[1]This is not the organization's true name.

[2]Hmong and American informants did not agree on who made decisions regarding items 1, 2, 4, and 5. In this list I have followed the perception of my Hmong informants. Data collection began late in the summer of 1982, so earlier events are based only on informants' reports, which do not always agree.

[3]"Hmong Artwork Association" is a name invented by the author to conceal the group's identity.

REFERENCES

Bar-Yosef, Rivka Weiss. 1968. "Desocialization and Resocialization: The Adjustment Process of Immigrants." International Migration Review 2(3):27-43.

Eisenstadt, S.M., and Louis Roniger. 1980. "Patron-Client Relations as a Model of Structuring Social Exchange." Comparative Studies in Society and History 22:42-77.

Hafey, Pamela, n.d. [1982]. "Southeast Asian Textiles." Flier.

Hanks, Lucian M. 1977. "The Corporation and the Entourage: a Comparison of Thai and American Social Organization." In Friends, Followers, and Factions, edited by Steffen W. Schmidt et al., pp. 161-166. Berkeley: University of California Press.

Harris, Jane. 1982. "Designs from Another World." Bellevue (Wash.) Journal-American, 28 June 1982.

Hendriksen, Georg. 1971. "The Transactional Basis of Influence: White Men Among Naskapi Indians." In Patrons and Brokers in the East Arctic, edited by Robert Paine. Toronto: University of Toronto Press.

Lande, Carl H. 1977. "Introduction: The Dyadic Basis of Clientelism." In Friends, Followers, and Factions, edited by Steffen W. Schmidt et al., pp. xiii–xxxix. Berkeley: University of California Press.

Lemoine, Jacques. 1972. Un Village Hmong Vert du Haut Laos. Editions du Centre National de la Recherche Scientifique. Paris: Ecole Pratique des Hautes E-tudes.

Paine, Robert. 1971. "Introduction." In Patrons and Brokers in the East Arctic, edited by Robert Paine. Toronto: Toronto University Press.

Thomas, Elaine. 1982. "Hmong and Mien Textile Art: Motif and Meaning." Unpublished manuscript.

Wells, Miriam J. 1979. "Brokerage, Economic Opportunity, and the Growth of Ethnic Movements." Ethnology 18:399–414.

THE HMONG RESETTLEMENT STUDY: A SYMPOSIUM

INTRODUCTION

Stephen Reder

This symposium is designed to present an overview of the Hmong Resettlement Study, a national project funded by the United States Office of Refugee Resettlement. The study was the joint undertaking of Northwest Regional Educational Laboratory (Portland), the University of Minnesota and Lao Family Community (Santa Ana). The major purposes of the study were to examine closely the resettlement of Hmong refugees in the United States, focusing on related issues, and to answer the following questions:

I. What has been the resettlement experience of the Hmong?

    -   How are the Hmong faring in terms of employment, dependence and adjustment?

    -   Are there areas of employment in which the Hmong have been particularly successful?

    -   What are the major problems that Hmong are experiencing in their resettlement and adjustment?

    -   What do resettlement workers and the Hmong regard as the major impediments to effective Hmong resettlement and self-sufficiency?

    -   What role does secondary migration (the voluntary move from the first city of resettlement to another) play in the resettlement of the Hmong? What are the reasons for resettlement of the Hmong? What are the reasons for secondary migration among this group? What are the implications for resettlement strategies?

II. What resettlement efforts and economic strategies have provided effective results for the Hmong?

-   How are problems being handled? What kinds of solutions are being tried by different resettlement communities and by the Hmong themselves?

-   What factors account for the effective resettlement of the Hmong in certain communities? Which resettlement efforts have proven to be the most promising?

-   How many and what kinds of entrepreneurial economic development projects involving the Hmong are currently in operation, e.g., farming projects, pa ndau cooperatives? How were they developed and how successful are they?

-   What kinds of Hmong employment strategies have been particularly successful?

III.   How might current strategies be changed to result in more effective resettlement and long-term adjustment of the Hmong?

-   How might resettlement be conducted differently for the Hmong? What new projects and approaches are being considered by those involved in Hmong resettlement? How would the Hmong want resettlement to be done differently?

-   How can the Hmong be resettled in a way that better utilizes their strengths and unique characteristics?

-   What do the Hmong want for themselves? What conditions do Hmong view as essential for effective resettlement? What are their goals for their own future and for that of the next generation of Hmong?

Research conducted in the project included analysis of existing data about the Hmong, compilation of information gathered through numerous informal face-to-face and telephone conversations with Hmong informants in nearly every Hmong settlement which could be identified across the country, and on-site observations, group meetings and personal interviews with Hmong individuals and families, as well as resettlement officials, service providers and members of the host communities. On-site studies of Hmong resettlement were conducted in seven selected locations: Orange County, California; Fresno, California; Portland, Oregon; Minneapolis-St. Paul, Minnesota; Dallas-Fort Worth, Texas; Fort Smith, Arkansas, and Providence, Rhode Island.

These communities were selected to exhibit a range of conditions pertinent to Hmong resettlement, including size of the host community, size of the local Hmong population, ability of the local economy to absorb the Hmong, and available welfare and social services.

Staff from the participating institutions worked as a team to carry out the overall project and the seven case studies.

The Northwest Regional Educational Laboratory team comprised Stephen Reder, project director; Mary Cohn, John Finck (also with State of Rhode Island), Mike Sweeney, Bruce Thowpaou Bliatout (also with City of Portland), Karen Reed Green and Marshall Hurlich (also with University of Washington).

The University of Minnesota Center for Urban and Regional Affairs team comprised Bruce Downing, Simon Fass, Doug Olney, Sarah Mason and Glenn Hendricks.

Project workers from Lao Family Community were Shur Vang Vangyi, Dang Vang and Thongsay Vang.

The results of the project are available to the public as a series of reports published by the United States Government Printing Office (GPO). Copies may be ordered from:

Dr. Allen Gall
Office of Refugee Resettlement
330 C Street, SW
Switzer Building, Room 1229
Washington, D.C. 20201

Mr. Bud Tumy
Refugee Materials Cntr.
U.S. Dept. of Education
324 E. 11th Street
9th Floor
Kansas City, MO 64104

Final Reports

Vol. 1: Summary
Vol. 2: Economic Development
Vol. 3: Exemplary Projects
Executive Summary (written in English)
Executive Summary (written in Lao)
Executive Summary (written in Hmong)

Site Reports

Orange County, California
Fresno, California
Portland, Oregon
Minneapolis-St. Paul, Minnesota
Dallas-Fort Worth, Texas
Fort Smith, Arkansas
Providence, Rhode Island

The purpose of this symposium is not to summarize detailed findings of the study--the series of public reports is available for that purpose. Within the time available, the participants in the symposium wish merely to highlight a few issues about selected aspects of Hmong resettlement in the United States.

Presentations will thus concern a number but certainly not all of the critical issues observed in Hmong resettlement: population trends, secondary migration, language issues, employment and welfare dependence, youth and future issues, and economic development. Although each presenter served a key role in the study, the research was not divided in a parallel fashion. For this symposium presenters have synthesized the results on their assigned topic from the range of case studies and other information on hand. In many cases they relied on case studies conducted by others and in some cases added their own opinions and evaluations of the issues. We hope the resulting diversity provokes a lively discussion.

POPULATION TRENDS

Douglas Olney

It is difficult to obtain accurate population figures on the Hmong in the United States or, for that matter, in the rest of the world. The figures put together for the Hmong Resettlement Study are from several sources including the United Nations High Commission for Refugees (UNHCR), the Federal Office of Refugee Resettlement (ORR), surveys done previously in Hmong communities and data collected in the course of this study. The figures are not to be taken as absolute, but they do provide a general picture of Hmong population trends.

Population Prior To Resettlement

Laos. Estimates of the prewar and preexodus population in Laos vary a great deal. An early 1960 census stated there were about fifty thousand Hmong, but a more accurate figure is that of Yang Dao, who states that the Hmong numbered over three hundred thousand or approximately ten percent of the total population of Laos.

Movement to Thailand. Table I shows the movement of hill-tribes to Thailand ("hill-tribes" or "highland Lao" include other Lao ethnic groups, but 90 to 95 percent are Hmong). In 1975, after General Vang Pao left, a great exodus occurred. In the next few years the flow diminished but it surged again in 1979, when pressure on Hmong in Laos again increased. This second wave peaked in early 1980 and then dropped off quickly in 1981 and the following years.

Table II shows the resettlement countries and number of hill-tribe people who have moved out of Thailand. Over one hundred ten thousand Hmong have left Laos since 1975, and there are still about fifty-two thousand in seven refugee camps in Thailand.

Table I HILL-TRIBE MOVEMENT TO THAILAND		Table II HILL-TRIBE RESETTLEMENT TO OTHER COUNTRIES (August 1983)	
1975	44,659	United States	53,950
1976	7,266	France	6,564
1977	3,873	French Guiana	1,413
1978	8,013	Canada	806
1979	23,943	Australia	317
1980	14,801	Argentina	222
1981	4,356	Other	289
1983 (May)	1,785		

TOTAL: 110,512   TOTAL: 63,561

THAILAND REFUGEE CAMP POPULATION, May 1984:   52,374

Movement to the U.S.   Table III and Figure I show the history of hill-tribe settlement in the United States.   The peak flow to the United States was in 1979 and 1980 following the second wave of exodus from Laos and corresponding to an increased awareness of the refugee problem in the United States.   Since 1981 Hmong arrivals have slowed considerably; it seems that the Hmong who remain in the camps do not want to resettle to third countries.

Table III
HILL-TRIBE RESETTLEMENT
TO THE UNITED STATES

1975	301
1976	3,058
1977	1,655
1978	3,873
1979	11,301
1980	27,242
1981	3,704
1982	2,511
1983	300

TOTAL: 53,950

Figure I

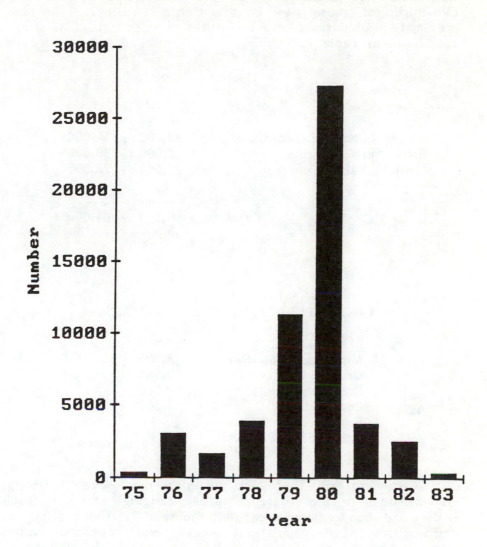

Population In The United States

General. As Table IV indicates there are between sixty-one thousand and sixty-five thousand Hmong current-ly in the United States; this includes a high level of natural increase in the number who were resettled here. California has about half of the Hmong population, and two-thirds of those live in the Central Valley. The approximate populations of the sites visited in this study are shown in Table V.

Table IV

Hmong outside California	32,000 - 34,000
Hmong in California	28,000 - 30,000
Central Valley	20,000 - 22,000

Total	60,000 - 64,000

Table V
HMONG POPULATIONS IN STUDY SITES

Fresno	10,000
Minneapolis-St. Paul	8,500
Orange County	3,000
Providence	2,500
Portland	1,000
Fort Smith	300
Dallas-Fort Worth	300

Communities. There are currently over seventy Hmong communities in the United States, ranging in size from under one hundred to over ten thousand. About fifty-six communities have populations under one thousand while there are only two with populations over eight thousand. While there are several distinct clusters of Hmong, many small Hmong communities are scattered across the nation.

A factor that contributed to the building of Hmong population centers has been the heavy sponsorship of Hmong by Hmong. In Portland it was found that eighty-five percent were sponsored by other Hmong and in the Twin Cities of Minneapolis-St. Paul, fifty-six percent. Of course we know that once the Hmong arrived in the city in which they were sponsored, they often moved on to other cities.

The wide variation in community size and the variation in other factors leads one to question whether there is a relationship between Hmong community size and economic and social self-sufficiency. Is there an optimum size for a Hmong community? Do different cities have different optimum populations which they can support?

Table VI
HMONG COMMUNITIES IN UNITED STATES

Size (persons)	Number
0 - 299	28
301 - 999	28
1000 - 1999	6
2000 - 2999	4
3000 - 3999	2
4000 - 4999	2
8000+	2

Birth rates. In the United States, the Hmong birth rate continues to be high, just as it was in the refugee camps. The rate is about 50 per 1000; this may be compared to the overall rate in the United States of 15.9 per 1000. While actual birth rates may be slowing, the availability of better medicine has reduced the infant mortality rate as compared to that in Laos. In the Twin Cities seventeen percent of a sample of 1,805 individuals were born in the United States. In addition to the general desire of Hmong to have large families, the high rate of marriage among Hmong teenagers contributes to the high birth rate. In several of the cities we visited it was reported that eight-five percent to ninety percent of the teenage girls were dropping out of high school to get married. This rapidly growing population may lead to further problems in attaining self-sufficiency. For example, continued large family size may drain family resources. On the other hand, it has been shown that the large Hmong family can be a resource in itself.

Age-sex characteristics. In the various samples collected, the Hmong population remains young: twenty-five
to thirty percent of the Hmong in the United States are
under five and over fifty percent are under fifteen,
while at the other end of the spectrum only about four
percent are over sixty. This age distribution suggests
consequences in several important areas of Hmong resettlement, particularly in the area of education. School
systems in which there are substantial numbers of Hmong
should expect continued enrollment of Hmong children as
those under five reach school age. Subsequently we should
see a larger, historically unprecedented proportion of
Hmong who will have had some education. The sex ratio of
the Hmong seems to be fairly even; in the Twin Cities
fifty-four percent were male and forty-six percent female. In general, families seem to be intact although in
the Twin Cities twelve percent of Hmong households are
headed by women. (Sources: UNHCR Monthly Statistics, ORR
Hmong/Highland Lao Workshop, Hmong Resettlement Study).

SECONDARY MIGRATION
TO CALIFORNIA'S CENTRAL VALLEY

John Finck

Approximately one-third of the Hmong in the United
States moved from one city to another between the time of
the first Hmong Research Conference, held in October
1981, and this second conference, held two years later.
What drew twenty thousand Hmong to the Central Valley of
California in so short a period? In the space of two
years, an estimated two thousand Hmong left St. Paul-
Minneapolis, and half of the Hmong population of Portland, Oregon, about two thousand people, moved to Central
Valley towns such as Fresno, Stockton and Merced. Fresno
has already replaced the Twin Cities as the largest resettlement site of the Hmong in the United States and is
reported to have the largest peacetime concentration of
Hmong in history.

Although the concentration of so many Hmong in one geographical area has permitted the reunification of many families and friends, it has not been without some problems. Fresno also has the largest number of Hmong on welfare of any county in the country. The numbers on cash assistance have grown exponentially. In July 1980, there were 168 Hmong individuals on public assistance in Fresno. Three years later, Fresno had over seven thousand Hmong on assistance. Unfortunately, Fresno's agriculture and service-based economy has not yet been able to absorb the new arrivals. Some individuals are concerned about the potential for Hmong becoming permanently dependent on welfare in the Central Valley.

Migration to the Central Valley appears to have been largely an unplanned, spontaneous choice by dozens of lineage and sublineage groups who moved for a variety of reasons. As Cheu Thao reported at the first Hmong Research Conference, the Hmong have a long tradition of what he termed "moving for betterment." With this understanding, we can conclude that the migration into the Central Valley stems in part from family reunification and in part from the perceived lack of opportunities in the primary host communities. The apparent irony lies in the fact that the Central Valley seems to be one of the least desirable sites in the country at present for employment and eventual self-sufficiency of large numbers of undereducated refugees. Their decisions to move to the Central Valley appear to have been based largely on the shortcomings of the sending communities rather than on knowledge of what might lie ahead in Fresno or Merced.

Interviews with Hmong informants in Fresno revealed several reasons for moving, including:

a) <u>The absence of jobs or a history of repeated layoffs in the host community</u>. The national recession in the last two years hit the Hmong particularly hard. Even Hmong with employment histories were subject to on-again, off-again hirings and firings. Frustration with the job market led many Hmong to consider moving. However, the job situation in the Central Valley was bleaker than what most Hmong left behind in other states. In 1983, about 5 percent of the employable Hmong in Fresno were working. By comparison, about 20 percent indicated they had held jobs before coming to Fresno.

b) <u>The desire for English classes and vocational training</u>. There is some evidence to suggest that refugees in other parts of the country assumed that what was once widely available in Orange County, California--namely, vocational training and English language classes--was also available in Fresno. Unfortunately, Fresno, as late as spring 1983, had no vocational training and only limited English as a Second Language (ESL) classes for Hmong.

c) <u>The dream of farming</u>. Perhaps half of the Hmong came to Fresno with the idea of farming. After seeing firsthand the requirements for capital, knowledge of modern farming techniques and marketing experience in the Central Valley, less than 20 percent of those who came with farming in mind indicated a continued interest. The costs and risks are great. The failures have been many. The minority of families who have successfully broken into farming in Fresno have inspired many others to try. And some progress is under way. But agriculture will likely support only a fraction of the Hmong population present in the valley.

d) <u>The change in national policy for cash assistance</u>. The federal government reduced the period of refugee cash assistance from thirty-six to eighteen months in the spring of 1982. Those states without welfare programs that paid benefits comparable to refugee cash assistance to unemployed two-parent families, were obliged to cut many refugees from their welfare ranks. A significant number of families without jobs in cities like Seattle and Portland therefore had to find other means of support, which in most cases turned out to be a general public assistance program that accepted intact families in a neighboring state.

e) <u>The snowball effect of family reunification</u>. Large numbers of Hmong families in a single location usually tend to attract additional families. This is the well-known experience of secondary migration. Younger family members find it difficult to resist the call of their elders either to move with a group or to join the group in a new setting. To some extent, migration to the Central Valley took on a life of its own that soon spread

to all parts of the country. Even Hmong leaders who advised against moving saw their counsel go unheeded in the
contagion of the impulse to move to California.

LANGUAGE ISSUES

Bruce Downing

The Hmong Resettlement Study addressed questions
concerning the acquisition of English and of literacy by
the Hmong and its importance to more general economic and
social adjustment. Some of these issues will be discussed here briefly.

1. The Value of English for Economic and Social Self-Sufficiency.

As in virtually every previous study we found that
learning English was considered both very important and
very difficult by the Hmong interviewed.

The Hmong see language as the principal barrier to
employment as well as other social adjustment. In the
Twin Cities Hmong Community Survey (University of
Minnesota, August 1982), respondents were asked to name
the problems facing them or their families. "English"
was the problem most often named, by 58 percent of all
respondents--and by 71 percent of the women respondents.
(The second most-often-named problem was "no job," mentioned by 46 percent.)

In Orange County it was found that "in spite of many
individual successes in learning English in a short time,
the community as a whole sees inadequate English as an
overwhelming problem. English is seen as necessary for
entry into jobs, for promotion on the job, for making use
of job training, for higher education and for acceptance
by the American community."

While some considered job acquisition to be the most
important problem facing the Hmong, training and English
were seen as the keys to obtaining jobs, and ability to
speak and read English was considered essential in most

job-training programs; thus, the primary factor in many cases turns out again to be English. In the Twin Cities it was found that nearly two-thirds of unemployed Hmong household heads were not actively seeking a job. Of the reasons given for not looking for employment, the most frequent (mentioned by 32 percent) was "limited English."

In a few areas, such as Dallas, Texas, it has been relatively easy to obtain jobs without knowing English and without special job skills. But now many of those Hmong who have had jobs are worried that if they are laid off they will not be able to regain employment.

Figure I (based on data from the Twin Cities Hmong Community Survey) shows graphically the relationship between proficiency in English and employment.

Figure I

JOB HOLDING IN UNITED STATES
BY SELF-RATED ENGLISH PROFICIENCY:
TWIN CITIES HMONG HOUSEHOLD HEADS

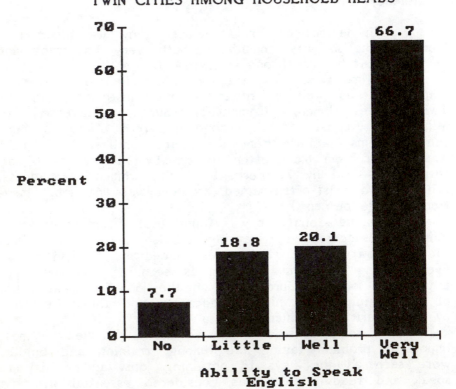

2. Educational and Linguistic Background.

A major concern in providing English language instruction has been the educational and cultural experiences the Hmong had in Laos and in the refugee camps, and how they affect their ability to learn English.

Some data are presented in Figure II (based on the Twin Cities Hmong Community Survey).

Figure II

EDUCATIONAL ATTAINMENT OF HMONG OVER 12

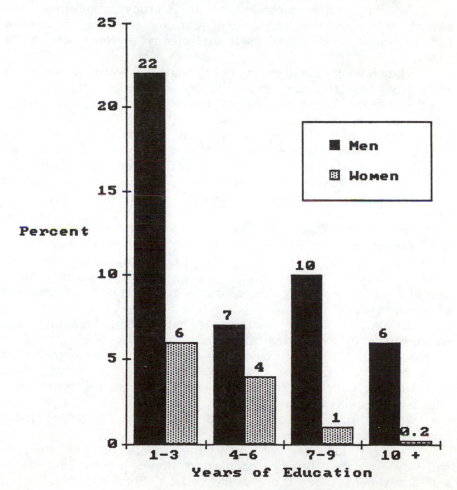

Fifty-five percent of the men and eighty-nine percent of the women had no schooling in Laos.

The importance of background factors such as literacy in Hmong, literacy in any language, knowledge of a second language, and level of education to the learning of English was brought out very clearly in papers by Barbara Robson and Stephen Reder (1982) at the first Hmong Research Conference and need not be reemphasized here.

3. The Extent of English Proficiency and Literacy of the Hmong.

An important question in this study concerned the extent to which the Hmong are learning the English needed for economic and social self-sufficiency.   Here are some cases.

The Hmong families in Fort Smith, Arkansas, were all originally resettled in some other location.   Nearly half of the Hmong household heads have never received formal instruction in English.   Hmong adults in Fort Smith believe that their limited ability to communicate in English is a major barrier to employment, yet none of the thirty-five men who attended a meeting for the study had attended ESL classes in Fort Smith.   Asked if they would like to have additional English instruction, all said they would.

In Orange County a local study showed that eighty-six percent of the Hmong there had attended some type of class and in 1981 (the time of the survey and the peak year of Hmong population in Orange County) seventy-three percent of the Hmong were currently enrolled in training of some kind.

In Dallas, where employment rather than training was emphasized by resettlement agencies, only about two in three of the Hmong originally resettled there received instruction in English.   Despite the insistence of some resettlement workers in Dallas that ESL is not necessary, because the Hmong can pick up English at work, both men and women interviewed indicated that they could not learn English on the job.

Surveys intended to determine levels of English proficiency in the Hmong population have been limited to self-assessments by those surveyed.   For example, in a sample of Hmong household heads in the Twin Cities, where major efforts have been made to provide appropriate language instruction for the large local Hmong population (Hmong Community Survey), self-rated English proficiency was as follows. These responses are to the question "How well do you speak English?"

Not at all	31.2%
Very little	42.6%
Well	25.0%
Very well	1.2%

Rated proficiencies were slightly lower for "reading English," and slightly lower again for "writing English."

The Hmong Resettlement Study Final Report summarizes the situation in which the majority of Hmong find themselves this way: though not all jobs which the Hmong obtain require English or literacy skills, it is generally believed by the Hmong and educators and employers that most Hmong need to know more English to retain a job, to successfully compete for new jobs in case of layoffs, and to be promoted from minimum wage positions.

4. Practical Barriers to Learning English.

The Hmong Resettlement Study interviews revealed a number of important practical barriers to the learning of English by Hmong adults, distinct from the background factors already discussed. These include social isolation, difficulty in learning English on the job, unavailability of programs, and problems of access to the programs that do exist.

The assumption that if jobs are obtained the workers will learn English on the job is not warranted. Hmong who don't know English have obviously been hired only for those jobs where communication through language is not a part of the work setting--for example, repetitious jobs on the assembly line. Workers holding such jobs have little opportunity to use English. Where employers have hired a group of workers with one bilingual among them to handle communication, the bilingual gets lots of practice in using English; the others get none. And if there is no improvement in English on the job, then obviously there is no possibility of advancement to a more skilled job or a supervisory position for which English is clearly required.

Interviews with Hmong adults who have attended ESL courses support the view that six months or a year or even two or three years of ESL are not enough to get many of the Hmong adults to a point of self-sufficiency, to the point where they can compete for jobs on an equal basis with workers who speak English well, or to the point where they can handle jobs that pay enough to feed their families.

Other factors frequently mentioned by the Hmong interviewed for the Hmong Resettlement Study as barriers to studying and learning English included transportation, child care (a major barrier to both training and employment for women), psychological problems, and family responsibilities which leave little time for study. Finally, in many smaller communities and some larger ones, there are simply no ESL classes or none at the appropriate level or with an appropriate focus.

5. Improvement of Language and Literacy Efforts for the Hmong.

Hmong adults interviewed for the study had many suggestions for the improvement of ESL instruction, which must be listed without discussion here:

- a more concrete, structured, step-by-step teaching approach, with regular periodic assessments and feedback on progress, so students can know whether they are making progress;

- more attention to practical language use;

- more preparation for employment and for job training;

- more efficient use of class time including more effective use of bilingual classroom aides;

- beginning classes that start at a truly beginning level, especially in teaching literacy, perhaps with Hmong instructors to provide explanation in Hmong, or beginning classes taught by Hmong through mutual assistance associations;

- appropriately designed courses (rather than placing Hmong in courses designed for more advanced Spanish speakers or Vietnamese);

- coordination of ESL with specific job training or job experience;

- opportunities to practice English outside of class.

HMONG EMPLOYMENT AND WELFARE DEPENDENCY

Shur Vang Vangyi

Overview

It has been almost eight years since the first wave of Hmong refugees arrived in the United States. Most still have no idea about what types of jobs are available. Some want to work immediately after arrival; others feel they will never be able to get a job or it may take years before they can be ready to work. Among the many reasons for these feelings are "culture shock," language problems, and the fact that the work environment in this country is very different from that of Laos.

By 1982, when we started this project, there were about sixty thousand Hmong in the United States. In trying to document Hmong employment conditions, we have encountered several problems:

1. Hmong employment is not stable.

2. There has been widespread secondary migration of Hmong.

3. Those Hmong who are employed tend to have found their own jobs and thus have dropped out of official fig-

ures such as employment services registries and welfare rolls.

This study used many informants and documentary resources to draw a picture of Hmong employment in the sev-
en communities where case studies were done. Estimates
of data on local employment patterns were collected by
telephone from knowledgeable Hmong informants in almost
every other Hmong community in the country.

Local Differences

The rate of Hmong employment differs widely from
community to community. It depends on the number and
types of jobs available and the competition for those
jobs. For example, the rates of employment of Hmong in
Orange County and Fresno, California and the Twin Cities
of Minnesota are quite low compared with those of smaller
Hmong communities such as Providence, Dallas, and Fort
Smith.

Hmong employment is also quite vulnerable to variations in the local economies. In the case of Orange
County, for example, two years ago, over half of the
Hmong households had at least one adult working, but after the economy slowed down in 1981 and 1982, only a
quarter of the families were working. Hmong, like other
people, are always looking for better opportunities.
After changes occurred in refugee cash assistance policy,
many states without adequate public assistance programs
for intact, unemployed families lost their Hmong population to secondary migration. Families without jobs were
unable to stay in these areas. Most moved to California
even though there were no jobs there; they wanted to move
away from the frustrations and depression of waiting for
work. At least in the Central Valley, they thought, they
could start doing some farming.

Individual Differences

Hmong are employed at a variety of jobs. Most of the
jobs are entry-level positions in light manufacturing,
requiring little previous training. Examples are elec-

tronic assembly, jewelry grinding, machine operation, sorting and collating, and food processing. Hmong are also employed at minimum wages in other industries, particularly nursery work, carpentry and industrial sewing. Most of the jobs obtained thus far require minimal English either to learn or to perform.

At the beginning of Hmong resettlement, during 1978-79, employers would hire refugees as long as there was someone in the company who could communicate with them in their native language. But that flexibility did not last very long. From 1980 to the present, because of the downturn in the economy, many companies have been forced to reduce operations or close down. As a result, employers became more selective and were reluctant to hire anyone who could not speak English.

People who took unskilled or semiskilled entry-level positions commonly did not encounter much opportunity for advancement. Wages received for those entry-level jobs varied between $3.50 and $5.00 per hour for men, and $3.50 to $4.50 for women. Few received any medical benefits. In California, many Hmong seemed to be laid off without adequate explanation when their wage reached $6.00.

A minority of the Hmong had better experience in the labor market. A small group of Hmong who spoke enough English took vocational training for positions as electronic technicians and machinists. These workers received somewhat higher wages, ranging from $7.00 to $10.00 per hour, and usually were offered health benefits. Another group includes the Hmong bilingual social service and paraprofessional educational workers. The average wage for this group is almost $4.50 to $6.00 per hour, occasionally reaching up to $15,000 per year. Another even smaller group included white-collar positions such as insurance sales and secretarial work.

The general picture, then, has the majority of Hmong employees working at minimum wage jobs and a small number in more highly skilled labor and technical or white-collar jobs. About 80 percent of the adult Hmong in California are not employed at all, compared with less than fifty percent of those who are outside of California.

Welfare Dependency

In some parts of the country, Hmong have had sponsors who found jobs for them as soon as they arrived. In
other states where there were no individual sponsors, the
Hmong refugees have had to go onto public assistance.
The resettlement agencies have tried to avoid such dependency by providing cultural, social and vocational orientation to the refugees. Unfortunately, the training often takes six months to one year to be effective, longer
than most can survive without cash assistance.

Many efforts have been made to find jobs for Hmong,
but it has been difficult. There are not enough suitable
jobs for them. Not only Hmong, of course, but many of
their American peers, too, cannot get jobs. Across the
country, wherever we met with Hmong groups and individuals, they expressed their concerns that the American
people may think that Hmong are lazy. Hmong have a strong
desire to work, to get off welfare, to take any job with
which they can support their families. However, because
the cost of health care is so high for large families,
many need subsidized medical care for their families.
Policies linking medical assistance to cash assistance (a
national welfare policy) make it very hard for large
Hmong families to get off welfare. Transitions from welfare to self-sufficiency are further hindered by the arbitrary 100-hour limitation on earnings regardless of
level of need. Hmong who have found good jobs do not want
to quit, but for some there have been no other viable alternatives.

Many Hmong feel the welfare system serves to keep
them on welfare and to keep them poor, and they recognize
the irony in that situation. In many states, the federal
government has spent a lot of money to help the Hmong and
other refugees to become self-sufficient, but this assistance has not been effective because of too much red tape
and too many political clouds and arbitrary restrictions.

Despite the many obstacles, the Hmong still share
the major goal of refugee resettlement in this country:
self-sufficiency.

HMONG YOUTH AND THE HMONG FUTURE IN AMERICA

Mary Cohn

The Hmong population profile shows that the Hmong in America are a young and rapidly expanding population, with the proportion of relatively younger members of the community growing each year. What the future holds for the young Hmong will eventually determine the outcomes of Hmong resettlement. As Hmong discussed the future of the younger generation in the course of this study, the two interrelated issues of education and cultural adjustment emerged as crucial.

Education Issues

In a very short time education has come to be tremendously valued by Hmong in the United States. Many Hmong who have given up hope of rebuilding their own lives pin their hopes for the future of the Hmong in America on the education of their children.

Though there are many individual exceptions, study interviews indicate that there are three different need groups of Hmong children and adolescents currently in the educational systems.

The first group is made up of children who are entering schools with English skills and who thus can quickly participate in the mainstream of the school system. These children appear to be adjusting well to schooling and to be succeeding in their studies. The second group is made up of young Hmong children, many born in the United States, who are entering schools with no English skills. These children apparently learn English quickly, but need special attention and recognition of their limited English proficiency as they first enter school. Besides English problems, some of the children who have had no previous contacts with non-Hmong have cultural adjustment problems as well. The third group is made up of older Hmong children and adolescents, aged about thirteen to twenty-one, who arrived in the United States with no previous education, having spent most of their school-aged years in flight from war or in refugee camps. These students, generally placed in grades by age rather than skill level, typically have great difficulties catching up to their classmates in time to graduate. The dropout rate for these adolescents is very high, and if they graduate they are often still unprepared to look for a job or to continue their education.

The very high dropout rate among Hmong teenagers is an issue of great concern among the young people, their parents, leaders and teachers. Though the attrition rate varies from locale to locale, being quite low for example in Dallas, it remains high in most areas. Hmong youth, leaders and educators identify several contributing factors to school dropout. These include academic difficulties in school, inadequate direction and counseling, welfare disincentives and early marriage and pregnancy.

Students relate problems in reaching competencies for the exit examinations now required by several states, including California and Oregon. Faced with failure in these exams, some students simply leave school. Even students who stay in high school indicate they have great difficulty in classwork which involves more advanced reading and writing skills, such as social studies and American history.

Hmong teenagers regularly identify a need for counseling in school, particularly career counseling. Students feel this direction must come from the schools, since their parents are still unfamiliar with the American educational and work world. Many students also suggest that their parents would benefit from some education about the American school system, since parents now have little idea of how best to participate and encourage their children in school.

Some youth see slow changes taking place in traditional marriage patterns. Yet in spite of some efforts by youth groups and Hmong leaders to encourage young people to marry a bit later, the Hmong traditional pattern of early marriage and childbearing persists. Essentially at odds with the design of American school systems, early marriage and pregnancy mean that the dropout rate for Hmong high school girls is very high. Nationwide it is probably at least fifty percent; in some impacted areas visited it is as high as eighty or ninety percent. (Again, Dallas exhibits a much lower dropout rate.) In group meetings with researchers, teenagers indicated they are interested in but have very little knowledge of family planning and do not have the information to make choices about the size or spacing of their families. Ironically, in many of the schools Hmong attend, sex education or birth control information is not taught until the junior or senior year of high school, by which time many Hmong girls have already dropped out, married and given birth to one or two children.

Cultural factors and education are interrelated: for those young Hmong men and women who are already experiencing difficulties in school, and have little future orientation, the culturally accepted patterns of marriage and family become more attractive. Teenage marriage poses long-term problems for integration into American life: young men and women with education far below the norm for this society will continue to have difficulties competing for jobs, and large young families without two incomes may continue to live at the margins of poverty.

Hmong leaders see an intergenerational pattern of poverty developing that they want aborted now. In families currently dependent on welfare, youth and their parents see AFDC policies as a substantial disincentive for Hmong adolescents from poor families to complete high school, particularly in California. Older youth who are behind in high school skills are often not able to graduate by their nineteenth birthday, when their AFDC grants may be cut. Under these conditions many young people feel they must quit school and go to work, only to find that they cannot find a job without a high school diploma.

Higher Education

In spite of the difficulties for Hmong youth, many highly motivated young Hmong across the country see higher education as their main hope for the future; a few school systems have also made laudable efforts to help Hmong young people of limited educational background. Among those Hmong students who have achieved success in high school and are able to go on to college, there is a very strong feeling of responsibility to share the education they receive by giving it back to the Hmong community. There are several youth groups in the country that tutor other Hmong students, advise them on educational plans, and give Hmong-language workshops for their elders on such topics as American government and economics.

Based on the nationwide telephone poll conducted as part of this study, there are three hundred to four hundred Hmong students attending colleges full-time. This number constitutes a tiny elite--less than five percent of the Hmong population of college age, although many more students are probably attending colleges part-time. The major barriers to higher education which Hmong students identify are graduating from high school, financial problems and family responsibilities. For those students who are admitted into college, lack of funds seems to be the largest problem--most Hmong college students use federal Basic Educational Opportunity Grants (BEOG) and live at home with their families.

Cultural Adjustment

Hmong young people straddle two cultures. They often feel conflicts between the values of independence in the American society they encounter in school and in their neighborhoods, and the traditional values of interdependence in their own families. Along with a strong attachment to their families and to "being Hmong," young people also voice a desire to be accepted as American. For example, teenage girls told us of problems they have "fitting in" with their peers. Many said they would like to join school clubs and go out with American friends, but they have to be home to take care of younger siblings, and their family responsibilities come first. Some of the cultural adjustment problems that arise in families are due to the discontinuities between the experiences of Hmong parents and new experiences of their children. In America, traditional family authority and boundaries no longer seem clear-cut.

The Future Of The Younger Generation

The Hmong youth's current experiences with adjustment and education have important implications for their future. In the short-term future, the specter of welfare dependence looms large for those young people aged about fourteen to twenty-five who have incomplete schooling and insufficient skills to compete for jobs.   Early marriage and large families mean that this new generation of Hmong parents may also experience difficulty, not only in becoming self-supporting, but also in integrating social and economic life into the mainstream resettlement community.   The younger Hmong children are likely to experience more success in school than their older brothers and sisters, though they may continue to lag behind their peers in language skills.   Whether or not this group will continue to marry young, drop out and start large families is uncertain, but the way this issue is resolved may have a large impact on their own self-sufficiency and adjustment and on the economic and social adjustment of the next generation of Hmong.

One attitude clearly emerges in interviews with young Hmong people: in spite of the uncertainty about their future, they feel responsible for helping themselves and helping their community.   Although they feel some conflicts with the values of American society and their roles within their own families, they still intend to take on responsibilities for their families; they would like to be able to support their parents in their parents' old age; they wish to use the skills they gain through better education to help the Hmong.   Most young people see themselves as Hmong and they wish to remain Hmong, but they also want to be armed with the skills and knowledge of the larger society in which they now live. The choices that they face are tough and often confusing. As one young man told us:

> I think we know it's hard, and we all want a college education.   We understand that we might go in the wrong direction and we are worried about that.   We want to go in the right direction.

ECONOMIC DEVELOPMENT AND EMPLOYMENT PROJECTS

Simon M. Fass

Against a backdrop of high unemployment and welfare dependency, Hmong across the country are attempting to promote self-sufficiency through a variety of innovative economic development projects. About one hundred sewing ventures, farm projects and small businesses are now under way. They touch the lives of twenty-five hundred families, or 25 percent of the Hmong population.

Sewing

Beginning with two ventures in 1978, the number of sewing projects rose to twenty-eight by 1983, and the twenty-three hundred women involved were generating annual sales of over $700,000 in fifteen states.

American women initiated most projects. They viewed them primarily as methods to preserve ethnic art or to help Hmong with psychological adjustment to the United States. As men's difficulties in securing employment grew evident after 1981, project participants found themselves under growing pressure to maximize their contribution to family income.

Three strategies to increase earnings arose from this pressure. The first was to emphasize marketing of traditional crafts produced at home or imported from relatives in Thailand. Participation in street fairs, church bazaars and gallery displays, and advertising led to an increase in sales. A few women succeeded in earning $3,000 a year or more, but the majority made less than $75.

To address the needs of these women, as well as to expand sales in general, the second strategy focused on design, production and marketing of inexpensive utilitarian items, like belts, aprons, eyeglass cases or fashion clothing that incorporated ethnic decorations. Some products did not sell. Others, like eyeglass cases, became quite successful. Earnings remained low, averaging $240 a year for each woman, but this constituted a sizable increase for those unable to market traditional craftwork.

The third strategy focused on training women in commercial sewing skills, such as dressmaking and tailoring, and then marketing their services, e.g., contract alterations. Initial results from the handful of projects that pursued this approach were promising, with individual monthly earnings of $100 to $200 not uncommon.

In implementing these strategies the projects had to overcome many difficulties. Some refugees were afraid of failure and unenthusiastic about changing their traditional methods of craftwork. Americans with ethnic art and social service backgrounds found themselves ill-prepared to transform sociocultural projects into what were essentially small businesses. They did not have prior exposure to market assessment for new products, patterns or colors, or to methods of marketing. Moreover, most projects were underfinanced. After paying refugees 60 percent to 80 percent of the value of sales, the American initiators had little left over to finance new product lines, to advertise or to acquire sewing machines.

Eleven ventures secured some external funding, and fared better than projects entirely dependent on internal resources. Externally supported projects, with resources to pay for full-time managers, materials and equipment, marketing expenses and training stipends, generated five times more in sales and two and a half times more in refugee income than the others: $303 a year for each woman vs. $117. The better-endowed projects were not, however, financially viable. In all but two cases expenses exceeded revenues. Preliminary indications nevertheless suggested that outside assistance, in terms of funds and staff with business experience, could make a significant difference to refugee income.

Farming

Families began gardening soon after their arrival, and almost every Hmong community enjoyed at least one season of growing vegetables for family consumption. Agricultural extension services, community organizations and self-help associations assisted the Hmong in most of these farming projects. The gardens provided households with in-kind incomes of $100 to $700 in retail value each season.

Pressure to secure alternative sources of income, noted above, and Hmong success at producing crops, led Americans and refugees to initiate eleven major projects in five states. At the end of 1983, these initiators were attempting to assist 230 households, and planned to cover another 70 to 80 within two or three years.

Project characteristics varied considerably. Participants ranged from three to sixty families, farm size from five acres to thirteen hundred acres, and initial investment from $7,000 to $425,000. In general these projects pursued one of two goals. The first type of project tried to create a financially viable source of secondary income: a seasonal venture on rented land to provide wage income for unemployed adults, unemployable women and elders, and out-of-school children. One project in Iowa collected $16,000 from private foundations in 1982 and launched sixty families into commercial farming on fifteen acres. It generated an average income of $200 per family, but lost $12,000. The project expanded to twenty-five acres in 1983, diversified its production, yielded $400 per family, and set aside funds to begin again in 1984 without extensive recourse to outside support.

The second type of project tried to provide complete self-sufficiency. A twenty-two-acre venture in Washington used almost $90,000 in 1982 to generate $13,000, or $1,100 each for a dozen participating families. In 1983, after infusion of another $70,000, it yielded $46,000 in sales, and $3,000 per family in net earnings. Income goals for 1984 called for $9,000 per family.

Another scheme, a four-year, $6 million effort for up to ninety families, organized by the University of Minnesota Agricultural Extension Service, started in 1983 with an initial investment of $472,000. The project successfully produced over $200,000 in crops, but could harvest and sell only $70,000. Among other factors, communication difficulties between Americans and refugees prevented Hmong from providing the amount of field labor required for complete harvesting.

Experiences in the Iowa, Washington and Minnesota projects were typical, and dampened the original enthusiasm about agriculture as a rapid mechanism for self-sufficiency. Participants learned that commercial agriculture was a more formidable challenge than consumption-oriented vegetable gardening. To greater or lesser extents the projects had to overcome constraints imposed by inadequate knowledge of commercial farming practices, insufficient financial resources, lack of contacts with neighboring farmers or extension agents, absence of marketing channels, communication breakdowns, weaknesses in financial planning and organizational management, problems in community relations, and administrative complications arising from the status of refugees as welfare clients.

The constraints proved surmountable, however, and experiences of initial seasons served to improve subsequent performance. Participants in the projects believed that ultimate outcomes would prove successful. This belief spread, and twelve new projects in eight more states were to begin in early 1984.

As with sewing, none of the farming projects are old enough to warrant judgments about effectiveness in promoting self-sufficiency. Rather, the ventures have thus far served the basic purpose of pointing efforts in a direction that might otherwise have been overlooked, particularly with regard to assisting families whose adult members cannot easily find work in the regular job market.

Small Business

Hmong entrepreneurship grew slowly. The number of grocery stores climbed from one in 1980 to over thirty in 1984, but other business ventures tended to fail or stagnate more often than they succeeded. Fifteen starts since 1980 yielded only two clear instances of success by 1984.

Most grocery stores were food-buying cooperatives established with the savings of kinship groups, and organized by younger community leaders. Besides providing families with Oriental foodstuffs at lower prices, cooperatives served as social gathering places, as symbols of community cooperation, and--at least in theory--as sources of financial return on community investment.

Sixteen stores that functioned as cooperatives in 1983 started with average investments of $20,000, and generated gross monthly sales of $5,400. Narrow operating margins permitted only six to offer paid employment, and five managed to generate small profits. The stores' contribution to self-sufficiency, therefore, took the form of providing families with expenditure savings, and, increasingly after 1982, of providing outlets for gardens and farm project output.

The profit-oriented grocery stores were capitalized from personal savings of employed refugees and their relatives. These stores began with investments 50 percent higher than the cooperatives, had monthly sales four times higher, employed more people, and usually yielded profits. The more viable status of these stores resulted from a variety of factors, including prior experience of owners in working for other businesses, their higher education levels, and placement of the goal of profitability above that of community service.

Other types of businesses in operation in 1983 were either embryonic or stagnant. The embryonic businesses included a community credit union, a bakery, and a woodcrafts enterprise established with the help of two Rotary Clubs. The stagnant operations included a jeweler, a housecleaning service, a stuffed-animal subcontractor, a supermarket and a videotape store/theater. Earlier ventures no longer in operation included a restaurant, an auto repair shop, a medical equipment subcontractor, a fishing gear subcontractor and a jewelry store.

One success story began in 1981 when six Hmong pooled $80,000 in personal and borrowed funds to open a restaurant. They opened a second facility in 1983 with another $60,000. By 1984 the two units employed eighteen people, and were training more for a third outlet under construction. Another success was a security guard service that began with a $350,000 loan to a Hmong accountant by American friends in 1981. After coming to within a week of bankruptcy in 1982, the service expanded rapidly. By 1984 the firm employed fifty-five people and planned expansion to another state. Five stores and other businesses received informal assistance from American or other refugee business people. Although most Hmong entrepreneurs also sought technical help from agencies like the Small Business Administration, that help was not forthcoming. As in other projects, entrepreneurs moved ahead at a pace dictated by the speed at which they learned from experience about business operations.

Employment Projects

A few Hmong may benefit from the enterprises mentioned above in the near future, but most depend for their self-sufficiency on employment services that provide job training, development, placement and counseling. While these services have not served Hmong as well as they've served others, in some cases, where innovative approaches were used, the employment services were quite effective.

In Minnesota a sponsorship agency worked with seventy volunteers tied into one thousand churches. Besides its ability to link with a large number of church-going employers, a major strength of the project was its assumption that every Hmong had a remunerative skill. The problem was to identify the skill clearly and then match it with an employer. Placement costs in the state during 1982-83 ranged from $600 to $1,200 per individual. The project placed 510 people at a cost of $270 per refugee in the same period.

Hmong in Missoula, Montana, had high unemployment in 1982 due to the recession. Working with a social service agency, a self-help association searched for job openings in Billings, 350 miles away, and moved families there at a cost of $570 per job, including transportation subsidies. This regional approach to employment worked well, and about 80 percent of the families who moved were self-sufficient at the end of 1983.

Focusing on the need to help Hmong become accustomed to the culture of the American work environment, a project in the State of Washington combined on-the-job acculturation with housecleaning and lawn-care work in a small business operation, and then placed "graduates" in regular jobs. Attention to the stresses imposed by work environments, a major impediment to Hmong employment, helped refugees retain their jobs. Organization of the project as a service business kept net project costs to $870 per placement in 1983, about twenty-five percent less than the cost of other training placement efforts in the state.

Corporate leaders collaborated with media and service organizations in Wisconsin to raise consciousness among employers of the benefits of hiring refugees who believed in the American work ethic and were more than willing to work diligently at the minimum wage. Business managers, convinced by this argument, instructed their personnel departments to open doors to Hmong and to help them adjust to the workplace. The project generated 140 jobs in 1982 at an out-of-pocket cost of $21 per placement to the business people involved.

While the cost-effectiveness of these employment efforts must await future assessments, the important interim aspect is that creative talents are searching for formulas to benefit Hmong more quickly.

Conclusion

Hmong and American project participants launched themselves into undertakings that were new to them. Some came prepared with prior training or experience, but most did not. The Hmong had no exposure to the basics of income-generation in the United States. Most American participants knew little at the beginning about analyzing markets, merchandising, minimizing costs, using creative placement techniques, preparing plans and contingencies, etc.

Lack of prior knowledge among participants suggested that, notwithstanding the slow pace of progress, recent efforts constituted important first steps in a difficult process of self-learning. Project difficulties seemed less important than the processes by which participants learned from errors so that they did not repeat them, and learned from successes so that they pressed these into service again.

While learning from experience appeared essential, it was not enough. Projects needed outside assistance in order to move forward more quickly. Unfortunately, many participants were not able to pinpoint their own limitations, and could not describe the help they needed. When they could, they did not know how to secure it. One compelling need was for guidance in how to harness locally available human resources for the benefit of a project and its participants.

This problem may be taking care of itself. Efforts of private and federal and state government agencies to bring together Hmong and Americans from projects around the country, are yielding a network of experienced individuals who can assist each other over the course of time. Workshops organized in 1983-84 brought participants of sewing and farming projects together with others who were planning new initiatives. A network of people involved in different projects is beginning to take shape.

This kind of process has historical antecedents. The National Alliance for Polish People provided insurance coverage for members of its own ethnic group; Jewish groups developed their own savings and loan associations. Hmong may face greater obstacles than their predecessors in moving into the economic mainstream, but similarities in the paths taken by earlier migrants and now the Hmong, and the help being extended by Americans, provides cause for optimism. Optimism encourages continued effort, and effort is the key to progress.

REFERENCES

Reder, Stephen. 1982. "A Hmong Community's Acquisition of English." The Hmong in the West: Observations and Reports, Papers of the 1981 Hmong Research Conference, edited by Bruce T. Downing and Douglas P. Olney, pp. 268-303. Minneapolis: Center for Urban and Regional Affairs, University of Minnesota.

Robson, Barbara. 1982. "Hmong Literacy, Formal Education, and Their Effects on Performance in an ESL Class." The Hmong in the West: Observations and Reports, Papers of the 1981 Hmong Research Conference, edited by Bruce T. Downing and Douglas P. Olney, pp. 201-225. Minneapolis: Center for Urban and Regional Affairs, University of Minnesota.

PART THREE

Language and Literacy

INTRODUCTION

Bruce Downing

The papers in this section reflect the interest of a number of researchers in the Hmong language and the problems Hmong face in learning English.

In the first area, the arrival in the United States of more than fifty thousand native speakers of Hmong opened up new opportunities for linguistic research. The Hmong language, virtually unknown in the West prior to 1975, has provided a fertile field of investigation for linguists interested in uncovering its structure and in adding a clearer understanding of this fascinating language to our storehouse of knowledge about the whole array of extant human languages.

On the more practical side, the fact that the Hmong came to America in most cases with very little knowledge of English and with little if any acquaintance with writing meant that professionals in teaching English as a second language, in adult basic education, and in teaching public school children with limited proficiency in English were faced with a new and challenging set of problems to be solved. These problems have drawn the attention of both educational researchers and persons interested in the social functions of literacy and of bilingualism.

A good sampling of the work being done in these two areas of research is represented here.

The first group of papers, by Ratliff, Owensby, Jaisser, and Fuller, are all descriptive studies of Hmong grammar. For non-linguists, reading about grammar may seem as dull and as difficult as reading someone else's computer programs or trying to get through a study in astrophysics when you don't know physics and your only astronomy class was 20 years ago. But the glimpses of the inner workings of the Hmong language presented here are well worth the reading. Language is an aspect of culture, and we find here that the linguistic aspect of Hmong culture is just as interesting, in its subtlety, its complexity, and its differences from a European language

like English as the other cultural characteristics of the
Hmong discussed elsewhere in this volume.

Martha Ratliff's paper beautifully illustrates the
linguist's aim of discovering structure--a system--in
what may at first appear to be only a welter of words.
She takes a set of two-word expressions in Hmong, examples of which are listed as "intensifiers" in Heimbach's
White Hmong Dictionary, and shows us that far from being
idiosyncratic and unpredictable, these expressions are
constructed according to very clear patterns.   Like little poems, they follow strict rules for the arrangement
of sound and syllables, and, also like poetic expressions, they serve to add nuances of expressive meaning--
reflecting sound, movement or the speaker's attitudes--to
the basic meaning of a sentence.

Americans in many places are studying the Hmong language in a practical way, hoping to be able to speak at
least a little of the language of their Hmong friends,
co-workers, or students.   A person doesn't get very far
in the study of Hmong before encountering a grammatical
pattern very unlike English: sentences in which one
clause, with just one subject, contains two or more
verbs, not related as conjoined predicates with and or or
to tie them together.   Laurel Owensby calls this pattern
"verb serialization," and her paper makes clear, with
many examples, what these sentences are and what they
mean.

Annie Jaisser addresses a puzzle in the analysis of
some complex sentences of Hmong containing the word kom.
(She refers to kom as a "morpheme," using the technical
word for a indivisible meaningful unit.)   The question is
whether kom is a verb meaning 'tell' or 'command,' whose
object is a clause, or whether it is a part of the subordinate clause, namely, a "complementizer" or subordinat-
ing conjunction that begins that clause.   She sorts out
the confusion with a series of neat arguments that lead
to a clear answer: sometimes kom is a verb, but at other
times it is in fact a complementizer introducing a new
clause.   The reader not only is led through this analysis
step by step, but along the way is shown quite a bit
about how "sentence embedding"--the construction of sentences that contain both a main clause and an embedded or
subordinate clause, is done in Hmong.

The paper by Judith Fuller is concerned not only with description of Hmong but also with the question of where this language fits with respect to a typology of languages that classifies them as "topic-prominent," like Chinese, or "subject-prominent," like English.   In this case the answer is not so clear-cut; Hmong falls somewhere in between, meaning that in Hmong the syntactic arrangement of a sentence is determined in part by the "topic"--what a whole section of a discourse is "about," and in part by consideration of which word is the grammatical "subject" of a sentence.

The linguistic papers are illustrated with a large number of example sentences, written in the Romanized Popular Alphabet (RPA), the writing system most widely used by the Hmong, at least in the United States.   Each sentence is translated into English, first word by word and then, on the next line, with a free translation into idiomatic English.   Grammatical terms used to identify Hmong words, e.g. comp. for "complementizer," are identified by each author in a footnote. The general correspondences between the RPA orthography and the sounds of Hmong are summarized in the "Note on Orthography" at the end of this introduction.

The last two papers of this section, although written independently, form a set that can be read together for a rather thorough introduction to questions of Hmong literacy and in particular the learning and use of literacy in English.

Gail Weinstein provides an overview of some of the issues concerning literacy as they have been discussed in the literature pertaining to basic literacy for adults. This background material is related to the situation of the Hmong refugees through an appended report on her first-hand observations of the uses of literacy and the "social consequences" of literacy on the part of the Hmong refugee community in Philadelphia.

In the final paper, Karen Green and Stephen Reder present preliminary results of a detailed longitudinal study of the acquisition of both spoken English and English literacy by Hmong adults in another part of the United States.   Their analysis focuses on an attempt to identify background factors and concurrent factors that can be statistically related to the rate of acquisition. Their results are important because so little of the pre-

vious research that informs theories of adult second language acquisition has been concerned with the less educated adults commonly found in third-world refugee populations.

A NOTE ON HMONG ORTHOGRAPHY

All references to elements of the Hmong language in this volume are presented in the Romanized Popular Alphabet (RPA), which has become the standard orthography for Hmong at least in the West.

The RPA was devised by American and French missionaries and introduced in Laos in 1953. It represents all of the consonant, vowel and tone distinctions of Hmong with ordinary Roman letters, entirely avoiding special symbols and diacritics.

Words in Hmong are generally monosyllabic. The orthographic representation of any syllable has the following general characteristics:

1. Each word includes one or two vowel letters (e.g., a, e, u, ai, ia) representing a simple or diphthongal vowel nucleus.

2. Doubling of the same vowel letter (ee, oo) indicates nasalization of the vowel and possibly, depending on the dialect, a syllable-final consonant sound like orthographic -ng in English. (There are no other final consonants in Hmong.)

3. Preceding the vowel there may be one to four consonant letters, indicating an initial consonant or consonant cluster. The letter h following another consonant indicates aspiration of the preceding sound, so that ph is similar to the English p in pat (in contrast with the unaspirated p in speak). An initial h (in the sequences hm, hn, hl) marks the sound it accompanies as voiceless. The letter n preceding another consonant indicates prenasalization; it is pronounced as m before p; n before t, d, and r; and ng before k.

4. A consonant letter as the last letter of a syllable or word represents the tone on which the vowel is produced, as follows:

217

-b   high tone
-j   high falling tone
-v   mid rising tone
--   mid tone
-s   mid-low tone
-g   mid-low breathy tone
-m   low glottalized tone
-d   low rising tone (a predictable variant of m)

Apart from this special use of final letters to mark tone, the consonant and vowel letters generally have familiar international values, the principal exceptions being:

x   pronounced like English s
s   pronounced like English sh or the s in sugar
z   pronounced like the English z in azure
r   a retroflex stop sound more like English t or d than English r
c   a sound like the t-y sequence in English fit youth
q   a sound like k or g but pronounced with the back of the tongue further back in the mouth
w   a vowel similar to that in English but or unstressed just
aw   a diphthong similar to w but prolonged.

One final caution to the reader: two distinct dialects of the Hmong language are spoken by refugees in the United States. These are usually referred to as Green Hmong and White Hmong. In addition there are many regional differences of pronunciation, vocabulary and grammar. The RPA orthography was designed to provide a single standard written form of each word; it will not therefore correspond to an individual's actual pronunciation in many cases.

TWO-WORD EXPRESSIVES IN WHITE HMONG

Martha Ratliff

The data which I have collected from three speakers of White Hmong and from Heimbach's dictionary reveal the existence of a formally well-defined set of word pairs associated with certain kinds of meanings. A formal description of these word pairs is much easier to deliver than an adequate account of their meanings. In general, they add immediacy and vividness to a description; they usually reflect the sensory experience of the speaker or his attitude toward what he is describing; and that sensory experience or attitude often determines the consonants and tones and perhaps (but less clearly) the vowels of the words chosen. A large set of related single words exists, such as dhev, lug and nthi, some of which participate in the word pairs described here. Both the word pairs and the single words are usually found in clause final position, and the functions and meanings of the two seem to be similar. The single words are more abstract, however, and are much less likely to have a close connection between meaning and sound.

The term "expressive" is taken from the work of Gérard Diffloth (1972, 1976, 1979), whose insightful and detailed descriptions of the expressives of some Mon-Khmer languages (Semai, Khasi, Sre and Bahnar) and the expressives of Korean make it clear that a similar word class exists in Hmong.[1] They have been called variously "descriptive words" or "aspect words" by Ts'ao (1958), "post verbal intensifiers" by Heimbach (1979), and "restricted modifiers" by Lyman (1974) in their descriptions of Hmong. They are related to the "ideophones" of the Bantu and other African languages; they exist in Japanese, some Dravidian languages and some Austronesian languages as well.

Expressives are formally and semantically differentiated from the language of propositions, the language proper, where utterances can be reduced to predicate and arguments, and words participate in relations of synonymy and antonymy. They are more likely than nonexpressive words to reflect in their phonetic composition the speaker's (and his speech community's) perception of one aspect of the object being described: either its sound, its appearance, another one of its innate characteristics, or his attitude toward it.   The relationship between word and meaning is likely to be more iconic; that is, the word, to the speaker's mind, resembles the thing he is describing; zig zuag, because of the initial consonants and the whispery tone, sounds itself like "walking through high grass."   The relationship between word and meaning in the majority of words in any language is, on the other hand, predominantly arbitrary and conventional: any string of sounds would suit equally well to express the meaning of "house," for example, and it is only history and custom which determine that that string should be tsev.

Iconicity in Hmong, or the direct reflection of meaning in phonological representation, is also apparent (1) in reduplication of nonexpressive words to convey the idea of augmentation; (2) in the vowel gradation in the classifiers of Weining Hmong described by Wang (1957); and perhaps, too, (3) in the vowel gradation and tone patterns in the second and fourth member of the four-syllable coordinative constructions, or lus ua txwm ("paired words") described by P'an and Ts'ao (1958), Mottin (1978), and Johns and Strecker (1982).   Since in these instances an effort is made to bend the prosaic language to mirror the natural world, a language which has a well-developed expressive system can be expected to have other kinds of "word play," or evidence of the language craftsman's skill: this is certainly true of Hmong, in which pig latins (secret languages) abound, and a highly sophisticated and elaborate oral literature exists.

The class of expressive words in Hmong is indeed a class separate from noun, verb, adjective, adverb and other classes Westerners are comfortable with.   Ts'ao felt Chinese scholars also needed to be warned about the nature of this word class which has no clear analogue in Chinese, except perhaps in Chinese color-word modifiers. Expressives have their own roots, and are only accidentally homophonous, on occasion, with words of another class.   Expressives are usually found at the ends of clauses, outside the Subject Verb Object (SVO) matrix and hence isolated from the structure of the proposition. Onomatopoeic expressives in Hmong, at least, are introduced by what have been called in other languages "carriers," words which effectually underscore this separation from the rest of the sentence: these are <u>nrov</u> ("sound") verbs of sound-making, e.g. <u>quaj</u> ("cry"), <u>hais</u> ("speak") and <u>poob</u> ("fall"). The two-word expressives can be said to have their own morphology; that is, the two words have a characteristic shape which involves the binding of their respective parts--their consonants, vowels and tones, which, despite the creative element inherent in all expressive language, is part of the system and cannot be altered at the whim of the speaker. In these respects, Hmong expressives are like those of Semai (Diffloth 1976), Korean (Martin 1962; Diffloth 1972; Kim 1977) and Bini (Wescott 1973). Most importantly, these words are part of every speaker's everyday speech; they are not reserved for poetry, song or ritual, although some individuals, those considered to be good storytellers, may be known to make more extensive use of them than others. The meanings of the expressives I have collected are overwhelmingly onomatopoeic, but I am not convinced that this is a representative sample of the whole corpus of Hmong expressives. Heimbach's appendix lists onomatopoeic phrases as a subclass of post-verbal intensifiers. According to Ts'ao, more Mhu expressives are "descriptive" than onomatopoeic. Based on his studies of the Mon-Khmer languages, Diffloth (1976, p. 262) has observed that most expressives do not describe noises. Nonetheless, sounds are easy to demonstrate and discuss in an interview, and therefore a disproportionate amount of time was spent collecting them. Although I probed for other kinds of expressives, I generally discovered them indirectly, i.e., when I was told that an onomatopoeic expressive could also be used to describe the appearance of something, or someone's behavior. For example, <u>dis daws</u> was first explained as a kind of continuous sound, perhaps because we had been talking about sounds, and secondarily as the appearance of a long line of people.

The multiple associations I was given for some of these expressives are fascinating, but are also a nightmare for the lexicographer. These words do not have definitions in the same way words in the prosaic part of the language do, and they are almost impossible to translate.

This seems to be true of expressives generally:

> The meanings of expressives seem to be extremely
> detailed and idiosyncratic, describing a situa-
> tion perceived as a whole, as an independent
> clause would. On the other hand, the same expres-
> sive can be used to describe a variety of situa-
> tions which at first glance seem to be quite dif-
> ferent but share a common core which could be de-
> fined as a cluster of elementary sensations. For
> instance, /klknare:l/ is used to describe an
> arrow or knife stiffly vibrating after embedding
> itself into a piece of wood; it can also describe
> the walk of a tall, skinny old man. The cluster
> of sensations common to both meanings (and recog-
> nized by informants) are: stiffness, perpendicu-
> larity, and repeated small oscillations. [Diff-
> loth 1976, p. 257]

Accordingly, at this early stage in the study of Hmong
expressives, in Heimbach's dictionary and in the data in
this paper, either a very specific association will be
given, e.g., txij txej, "a rat or mouse crying out in a
snake's mouth," or a very vague, general abstraction will
be given, e.g., quj qees, "perseveringly." Neither gives
enough information for the expressive to be well understood. There is a question as to whether the meaning of
an expressive can always be reduced to "a cluster of ele-
mentary sensations," with all associations having equal
status with regard to each other. Perhaps one sense is
basic and the others derived. For example, hawv huav has
these associations: (a) sound of animals growling, ready
to bite, (b) human panting, and (c) nervous, tense pac-
ing. The sense of sound may be basic and apprehension of
the related behavior may be secondary; similarly, the behavior of the animals may be basic and the behavior of
the humans may be perceived as animal-like. We know
enough of expressive meaning nonetheless to discontinue
use of the term "intensifier." These words particular-
ize; they are eyewitness accounts of the passing scene
and, as such, give immediate apprehension to stories and
characterizations. They do not intensify in the sense of
giving more of some aspect of meaning that is already in
the utterance without the expressive. That is the func-

tion of reduplication in Hmong.

The two-word expressives in Hmong have a character-istic morphology which makes them easily recognizable. The two words have identical initial consonants or conso-nant clusters, but dissimilar vowels. Either the two tones will be the same, or the first will be high falling (-j) and the second any other tone. If the tones of the two words are identical, the vowel of the first word will be /-i-/; if the tone of the first word is high falling and the tone of the second word is some other tone, the vowel of the first word will be /-u-/. From the semantic associations I was given by my tutors, there seems to be clear tonal iconicity in the more well-represented tonal patterns. For that reason, the data are organized by tonal patterns, and rough impressions of the meaning range for each group are given.[2] The pattern -g/-g is associated with low-pitched, echoic, hollow, diffuse or airy sounds: dig dug, "boiling of thick liquid"; plig plawg, "a bird rising from its nest on the ground"; vig vwg, "the roar of a fire; strong wind; fast traffic." -j/-j is associated with energetic, fast, short sounds which are not necessarily sharp, high or falling: fij fwj, "a bird or plane whizzing by"; nthij nthooj, "cow's or children's heads butting"; ntsij ntsiaj, "pushing-pulling bolt on an M-16"; tij tauj, "raindrops." -s/-s is associated with flat, continuous, unending sounds and sights: dis daws, "a continuous mixed sound; the appear-ance of a long line of people"; lis loos, "bees buzzing." -j/-v has a double orientation--back and forth, in and out: dhuj dheev, "whimpering on and off; rising from and falling back into unconsciousness; almost remembering, then forgetting again"; nyuj nyav, "whining; smile with double meaning; bittersweet feeling of longing"; quj qev, "the sound of a creaky door." -j/-s suggests both back and forth (-j/-v) and level and steady (-s/-s): luj laws, "a big, continuous humming sound; continual complaining to oneself"; vuj vias, "unsteady walk; going back and forth on a swing." I have no sense of the nature of the iconicity, if any, associated with the minor tonal pat-terns.

As a check to the validity of my generalizations about the meanings associated with particular tonal pat-terns, I asked my tutors if they knew of two-word expres-sives for certain meanings I proposed, which I guessed

would be typical of certain tonal patterns. My predictions were not always right, and usually there was no expressive for the meanings I proposed, but if one did exist it matched my prediction with more than chance frequency. For example, I predicted thunder would have a
<u>-g/-g</u> pattern (<u>ntig ntwg</u>), the movement of a snake a
<u>-j/-v</u> pattern (<u>xuj xuav</u>), hiccups either a <u>-j/-j</u> or a
<u>-v/-v</u> pattern (and I was given both <u>ij awj</u> and <u>iv awv</u>!).
Needless to say, I did not tell my tutors which pattern I
was expecting.

The <u>-j/-v</u> or "double orientation" pattern is especially interesting because of its analogues in Semai and
Bini, a Nigerian Kwa language. In Semai, if there is
vowel disharmony between corresponding morphemes in a
two-word expressive, the associated meanings have to do
with randomness, sloppiness, or imbalance, e.g., <u>klicwŭc-
klicwĕc</u>, "random kicking, as of a turtle in sand" (Diffloth, personal communication). In Bini, polysyllabic
expressives with alternating high and low tones are associated with "irregular shape or motion," for example the
expressives for "staggering," "fluttering," "twisted,"
"crippled" and "jerky" (Wescott 1973, pp. 200-201). The
iconic relationship here between irregular form and irregular meaning can be said to be diagrammatic; that is,
the relation of the parts of the object, motion or sound
represented corresponds to the relation of the parts of
the phonological string.

In Hmong two-word expressives, then, tones are mean-
ingful--not only in their power to distinguish morphemes,
but in themselves. Linguists have been aware for a long
time that parts of morphemes can be meaningful, and can
stand in relation to the other parts of the same morpheme
much as words stand in relation to one another in a sentence (Bolinger 1950, Jakobson 1966, McCarthy 1983).

When we look beyond the White Hmong dialect to the
Hmongic family, the details of expressive morphology here
described do not seem as important as the fact that this
word class, with these kinds of meanings associated with
a pattern of some kind, exists. Ts'ao's description of
the Mhu of Lushan in eastern Guizhou province in China
reveals the existence of both one- and two-word expressives with meanings reminiscent of the expressives of
White Hmong. While the tones of the words in each two-
word expressive reported in Ts'ao's article are identi-

cal, the words have identical vowels and dissimilar initials, the mirror image of the morphology of the White
Hmong expressives!

The connection between meaning and tone is often reinforced and refined by consonantal iconicity. I can only
cite isolated examples of this, where my perception of
the phenomenon being described matches some aspect of the
acoustic or articulatory properties of the consonant involved or where expressives with similar meanings can be
compared.   As yet, I see no system of consonantal iconicity such as Diffloth describes for some Mon-Khmer languages and Korean, but that does not mean such a system
does not exist.   Zero-initials seem to involve cries and
involuntary sounds originating from within with no oral
(consonantal) impediment: ig awg, "wild pigs fighting in
close combat, a gobbling sound"; ij aj, "babies crying";
ij awj, "hiccups"; iv awv, "dogs' hunting bark; hiccups."
The "liquid" consonant /-l-/ may be actually felt to be
associated with water; witness the contrast between pij
pauj, "fruit falling on the ground," and pliv ploov,
"fruit falling in water."[3]   The contrast between tsig
tsuag, "monkeys jumping through the treetops, separate
abrupt jumping noises," and zig zuag, "monkeys swishing
through the treetops, continuous sound," lies only in the
iconicity of the consonants: the initial of the former is
an affricate, which consists of a stop (hence the abrupt
jumps) and a fricative, whereas the initial of the latter
is a simple fricative, one of the continuant class (hence
the continuous swishing).   The idea of heaviness may be
associated with /-ŋ/, witness pig poog, "bomb impact";
tig toog, "heavy footsteps"; vig voog, "a herd of animals
stampeding"; and pliv ploov, "fruit falling in water."
Many such guesses can be made upon inspection of the data.   The vowel of the second word has not yet been analyzed, but is also a likely factor in the iconic equation.

The exceptions to the canonical form of the two-word
expressive involve phrases which have characteristically
expressive meanings but which either do not have identical initials or dissimilar vowels, or do not have one of
the tone patterns described above. It may be that the inventory of tone patterns will have to be increased and
refined when more examples are collected.   I doubt,
though, that the observation that these words have iden-

tical initials will have to be modified; in most instances where the two words of a phrase had different initials, one or both of the words were found to be non-expressive words being used metaphorically. For example, nrov ncha ntws, a loud sound which "flows" or reverberates, contains ntws, which can also be a regular verb meaning "to flow" and which my tutor believes to be a verb in that context. I expect that we may find other explanations which will account for the few remaining forms which appear to be exceptions.

In the expressive domain, where meaning is so elusive and so intimately involved with culture and world view, it is necessary to have the insight that only native speakers can bring to the problem of isolating the essence of each expressive and of describing the semantic range of the class as a whole. As an outsider, I can only comment with confidence on those formal patterns which forced themselves on my attention while gathering the data. An analysis of the one-word expressives will be necessary, too; for their own sake and because they often serve as constituents of the two-word expressives. To my knowledge, no work at all has been done on them. Heimbach has performed an invaluable service in simply listing them in his dictionary, wisely not attempting to analyze how many of them alter the meaning of the sentences in which they appear. Native speakers have a hard time doing this, too. It may be that the one-word expressives are very old forms and whatever clear meaning they once had has been lost through constant use and increased abstraction. One clearly delimited expressive group serves to fine-tune colors; it would be a pleasure to have a preliminary analysis of the way this is done.

ILLUSTRATIONS

(The following are associations or [possibly incorrect] abstractions; they are not definitions. "+" indicates that an expressive is partially or solely associated with a sense other than sound. "*" indicates that an expressive makes use of phonological contrasts not usually employed in the language.)

-b/-b: (high level/high level) high pitched, short
        sounds.

nplhib nplheeb	a) silverware rattling (or other metal on metal); b) pin coming out of a hand grenade
plib pleb	wood crackling on a fire
zib zeb	a big pig fighting

-g/-g: (falling "whispery" / falling "whispery") productive; low-pitched, echoic, hollow, diffuse or
airy sounds.

ig awg	wild pigs fighting in close combat (gobbling sound)
dig dug	boiling of thick liquid like oatmeal, corn mash (thick, ponderous bubbles)
kig kuag	mice feet on an empty box
mig mog	a) a cow mooing; b) tigers playing
mlig mlog	(associations unclear)
ntig ntwg	thunder
pig poog	bomb impact (cf. ntij ntoj)
plig plawg	a bird rising from its nest on the ground
plig plog	someone jumping into water
sig suag	rain on a thatch roof
tig toog	heavy footsteps
tsig tsuag	a) a downpour; b) monkeys jumping through the treetops--discontinuous (cf. zig zuag)
vig vag	the sound a tree makes as it brushes through other trees and growth while falling
vig voog	a herd of animals stampeding, running scared (cf. nqaj nqug)
vig vwg	a) the roar of a fire; b) strong wind; c) fast traffic; d) small airplane motor
zig zawg	a) asthmatic breathing; b) snoring; c) panting (cf. hawv huav)

zig zuag   a) walking through high grass
                           (cf. rhij rhuaj);
                           b) drizzling rain;
                           c) monkeys jumping through the
                           treetops--continuous sound (cf.
                           tsig tsuag)

-j/-j: (high falling/high falling)   very   productive;   en-
         ergetic,   fast,   short   sounds   (not   necessarily
         sharp   or   high);   perhaps   surface   contact   as
         opposed to contact and penetration; not necessar-
         ily falling sounds.

ij aj   babies (baby animals?) crying (cf.
                           gij gaj)
ij awj   hiccups (cf. iv awv)
dhij dhuj   breathing with a full nose
fij fwj   bird or plane whizzing by (cf. mij
                           mẽwj)
*gij gaj   babies crying (cf. ij aj)
hij haj   a) laughing;
                           b) fighting
mij mej   mosquitoes or other insects flying
                           around your ear
*mij mẽwj   bullet whizzing past (cf. fij fwj)
nphij nphooj   a) pop of bamboo in fire (cf. plij
   (=*bhij bhooj)   ploj;
                           b) sound of a lot of popcorn
                           popping (full pan, not much room)
                           (cf. plij plej)
nplij nploj   a) foot pulling out of tar (cf.
   (=nplij nplooj)   txij txej);
                           b) pop of chewing gum;
                           c) clap of bamboo
nplij npluaj   (associations unclear)
ntij ntawj   fast, sharp typing
   (=nrij nrawj)
ntij ntoj   low impact sound, as cut lengths
                           of bamboo rolling down a mountain
                           (cf. plij ploj, nqaj nqug)
nthij nthooj   heads butting (cows, children...)
ntsij ntsiaj   pushing-pulling bolt on an M-16

pij pauj	hail or fruit falling to the ground
plij plej	just a little popcorn popping (a lot of room in the pan) (cf. nphij nphooj)
plij ploj	a) bullet impact (cf. ntij ntoj); b) bamboo bursting (cf. nphij nphooj)
plhij plhawj	a) helicopter propellers; b) birds making short flights (e.g. pigeons flying from one roof roost to another)
+rhij rhej	light and sound combination: a) lightning (light and crack); b) small amount of water on grease or vegetables frying (cf. rhuj rhev)
rhij rhuaj	foliage or grass rustling as a person or animal walks (cf. zig zuag)
tij tauj	raindrops
txij txej	a) rat or mouse crying out in a snake's mouth; b) foot pulling out of mud (cf. nplij nplo(o)j)
vij vawj	dogs barking at something (cf. iv awv)

-s/-s: (low level/low level) clear group, although not large; flat, continuous, unending sounds and sights.

is ws	a) everyone saying "ws"; b) speaking in a monotone; c) little pig running after its mother
is as	(associations unclear)
chis chaus	(associations unclear)
+dis daws	a) a continuous mixed sound: e.g., a group of monkeys chattering and jumping around, heard at a distance; many people walking on a mixed surface--twigs, rocks, soil;

	b) the appearance of a long line of people
lis loos	bees buzzing (cf. luj les)
mlis mlas	cat meowing (cf. mluj mlob)

-v/-v: mid rising/mid rising) vowel of first word ˙may also be /-aw-/.

iv awv	a) dogs' hunting bark (cf. vij vawj);
	b) hiccups (cf. ij awj)
dhawv dhev	whimpering; separate whimpers (cf. dhuj dhev, dhuj dheev)
+hawv huav	a) sound of animal growling, ready to bite;
	b) human panting (cf. zig zawg);
	c) nervous, tense pacing
+khawv khuav	steady run
pliv ploov	a) ducks diving underwater;
	b) submerged bottle filling up with water;
	c) fruit falling in water (cf. pij pauj)
qiv qawv	manner of grinding teeth
qhuav qhawv	(associations unclear)
txiv txev	rats or birds chirping (cf. ntuj ntiv)
xyav xyov	(associations unclear)

-j/-b: (high falling/high level).

+chuj chiab	working absentmindedly (cf. nrhuj nrhawv)
mluj mlob	a) whining (cf. nyuj nyav);
	b) cat meowing (cf. mlis mlas)
+ncuj nciab	grudgingly
zuj zeb	little hungry pigs squealing

-j/-g: (high falling/falling "whispery").

duj dog

+nqaj nqug   a) the sound of a number of trees
                          falling one right after another
                          and their appearance, overlaid,
                          on the forest floor;
                          b) a big herd of cows stampeding
                          (cf. vig voog);
                          c) everyone talking at the same
                          time in small groups;
                          d) bamboo rolling and sliding
                          down a mountain (cf. ntij ntoj)

 zuj ziag   a) pulling a metal chain over
                          something;
                          b) a cicada singing

-j/-m: (high falling/low glottalized).

 duj duam   manner of walking (?)
 qhuj qhem   (associations unclear)

-j/-s: (high falling/low level) suggests both back and
         forth (-j/-v) and level and steady (-s/-s).

+luj laws   a) big, humming sound, continuous
                          (e.g. an electric generator)
                          b) continual complaining to one-
                          self;
                          c) hais luj laws = to speak
                          without expression, but not
                          without feeling

 luj les   a) bees buzzing (cf. lis loos);
                          b) airplane;
                          c) vacuum cleaner

+nkuj nkaus   back and forth (e.g., nthos nkuj
                          nkaus = to snatch and put back
                          quickly)

+nkhuj nkhoos   a) sound of chopping dead or
                          hollow tree (or log) with an axe;
                          b) sound of a dog gnawing a bone;
                          c) appearance of an old person
                          with a bent back

+nplhuj nplhoos   a) sound of a boar grunting;

	b) putting off duty, doing things to avoid performance of duty
+quj qees	a) perseveringly; b) gradually building (e.g., <u>chim quj qees</u>)
+vuj vias	a) unsteady walk; b) going back and forth on a swing (movement)

-j/-v: (high falling / mid rising) double orientation: back and forth, in and out, up and down.

dhuj dhev	continuous whimpering (cf. <u>dhuj dheev</u>, <u>dhawv dhev</u>);
+dhuj dheev	a) whimpering on and off (cf. <u>dhuj dhev</u>, <u>dhawv dhev</u>) b) rising from and falling back into unconsciousness; c) <u>nco dhuj dheev</u> = almost remembering, then forgetting again
+khuj khuav	deliberate, slow manner
nruj nreev	a) sound of tree popping (fast) before it falls (cf. <u>nrhuj nrhawv</u>); b) sound of tight bow string twanging after arrow is released
+nrhuj nrhawv	a) sound of tree popping (slow) before it falls (cf. <u>nruj nreev</u>); b) with difficulty, slowly; absentminded walking (cf. <u>chuj chiab</u>)
ntuj ntiv	rats eating (cf. <u>txiv txev</u>)
+nyuj nyav	a) <u>quaj nyuj nyav</u> = whining (cf. <u>mluj mlob</u>); b) <u>luag nyuj nyav</u> = smile with double meaning; c) bittersweet feeling of longing
quj qev	a creaky door
+rhuj rhev	lightning and thunder (light; pause; sound) (cf. <u>rhij rhej</u>)
rhuj rhuav	a) sound of cutting vegetation; b) sound of bird shuffling through leaves looking for insects

tuj tauv	a) water dripping from a leaky roof (inside the house); b) the sound of a voice engaged in flattery
tuj tev	unclear speech; muttering, but not necessarily all low pitched
+xuj xuav	a) a long, easy, all-day rain; b) the undulating movement of a snake moving slowly

Some apparent exceptions to the canonical form of the two-word expressive:

+daws duam	mus <u>daws</u> <u>duam</u> = manner of walking
+nqhawv nqho	a) <u>quaj</u> <u>nqhawv</u> <u>nqho</u> = animals growling and panting; b) <u>ua</u> <u>nqhawv</u> <u>nqho</u> = to do everything in a hurry
+nrawv nroos	one after another
+nrawg nroos	equally well
qos qawv	<u>tom</u> <u>hniav</u> <u>qos</u> <u>qawv</u> = manner of gnashing teeth

ACKNOWLEDGEMENTS

I am grateful for the suggestions of Gérard Diffloth, who taught the seminar on expressives at the University of Chicago in the spring of 1983, in conjunction with which I began this study. I would like to thank my two primary Hmong tutors, Xab Xyooj and Kuam Yaj, for their patience, hard work and good humor. I would also like to thank Nancy L. Dray, Miriam Lykke and David Strecker for their criticisms of an earlier version of this paper.

NOTES

[1]Diffloth's intellectual debts, and therefore mine, can be traced back through Jakobson (1966) to the American philosopher Charles Sanders Peirce (1931), whose study of the various relationships between form and meaning includes the notion of iconicity, which is of key importance here.

[2]It may be accidental, but onomatopoeia predominates in the patterns where the tone is identical in the two words, and other senses and attitudes, or multiple senses, are much better represented in the patterns where the tones are dissimilar.

[3]See also plig plog (someone's body hitting the water). Two other associations with pliv ploov also involve water: the sound of ducks diving underwater and the sound of a submerged empty bottle filling up with water.

REFERENCES

Bolinger, Dwight. 1950. "Rime Assonance and Morphemic Analysis." Word 6:117-36.

Diffloth, Gérard. 1972. "Notes on Expressive Meaning." Papers from the Eighth Regional Meeting of the Chicago Linguistic Society, pp. 440-47. Chicago: Chicago Linguistic Society.

_____. 1976. "Expressives in Semai." Austroasiatic Studies, Oceanic Linguistics Special Publication No. 13, pp. 249-64. Honolulu: The University Press of Hawaii.

_____. 1979. "Expressive Phonology and Prosaic Phonology." Studies in Tai and Mon-Khmer Phonetics and Phonology, edited by Thongkum et al. pp. 49-59. Thailand: Chulalongkorn University Press.

Heimbach, Ernest E. 1979. White Hmong--English Dictionary, revised edition. Linguistics Series IV. Southeast Asia Program Data Paper No. 75. Ithaca: Cornell University, Department of Asian Studies.

Jakobson, Roman. 1966. "Quest for the Essence of Language," Diogenes 51: 345-59.

Johns, Brenda, and David Strecker. 1982. "Aesthetic Language in White Hmong." In The Hmong in the West: Observations and Reports. Papers of the 1981 Hmong Research Conference, edited by Bruce T. Downing and Douglas P. Olney, pp. 160-69. Minneapolis: Center for Urban and Regional Affairs, University of Minnesota.

Kim, Kong-On. 1977. "Sound Symbolism in Korean." Journal of Linguistics 13:67-75.

Lyman, Thomas Amis. 1974. Dictionary of Mong Njua. The Hague: Mouton.

McCarthy, John J. 1983. "Phonological Features and Morphological Structure." Papers from the Parasession on the Interplay of Phonology, Morphology and Syntax, pp. 135-61. The 19th Regional Meeting of the Chicago Linguistic Society. Chicago: Chicago Linguistic Society.

Martin, Samuel E. 1962. "Phonetic Symbolism in Korean." American Studies in Altaic Linguistics, pp. 177-89. Bloomington: Indiana University.

Mottin, Jean. 1978. Elements de grammaire Hmong blanc. Bangkok: Don Bosco Press.

P'an Yüan-en and Ts'ao Ts'ui-yün. 1958. "Four Syllable Coordinative Constructions in The Miao Language of Eastern Kweichow." In Miao and Yao Linguistic Studies, edited by Herbert C. Purnell, pp. 211-34. Ithaca: Cornell University Department of Asian Studies.

Peirce, Charles Sanders. 1931. Collected Papers. Cambridge: Harvard University Press.

Ts'ao Ts'ui-yün. 1961 "A Preliminary Study of the Descriptive Words in the Miao Language of Eastern Kweichow." In Miao and Yao Linguistic Studies, edited by Herbert C. Purnell, pp. 187-210. Ithaca: Cornell University Department of Asian Studies.

Wang, Fu-shih. 1957. "The Classifier in the Wei Ning Dialect of the Miao Language in Kweichow." In Miao and Yao Linguistic Studies, edited by Herbert C. Purnell, pp. 111-85. Ithaca: Cornell University Department of Asian Studies.

Wescott, R. 1973. "Tonal Icons in Bini." Studies in African Linguistics 4: 197-205.

VERB SERIALIZATION IN HMONG

Laurel Owensby

As fellow linguistics students and I began studying the Hmong language, looking at folk tales (Johnson 1981) and working with a bilingual informant, I remember often being surprised at the way verbs seemed to be "strung together." My surprise at finding so many verbs within a single sentence has developed into this report on verb serialization in Hmong.

The phenomenon of verb serialization has been described as a feature of many of the world's languages. Verb serialization has been defined by Isaac George (1975-76) as "essentially a surface sentence containing a row of two or more verbs or verb-phrases without any connective word between them."

Charles Li and Sandra Thompson, in their work on serial verb constructions in Mandarin Chinese (1973:97), use the following definition:

> Serial verb sentences consist of a subject followed by two predicates where the first subject is the subject of both predicates.[1]

NP	V (NP)	V (NP)
Subject	Predicate1	Predicate2

William Welmers, in his studies of African languages (1973), found that serial verb constructions are used for actions which are closely related to each other, and that serialized verbs are often translated by one English verb and a preposition or sometimes just one verb.

I have used three criteria in identifying examples of verb serialization in Hmong: one subject, with two or more verbs or verb phrases, and no conjunction between them. Examples thus identified seemed to divide up into various distinct types.

What at first glance seemed the simplest type of serial verb construction involves what linguists call reduplication. This is when the same verb is repeated. Reduplication occurs frequently in Hmong, with adjectives and adverbs, and with verbs as well.

Reduplication is not true serialization, according to the usual more narrow definitions, because the two parts make up a single, compound verb. Thus, it does not satisfy the definition of Li and Thompson, cited above, which requires that there be two distinct predicates for a single subject.

Reduplication of verbs in Hmong may serve a variety of purposes. It may mark an action repeated over and over again, an action in progress, or an action that occurs often. The function of reduplication of verbs may vary according to semantic classes of verbs.

Certain verbs in English, like slap, jump, cough and shout, signify a single occurrence of an action. When we hear "I sneezed," for example, we assume one action, in a brief period of time, unless it is marked otherwise, like "I sneezed and sneezed" or "I was sneezing." Verbs of this type can be reduplicated in Hmong to show a continuing action, rather than a single occurrence of an action, as in examples (1) to (3) below.

(1) Mas   nroj   niam   nplawm nplawm thiab   ntaus   ntaus
     Part. weeds   slap   slap   and   hit   hit

     nplej thiab pob kws.
     rice   and   corn

     "The weeds are fighting with the rice and corn."
     (From the folk tale, "The First Farmer")

(2) Nws dhia dhia.
     she jump jump
     "She jumped many times."

(3) Kuv tau   qw   qw.
     I   past shout shout
     "I shouted (for a long time)."

Reduplication may also be used to show that an action is in progress, while something else occurs, as illustrated in (4).

(4) Thaum nws tseem   *cheb* *cheb* tsev muaj ib tug
    then   she action in sweep sweep house have one clf.
           progress

    neeg muaj txiag tuaj txog   ntawm nws lub
    man have money come arrive there her clf.

    qhov rooj.
    door

    "While she was sweeping, a rich man came to her
    door." (From the folk tale, "The Woodcutter")

Some verbs are not usually reduplicated, like _noj_
'to eat.'

   (5) *Nws noj noj.
       He eat eat

Our Hmong informant said this sentence would be acceptable if it had something else before it that happened
while he was eating, like _nws txham_ 'he choked.' Thus _nws
txham nws noj noj_ could be used to indicate "He choked
while he was eating."
   The reduplication of a verb can also mean that an
action is something that's usually done:

   (6) Nws ua   ua   paj ntaub.
       She make make pa ndau.
       "She makes pa ndau (more than she does anything
       else)."

Another type of construction, this time an instance
of true serialization involving two distinct verbs, is
used with instrumentals. In Hmong, as well as in other
languages, two verbs are used with instrumentals, rather
than a verb and a preposition, as in the English "do
(something) _with_ (something)." This construction is illustrated in (7) to (9).

   (7) Tus neeg caum nqaij _xuas_ phom _tua_ tus noog.
       clf. man chase meat use gun shoot clf. bird
           (hunter)
       "The hunter shoots the bird with a gun."

(8) Kuv tus   tij   lauj   siv hlua nce   ntoo.
    My clf. older brother use rope climb tree
    "My older brother climbs the tree with a rope."

The verb muab 'to take in hand' is used frequently
with instrumentals also.

(9) Muab hmuv nkaug ntiaj teb ...
    take spear stab   earth
    "Stab the earth with a spear ..."

This verb muab is found frequently in other serial
verb constructions with an object, as in (10):

(10) Ces nkawd txawm muab pob zeb dov saum roob
     so they2 then take stone   roll top mountain

     lawm   nram kwj ha.
     compl. down valley.

     "So they rolled the stone down the mountain."

It occurs before an object that is being manipulated
somehow by first picking it up, which is then followed by
another verb.   This is possible even when the object is
not expressed.

(11) (they)••• tau muab txhoov ua   tej daim   coj
               past take cut up make many pieces take

               mus tso rau ghov txhia chaw.
               go put to clf. all   place

               "They chopped it into pieces and put them
               everywhere."

Notice that in this last example there are two series of
three verbs each, all associated with a single subject.
(Examples (9) to (11) above are from the folk tale, "The
Flood.")
     The most frequently occurring type of verb seriali-
zation I've observed is the use of the verbs mus 'to go'
and los 'to come' after verbs of motion.   These verbs
mark the direction of the action, toward or away from the
speaker or point of reference, as shown in (12) and (13).

(12)   <u>Nga</u>   taw   <u>mus</u>.
        carry wood   go
        "Take the wood."

(13)   <u>Nga</u>   taw   <u>los</u>.
        carry wood   come
        "Bring the wood."

This use of <u>mus</u> and <u>los</u> tells us where the speaker is in relation to the listener.

A somewhat different example is (14).

(14)   Nws <u>mus nyooj lawj</u> ua   av   <u>nqeeg nkaws</u> <u>los</u>.
        He go   growl   make earth shake   come
        "The tiger went and growled and made the earth shake."

In this example, because it is a story being told, the point of reference is the participants in the story itself. The tiger went away from the other animals and growled. He made the earth shake and the shaking reached them, as indicated by <u>los</u>.

<u>Mus</u> and <u>los</u> after a location are used to mark <u>from</u> what place and <u>to</u> what place an action is going. Consider the sentences (15) and (16).

(15)   Nws <u>nkag</u> hauv   txaj <u>mus</u>.
        She crawl inside room go
        "She crawled out of the room."

(16)   Nws <u>nkag</u> hauv   txaj.
        She crawl inside room
        "She crawled into the room."

This pair of examples indicates that <u>mus</u> after a location means that the subject is leaving from that place. Without that indication of direction, the location is assumed to be the goal of the action.

<u>Los</u> means not only 'come' but 'come to a place where you belong or where you've been before.' Compare sentences (17) and (18):

(17)   Koj <u>mus</u> qhov twg <u>los</u>?
        You go   where come
        "Where are you coming back from?" (to someone in
        your household).

(18)   Koj <u>los</u>   qhov twg <u>los</u>?
        You come   where come
        "Where are you from?" (to someone you don't know
        very well, but you knew a long time ago).

This meaning of <u>los</u> is in contrast with <u>tuaj</u> which also
means 'come' but doesn't imply where something belongs:

(19)   Koj <u>tuaj</u> qhov twg <u>tuaj</u>?
        You come   where   come
        "Where are you from?" (to a stranger).

My study of verb serialization has involved, first,
finding examples of sentences with two or more verbs or
verb phrases after a subject.   Second, I have tried to
classify them by type: reduplication, and "true" serialization involving instrumentals and directional markers.
Further study is needed of verb "compounds" that don't
yet fit neatly into categories.   Yet verb serialization
can definitely be seen as an important characteristic of
sentence structure in Hmong, with a variety of syntactic
functions.

ACKNOWLEDGEMENT

Mr. Tong Vang has been an invaluable consultant in
this data collection and interpretation.

NOTE

[1]NP indicates noun phrase and V = verb.   Other abbreviations used in the glosses of the example sentences can
be explained as follows: part. = participle,   clf. =
classifier, they2 = third person dual and compl. = com-
pletive aspect.

REFERENCES

Li, Charles N., and Sandra A. Thompson. 1973. "Serial Verb Constructions in Mandarin Chinese: Subordination or Co-ordination?" In You Take the High Node and I'll Take the Low Node: Papers from the Comparative Syntax Festival. A paravolume to Papers from the Ninth Regional Meeting of the Chicago Linguistic Society, edited by Claudia Corum, T. Cedric Smith-Stark and Ann Weiser, pp. 96-103. Chicago: Chicago Linguistic Society.

George, Isaac. 1975-76. "Verb Serialization in Kwa-Type Languages." Dissertation Abstracts International 36: 3633.

Johnson, Charles. 1981. Hmong Folk Tales. St. Paul: Linguistics Department, Macalester College.

Welmers, William E. 1973. African Language Structures. Berkeley: University of California Press.

THE MORPHEME KOM: A FIRST ANALYSIS AND LOOK AT EMBEDDING IN HMONG

Annie Jaisser

The intent of this paper is to give a syntactic and semantic analysis of the morpheme <u>kom</u> in Hmong in an attempt to gain insights into sentence embedding.[1] In his section on subordinate clauses, Mottin (1978) has described <u>kom</u> as the conjunction "so that, in order that" heading a resultative clause. Heimbach (1979) has described <u>kom</u> as a verb meaning "cause, bring into effect." Bertrais (1979) listed <u>kom</u> as a verb meaning "make, want," followed by a subordinate clause. Yang Dao (1980) has described <u>kom</u> as either a conjunction expressing "so that, in order that" or a verb, "want," followed by a subordinate clause. These descriptive statements (demonstrated by example sentences) afford no coherent syntactic analysis. In an attempt to arrive at such an analysis, I looked at the example sentences given by these authors as well as data found in the folk tales (Johnson 1981) which we used in a seminar on Hmong syntax. I then formulated hypotheses which I tested out with my informants. Results from this study, to be presented below, show that <u>kom</u> can function as a higher verb meaning "tell, order (somebody to do something)"; as a complementizer introducing an embedded sentence; and, when followed by the "can/able to" particle <u>tau</u>, as an element of an idiomatic phrase. I will look at each of these, using as a framework for analysis the "Standard Theory" of generative grammar developed in the work of Noam Chomsky and others.

<u>KOM</u> AS A HIGHER VERB

Let us consider one of the examples Mottin gives (p. 130):

(1) Kuv kom   nws mus.
     I   order him go
     "I ordered him to go/I told him to go."

Mottin claims that "as in reported speech, the main verb can be understood" and that "when this is the case, the understood verb is always qhia 'tell.' In other words, kom by itself can be translated by 'tell' (my translation). There is no solid syntactic evidence in Mottin's statement to disprove the hypothesis that kom might simply be the main verb in the example he gives. According to my informants, qhia could indeed be inserted before kom; this, however, would yield a different sentence, in which kom functions as a complementizer (see discussion in the next section).

My hypothesis that kom could be a main verb was strengthened by sentences in the data I collected which followed the same pattern as Mottin's example and by a sentence Heimbach gave (p. 85):

(2) Kuv tsis kom nws mus.
     I   NEG make him go
     "I won't make him go/I won't cause him to go."[2]

In Heimbach's example, the negative particle tsis occurs before kom; this is a practical test for determining whether an entity is a verb or not. I double-checked this example with my informants and used the further syntactic tests discussed below to check out the hypothesis that kom is a main verb. All these tests help determine if an entity is a verb or not.

Negative Insertion

In Hmong the particle tsis is placed in front of the verb to negate a statement, as seen in:

(3) Kuv tsis   mus.
     I   NEG go
     "I don't go."

The insertion of tsis in Mottin's example yields the sentence Heimbach gave:

(4) Kuv tsis kom   nws mus.
    I   NEG order him go

According to my three informants, this sentence is grammatically acceptable and means "I didn't order/tell him
to go."

Question Formation

Inserting the particle <u>puas</u> before the verb turns a
statement into a question, as illustrated in:

(5) Koj puas mus?
    you Q   go
    "Did you go?"

The insertion of <u>puas</u> works in Mottin's example as well:

(6) Kuv puas kom nws mus?
    I   Q   tell him go
    "Did I tell him to go?"

Past Tense Formation

In Hmong the appearance of the particle <u>tau</u> before
the main verb makes it overtly past, as seen below:

(7) Kuv tau mus.
    I   past go
    "I went."

The insertion of <u>tau</u> is acceptable in Mottin's example:

(8) Kuv tau kom nws mus.
    I   past tell him go
    "I told him to go."

Future Tense Formation

The insertion of <u>yuav</u> before the verb puts the action overtly into the future, as illustrated in:

(9) Kuv yuav mus.
     I   fut. go
     "I will go."

This, too, works in Mottin's example:

(10)   Kuv yuav kom nws mus.
        I   fut. tell him go
        "I will tell him to go."

Negative Imperative Formation

Hmong insert the negative particle _tsis_ followed by the particle _txhob_ in front of the verb to turn a statement into a negative command. _Tsis_ is optional and _txhob_ is obligatory, as seen in:

(11)   (Tsis)   txhob mus!
        NEG   NEG   go
        "Don't go!"

This test is positive with _kom_:

(12)   (Tsis)   txhob kom nws mus!
        NEG   NEG   tell him go
        "Don't tell him to go!"

These tests strongly suggest that _kom_ is a verb. However, all the particles used are preverbal and don't exclude the possibility of there being a deleted main verb (_qhia_) before _kom_, as Mottin claims. So (4) _Kuv tsis kom nws mus_ could be analyzed as _kuv tsis Ø kom nws mus_ with Ø being the site of the deleted _qhia_. We need further evidence to support the hypothesis that _kom_ can be a main verb.

The "Can/Able To" Modality Test

Inserting the particle _tau_ after the verb adds the modality "can/able to" to it, as seen in:

(13)   Kuv mus tau.
        I   go can
        "I can go."

When applied to Mottin's example, the result is ungram-matical:

(14a)   *Kuv kom tau nws mus.
         I   tell can him go

Although we can't have (14a), we can have:

(14b)   Kuv kom nws mus tau.
         I   tell he go can

According to one of my informants, tau can go either with kom, yielding "I could tell him to go" or with mus, yielding "I told him he could go." The structure in (14b) supports the hypothesis that kom functions as a main verb and suggest that tau can be attached at the end of the sentence to affect the higher verb. Further research is necessary to confirm the latter point, however.

Tag Formation

Hmong use a negative duplicating the main verb, as illustrated in the following example from Mottin (p. 88):

(15)   Koj mus los tsis mus?
        You go or   NEG go
        "Are you going or not?"

When this tag is attached to (1), kom shows up in the tag:

(16)   Kuv kom nws mus los   tsis kom?
         I   tell him to   or   NEG tell
        "Did I tell him to go or not?"

If we put qhia before kom in (16), qhia shows up in the tag:

(17)   Kuv qhia   kom nws mus los tsis qhia?
        I   instruct   comp. he go or NEG instruct
        "Did I instruct him to go or not?"

The fact that kom shows up in the tag in (16) is the most
persuasive piece of evidence to support the hypothesis
that kom can be a main verb.
        The occurrence of the preverbal particles tsis,
puas, tau, yuav and (tsis) txhob before kom (4, 6, 8, 10,
12) and, most of all, the duplication of kom in a negative tag (16) confirm the hypothesis that kom can be a
main verb.   Mottin was right when he said that "kom by
itself can be translated by 'tell'" (p. 130), but not
because qhia is the understood main verb.   The syntactic
tests mentioned above show that kom can function as a
higher verb meaning "tell, order" in its own right. When
used as such, it implies a strong command.   This is illustrated further in the following sentence from a folk
tale:

(18)   Ces Txiv Nraug Ntsuag txawm kom niag Niam
        and the Orphan boy   then order   Nia

        Nkauj Kub Kaws mus ntov ntoo
        Ngao Kou Ker go cut tree

        "And then the Orphan ordered Nia Ngao Kou Ker
        to go and cut down trees."
        (From Nia Ngao Zhua Pa, 1st version by Lou Lee,
        p. 18)

Semantic incompatibility between the modal tau "can/able
to" and the verb kom "tell, order" accounts for the un-
grammaticality found in (14).

KOM AS A COMPLEMENTIZER

        In this section I will look at sentences in which
kom is inserted between a higher verb and an embedded
sentence and discuss the hypothesis that kom is a complementizer in that case.   Mottin makes a distinction between the following two sentences (p. 130):

(19a)   Kuv xav   mus.
         I   want go
         "I want to go."

(19b)   Kuv xav   kom   nws mus.
         I   want comp. him go
         "I want him to go."

In the first sentence we will assume that the subjects of
the higher and the lower verbs are coreferential and an
"Equi-NP deletion"[3] rule controlled by the higher subject
deletes the lower subject.   According to Mottin, the insertion of <u>kom</u> in (19b) "implies an intention, a sense of
will towards another party" (p. 130).   From a syntactic
standpoint, <u>kom</u> seems to function like a complementizer
introducing an embedded sentence.   Native speakers' in-
tuitional feedback on constituent breaks is helpful in
determining where the higher sentence stops and the lower
one begins.   When asked where (19b) could be "cut in
two," my informants said after <u>xav</u>.   They always separated sentences following the same pattern after the main
verb.   Additional syntactic evidence to support the hypothesis that <u>kom</u> is a complementizer is provided by applying the negative insertion, question formation and
"can/able to" modality tests defined in the first section
of this paper to the following sentence:

(20) Kuv qhia   kom   nws mus.
     I   instruct   comp. him go
     "I instructed him to go."

Negative Insertion

(21) Kuv tsis qhia (*tsis)   kom   nws mus.
     I   NEG instruct   comp. him go
     "I didn't instruct him to go."

The negative particle <u>tsis</u> is inserted before the higher
verb; it cannot occur before <u>kom</u>.

Question Formation

(22) Kuv puas qhia (*puas) kom   nws mus?
      I   Q   instruct   comp. him go
      "Did I instruct him to go?"

The question marker puas can be inserted before the higher verb but cannot occur before kom.

"Can/Able To" Modality Test

(23) Kuv qhia   tau kom   nws mus.
      I   instruct can comp. him go
      "I can instruct him to go."

Tau is grammatically inserted between the higher verb and kom, as expected.   It can also follow kom; the resulting pattern, i.e., main verb plus kom tau, changes the meaning of the sentence and will be discussed in the next section.
     The facts that tsis and puas are inserted before the higher verb and that tau is inserted between the higher verb and kom show that kom in these examples functions as a complementizer.   This justifies Mottin's classification of kom as a subordinate conjunction (p. 130).   Mottin lists a few verbs which can be followed by kom (p. 131):

hais	'say, speak'
qhia	'inform, instruct, teach, tell'
txib	'tell somebody to do something'
thov	'ask, beg'
xav	'want'
kheev	'be willing, consent to'
ua	'make, do on purpose'
txhib	'excite, entice'
yuam	'compel'

There were numerous sentences with kom in the data I collected. The verbs preceding kom are listed below:

ntuas	'advise'
ntiab	'drive away, drive out'
nyiam	'like'

xov	'enclose with a fence'
thawb	'push'
cheb	'sweep'
tos	'wait'
pab	'help'
txwv	'forbid'
noj	'eat'
txiav	'decide'
foom	'curse'
ntaus	'strike, hit, beat'
tsoo	'hit, crush'
tua	'fire, weapons'
sau	'write'
kawm ntawv	'study'
piav	'explain'
nyeem	'read'
qw	'shout, yell'
tso	'send'
yuam	'force'
ua	'make, do'

This is a great variety of verbs. What do they have in common? They can all be followed by an embedded sentence introduced by kom and conveying a result, an intention or an implicit command. It is difficult to narrow down the semantics of kom to a single word translation when it is used as a complementizer. Mottin and Yang Dao came closest to doing so when they translated kom by "so that, in order that." In all the sentences in which kom functions as a complementizer, the higher subject NP affects the behavior of the lower subject NP via a great variety of verbs. It is my contention that any verb whose semantics allows the subject to affect the behavior of the lower subject can be followed by kom.

Having discussed the semantics of kom as a complementizer, I will now turn to structural patterns. The basic pattern is the following:

(NP) main verb   [-kom NP VP] -

This pattern applies to all the verbs I listed earlier and is illustrated below:

(24) Hais kom   nws khiav   mus.
     say comp. her depart go
     "Tell her to go away."
     (From The Orphan and Ngao Zhua Pa, Level 1:20)

(25) Peb tos   kom   hnub tuaj siab siab tso   puas
                                                tau?
     we wait comp. sun rise high high first Q can
     "Can we wait until the sun is high up?"
     (From The Monkeys and the Grasshoppers, Level
     2:9)

(26) Kuv qw   kom   kws   ceevfaj.
     I   shout comp. he be careful
     "I shout so that he's careful."/"I shout for
     him to be careful."
     (From Tong Vang, informant)

When the higher and lower subjects are coreferential, the lower subject is deleted, as seen below:

(27) Peb kawm ntawv kom   tsawj ntawv.
     we study   comp. be knowledgeable
     "We study in order to be knowledgeable."
     (Bertrais 1979: 104)

(28) Peb tua   kom   yeej cobtsib
     we fire weapons comp. win Vietnamese

     kom tshaj.
     communist

     "We fire weapons in order to defeat the Vietnamese
     communists."
     (From Tong Vang, informant)

According to my informants, it is possible but not necessary to keep peb in the lower sentence in (27) and (28).
In that case, the translations would be: "We study so
that we are knowledgeable" for (27) and "We fire weapons
so that we defeat the Vietnamese communists" for (28).
     The lower subject is also deleted when it has been
mentioned previously, as seen in the following excerpt
from a folk tale:

(29) Kuv nyiam kom   sawv daws nyob   ua ke   li no
     I   like   comp. everybody live   together like

mus li.   Tab sis kuv nyiam kom (sawv daws)
this forever.   But   I   like   comp.

ua   suab   sab...
make noise   loud

"I'd like for all of us to live together like this
forever. But I also like for us to make loud
noises..."
(From <u>Shao and His Fire</u>, Level 2:8)

In sentences where the main verb is followed by an
indirect object NP, which is also the subject of the lower sentence, the lower subject is retained (30), pronomi-
nalized (31) or deleted (32,33):

(30) Hais rau nws kom   nws mus cheb tsev   zoo   zoo.
     say to her comp. she go   sweep house well well
     "Tell her to go and sweep the house carefully."
     (<u>Yao the Orphan</u>, Level 2:13)

(31) Hais rau koj   poj niam kom   nws khiav   mus.
     say to your wife   comp. she depart   go
     "Tell your wife to go away."
     (<u>The Orphan and Ngao Zhua Pa</u>, Level 1:19)

(32) Kuv qw   rau nws kom   ceevfaj.
     I   shout at him comp. be careful
     "I shout at him so that he's careful."
     (From Tong Vang, informant)

(33) Nws foom rau yeej kom   txhob tau zoo.
     he curse at man comp. NEG   have good for-
                                        tune
     "He cursed the man so that he would not have good
     fortune."
     (From Tong Vang, informant)

The lower subject could also be deleted in (30) and (31).
A syntactically interesting phenomenon came up with regard
to one of the examples Mottin gives in his section on <u>kom</u>
(p. 130).

(34) Kuv ntuas Lis kom   mus
      I   advise Lee comp. go
      "I advised Lee to go."

= (35) Kuv ntuas   kom   Lis mus.
        I   advise   comp. Lee go

According to Mottin, there is no difference between (34)
and (35). This was confirmed by my informants. The corresponding information question is:

(36) Koj ntuas Lis li cas?
      You advise Lee what
      "What did you advise Lee to do?"

Example (36) shows that <u>ntuas</u> takes a main clause object
NP. It functions like a <u>force</u>-type verb in English, but
instead of obligatorily deleting the lower subject NP
using Equi-NP deletion, Hmong offers a choice of deleting
either the lower subject NP (34) or the higher object NP
(33). <u>Pab</u> "help" functions in the same way in the following example:

(37) Pab nws kom   hlob   zuj zus.
      help him comp. grow   little by little

= (38) Pab kom   nws hlob   zuj zus.
        help comp. he grow   little by little
        "Help him grow little by little."

I have found other verbs in the data which offer the same
choice when they are followed by <u>kom</u>:[1]

ntiab	'drive out, drive away'
qhia	'inform, tell, instruct, teach'
txwv	'forbid'
xov	'enclose with a fence'
thawb	'push'

Further subcategorization of verbs that can take this
structure and a study to determine what accounts for the
deletion choice would be interesting topics to pursue.
     To conclude this section I will mention an interest-
ing fact concerning negative formation in embedded sen-

tences introduced by kom. In all the sentences I collected in which the lower verb is negated, this verb is preceded by txhob rather than tsis. This is illustrated in the following example from Mottin (86):

(39) Nws pab kom   tus   tsov txhob tom kuv.
     he help comp. clf.   tiger NEG   bite me
     "He helped me so that the tiger wouldn't bite me."

Mottin (1978) and Heimbach (1979) have described txhob as a particle used before the verb to express a strong negative command. The negative imperative thus formed can optionally be preceded by the usual negative marker tsis, as seen in:

   (40) Tsis txhob   txhawj.
         NEG NEG IMP   worry
         "Don't worry"

= (41) Txhob   txhawj.
        NEG IMP worry
        (From How We Got Grain and Meat, Level 1:11,24)

    I formulated the hypothesis that tsis could also be optionally inserted before txhob in embedded sentences starting with kom. This was confirmed by my informants, with no difference between the kom (NP) tsis txhob V and kom (NP) txhob V patterns.
    I further hypothesized that (tsis) txhob was the obligatory negative marker in lower sentences introduced by kom and that tsis alone could not be used in that case. My informants, however, accepted the kom (NP) tsis V pattern, stating that the sentences were grammatical but that they did not convey as strong a negative as the kom (NP) (tsis) txhob V pattern. Considering the facts that all the sentences I found in the data followed the kom (NP) (tsis) txhob V pattern and that my informants preferred this pattern to the kom (NP) tsis V one, I will suggest that the former is the unmarked (preferred) pattern and the latter the marked pattern for negative formation in embedded sentences introduced by kom.

THE IDIOMATIC PHRASE <u>KOM TAU</u>

As seen in (14), the modal <u>tau</u> "can/able to" cannot
follow <u>kom</u> when <u>kom</u> is a main verb, presumably because of
semantic incompatibility between the modality and the
strength of the command in <u>kom</u> "order, tell (somebody to
do something)." <u>Kom</u> can, however, appear between a main
verb and <u>tau</u>. In that case, the sequence <u>kom tau</u> seems to
function as an idiomatic phrase.   This point is illustrated below:

(42)   Kuv mus tau.
       I   go   can
       "I can go."

(43)   Kuv mus kom tau.
       I   go
       "I will make myself go." (no matter what)

When <u>tau</u> alone follows the main verb (13), it simply
expresses the "can/able to" modality, as seen earlier.
When <u>kom</u> is inserted between the verb and <u>tau</u> (43), it
changes the modality and implies a command, something to
the effect "not only can I do it, but I have to carry out
the action, no matter what the circumstances are."   <u>Tau</u>
goes with <u>kom</u> in that case, according to my informants,
and the sequence functions as a separate semantic unit.
<u>Kom tau</u> can follow a variety of verbs, as seen in the
following examples from Tong Vang, one of my informants:

(44)   Kuv nqa kom tau lub   pob zeb ntawd.
       I   lift   clf. rock   that
       "I have to be able to lift that rock."

(45)   Peb caum kom tau lub tsheb daj   tod.
       we chase   clf. car   yellow that
       "We have to be able to catch up with that yellow
       car."

CONCLUSION

Using the results of preverbal particle and tag-
formation tests, I have shown that <u>kom</u> can function as a

higher verb meaning "tell, order (somebody to do some-thing)." I have also shown that <u>kom</u> is used as a comple-mentizer and discussed structural patterns. Finally, I have shown that, when preceded by a main verb, <u>kom tau</u> functions as an idiomatic phrase meaning "can and will..., no matter what."

NOTE

[1]This paper is drawn from my M.A. thesis (San Diego State University), in progress, on complementation in Hmong.

[2]NEG=Negative. Other abbreviations used in the glosses of the example sentences are as follows: Q = question, comp. = complementizer, fut. = future, NP = noun phrase, VP = verb phrase, IMP = imperative, V = verb, clf. = classi-fier.

[3]Equi-NP deletion refers to the deletion of one of two identical noun phrases in a sentence.

REFERENCES

Bertrais, Yves. 1979. <u>Dictionnaire Hmong-Français</u>. Bang-kok: Assumption Press, Sangwan Surasarang Publisher.

Heimbach, Ernest E. 1979. <u>White Hmong-English Dictionary</u>, revised edition. Linguistics Series IV. Southeast Asia Program Data Paper No. 75. Ithaca: Cornell University, Department of Asian Studies.

Johnson, Charles. 1981. <u>Hmong Folk Tales</u>. Saint Paul: Linguistics Department, Macalester College.

_____. 1984. <u>Dab Neeg Hmoob: Myths, Legends and Folk Tales from the Hmong of Laos</u>, Saint Paul: Linguistics Department, Macalester College.

Mottin, Jean. 1978. <u>Elements de grammaire Hmong blanc</u>. Bangkok: Don Bosco Press.

Yang, Dao.   1980.   Dictionnaire français-Hmong blanc.
     Paris: Comité National d'Entraide.

Yang Dao, Se Yang and Tong Vang, personal communication.

ZERO ANAPHORA AND TOPIC PROMINENCE IN HMONG

Judith Wheaton Fuller

Mottin, in his grammar of Hmong, noted that "personal pronouns are often omitted when the sense is clear" (Mottin 1979:44; original in French). In this paper I will examine what this statement means in a variety of pronominal contexts, and consider the implications of this absence of pronouns (called zero anaphora) in Hmong for typological statements about the Hmong language. I will first outline some facts of zero anaphora in Hmong, then relate these facts to the concept of topic-prominence.

SENTENCE-LEVEL ZERO ANAPHORA

Let us look first at some sentence-level ellipsis phenomena. Sentences with zero noun phrases occur in several situations; I will note these structures and divide them into two groups. The first pronoun omission type, EQUI NP DELETION,[1] is illustrated in examples (1) and (2), where zeros are used to indicate the position of the missing noun phrase.[2]

(1) Kuv xav ∅ mus.
     1ps want go
     "I want to go."

(2) Kuv yuav pab koj ∅ cog   nplej.
     1ps will help 2ps   plant rice
     "I will help you (to) plant rice."

A sentence like (1) has traditionally been analyzed as having the underlying structure [I want [I go]], where the second instance of the first person pronoun is deleted by the rule of EQUI NP DELETION. The omission here of the subject of mus 'go' is controlled by the identical subject of the higher verb xav 'want.' In (2), the omission of the subject of cog 'plant' is controlled by the

subject of the higher verb pab 'help'. In these cases
the "sense is clear" because the verbs xav 'want' and pab
'help' are understood to require the deletion of the subject of their complements under identity with the subject
and object, respectively, of the higher verb; recovera-
bility of the complement subject is thus assured.

IMPERATIVE SUBJECT OMISSION is also common (though
not mandatory) in Hmong, as shown in (3-4).

(3)   Ø Muab rau kuv.
          give to 1ps
       "Give it to me."

(4)   Ø Cia   nws ua nws li.   (Heimbach:14)
          allow 3ps do 3ps like
       "Let him do as he likes."

In (3-4) the "sense is clear" because the omitted pronoun
is predictably the addressee, again assuring recoverabil-
ity. If nws or peb, for example, were meant, those pronouns would have to appear on the surface.
       Zero noun phrases also occur in VERB SERIALIZATION,
as shown in (5).

(5)   Thaum ntawd lawv mam thiaj li   yuav Ø nce
          time   that 3pp then consequently want   ascend

       Ø tuaj Ø mus.
          come   go

       "At that time, they will want to better themselves."

In (5), if each verb is interpreted separately, its subject is deleted under identity with the subject of the
initial verb.

DISCOURSE-LEVEL ZERO ANAPHORA

Another type of zero noun phrase which occurs in
Hmong is main clause DIRECT OBJECT OMISSION. Examples
are given in (6-9).

(6)   Kuv tsis nyiam ∅.   (Heimbach:219)
       1ps NEG like
       "I don't like (it)."

(7)   Kuv tsis tau ua ∅.   (Heimbach:307)
       1ps NEG ASP do
       "I didn't do (it)."

(8)   Nws mob. Mas koj puas mus xyuas ∅?   (Heimbach:417)
       3ps pain Prt 2ps Q   go visit
       "He's ill. Will you go to visit (him)?"

(9)   Kuv tsis tau hnov ∅ dua.   (Heimbach:70)
       1ps NEG TM hear   before
       "I have never heard (it) before."

In (6-7), pronominal object omission with the meaning
given is obligatory.   In (8), the object omission is completely optional.   In (9), the missing object refers to a
nonhuman sound; if <u>nws</u> is inserted in the missing object
position, this pronoun must refer to a person.   While the
animacy restrictions governing optional vs. obligatory
omission are not entirely clear, object omission in general is governed by its reference to a <u>topic</u> in the preceding linguistic or nonlinguistic context.   Thus the referent cannot be recovered by looking at sentence level
facts alone.

Main clause SUBJECT OMISSION, independent of IMPERA-
TIVE SUBJECT OMISSION, is also a frequent phenomenon in
Hmong, as shown in (10-13).

(10)   ∅ Tsis tau sib   fim.   (Heimbach:45)
         NEG ASP RECIP meet
       "(We) haven't met yet."

(11)   ∅ Tabkaum koj   haujlwm.   (Heimbach:77)
         hinder 2ps work
       "(I) have hindered you."

(12)   ∅ txujkum dim   oj?   (Heimbach:4)
         how   escape Q PRT
       "How will (he) escape?"

(13)   Niaj   hnub ∅ mus laij   teb.   (Lyman:47)
        every day   go   plow field
        "Every day (they) went to plow the field."

In (10-11), the omitted subject is presumed to be the
speaker (or speaker and hearer).   In the cases of third
person subject omission in (12-13), interpretation of the
zero subject pronoun is not possible from the sentence
alone, but requires additional linguistic or extralinguistic context.

        In (14), both object and subject are omitted.

(14)   Kuv thawb ∅ ∅   ntog.   (Heimbach:190)
        1ps push   roll over and over
        "I pushed (it) and set (it) rolling."

        Again, the omitted word or words do not refer to a
noun phrase in the same sentence; the referent is in the
previous linguistic or extralinguistic context.
        While all of these processes delete noun phrases,
main clause SUBJECT and OBJECT OMISSION function differently from EQUI NP DELETION, IMPERATIVE SUBJECT OMISSION
and VERB SERIALIZATION.   The latter three principles are
controlled by easily specifiable syntactic conditions referring to grammatical relations and operating within the
sentence. The conditions for SUBJECT and OBJECT OMISSION,
on the other hand, are not easily specified, their domain
is extrasentential, and they are controlled by the topic.
Since a topic can be and often is mentioned in one sentence and referred to in subsequent sen-tences, the domain of topic-controlled deletion is necessarily beyond
the sentence.   In fact, SUBJECT and OBJECT OMISSION are
not very good names for this type of deletion, since the
fact that the deleted NPs are subjects or objects is irrelevant.   A better designation encompassing both would
be TOPIC-NP DELETION, as we will show.
        Tsao (1979), in his description of Chinese, has re-
ferred to TOPIC-NP DELETION as a process operating within
a topic chain.   When the domain of a topic extends over
several sentences, Tsao refers to the sentences in that
domain as a topic chain.   Within a topic chain, the topic
is mentioned once, then may be omitted in subsequent mention.   It is this type of deletion process, TOPIC-NP DE-
LETION (rather than the EQUI type of deletion that is

controlled by the sentential subject or object) that I am particularly concerned with in the discussion of zero anaphora in Hmong.

A topic chain with TOPIC-NP DELETION is illustrated in (15) (from Lyman 1979:47–48).

(15) Muaj   ob tug txiv neeg mas yog ob tug twv tij.
     there 2 CLF people   PRT BE 2 CLF brothers

Niag hnub Ø mus laij teb.
every day   go plow field

Hnub laij tas,   ib hmos tagkis Ø rov   mus saib.
day plow finish   one night tomorrow back go   look

Muaj   ib hmos thiaj li Ø mus zov   saib yog
there was 1 night than   go watch see was

ua li cas.
how

"(Once) there were two people who were brothers. Every day (they) went to plow the field. After each day's plowing, when night-time was over and dawn had arrived, (they) would go back to look at the field.... Then one night (they) went and watched to see what happened."

Within a topic chain, the question arises as to the predictability of omission of noun phrases coreferential to the topic. In a prototypical topic chain model, the topic is initially expressed as a full noun phrase, and subsequent references to the topic are deleted under identity with (or reference to) the topic noun phrase. However, under certain circumstances, perhaps if the topic chain becomes long, or competing noun phrases appear, a pronoun or a repeated or substitute noun phrase may be used to refer to the topic. This raises the question whether there are definite rules governing TOPIC-NP DELETION, or whether deletion is always optional.

Li and Thompson (1979), in their study of zero anaphora in Chinese, took the view that zero anaphora was the norm, and it was the presence of a pronoun (or fully referring noun phrase) in a discourse that required explanation. They conducted an experiment in which they excerpted short narratives from a Mandarin text, took out all pronoun occurrences, and gave them to native Mandarin speakers to read, asking them to insert pronouns where they felt they were needed. The results confirmed Li and Thompson's claims that zero anaphora is the norm, and that native speakers vary in their judgments about where pronouns are needed (1979:388). They found that one predictable factor in pronoun insertion was degree of conjoinability: "the lower the degree of conjoinability between two clauses, the higher is the likelihood of a pronoun occurring in the second clause" (1979:334). They concluded that since conjoinability depends on individual judgments, predictions of pronoun insertion are only possible statistically, for groups of speakers, rather than for individual speakers.

Following Li and Thompsons's procedure, I removed pronoun occurrences from a Hmong narrative written in RPA and submitted the narrative to a small number of native Hmong speakers, asking them to insert pronouns where they thought pronouns were needed. The results indicated that native speaker judgments about the appropriateness of pronoun placement were indeed variable. While no pronouns were inserted in EQUI type positions, which are sentence-level and subject-controlled, pronoun insertion occurred in TOPIC-NP DELETION positions, which are discourse-level and topic-controlled. There was no unanimity of judgment about where the pronoun insertion occurred. For example, in the segment referred to in (15), which is part of the text used in the experiment, one respondent felt a pronoun was required in the last sentence, following some omitted material, while another respondent and the original text used no pronoun in that position. Use of a pronoun in such positions may depend on speaker judgments of intelligibility, which may vary with speakers. Constraints on zero pronouns in these situations appear to be primarily topic-oriented.

I also submitted another Hmong narrative written in RPA (a Hmong folk tale edited by Charles Johnson) to a native Hmong speaker, asking him to remove pronouns in the narrative that he felt could be omitted. Using this procedure it seemed clear that intelligibility was not the only criterion used to determine acceptability of sentences without coreferential pronouns; even where co-

referentiality was clear, pronouns were sometimes required, apparently for syntactic reasons.[3]   This situation is shown in (16), where <u>nws</u> in the second sentence
is obligatory, according to this native speaker.

(16)   Nws hle   nws cev ris tsho   zoo cia.
        3ps take off 3ps CLF clothes   good put aside

        Nws hnav   nws cev   ris tsho   tawv nas tawv
        3ps put on   3ps CLF   clothes   skin rodent skin

        noog.
        bird

        "He took off his good clothes.   He put on animal
        skins."

Zero pronouns are more acceptable when the sentences with
coreferential NPs are not merely conjoinable but when a
transition word is used, as in (17), where <u>Sib Nab</u> may be
omitted in the second sentence if <u>ces</u>, 'then', is inserted.

(17)   Sis Nab ntsia   saum Nkauj Ntsuab lub qhov rai
        Sis Na gaze   up   Ngao Njua   CLF window

        Sis Nab ∅ ces   txawm tshuab tshuab qeej.
        Shee Na   then PRT   blow   kheng

        "Shee Na looked up at Ngao Njua's window.   He then
        played his kheng."

Constraints on omission here appear to be syntactic as
well as topic-centered.   However, much more study is
needed to uncover and interpret the facts of these deletion constraints.
        Languages differ in the restrictions they place on
zero anaphora.   English, for example, restricts zero anaphora quite severely.   While (18-19),   showing a type of
deletion that Tsao calls SPEAKER AND HEARER DELETION, are
acceptable in informal speech, (20-24) are either unacceptable, (marked by an asterisk) or marginally acceptable, (marked by a question mark).

(18)   Ø Went to the store while you were gone.   Ø Bought some blueberries.

(19)   Ø Go to the store while I was gone?   Ø Buy any blueberries?

(20)   *When I saw John yesterday, Ø realized that he was sick.

(21)   That table is ugly. *I don't like Ø.
        ?Ø Doesn't go with the buffet.

(22)   *Regarding that table, Ø isn't big enough to serve this many people.

(23)   *Regarding that table, I want to refinish Ø.

(24)   ?Before you set the table, put a tablecloth on Ø.

On the other hand, in a language like Chinese, as we have noted, zero anaphora is much less restricted. According to our investigations so far, Hmong falls somewhere between Chinese and English in having zero anaphora in more contexts than in English, but with more restrictions than Chinese.

TOPIC-PROMINENCE AND ZERO ANAPHORA

Gundel (1980) has classified a number of languages according to the degree to which they restrict zero anaphora. This classification is shown in (25).

(25)

I		II			III
Lisu	Chinese	Numbami	Hebrew	Spanish	English
Lahu	Japanese	Kekchi	Arabic	Italian	French
Thai	Korean	Yukatan	Turkish	Baltic	German
Vietnamese		Fijian	Latin	Slavic	

Languages with least restricted zero anaphora are shown at the left in I, those with most restricted zero anaphora at the right in III.   Those in the middle, in II, are intermediate, allowing zero anaphora only in some situations.   As Gundel points out, an interesting feature of this classification is the degree to which it corresponds to the classification of subject-prominent and topic-prominent languages developed by Li and Thompson (1976):   the languages that have the least restricted zero anaphora are the same languages   that are the most topic-prominent, and the languages which have the most restricted zero anaphora are the ones that are the least topic-prominent.   Gundel's generalization stating   this point is given in (26).

(26)   The more topic-prominent a language, the less restricted its use of zero anaphora (Gundel 1980).

Li and Thompson have proposed the typology of topic-prominent versus subject-prominent languages as a tool for examining the sentence structure of languages to determine whether the language is more fruitfully described in terms of topic-comment structure or subject-predicate structure (1976:460).   Li and Thompson characterized topic-prominent languages as shown in (27).

(27)   Characteristics of topic-prominent languages:

       a)   surface coding of topic
       b)   passive construction nonexistent or marginal
       c)   no "dummy" subjects
       d)   existence of "double subjects"
       e)   topic controls coreferential constituent deletion
       f)   verb-final
       g)   no constraints on what may be topic
       h)   topic-comment sentences are part of the repertoire of basic sentence types.

Subject-prominent languages, by contrast, typically do not code topics; they have processes such as passivization, which refer to subject, and they require "dummy" subjects to fill subject position.   Subject in subject-

prominent languages is important in controlling coreferential deletion, subject-predicate division rather than
topic-comment division is characteristic of sentence patterns, and constraints may be placed on the expression of
topic (for example, the topic may have to be a subject).

I would now like to examine Hmong sentences according to Li and Thompson's characteristics of topic-prominent languages, and then use Tsao's criticisms of Li and
Thompson's statements about Chinese to show that zero anaphora is the most relevant of these characteristics in
assessing the "topic prominence" of a language.

(a) Surface coding of the topic is an indication
that the language requires the topic to be salient. Coding may be a morphological marker, as in Lisu, Japanese
and Korean, or position (invariably initial sentence position), as in Chinese. Hmong has no invariant morphological topic marker. Topics are often made explicit by
the introductory expressions <u>hais</u> <u>txog</u> or <u>hais</u> <u>tias</u>, as
will be illustrated below.

(b) Hmong has a passive construction containing the
word <u>raug</u> which is sometimes translated into English as
passive and appears to be regarded by Hmong speakers as a
passive. Examples of its use are shown in (28-31).

(28)   Pov tau raug nees   tuam nws.
        Pao TM   horse kick 3ps
        "Pao got kicked by a horse."

(29)   Naghmo   kuv lub qhws ntsej raug luag
        yesterday 1ps CLF earring   somebody

        nyiag lawm.
        steal TM

        "Yesterday somebody stole my earring."

(30)   Nws raug tua   tuag tawm.
        3ps   kill die TM
        "He was killed."

(31)   Tooj raug luag   ntes.
        Tong   someone catch
        Tong was caught by someone."

However, the passive word <u>raug</u> cannot be used in translating English sentences such as "The room had been cleaned by Ntxhais" or "A new kind of rice was studied by the scientist."   These sentences must be rendered in Hmong in active form, as in (32-33).

(32)   Ntxhais tau cheb chav pw.
        Ntxhais TM clean room-bed

(33)   Tus kws txuj   tau kawm ib   hom nplej tshiab.
        CLF scientist TM study one kind rice   new

The types of verbs in use with <u>raug</u> suggest that PASSIVE in Hmong is limited to an "adversity" situation.   In addition, the word <u>raug</u> is not specifically a passive marker, but a verb with the meanings "to encounter," "to meet up with," "to incur" or "to suffer," according to the Heimbach dictionary.   Other facts bolstering the identification of <u>raug</u> as a verb are its placement in verb position in the sentence, and its use with the aspect marker <u>tau</u>, as in (28).   Passive in Hmong is thus either nonexistent or quite restricted, to the extent that one can read many pages of Hmong texts of various types without encountering a single instance of <u>raug</u>.   The passive construction in Hmong thus conforms with Li and Thompson's characterization of passive in topic-prominent languages.

One use of passive constructions is to make nonsubject noun phrases into subjects so that they can serve as topics.   Li and Thompson state that the reason passive is not needed in topic-prominent languages is that "any noun phrase can be the topic of a sentence without registering anything on the verb" (1976:467).   However, the existence of the topic chain   suggests another mode for registering a noun phrase as a topic in Hmong.   If, for example, <u>chav pw</u> 'bedroom' in (32) were to be a topic, it could appear in topic position in a previous sentence, then become zero in the following clause, as in (34).

(34)   Chav pw sw   heev (mas) Ntxhai   yuav cheb Ø.
        room-bed disorderly very (PRT) Ntxhais will clean
        "The bedroom is very disorderly, (so) Ntxhais will
        clean (it)."

Notice, however, that this expression of topic requires consideration of a domain beyond the simple sentence.

(c) "Dummy" subjects occur in English in sentences with nonreferential _it_ and existential <u>there</u>. Hmong appears to have no dummy subjects.[4] The verb <u>muaj</u> 'to have' is used clause-initially in an existential sense; (15) in the narrative given previously is an example of this.

Expressions such as "It might rain today" are typically given in Hmong as (35).

(35)   Tej zaug hnub no yuav los   nag.
         maybe   today   will come rain

(d) The occurrence of double subjects, typical in a topic-prominent language like Chinese, appears to be marginal in formal and written Hmong, although it may be more acceptable in conversational spoken language.   For example, (36) is an acceptable Hmong sentence, while (37) is better re-phrased as (38).

(36)   Kuv lub   tsev   mas   kuv tau yuav   tsaib   no.
         1ps CLF house PRT, 1ps TM buy   last year   this
         "I bought my house last year."

(37)   Tsheb   mas   cov Toyota thiab Datsun zoo   heev.
         car   PRT CLF Toyota and   Datsun good very
         "Cars, Toyota and Datsun are very good."

(38)   Hais   txog   tsheb mas, cov Toyota thiab Datsun zoo
         speak about car   PRT CLF Toyota and   Datsun good

         heev.
         very

(e) Regarding   coreferential   deletion,   it   is   clear from the preceding discussion that both subject and topic can control coreferential deletion in Hmong.   The crucial cases here involve sentences with distinct topic and subject, and a subsequent zero pronoun which could potentially refer to either, as in (39).

(39)   (Hais txog)   daim teb / thav av   ntawd (mas),   tsob
         (speak of)   CLF field / CLF land that   (PRT)   CLF

         nplej tuaj   loj loj   yog li no   mas Ø muaj nqi heev
         rice   grow big   consequently PRT   valuable very

"That field/land, rice grows very big, so (it) is very valuable."

Li and Thompson's claim is that in these cases, in topic-prominent languages, topic overrides subject as controller of deletion, and where subject must control deletion, the sentence is unacceptable. In Hmong, the zero pronoun in (39) can refer to either the topic- or the subject. Thus Hmong is equivocal about topic or subject-prominence with regard to coreferential deletion.

(f) Li and Thompson characterize topic-prominent languages asverb-final. Although it is true that the languages they identify as topic-prominent are verb-final,[5] it is not clear what relevance this fact has to topic-prominence. Hmong is verb-medial, although it has, as we have seen, some topic-prominent characteristics.

(g) Hmong can have objects as well as subjects as topics, as shown in (40).

(40) Hais   txog tsheb mas, kuv tsis nyiam tsav ∅.
      speak about car   PRT 1ps NEG like   drive
      "Speaking of cars, I don't like to drive (them)."

With respect to the range of phenomena Li and Thompson consider, then, Hmong does not constrain heavily what can be topics.

(h) Regarding sentences which are basic in Hmong, sentences (36-38) show that overt topic-comment sentences of the Japanese/Chinese type are possible but somewhat marginal in Hmong.

What Li and Thompson have shown in their typology is an interesting correlation between certain properties of sentences and a predilection for a language to organize its structure according to topic-comment relations. Some of these sentence-level properties, such as surface coding for topic and topic-comment sentences as basic, are a manifestation of topic-prominence. Other cases, such as no dummy subject and verb-final, show an interesting correlation, but no apparent intrinsic relationship to topic-prominence, although a dummy-subject requirement is intrinsically related to subject-prominence. The inclusion of some properties, such as no passive, no dummy subjects, and topic-comment sentences as basic seemed designed to show that in these languages the subject is of little importance.   In fact, Li and Thompson take pains to show that in Lisu and in Mandarin it is sometimes impossible to identify a sentence subject.

However, there is no reason to assume that a language which gives a prominent role to topic must give a lesser role to subject.   Japanese and Korean mark both subjects and topics, and Li and Thompson themselves consider these languages to be both topic-prominent and subject-prominent.   It is also clear that a language like Hmong, which has some topic-prominent characteristics, also gives the subject a well-defined role: subject has a characteristic sentence-initial position, and controls coreferential deletion in sentence-level processes, as we have seen.

Tsao (1979:91) makes a crucial point in comparing subject and topic influence when he states that subject and topic "belong to different levels of grammatical organization."   Subject is relevant at the sentence level, while topic is relevant at the discourse level.   Thus, regarding sentence-level structural facts, while they may show interesting correlation with topic organization and may indeed be related to it, the relationship is indirect.   For example, as I have suggested, a language like Hmong may have a marginal passive not because the topic rather than the subject is important in Hmong, but because organization at the discourse level, where subject is not relevant, obviates the necessity for the use of the passive construction, or because constraints on the PASSIVE morpheme force the use of alternative constructions.   The grammaticality of topic-comment sentences as such is clearly a sentence-level matter; the rarity of such sentences, even if they are "basic", can only be explained on the discourse level, where the notion of the topic chain shows clearly that explicit topic-comment expression only occurs when the topic is introduced.

Li and Thompson's characteristics of topic-prominent languages are all sentence-level characteristics, with one exception.   Control of coreferential deletion in coordinate clauses is, although Li and Thompson do not present it this way, clearly related to discourse processes.   This type of coreferential deletion is similar to that occurring in topic chains in that deletion occurs under coreference with the topic.

Because of its direct connection with the organization of topic in discourse, then, zero anaphora is the most relevant of Li and Thompson's characteristics for assessing topic-prominence. The definition of "topic-prominent" can thus be extended to mean that such a language has certain ways of organizing discourse topics, including use of zero anaphora, and that certain sentential structures provide signals of this organizational pattern.

While many of these matters require further study, it is clear that the term "topic-prominence" is separable into sentence-level and discourse-level processes. Since, as Tsao points out, the proper domain for topic is discourse, it is appropriate to look to discourse-level processes such as zero anaphora for defining features of a topic-prominent language.

CONCLUSION

In conclusion, I have shown that zero anaphora in Hmong is less restricted than in English, since subject and object NPs may be zero when the referent is the discourse topic. Zero anaphora is, however, more restricted than in Chinese, since a connection between sentences rather than mere conjoinability is sometimes required for acceptable sentences with zero NPs. While topic clearly controls coreference in topic chains, in the crucial situation where a sentence has both subject and topic as in (39), the results are equivocal: control by either subject or topic is possible. Hmong thus occupies an intermediate position with regard to coreferential deletion: between English, a prototypically subject-prominent language, and Chinese, a prototypically topic-prominent language. It is interesting that this intermediate position is also reflected in characteristics: Hmong has a marginal passive and does not use "dummy" subjects, characteristics of topic-prominent languages; but is not verb-final, and it is not entirely clear that double-subject sentences are basic. Sentence-level and extrasentential processes thus reinforce each other in elucidating the role of topic in Hmong.

ACKNOWLEDGEMENTS

I would like to thank Vang Vang and Yang Dao for their help with the Hmong sentences and texts, and Bruce Downing, Jeanette Gundel, Martha Ratliff and Cynthia Perry for their helpful comments on earlier drafts of this paper. Any remaining problems are, of course, my own.

NOTES

[1] EQUI NP DELETION is a term used to indicate the deletion of one of two identical noun phrases in a sentence.

[2] Other abbreviations used in the glosses of the example sentences are as follows: 1ps refers to the first person singular pronoun, 2ps to second person singular, 3ps to third person singular, 3pp to third person plural, NEG = negative, ASP = aspect or tense marker, PRT = particle, Q = yes-no question word, RECIP = reciprocal, CLF = classifier, BE = any form of the verb be.

[3] Charles Johnson has pointed out to me that narratives such as these may require more pronoun use than other types of speech.

[4] Some speakers accept sentences with dummy subjects, but say they are seldom, if ever, used. Other speakers reject nonreferential nws completely.

[5] Chinese, a Subject-Verb-Object language, is the exception. Li and Thompson argue that Chinese is becoming verb-final.

REFERENCES

Gundel, Jeanette K. 1980. "Zero NP-Anaphora in Russian: A Case of Topic-Prominence." Papers from the Parasession on Pronouns and Anaphora. Chicago: Chicago Linguistics Society.

Heimbach, Ernest E. 1979. White Hmong-English Diction-ary, revised edition. Linguistics Series IV. South-east Asia Program Data Paper No. 75. Ithaca: Cornell University, Department of Asian Studies.

Johnson, Charles, ed. 1981. Nkauj Ntsuab thiab Sis Nab: Dab Neeg Tiaj Rhawv Zeb. Ngao Njua and Shee Na: The Story of the Plain of Jars. St. Paul: Lingustics De-partment, Macalester College.

Li, Charles N., and Sandra A. Thompson. 1976. "Subject and Topic: A New Typology of Language." Subject and Topic, ed. by Charles N. Li, pp. 457-489. New York: Academic Press Inc.

_____. 1979 "Third-Person Pronouns and Zero-Anaphora in Chinese Discourse." Syntax and Semantics 12: Dis-course and Syntax, edited by Talmy Givon, pp. 311-335. New York: Academic Press.

Lyman, Thomas Amis. 1979. Grammar of Mong Njua (Green Miao): A Descriptive Lynguistics Study. Published by the author.

Mottin, Jean. 1978. Elements de grammaire Hmong blanc. Bangkok: Don Bosco Press.

Tsao, Feng-Fu. 1979. A Functional Study of Topic in Chinese: The First Step Towards Discourse Analysis. Taipei, Taiwan: Student Book Co., Ltd.

INVESTIGATING LITERACY: APPROACHES, TOOLS, AND THEIR CONSEQUENCES FOR INQUIRY

Gail Weinstein

BACKGROUND

Chou, a young man of 25, sat patiently beside the pastor until it was time to give a Bible reading in Hmong. During his two-minute reading, the Hmong in the congregation looked up to listen, and the Americans seemed to relax and let the music of the language wash over them. After the service, someone introduced me to Chou as an English teacher who was interested in the refugees in the neighborhood. He invited me to visit at his home.

I took up the invitation despite a cold and a sore throat. After finding Chou's rowhouse, the only one intact in a row of gutted and abandoned structures, I rang the bell and waited. I was welcomed into a second-floor apartment. Two old beds, where two babies slept in heaps of blankets, had been pushed together against a wall. Plants crowded a table next to a TV against another wall. On the bathroom door, there was a magazine picture of a very muscular wrestler gritting his teeth. As soon as my cold became apparent, Chou's wife, Sai, cut some ginger root and rubbed it on my neck and arms. This marked the beginning of a lasting friendship. (The names of Chou, Sai and all other Hmong people in this paper have been changed to protect anonymity.)

Chou is among the better educated Hmong who fled from Laos. The son of a town merchant, he was able to attend school for four years before becoming a soldier. He guesses, with no aid from birth documents, that he was about twelve or thirteen when he left school to become a soldier. By then, he had already had what would prove to be some precious experience with reading. Sai, on the other hand, did not encounter printed materials until she was an adult in a Thai refugee camp. Unlike Chou, whose first written language encounters were with Lao, Sai read and wrote her first words in English shortly before her journey to the United States.

The Hmong in Philadelphia, like many other recent Hmong refugees, are faced with the transition from farming in the hilltops of Asia to coping with the people and institutions of a Western urban center. If we are to understand their situation, what are we to watch for? How do we make sense of what we see? What is the role of literacy in adaptation? How do we interpret the processes by which Chou and Sai and their kin grapple with their new lives?

PERSPECTIVES ON THE ROLE OF LITERACY

Anthropologists have long contended that it is not only difficult to shed our cultural biases and observe "objectively"--it is impossible. As effective social scientists, the best we can do is to recognize what those biases are, and to take into account what effect they will have on what we find.

The first section of this paper very briefly reviews the work of some researchers and scholars who have pondered the role of literacy in human cognitive and social development. By looking at their burning questions we can detect their underlying assumptions. By scrutinizing their research tools, we can better evaluate the scope and limits of the tools available to us.

Literacy and Evolution: The Great Transformation

Earliest discussions about literacy centered on its consequences on human cognition. Havelock (1963) argues that alphabetic writing, which originated in Greece, changed the structure of human thinking and logic. Goody (1968) builds on Havelock's assertion that a phonetic alphabet is linked with the eventuality of abstraction, and its corresponding abilities. In their work among the Wolof, Bruner (1973) and Greenfield (1972) found that illiterates scored much lower on sorting and labeling tasks than their literate counterparts, and were more "context-dependent" in communication. They conclude from their research that writing promotes cognitive development, and suggest further that "technologies" available in a given culture determine the "range and abilities" of its members. "Symbolic technologies," they argue, "push cognitive growth better, earlier, and longer than others."

English teachers will be among the first to concur that Hmong students have considerable difficulty in the classroom. In view of these difficulties, some of these suggestions are compelling. Olson (1977) examines the "shift from utterance to text" as a phenomenon characterizing individual psychological as well as cultural processes. He argues that as individuals develop, spoken language becomes less ambiguous, more explicit, and more autonomous as a representation of meaning. Of individuals and social groups, Olson writes:

> The bias of written language toward providing definitions, making assumptions and premises explicit, and observing formal rules of logic produces an instrument of considerable power for building an abstract and coherent theory of reality. [P. 273]

This argument suggests that there exists a continuum along which one could map the stage of development of any individual or culture (whose concept of reality is correspondingly coherent or incoherent). Is this model accurate? Does it explain the difficulties that Hmong people face in the classroom? More important, is it useful?

Scribner and Cole (1981) address themselves to the "writing crisis" in the United States in a manner that provides a new framework that is useful for examining literacy. In a discussion of the Vai of northwest Liberia, Scribner and Cole demonstrate that the effects of literacy are often confused with effects of formal schooling. In an extensive study (1981) they question traditional evaluative measures for testing consequences of literacy. They find that those Vai who are literate without schooling do better in some cognitive tasks than nonliterates, but only in tasks involving closely related skills. Some literacy skills are transferred to other tasks, but within a very specific range. "Logic," they find, is little affected by nonschooling literacy in the Vai people.

Scribner and Cole examine uses of literacy in English, Arabic and Vai scripts in a functional framework, looking to see which skills are used by whom for which particular ends. Their aim is to learn about cognitive consequences of literacy, specifically in areas where previous scholars have made assertions without empirical evidence. By examining the uses and functions of skills in context, Scribner and Cole are able to demonstrate how social organization creates the conditions for a variety of literary activities. With these kinds of questions in mind then, it becomes possible to examine the social organization that encourages or restrains uses of literacy as well as the social and intellectual significance of these skills.

Trouble at School: Approaches For Problem Solving

Scribner and Cole examine uses of oral and written language as well as schooled and nonschooled literacy to discover intellectual effects. Other scholars have studied these distinctions to understand and explain the difficulties faced by children as they navigate their way through urban schools. Cook-Gumperz and Gumperz (1977) argue that the move from home to school demands a change in communicative tasks in which children are required to process "decontextualized" information in new social and linguistic codes. That is to say that a formal school setting involves introduction of information that is not of immediate relevance to the social situation. While language in the home might center around immediate concerns such as preparation for mealtime or hours of available sunlight for grandma's sewing, the language of schooling is removed in content from immediate experience, and is structured in different ways.

Scollon and Scollon (1981) contrast their two-year-old daughter with other children at Fort Chipewyan in Alberta, Canada. They discover that she has skills in "decontextualization of the information structure," including fictionalizing her own role in narration. She tells a story about an experience she had, referring to herself in the third person. In a fascinating discussion, Scollon and Scollon demonstrate how a preschooler has an orientation that is characteristically literate compared with a ten-year-old Chipewyan child who can read, write and even type! That is to say, literacy is not a set of mechanical coding and decoding skills, but rather a way of processing information which will affect ways of interacting.

Scollon and Scollon conclude, as do others, that these skills are the result of specific socialization patterns in the forms of conscious parental instruction. They suggest that prose, or "essayist literacy" is under-lying our (middle class) caretaker talk, and language and activity structures of Western schooling. Michaels (1981) examines language in classrooms with black and white children. She finds that white teachers interpret black children's differences in narrative style during "show and tell" time as behavioral or cognitive deficits. While the work of Scollon and Scollon and Cook-Gumperz and Gumperz make it clear that there are a variety of orientations that are socially and situationally deter-mined, Michaels raises the dilemma that only one style is legitimized in certain settings.

Researchers who have approached literacy with the purpose of understanding and solving problems of children in schools have raised new questions and challenged old ways of viewing literacy. They suggest that literacy is not only a set of mechanical skills residing in individu-als. Rather, new insight can be gained by viewing liter-acy also as a mode of communication that takes on meaning within specific social contexts.

Literacy and the Social Order

Scholars who have investigated literacy practices in traditional societies--Goody (1968) among them--have found that writing is associated with a wide variety of political, social and economic activities. Reder and Green (1983), in a thorough study of literacy activities in an Eskimo fishing village, follow two major historical strands in the development of literacy on the island: Russian and English. By observing the practice of liter-acy—that is, who writes what, where and under what con-ditions--they discover that there are distinct domains of literacy activity associated with each strand. In this study, Reder and Green present an analysis in which they demonstrate that social activity both shapes and is shaped by the distribution of literacy activities. Therefore, literacy provides a window into the structure of the social order, and the social arrangement furthers the understanding of literacy practices in cultural context.

Heath (1980) brings the framework closer to home. Examining the functions and uses of literacy in a black working class community in the southeastern United States, she argues that there are discontinuities between the meanings of reading and writing for families in the community as opposed to in the schools where their children are enrolled.

Ogbu (1980) makes a very strong case that cultural discontinuity alone cannot explain the "failure" of black children in American schools. He argues that blacks, and other "caste-like" minorities find themselves in a society with such strong gatekeeping mechanisms (e.g., job ceilings) that no amount of mastery of literacy skills in "essayist" or any other style is likely to affect or alter their position in the economic order. By looking at the black example, it becomes apparent that observing the functions and uses of literacy within a minority group is not sufficient for understanding the role of literacy in adaptation. It is also necessary to examine the social and economic context within which the minority must operate.

Literacy and Adaptation: Preparation for Inquiry

Much of the literature on literacy and "oral/literate" cultures makes generalizations that are broad and far-reaching. These generalizations, while appealing, become problematic in light of the bothersome details that are yielded when researchers study the use of language in everyday life. For these reasons, I argue that researchers should bring several assumptions to the task.

1. The meaning of reading and writing are problematic. Studies of people in communities show that definitions of reading, writing and literacy are problematic both within and between groups. As Gilmore (1982) listens to classroom teachers lament that the kids don't know how to write, she observes the children passing a series of elaborate notes to one another under their desks. The social context will determine what kinds of reading or writing "count" or not.

2. The relationship of speech and text are also problematic. While Olson's distinctions between the nature of utterance and text are stimulating, researchers who study actual language use find that even these distinctions become fuzzy. Tannen (1982) finds that features used earlier to characterize text versus speech could be found to differing degrees in the speech of two different groups. Lakoff (1982) reflects on ways in which writers use both oral and literate strategies in written communication to achieve specific effects. Observations of some Hmong families reveal that oral and written modes of communication are being used in interesting ways. Letters that relatives in other states or countries send to these families are usually read out loud to several listeners. Letters often include cassette tapes with oral messages. Speech and text are not distinct entities with clear boundaries. They are modes of communication within a communicative economy, in which changes in technology and/or social organization change the balance of how these modes are used and how they interact.

3. The third assumption is twofold: first, that individuals are rational beings whose behavior reflects rational choices within their perceived options, and second, that inquiry into human behavior must take into account the individual, the group(s) to which s/he belongs, and the wider social context in which the group(s) operate. The "orality" or "literacy" of cultures is meaningless if we know nothing of those who participate in them. Accounts of individuals are meaningless without recognition of the wider context in which they operate.

4. Investigation must have an empirical base. Suspicions about the nature of literacy are interesting, but investigation of real people using language for specific ends holds the most promise for discovery, and for interesting surprises.

We are fortunate, indeed, to have the opportunity to explore the nature of literacy in our own backyard. What is most fortunate is that we have the chance to collaborate with our rugged, resourceful new neighbors--the Hmong.

SOME SOCIAL CONSEQUENCES OF LITERACY: REFLECTIONS OF A BACKYARD ETHNOGRAPHER

To begin to explore the role of literacy in everyday life, I arranged to spend four weeks with Chou and Sai and their two children. On weekdays, after our respective days of studying, childcare and teaching, we shared the evening meal. Weekends afforded more time for visiting, sewing, and excursions (i.e., to Reading to visit a sick brother or to the Spectrum for an evening of wrestling).

I discovered that four weeks was time enough to do little more than lay the foundations of a friendship--if friendship grows from sharing not only great adventures, but also daily routines. Also, as I looked on while Chou and Sai navigated their way through welfare and educational bureaucracies, community activities and a variety of interactions with both Americans and Hmong, I made many discoveries.

I will suggest in these pages that literacy, as one among many modes of language, can be viewed as (1) a tool used for negotiating with new institutions, (2) a tool possessed by those who mediate between culture groups, and (3) a tool associated with articulating new social status in a changing social order.

By describing some glimpses I have caught through my tiny keyhole, I hope to create a framework in which literacy can be examined as an addition as well as an agent of change in a whole communicative economy, with profound effects on the relationships of the participants.

Literacy As a Tool for Negotiating with New Institutions

One Tuesday afternoon, Chou received a letter from his caseworker saying that he had to show up at her office Friday morning, or his "case" would be "closed." The letter instructed him to bring four documents with him, including one which had to be stamped by an agency several miles away (and not easily accessible by public transportation), and others which required picking up various forms with signatures from different places.

Chou had already planned to take off from school on Thursday afternoon to pay phone and electric bills.   He says he has to pay them in cash because if he puts more than a very small amount of money in a checking account, his benefits will be cut.   This left only Thursday morning, since he had a test in school on Wednesday that he felt he could not miss.

That evening, Chou spent time usually set aside for homework to fix his bicycle.   He knew that he could not cover all necessary bases on foot in one day.   He called his English teacher to tell her he would be absent on Thursday and Friday.

On Friday, Chou reported to his caseworker with all of the forms that he had gathered.   Both his signature and Sai's were required, and both had to be made in the presence of the caseworker.   So when Chou got home at about midday, he took over the child care so that Sai could repeat the journey.   We took the Broad Street subway.   I showed Sai how to distinguish the northbound from the southbound train, and how to find the right stop for future reference.

At the welfare office, we waited in bolted-down wooden seats for Sai's name to be called.   On the wall across from where we were sitting were two written signs: "EFFECTIVE 11-8-81 Foodstamps will be given out only between 2:30 and 3:30 p.m." and also, "PLEASE NOTE: Any foodstamps not picked up within five days will be returned to Harrisburg."   Sai's name was called.   She signed the form and we left.

Chou comments that he likes his present caseworker because "she help us everything."   Just lucky, he reflects.   In his previous apartment in another neighborhood, the old caseworker "window broken, he don't care. No heat, he not do anything.   New baby born, he don't help extra money."   Some neighbors have difficulty even with the "good" caseworker.   An older woman living one floor below does not know how to decipher forms, letters or bills.   Preparing the required documents is an insurmountable task for her.   One evening Chou disappeared with a pan full of meat.   Returning to the apartment, he explained that he had intervened with the caseworker on the woman's behalf, getting $125 and $60 for gas on two occasions.   Therefore, the woman lets Chou and Sai use her oven from time to time to help them save money on their own gas bill.

When the old woman cannot solve a problem, she sometimes brings it to Chou. When Chou is stuck, he turns to me or to another American in his church. He had done this on many occasions with puzzling bills or difficult homework. Sometimes a favor is returned in kind, as illustrated above with the gas money. Other requests for help cause conflict.

Chou had been complaining for a couple of days about a man who wanted him to write a fraudulent letter to welfare. The man, who lived six blocks away, had asked Chou to claim that he lived with him so that he could pick up a welfare check at Chou's address. I arrived one afternoon to find the two in frank discussion. When the man left, Chou was angry. "He want me to cheat for him.... He not my relative, he never help me anything. He just make trouble for me." Chou felt that the request was inappropriate, and that it jeopardized his own standing with welfare. I advised him not to do it, as had another American.

I'm not sure why Chou was called upon for this favor. He is neither a neighbor nor a clan member. I suspect it may be related to the fact that Chou is among the few literate household heads who would be able to perform the task.

Chou later received a call from a man who he explains has a leadership position in Philadelphia. As in many other cities, social service agencies hired the earlier Hmong arrivals who became bilingual to work in the resettlement process. These people have become the prime mediators between the caseworkers and the Hmong population in the area. Not coincidentally, Chou tells me, the members of some clans seem to fare best in matters that require attention from the social service system. For example, Chou said that when he first arrived, the leader called the police when Sai was in labor. He did not take the time to accompany the couple to the hospital as he did for certain other families. Because he spoke very little English at the time, Chou felt helpless when the doctors decided to perform a Caesarean section on Sai. He is sure that it could have been avoided with the right advocacy. In Laos, this leader would appropriately be expected to aid members of his own clan. As a caseworker in Philadelphia, however, he is seen by Americans as a representative of "the Hmong" and is asked to be an advocate for members of many clans. The old and new expectations do not always harmonize.

The leader, then, asked Chou to do this welfare letter for the young man. While listening to the Americans on one hand, Chou felt, I suspect, trapped by powerful social and political pressures from within the Hmong community. The dilemma had no clear solution. As the phone continued to ring, and Chou's homework lay neglected, he shouted in exasperation, "Too many calls! Too many questions!" With that, he pulled the phone wires out of the wall and sat down to do his homework, complaining, "Everybody want something from me!"

From these examples, it becomes clear that decoding and composing documents play an important role in economic survival. Those who have literacy skills must use them to gain and maintain benefits, and those who don't must often rely on those who do. Who may rely on whom is problematic. Whereas dependence relationships once resided within families and clans, new categories such as caseworker/client, cotenant/client or urban neighbor/client pose new possibilities and pressures for different kinds of interaction in this new setting.

Literacy As a Tool Used by Those Who Mediate Between Culture Groups

Members of Chou's church feel their way as they accommodate the hefty new population of refugees. Incorporating the Hmong into religious life was a priority. On any given Sunday, one or several Hmong couples are baptized, becoming full members of the "church family" (a term used by one of the Sunday school teachers).

Chou used to spend several hours each Saturday studying the Bible with the pastor. Thus prepared, he led Sunday school Bible lessons in Hmong for those who could not understand English. The group consists mostly of new arrivals, women and older men. With the Lao Bible and English Bible close at hand, Chou is able to synthesize each lesson to convey it to the group.

Until their language mastery improves, newcomers depend on interpreters like Chou to open a sort of lifeline with the church, permitting exchange of information and participation that would otherwise be impossible. In a conversation with me over a year ago, the pastor confided that he was having difficulties at that time because the Hmong leader/translator had just moved with many in his clan to resettle in Rhode Island. To his relief, Chou has moved into the vacant position, bringing "wisdom" from the American religious leader into the world of the Hmong, and providing a way for the Hmong to become part of the church community.

When Chou does his short reading for the whole congregation, he is, in another sense, bringing a bit of Hmong culture over for consumption by Americans. His seat next to the pastor during the service, and his name printed in the service program legitimize both the task and Chou himself as mediator in the exchange.

Because his knowledge of English makes him accessible, I suspect, several congregation members have called Chou to offer him small wages for doing work in their homes. When he is unable to comply with all offers on his one precious Saturday, he is usually free to supply the name of an alternate.

Chou's role as mediator extends past the boundaries of the church. During my stay at Chou's home, a social worker from a neighboring church called, asking him to translate a sign that requested users of a free clothing room to limit the amount that they took, from English to Hmong. Chou had been identified to her as an able writer, and she contacted him immediately. That evening he put aside his homework and wrote and rewrote the message until he was satisfied that it was well done. The social worker picked it up that same evening, thanking him for the effort.

This woman, a community worker, depended on Chou to convey information to Hmong people who were using the services of her own church. Chou is therefore becoming a mediator for the neighborhood as well as for his own church.

Chou spends time deliberately cultivating relationships with Americans. Before I moved in with him and his family, he would often call me on the telephone for no apparent reason except to chat. One afternoon during my four-week stay, when I returned to his apartment, I found him going systematically through his memo-pad phone directory calling each American on his list, one by one.

The content of each conversation was more or less the same, as he asked each person what was "up" and spoke of his own state of affairs.   My impression was that he enjoys trying to keep his American "friends," including teachers, church members--and oddballs like ethnographers--engaged as long as possible.   The decision he and Sai made to let me live with them for a month was another daring move to allow an American into his world.

Incorporation of Americans into Chou's life surely has its benefits, but it must also have its price.   After I moved in with Chou and Sai, a young Hmong man began "accidentally" kicking Chou repeatedly during soccer games.   Sai found herself the object of suspicious questions at church.   Chou and Sai asked which Hmong people I had told about the stay, and asked that I keep the arrangement private.   I didn't know whether the conflict arose out of jealousy, suspicion or some other factor.

At one point, I asked Chou and Sai if they wanted me to leave.   They assured me that I could stay, but their request for my discretion made it clear what a sensitive issue this was.   There is surely ground for much investigation to better understand the gains and sacrifices involved in becoming a bridge between two culture groups.

Literacy As a Tool Associated with Articulating New Social Status In a Changing Social Order

The New Year: Tradition and Change.   One November, my oldest student, fifty-eight-year-old Jou, invited me to join her in New Year's preparations.   She led me to a home on Powelton Avenue where thirty Hmong women were crowded into one room, wrapping colorful sashes over their black velvet garb.   Coin- and silver-bedecked children ran in and out from the street, playing with each other.   Jou's daughter helped the other women bind their hair in dark turbans with striped bands criss-crossed over them.   One lovely teenager, who was heavily laden with coins and beads and had black velvet wrapped around her calves, threw a shiny green silk jacket on over her dress.   Across the back, in large letters, was printed "ROLLER DISCO".

A couple of months before this New Year celebration, a meeting of the Hmong Association was called.   A couple of hundred Hmong went by bus to gather at the Indochinese

Center. The association was then headed by a young man
who is in his thirties. Jou's son showed me a flyer, in
Hmong, with instructions and news of committee responsibilities for different aspects of the affair. It outlined financial arrangements, job responsibilities and
subsequent meeting times.

In the hills of Laos, New Year was an event anticipated all year. Heads of clans in each village, always
the eldest men, met to arrange the event. Apparently New
Year's festivals were planned at different times for different places, in order that villages might reciprocally
invite one another to their activities. Young men and
women would line up in rows facing each other, throwing
back and forth a cloth ball that the girls had made from
their sewing scraps. Boys would sing, serenading, beginning a process of courtship that would become manifest
with a rash of marriages following the New Year.

How has literacy as a new communicative mode played
a part in changing the social order? Previously, a household head would call the meetings by word of mouth. Responsibilities were delegated and carried out accordingly. As Hmong people find themselves spread throughout a
city, written materials become useful to organize meetings and arrange for bus transportation. As information-
sharing begins to depend on a literate mode, what happens
to the role of elders in leadership? How will decisions
be made when young people are the only ones who have direct access to information and resources?

On the second day of the New Year festivities, cos-
tumed young men and women line up facing one another on a
strip of park grass in Philadephia's Germantown. They
threw green tennis balls back and forth. Jou complained
that the boys didn't know the words to the traditional
songs anymore. But can a Hmong boy still impress a girl
with blessings and prayers he has memorized? These
skills will no longer be crucial to prove himself a good
husband. In an environment where information is recorded
on paper, what traits will be sought or desired in a
mate?

The Craft Sale. It takes time for an outside observer to discover the talents of Hmong women. Returning
to the apartment in the afternoons, I would often find
Sai sewing decorative squares while she rocked her youngest child on her back in a brightly embroidered baby car-

rier.   Characterized by tiny precise stitches, reverse applique and stunning colors, the handiwork is awesome. To my delight, Sai often works with her sister and mother, as well as other passers-through.   All are happy to chatter or sit quietly as I join them with my crocheting. From such gatherings, I got the idea of inviting my friends to a party at which the Hmong women could display their pieces for sale.   So I planned one.   The party succeeded to the tune of $700 of collective sales.   The money was distributed to the individual artists whose pieces were sold.

I suggested to Chou and Sai that each woman contribute one or two dollars for a kitty to cover refreshments for the party, and to start some collective savings for renting craft tables or even eventually saving for a storefront.   Chou spoke out: "Hmong people can pay for food at the party, but not to save money together.   My name _____ (clan name), I help _____ (members of same clan).   We don't trust money together."

There were the divisions, starkly clear.   Family helps within family, clan helps within clan.   Cooperation was only possible to repay the American authority.   An interesting conflict then arose.   By miscommunication between myself and another American who was keeping books, money was not collected for reimbursing me for the refreshments.   I brought it to Chou's attention.   "Don't worry," he comforted me.   He would collect the money from the people in Sunday school.   He could not collect from the other sale participants.   "They not obey me," he said.   "But people in my church, I think we can help you." A new unit of cooperation is being formed--members of a congregation who can be influenced to act by a young man who may or may not share their name.

Chou once commented to me, "I don't have family here--I have my church.   People help me, give me a desk, dresser, chair...."   Indeed, the church has been a source of furniture and clothing for Chou and Sai.   During my short stay at their home, individual congregation members lent a space heater when the heat was broken and moved to investigate the delay in bringing Chou's brother over from Thailand, among other things.   They have provided those things for which, in the past, Chou could only turn to "family" or clan.

It remains to be seen how, as Hmong refugees adapt to their new urban environment, literacy will take its place within the communicative economy. Likewise, as the new mode of communication enters the social fabric, it will be interesting to note what impact literacy has on the process by which relationships between people evolve and change.

NOTE: On Being an Ethnographer

It would be easiest to say that I wanted to understand my students in order to be more effective as a literacy teacher, that I wanted to know how they processed things, what they could use, and what was important, so I could make the classroom work. The truth is, however, that I became an English teacher because I wanted to find out how these people made sense of the world--not the other way around! Peasant farmers, who once organized their lives around the rhythms of subsistence survival, find themselves in a foreign, literate city. How do they manage?

To many of the Hmong I have known, I am an English teacher. I help them unravel the language, tell them about their new city and decipher bills and other strange documents. To Chou and Sai I have been a frequent visitor, an unsuccessful language learner, an appreciative consumer of Hmong food, a source of rides, homework help and tickets to the Spectrum wrestling matches. I have also been a hostess to parties where Hmong women can sell their crafts. And I am one who does not understand the relationships between actors in the "Hmong Community"-- community being my own choice of word and perhaps not one that the Hmong would use to describe themselves. I have also been a source of conflict for Chou and Sai, whose hospitality has caused various tensions for them with others in the community. I don't know what other things I am to them. A source of favors? A social worker? An enigmatic curiosity? A lone person to take in and nurture? A source of language input and help? A friend?

To me, Chou and Sai have been many things. They are model survivors. From Laos, across the Mekong, to boring dirty refugee camps, to Powelton where they were robbed and their neighbors' children beaten by angry black kids,

they somehow managed to continue with gentleness, cour-
tesy and good humor. They are a keyhole into a complex
world that I have barely glimpsed. They are young people, making decisions about how to balance the old and
the new. They have been hosts who have fed me, housed
me, invited me to sleep next to them when it was cold.
They are fun companions to watch wrestling with, and they
are family to share good meals with. They are newcomers
who need tips about getting around, and they are new language learners who can use my help in some areas.

I suspect that they have given me far more than I
can give them. The "homestay" is over, but the feeling
of home remains. In response to their obvious hurt/dis-
appointment when I prepared to move back home, I left my
nightgown for occasional overnight visits. That seemed
to appease their suspicion that I was pulling out forever. Indeed, if luck is with me, I will know Chou and
Sai for a long time--and have the good fortune to continue a process with them of having fun together, sharing
things, figuring each other out, and learning from each
other more about the world and how it can look from different eyes.

REFERENCES

Bruner, J.S. 1973. "From Communication to Language: A
Psychological Perspective." Cognition 3:255-287.

Cook-Gumperz, Jenny, and John Gumperz. 1977. "From Oral
to Written Culture: the Transition to Literacy". In
Writing: The Nature, Development, and Teaching of
Written Communication. Vol I: Variation in Writing:
Functional and Linguistic-Cultural Differences, edited by Marcia Farr Whiteman, pp. 89-109. Hillsdale, N.J.: Lawrence Erlbaum Associates.

Gilmore, Perry. 1982. "Gimme Room: A Cultural Approach
to the Study of Attitudes and Admission to Literacy." Ph.D. dissertation, University of Pennsylvania.

Goody, Jack. 1968. "The Consequences of Literacy." In _Literacy in Traditional Societies_, edited by Jack Goody. New York: Cambridge University Press.

Greenfield, P.M. 1972. "Oral or Written Language: The Consequences for Cognitive Development in Africa, the United States and England." _Language and Speech_ 15:199-77.

Havelock, Eric A. 1963. _Preface to Plato_. Cambridge, Mass.: Belknop Press of Harvard University Press.

Heath, Shirley. 1980. "The Functions and Uses of Literacy." _Journal of Communication_ 30(1): 123-134.

Lakoff, Robin. 1982. "Some of My Favorite Writers are Literate: The Mingling of Oral and Literate Strategies in Written Communication." In _Spoken and Written Language_, edited by D. Tannen, Norwood, N.J.: Ablex Publishing Corporation.

Michaels, Sarah. 1981. "Sharing Time: An Oral Preparation for Literacy." Presented at Ethnography in Education Research Forum, University of Pennsylvania.

Ogbu, John. 1980. "Literacy in Subordinate Cultures: The Case of Black Americans." Paper presented at the Literacy Conference, Library of Congress, Washington, D.C., July 14-15.

Olson, David R. 1977. "From Utterance to Text: The Bias of Language in Speech and Writing." _Harvard Educational Review_ 47(3): 257-281.

Reder, Steven, and Karen Green. 1983. "Contrasting Patterns of Literacy in an Alaska Fishing Village." _International Journal of the Sociology of Language_ 42: 9-13.

Scollon, Ron, and Suzanne Scollon. 1981. "The Literate Two Year Old: The Fictionalization of Self." In _Narrative, Literacy and Face in Interethnic Communication_. Norwood, N.J.: Ablex Publishing Corporation.

Scribner, Sylvia, and Michael Cole. 1981. "Unpackaging Literacy." In <u>Writing: The Nature, Development, and Teaching of Written Communication</u>. Vol. I: <u>Variation in Writing: Functional and Linguistic-Cultural Differences</u>, edited by Marcia Farr Whiteman, pp. 71-87. Hillsdale, N.J.: Lawrence Erlbaum Associates.

Tannen, Deborah. 1982. "The Myth of Orality and Literacy." In <u>Linguistics and Literacy</u>, edited by William Frawley. New York: Plenum Press.

FACTORS IN INDIVIDUAL ACQUISITION OF ENGLISH: A LONGITUDINAL STUDY OF HMONG ADULTS

Karen Reed Green and Stephen Reder

Within the past ten to fifteen years, adult second language acquisition has become the subject of a number of studies. Second language acquisition research in general has followed in the footsteps of studies of first language acquisition, primarily focusing on children learning a language and attempting to answer the question, "Is second language learning like the first?" (e.g., Ervin-Tripp 1974). Adults' experience with language learning has been compared with that of children. Studies have pointed out the similarities in the processes of first and second language learning (Chamot 1981; Krahnke and Christison 1983); they have also shown that children and adults tend to follow similar patterns in the order in which they acquire certain grammatical aspects of the second language (Dulay and Burt 1974; Bailey, Madden and Krashen 1974). Although comparisons of rate of acquisition and proficiency attained by children and adults appear to vary in their findings, in general such studies concur that adults and older children acquire the second language faster in the early stages, but that children will usually attain greater proficiency than adults in the long run (Krashen, Long and Scarcella 1979).

Considerable discussion has evolved regarding factors which may explain these differences in rate of acquisition and proficiency between children and adults, as well as individual differences observed among adults. Suggestions include characteristics such as language aptitude, verbal intelligence, sense of self-esteem, willingness to take risks, attitude toward the language or culture in which it is used (social and psychological distance), and motivation to acquire the language. Other factors beyond the individual also considered to be influential include social aspects of the interaction between the two language groups (relative size of the groups, attitudes toward each other, etc.). Researchers

299

generally agree on the importance of social and affective factors in second language acquisition (Gardner and Lambert 1972; Krahnke and Christison 1983; Lambert 1981; Schumann 1975, 1976; Stauble 1980). However, they have found such factors difficult to measure.

Despite the growing interest in adult second language acquisition, most of the research to date has been of only minimal utility to individuals who teach English to recent immigrants and refugees in this country. In part, this is due to the still limited number of studies which focus on adults. However, the major barrier to applying the research is the disparity between the characteristics of the adult subjects of most studies and the backgrounds of the many adults who have arrived in this country in the last five years. In general, researchers have examined the acquisition of a host country language by foreign students or educated foreigners (such as Americans living abroad). Such individuals have been highly educated in their own countries and enter at a high level into the educational system in the country in which they are studying. The differences are very clear between the educational attainment and other background characteristics of university-level foreign students and adult refugee English as a Second Language (ESL) students from third-world rural agricultural backgrounds.

The present paper contributes to the growing body of research on factors which influence adult second language acquisition by clarifying the important role of background characteristics in the acquisition of English. The backgrounds of the adults in this study contrast sharply with those of participants in other studies: the subjects here are Hmong refugees--slash-and-burn farmers from the mountains of Laos, individuals with little or no formal schooling and often no previous literacy skills. Through a combination of qualificative and quantitative methodologies, the study examines these individuals' acquisition of English in light of the differing background experiences each individual brings to the acquisition process and also considers the influence of each person's current activities.

Our research with the Hmong has been conducted in several phases:

1) ethnographic fieldwork and informal English classes with a cohort of 10 adults,

2)   a community survey of 332 households and

3)   a longitudinal study of the acquisition of English by the adults in 20 randomly selected families over a year's time.

We began our work with the Hmong by conducting informal English classes with five men and five women recently arrived in this country and settled in a large urban center on the West Coast. The classes were a rich source of information about English language and literacy acquisition and evolving perceptions about literacy, as well as a vehicle through which to network out into the students' extended families. During a year and a half, we participated in the adjustment of these people to life in their new environment and observed their growing use of English language and literacy skills in their daily lives. This first phase of the research revealed wide variation among Hmong adults in their acquisition of spoken and written English. To investigate these differences further, information was needed about the distribution of background variables and formative experiences among community members.

A community-wide household survey (reported in Reder 1982) was conducted to obtain a quantitative picture of the variation in factors that the previous ethnographic work had suggested might be critical in language and literacy development. Interviews were conducted with 332 household heads--approximately 90 percent of the community. Topics included the educational and linguistic backgrounds of family members over the age of twelve, family migration history, employment and English language training, economic and religious status, and any additional concerns voiced by the interviewees. Also included was a self-report measure of English proficiency by Hmong adult household members. The results of that survey indicated that the process of acquisition is heavily influenced by the background . characteristics (e.g., age, previous education, literacy) which individuals bring with them to learning a second language. In other words, people are differentially ready to acquire English when they enter this country.

To investigate the apparent causal links suggested by the household survey and to measure language profi-

ciency objectively as it develops over time, a longitudinal study was designed. This study complements both prior
phases of the research. On the one hand, by following a
smaller number of individuals over time, the longitudinal
work could achieve greater depth than the household survey; on the other hand, by focusing on objective assessment and documentation of individuals' language and literacy skills and knowledge at specific points of time, it
provides quantitative data which complement that obtained
in the ethnographic phase of the work.

     This paper will describe the methodology used to
trace this group of Hmong adults' acquisition of English
language and literacy over a year's time and then focus
on some of the study's preliminary results. Once we have
discussed the acquisition documented during this time
period, we shall examine the factors which seem to account for individual differences in acquisition of
English.

METHODS

Sampling Procedure

     From the comprehensive community survey population,
a random sample of twenty families was selected. Since
findings from the initial phase of the research had suggested that most Hmong adults acquire only minimal English language and literacy proficiency during their first
year in this country, the sample of families was strati-
fied by length of time they had been in the United
States. The households in the community survey were thus
divided into four groups, based on the length of time the
head of the household had been in the United States: zero
to five months, six to eleven months, twelve to seventeen
months and eighteen to twenty-three months. These strata
were then filled with families selected randomly--five
from each of the four time groups. This purposeful stra-
tification allowed observation of various periods of language and literacy acquisition: the observations during
the longitudinal study represented one year in four different segments of a three-year period of acquisition and
adjustment. That is, at the end of the study the families

had been in this country from one to three years, having arrived between early 1979 and early 1981.

Characteristics of the Study Population

The sample of twenty families included fifty-nine adults age eighteen and over who agreed to participate in the year of observation and assessment. Eight additional adults live in these households, but were not included in the study due to extreme age, physical or mental disabilities, or reluctance. The fifty-nine participants were nearly equally divided among women and men. Their ages ranged from eighteen to seventy-two; nearly half of the sample were between the ages of twenty-five and thirty-five. As indicated in Table 1, this group as a whole had rather limited experience with literacy and education: 80 percent had not attended school in Laos; 81.5 percent could not read Lao, a skill which was acquired through formal schooling in Laos. Literacy in Hmong, on the other hand, was acquired informally; 29.6 percent of this population reported having at least some proficiency in reading Hmong.[1] The ability to speak Lao could also be acquired informally, through social contacts and trade. Thus, more individuals could speak Lao than could read it--slightly over half the population.

Maintenance of the Cohort

During the course of this research, the Hmong community under study--like many other Hmong communities around the country--began to experience the flux of secondary migration. By the spring of 1982, approximately three-quarters of the population had moved to California. By the time of the study's second assessment visit (July and August 1982), 85 percent of the study participants had moved to one of four different cities in the Central Valley. Fortunately, they were all willing to continue to participate and we were able to follow them to their new homes. However, by the end of the year, 28.8 percent of the individuals who had originally agreed to participate in the longitudinal study had dropped out for varying reasons, including lack of time or interest, or health problems. In addition to that attrition, some individuals who remained with the study until its comple-

TABLE 1

Background Characteristics of the Longitudinal Study Population
Full Sample and After Attrition

Background Characteristics	Full Sample		Individuals Participating in Both First and Last Assessments	
Age*				
Range	18 - 72		18 - 71	
Mean	35.2		35.9	
	n	Percent	n	Percent
Sex				
Women	28	47.5	18	48.6
Men	31	52.5	19	51.4
Proficiency in Speaking Lao				
None	26	48.1	17	48.6
Some	28	51.9	18	51.4
Proficiency in Reading Hmong				
None	38	70.4	26	74.3
Some	16	29.6	9	25.7
Proficiency in Reading Lao				
None	44	81.5	29	82.9
Some	10	18.5	6	17.1
Education in Laos				
None	44	80.0	30	83.3
Some	11	20.0	6	16.7
Education in U.S.*				
Under 1 year	27	55.1	16	47.1
Over 1 Year	22	44.9	18	52.9
Length of Residence in U.S.				
0-5 months	13	24.5	9	25.7
6-11 months	24	45.3	16	45.7
12-17 months	12	22.6	9	25.7
18-23 months	4	7.5	1	2.9

Note: Unless otherwise indicated, these data were gathered during the
household survey conducted in April and May 1981.

*by the time of Assessment 2 (July and August 1982)

tion had been unable to participate in the first assessment. Thus, the number of people who were part of both the first and last assessments was reduced to 63 percent of the original group.

As seen in Table 1, this attrition fortunately had very little effect on the composition of the cohort in terms of background characteristics, length of residence in the United States or amount of schooling taken here.

Background Interviews

Prior to initiating bimonthly objective assessments of individuals' English capabilities, a series of in-depth interviews was conducted with each of the 20 families. These interviews focused on the families' backgrounds and experiences in Laos and Thailand and document the nature and extent of individuals' exposure to formal education, literacy and other languages prior to their arrival in the United States, as well as their knowledge and uses of literacy in the various environments. Information was gathered regarding who acquired literacy, who used it for various purposes and how they were perceived by others, how the uses and perceptions of literacy changed with the move from villages in Laos to camps in Thailand, etc.[2]

Bimonthly Assessment Visits

Once the background interviews were completed, we began to visit the families every two months, starting in late May and early June 1982, and thereafter continuing over a year's time. Several hours each visit were spent with each adult family member (men and women over the age of eighteen).

During an assessment visit, time was spent with each individual discussing activities and experiences which had taken place during the two months since the preceding visit. A series of assessment tasks was then conducted. Numerous tasks using varied materials were devised to assess individuals' oral English proficiency, their abilities to read and write in English, and their knowledge of the uses of English literacy in this country. In addition, proficiency in reading and writing Hmong and Lao were documented. Some tasks were conducted every visit to establish developmental trends, others only periodically, and some only during the first and last visits to capture overall changes.

A standardized ESL test (the Basic English Skills Test, or B.E.S.T., developed by the Center for Applied Linguistics for use with adult Southeast Asian refugees) was administered during the first assessment visit and again during the final (seventh) session. All other tasks were specially developed for these assessments; they include the oral identification of pictured English vocabulary items, recognition of written English vocabulary items, repetition of sentences of varying length and grammatical complexity, reading and writing of materials sampled from selected genres of written English, Hmong and Lao (e.g., a social letter, an agency form letter, a job application, a change of address form, a sample of driver's test questions, etc.), and demonstration of knowledge of the uses of written materials common in daily life in the United States.

In designing these assessment tasks, we drew on our previous experience in helping Hmong friends learn English. Care was taken to employ not only a broad range of written materials, but also diverse contexts and methods, since in this phase of the research it was not feasible to follow this group of adults (fifty-nine individuals dispersed into five different cities) out of their homes and into their interactions using new language and literacy skills in the surrounding host community. Thus, individual lexical items were presented in varied contexts-- e.g., as isolated vocabulary items as well as in the genre of a form letter, bill or street sign.

A "literacy portfolio" of frequently encountered written artifacts was compiled, consisting of actual newspaper ads, receipts, prescriptions, registration forms, bills, etc., and photographs of street signs, license plates, store windows and so forth. Items in this portfolio were discussed with study participants in English or in Hmong as the individual preferred, since the purpose of this task was not merely to determine the extent of each individual's ability to read these items, but rather his or her understanding of what they represent and what functions they serve. In addition to recognition of the item and specification of the way it is used, questions were asked about each participant's personal experience using it, frequency of use, need for assistance in using it, etc. In this way, information was gathered on individuals' exposure to a wide range of literacy items and the situations in which they are used as well as the social networks that have developed within the community to cope with the new demands posed by the wider literate society. The portfolio was presented at the beginning and end of the year of observation to document acquisition of knowledge and changes in experience with the items.

Other purposive data collection also took place throughout the year. Information about individual participants' educational and employment status was updated every two months. Twice during the year the types of activities outside the home in which individuals participated were discussed. The nature and frequency of the activity and the role, if any, which literacy (in English, Hmong or Lao) played in it were carefully noted. Preliminary analyses midway through the study indicated the importance of native language literacy as a predictor of both oral and written English proficiency. This finding, which substantiated earlier findings from the ethnographic and survey phases of the research, prompted the collection of additional information about the phenomenon of Hmong literacy. Discussions focused on the uses of Hmong literacy, methods and materials used for acquiring it, and the reasons some Hmong are continuing to learn to read and write Hmong in this country.

MEASURING ACQUISITION

Two of the objectives of this longitudinal study were, first, to observe and document the ongoing process of language and literacy acquisition in the Hmong community, and second, to identify factors which influence that acquisition. The results reported here are based on preliminary analyses of the first and last assessments of three of the measures mentioned above: (1) the Basic English Skills Test (B.E.S.T.), (2) the recognition of pictured English vocabulary items, and (3) the recognition of written English vocabulary items. Comparisons of each of these measures, between the first and last visits, indicate that acquisition took place over the year's time.

(See Figures 1-3.) The mean scores on these measures improved from 13.2 to 22.7 percent.

The B.E.S.T.

The B.E.S.T. Core Section is described as assessing five areas of skill: listening comprehension, communication, pronunciation, fluency, and reading and writing. All but pronunciation were scored in this study. The version administered in this study has a maximum possible score of 90. The highest score among these adults at the beginning of the year was 88, the lowest 1; by the end of the year the range was 0-83. Thus, both at the start and the finish of the year, the range of abilities in this population was quite wide. The group mean for the total score on the B.E.S.T. was 35.57 at the start of the year; by the end it had gone up 15 percent to 40.92. (See Figure 1.) Fifty-four of the fifty-nine adults in the longitudinal study took the B.E.S.T. at the beginning of the year, whereas thirty-eight took it at the end. Thirty-seven people took both tests; comparative analyses presented here include only these individuals.

Pictured English Vocabulary Recognition

This task used pictures to measure the acquisition of oral English vocabulary by Hmong adults. During each of six bimonthly visits, participating adults were asked to identify orally pictures of a randomly assigned set of vocabulary items in English. The population of pictures used in this task was taken from the Peabody Articulation Cards (PAC), originally designed for use with children and adults whose speech production requires further development or remediation.[3] These cards were selected for use here because of the clarity and realism of the pictures. Since the medium is pictures, the words are mainly nouns; some verbs and a few adjectives (colors) are included. The 350 pictured words in the PAC were screened to eliminate items which were ambiguous to Hmong adults. From a total of 210 acceptable words, six sets of thirty pictures were randomly generated. Fifteen additional words were selected for inclusion in all six assessments: ten randomly selected items and five items purposely chosen for their relative simplicity and frequency of use.

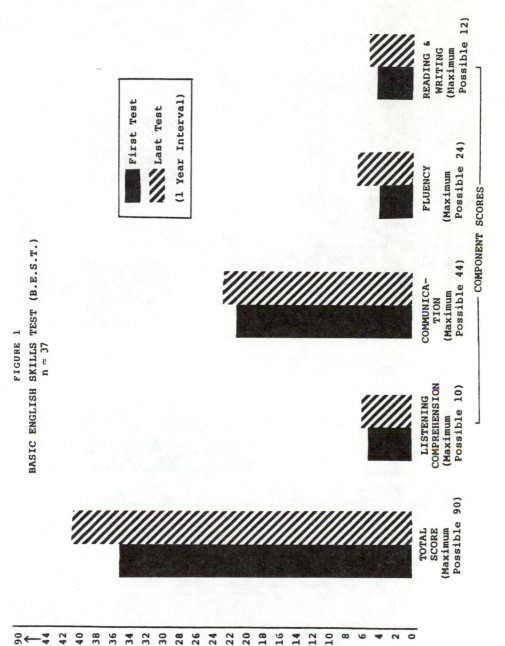

FIGURE 1

BASIC ENGLISH SKILLS TEST (B.E.S.T.)

n = 37

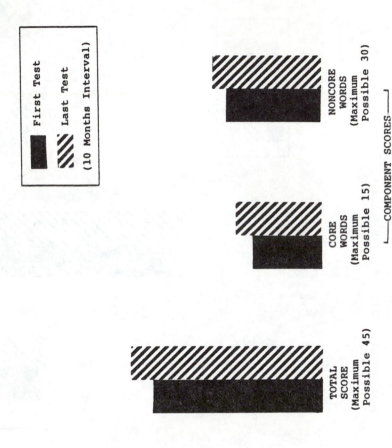

FIGURE 2

PICTURED VOCABULARY RECOGNITION

n = 34

FIGURE 3

WRITTEN VOCABULARY RECOGNITION

n = 34

First Test

Last Test

(10 Months Interval)

TOTAL
CORE
(Maximum
Possible 35)

CORE
WORDS
(Maximum
Possible 10)

NONCORE
WORDS
(Maximum
Possible 25)

────COMPONENT SCORES────

35
34
32
30
28
26
24
22
20
18
16
14
12
10
8
6
4
2
0

NUMBER OF CORRECT WORDS

The five "easy" items were included to ensure that every-one would know some words, thus preventing individuals at low levels from becoming overly discouraged.

Vocabulary growth was measured by assessing know-ledge of the six sets of words, one set per visit. Vari-ation in the order of these sets across individuals made it possible to avoid confounding the potential effects of order of testing with growth of vocabulary over time.[4] The fifteen "core" items were added to each set to be used as an indicator of change or acquisition from one assessment to the next, before the full six sets of words had been administered. Of course, repeated assessment of these fifteen core words every two months might confound the effects of repetition with those of spontaneous ac-quisition. However, once the six assessments were com-plete, the rate of growth of core and noncore items could be compared to determine approximately how much influence repetition over assessments might have had.

The scores on the noncore pictured vocabulary items ranged from 0 to 25 (out of a total of 30) on the first assessment and 0 to 26 on the last; core scores ranged from 0 to 13 and 0 to 15, respectively. As illustrated in Figure 2, the mean number of noncore words recognized increased from 11.82 on the first assessment to 13.38 on the sixth, up 13.2 percent. The mean number of core words recognized increased from 8.27 to 10.18, a rise of 23.1 percent. The larger increase among core items suggests that in addition to the overall vocabulary growth taking place, repetition of core items over sessions also had an effect on learning.

The interval between the first and last assessments of this and the task described below was approximately ten months. Thirty-four individuals participated in both first and last assessments of these tasks.

Written English Vocabulary Recognition

In this task, recognition of isolated written lexi-cal items was used as one measure of literacy. Using a procedure similar to that used to generate materials for the pictured vocabulary task, six partially overlapping sets of items were developed and represented to indivi-duals in varying orders over the six visits. Twenty-five items were unique to each set and ten were common to all six.[5] During each of six assessment visits, participants were asked to read and paraphrase each item in the given set of thirty-five English words, phrases and common abbreviations, written in boldface type on three-by-five inch index cards.

Scores on the noncore written vocabulary items ranged from 0 to 20 on the first assessment and 0 to 21 on the last; core scores ranged from 0 to 8 and 0 to 9, respectively. The group mean for noncore items rose 22.7 percent, from 3.88 words out of 25 to 4.77. (See Figure 3.) The mean core item score rose 29.3 percent, from 3.31 words out of 10, to 4.15. Clearly, this task was more difficult for the majority of participants than was the pictured vocabulary recognition: A full 50 percent of those participating in both first and sixth assessments recognized no noncore written words at all in the first session and that figure dropped only slightly, to 47 percent, during the last session. Thirty-eight percent knew no core written words the first time, 29 percent knew none the last. This contrasts greatly with the pictured vocabulary results, in which only one to two individuals knew no noncore items.

Relative Proficiencies

Beyond documenting the acquisition which has taken place, this study examined individual variations in acquisition. The Hmong's acquisition of English is by no means uniform. Like other immigrants before them, not all Hmong adults master the English language or literacy. A wide range of proficiencies and levels of functioning exist even among individuals who have been in this country for several years. As noted above, the range of proficiency among these longitudinal study participants is considerable: on each of the measures reported here, scores ranged from 0 to close to the maximum possible.

Such differences in learning need to be better understood. In general, individuals acquire some English proficiency early in their resettlement here. According to the results of this study, acquisition continues at a slow pace over time. Analyses of these results further show that the relative levels of proficiency within the group remain much the same as acquisition progresses. That is, individuals who scored low at the beginning of the year of observation continue at a low level relative to the group at the end of the year. The best predictor of how a person performs an assessment task at the end of the year is how he or she performed at the beginning. (On the B.E.S.T., for example, individuals' scores on the test at the first of the year predicted 89 percent of the variance in scores on the test at the end of the year.) When we consider the progress made by a smaller group of Hmong adults over the past three years (that of the Hmong adults to whom we taught English at the beginning of this research project), a similar pattern emerges: all have made progress over those three years, but their relative positions within the group with regard to their English proficiency remain the same today as they were three years ago.

FACTORS AFFECTING ACQUISITION

If individuals tend to maintain their relative level of proficiency (there are exceptions, of course), what accounts for the initial differences? That is, what factors underlie individual differences in the acquisition of English? Our analyses indicate there are many variables correlated with individual differences in acquisition. Many of these variables reflect differences in the experiences individuals had in Southeast Asia, prior to most Hmong's attempts to learn English;[6] others involve experiences concurrent with the learning process.[7] For example, a consistent pattern is evident between individuals' assessment scores and their personal background characteristics, particularly formal education in Laos and proficiency in reading Hmong or Lao. For the most part, the educated group scores higher than the noneducated and the literates higher than the nonliterates. (See Table 2.) Similarly, a consistent pattern emerges in relation to individuals' current activities, such as attending school, having American friends or using English at the store. (See Table 3.) All of these variables show a relationship to proficiency in the English language and literacy. The difficulty lies in determining which of these many correlations reflect causal relationships with English acquisition.

TABLE 2

English Proficiency Scores by Personal Background Characteristics

Proficiency Measures	Scale Values	Education in Laos		Proficiency in Reading Lao		Proficiency in Reading Hmong		Sex	
		None	Some	None	Some	None	Some	Women	Men
B.E.S.T. n	0-90	31	6	29	6	26	9	18	19
First Test Total		28.8	70.3	29.7	68.0	27.3	62.0	23.9	46.6
Last Test Total		34.4	74.7	35.2	73.5	32.2	69.3	27.4	53.7
Pictured Vocabulary n		30	4	27	4	24	7		
Noncore Words – First	0-30	10.8	19.3	11.1	20.3	10.8	17.4	n.s.*	n.s.*
Noncore Words – Last	0-30	12.5	20.0	12.8	21.8	12.5	19.0	n.s.*	n.s.*
Core Words – First	0-15	7.7	12.3	8.1	12.3	8.0	11.0	n.s.*	n.s.*
Core Words – Last	0-15					9.8	13.1	n.s.*	n.s.*
Written Vocabulary n		30	4	27	4	24	7	15	19
Noncore Words – First	0-25	2.2	16.5	2.6	15.3	2.3	11.0	1.3	5.9
Noncore Words – Last	0-25	3.1	17.0	3.6	16.3	2.9	13.1	n.s.*	n.s.*
Core Words – First	0-10	2.6	8.0	2.8	8.0	2.5	7.0	2.0	4.2
Core Words – Last	0-10	3.5	9.0	3.8	8.8	3.5	7.7	n.s.*	n.s.*

Note: Analyses of variance indicated differences in proficiency by these personal characteristics to be significant at least at the .05 level unless otherwise noted.

*Difference is not significant at the .05 level.

TABLE 3

English Proficiency Scores by Current Personal Activities

Proficiency Measures	Scale Values	Attending School Now or Within Last 2 Months		Have American Friends		Speak English With American Friends		Speak to Americans Daily		Speak English at the Store		Speak English to the Doctor	
		No	Yes	No	Yes	No	Yes	No	Yes	No	Yes	No	Yes
B.E.S.T. n	0-90	13	24	26	11	28	9	19	18	21	16	30	6
First Test Total		18.6	44.8	28.8	51.5	29.3	55.0	24.1	47.7	23.1	51.9	28.5	70.3
Last Test Total		17.5	53.6	34.6	55.9	35.0	59.3	26.5	56.2	27.2	58.9	34.2	74.7
Pictured Vocabulary n		10	21			24	7	15	16	16	15	25	5
Noncore Words – First	0-30	8.0	14.2	n.s.*	n.s.*	n.s.*	n.s.*	8.9	15.4	9.9	14.7	10.8	19.2
Noncore Words – Last	0-30	9.0	16.5	n.s.*	n.s.*	n.s.*	n.s.*	10.1	17.8	11.3	17.0	13.1	20.0
Core Words – First	0-15	6.3	9.8	n.s.*	n.s.*	8.0	11.0	7.1	10.1	7.2	10.2	n.s.*	
Core Words – Last	0-15	7.2	12.0	n.s.*	n.s.*	n.s.*	n.s.*	8.5	12.3	8.7	12.3	9.6	14.0
Written Vocabulary n		10	21	23	8	24	7	15	16	16	15	25	5
Noncore Words – First	0-25	.3	6.1	2.7	8.8	2.7	9.7	1.5	6.8	1.1	7.7	2.4	14.2
Noncore Words – Last	0-25	.2	7.6	n.s.*	n.s.*	n.s.*	n.s.*	1.5	8.7	2.1	8.6	3.6	14.2
Core Words – First	0-10	.7	4.9	2.8	5.5	n.s.*	n.s.*	1.6	5.3	1.9	5.2	3.0	7.0
Core Words – Last	0-10	1.8	5.9	n.s.*	n.s.*	n.s.*	n.s.*	3.0	6.0	2.8	6.4	3.9	8.0

Note: Analyses of variance indicated differences in proficiency by these personal activities to be significant at least at the .05 level unless otherwise noted.

*Difference is not significant at the .05 level.

Interpretation of the relationship between activities or experiences occurring at the same time as the acquisition being measured is problematic. At best, we can only say there is a positive association, since the influences may flow both ways. For example, ESL training has a very significant correlation with all of the assessment results to date. The mean score at the end of the year for individuals with less than a year of ESL in this country was 25.9 out of a total of 90 points possible on the B.E.S.T., whereas the mean for those with more than a year of ESL was 56.8. Similarly, those not taking ESL within the last two months had a mean of only 17.5; for those presently attending ESL, it was 53.6. Although it would thus appear that ESL training helps, we cannot say from these results whether continued attendance in ESL classes improves proficiency, or whether individuals who are having success with language learning in general (outside of school) are the ones who continue to take ESL, whereas others who are less successful get discouraged and drop out. The same difficulty of interpretation holds for other kinds of ongoing experiences, such as having American friends. Perhaps only those individuals who have reached a certain level of proficiency are willing or able to make social contacts with Americans. The fact that the people with American friends are also the ones who exhibit high levels of proficiency does not necessarily mean that having American friends increases one's proficiency.

Interpretation of associations between proficiency and prior characteristics or experiences is more straightforward. In such cases, it can be assumed that one variable is causally prior to the other (e.g., that age may affect English acquisition but English acquisition may not "affect" one's age). Using multiple regression analyses, we have found that individual differences in acquisition of English language and literacy are largely determined by such prior variables, that is, by individuals' English proficiency as measured by the assessment tasks described above--the B.E.S.T. and the pictured and written vocabulary recognition tasks. Although the degree of their influence varied from task to task (see Table 4), the following characteristics were found to exert the greatest influence on individuals' English proficiency:

TABLE 4

Regression Equations for Predicting English Proficiency

Proficiency Measures	Adjusted R²	Predictive Variables	b	Beta	F	Significance
B.E.S.T.						
First Test	.602	Proficiency in Reading				
		Hmong	5.943	.4228	11.406	.002
		Age	-.738	-.3598	9.824	.004
		Education in Laos	3.436	.2737	4.864	.035
Last Test	.544	Proficiency in Reading				
		Hmong	5.615	.3549	6.024	.020
		Age	-.920	-.3982	10.576	.003
		Sex	15.316	.2976	4.644	.039
Pictured Vocabulary						
Noncore Words						
First Test	.236	Proficiency in Reading				
		Lao	1.851	.3442	4.303	.047
Last Test	.342	Age	-.364	-.6035	16.612	.000
Core Words						
First Test	.258	Age	-.155	-.5319	11.443	.002
Last Test	.222	Age	-.161	-.4979	9.559	.004
Written Vocabulary						
Noncore Words						
First Test	.590	Education in Laos	1.256	.3917	7.701	.011
		Proficiency in Reading				
		Hmong	1.565	.3818	7.323	.012
		Age	-.150	-.2826	4.735	.040
Last Test	.582	Education in Laos	1.458	.4201	8.703	.007
		Proficiency in Reading				
		Hmong	1.663	.3750	6.945	.014
Core Words						
First Test	.416	Proficiency in Reading				
		Hmong	.911	.4548	8.752	.006
		Proficiency in Reading				
		Lao	.952	.3425	4.964	.034
Last Test	.436	Age	-.129	-.4494	10.008	.004
		Proficiency in Reading				
		Hmong	.872	.4168	8.608	.007

1)   proficiency in reading Hmong (a person literate in Hmong tends to score higher than someone who is not),

2)   age (a younger person tends to score higher than an older person), and

3)   education in Laos (an individual who received some formal schooling in Laos tends to score higher than someone who is not educated).

As seen in Table 4, one of these three variables or a combination of them was found to exert a significant influence on the results of each of the proficiency tasks reported here.   For example, these three characteristics predict 60 percent of the variance among individuals' performances on the B.E.S.T. at the beginning of the year.   At the end of the year, proficiency in reading Hmong and one's age are again important predictors.   (A minor variation occurs in the third variable to enter the predictive equation, but this variable--sex--only contributes 5 percent to the amount of variance predicted.) Age is a primary influence on individuals' performances on the pictured vocabulary recognition, and education in Laos and proficiency in reading Hmong are the major predictors in the written vocabulary recognition task.   To a lesser extent, proficiency in reading Lao--which was primarily acquired through formal schooling and is thus highly correlated with education in Laos (.79)--occasionally exerts a significant influence.

These results, based on objective measures of language and literacy over time, confirm what was suggested previously through the survey methodology and our prior ethnographic experience with the Hmong: the importance of background characteristics.   Thus, although this longitudinal study is based on a relatively small sample of individuals, the findings provide some insight about the relative influence--that is, the interrelationships--of factors which affect adult second language acquisition. That literacy, age and previous education are influential in adult language learning is not surprising.   These variables have long been thought to be important.   But exploring why and how they are influential and why other background factors are not may help us to understand further the process of second language acquisition by adults.

The finding that age, and sometimes sex, continue to play a role in predicting English proficiency--even after the effects of their correlation with other background experiences are statistically controlled--suggests the continuing influence of those historical, social and cultural factors which enabled only certain members (primarily young men) of current Hmong refugee communities to go to school when they lived in Laos. That is, the social expectation that young people (men, in particular) should go to school may be combining forces with the sense of inadequacy experienced by adults finding themselves in the midst of a totally different, complex, often unintelligible environment, and with the discouraging observation made by most parents that their children are learning faster and more than they are. Over and over again people expressed the belief that they were too old to learn (even though they were in their late twenties or mid-thirties). The continuing influence of age as a predictor may also be simply a result of the still preliminary stage in which most Hmong adults find themselves in their acquisition of English. Teenagers have arrived with more education and literacy than their parents and receive more concentrated schooling here. In addition, because of their rapidly increasing language and literacy skills, they are constantly being called upon by adults to use those skills. Thus, the idea that the young learn faster becomes a self-fulfilling prophecy.

One of the factors that is puzzling for its absence of influence is the amount of time individuals have been in the United States. While other background characteristics do predict acquisition, the passage of time in the United States per se does not appear to be a significant predictor. The reasons for this are not clear. The fact that time is not a predictor is not because individuals have stopped learning. The results reported here show acquisition taking place now--and these individuals have been here from two to four years.

Time is usually considered to be a significant factor in adult language acquisition because it is assumed to reflect the amount of individuals' linguistic input. But factors other than time may actually determine the amount of English input individuals receive. It is clear from our fieldwork that Hmong adults have very different opportunities for exposure to and use of the host language. Some Hmong have suggested, as one reason for not moving to areas of high Hmong concentrations in California, that the more heavily concentrated the Hmong population is in an area, the more socially isolated Hmong adults are from contacts with native English speakers. Following this theory, in areas like the Central Valley of California or the Twin Cities of Minnesota, adults would have less social contact with native speakers. Self-reported data on social contacts with Americans by study families before and after the move to California have been gathered, but have yet to be analyzed. Ethnographic work after the longitudinal study found that individuals in a heavily Hmong community in California felt they had infrequent contacts with native English speakers.

Another characteristic conspicuous for the absence of its influence is the ability to speak Lao. A common assumption is that experience learning a second language can facilitate learning a third. Ervin-Tripp (1973:95), for example, speaks of different learning strategies based on different language acquisition experiences. In multivariate analyses of our data, fluency in Lao does not play a significant role at all. The point to ponder here is the finding that previous literacy--Hmong literacy--exerts more influence on acquisition of spoken English than does previous bilingualism. The relatively limited influence of literacy in Lao is less difficult to understand. Once the relationship of Lao literacy to education in Laos is statistically controlled, previous education appears as a more influential factor than literacy in Lao.

We are still at a preliminary stage in analyzing the relationship of literacy in Hmong to acquisition of English. The nature of this relationship is not quite as clear-cut as that of some of the other background characteristics because acquisition of Hmong literacy is still taking place in this country: 47 percent of those who reported themselves as literate in Hmong have learned it or are still learning it here in this country. There may be some levels of mutual influence between English acquisition and Hmong literacy. For example, it is possible that acquisition of English (if one learns the alphabet) could facilitate subsequent acquisition of Hmong literacy. However, considering these results together with the previous survey results and our ethnographic experience with the Hmong, it seems likely that the primary influence is in the other direction--that is, that Hmong literacy is affecting English acquisition.

There are several reasons why Hmong literacy might affect English acquisition. An obvious one is that both English and Hmong literacy (as practiced by this group of Hmong) use the Roman alphabet. To individuals literate in Hmong, the characters used to write English at least look familiar. But since the Romanized Popular Alphabet (RPA) orthography for Hmong does not represent the phonology of English, it is not clear how familiarity with the alphabet itself would foster acquisition of <u>spoken</u> English. Several possibilities come to mind. First, adults' acquisition of oral and written English may be so intertwined that the obvious advantage which the familiarity of the Roman alphabet seems to bestow on English <u>literacy</u> acquisition carries over to spoken English as well. Second, many Hmong participate in formal ESL training, which relies heavily on the use of primers, worksheets, boardwork and other written materials, so that those familiar with the alphabet may progress more quickly and benefit more from formal training. Third, as previously reported, Hmong adults use their native script actively as a tool in learning English--copying new material, transliterating its pronunciation and translating it into Hmong. All of these applications of Hmong script are later studied at home. The social segregation of Hmong adults and their resulting isolation from native English speakers may well give a significant edge to those able to "study" English through the tool of Hmong literacy. If this is the case, the English proficiency gap between people literate in Hmong and those who are not might be expected to widen further in California.

Another kind of factor--an affective one--may be at work in the apparently powerful role of Hmong literacy in English language acquisition. Most individuals literate in Hmong script chose to become literate on a self-selected basis (in contrast, for example, to most of the individuals literate in Lao, who were sent by others to schools in Laos where Lao literacy was learned). Perhaps there is overlap between the motivations or aptitudes underlying acquisition of Hmong literacy and English; individuals who desire to learn Hmong script tend to be predisposed to learning English. The fact that many Hmong believe that literacy in Hmong script facilitates acquisition of English seems consistent with this line of explanation. In a surprising twist, the acquisition of native language literacy in Hmong may be seen not as an indicator of interest in cultural maintenance, but of openness to change, if not assimilation.

CONCLUSIONS

This longitudinal study set out to document English acquisition by a group of Hmong adults over a year's time and to explore the factors which appeared to be affecting their progress. Based on the three measures reported here, we found that acquisition was indeed taking place-- that people were learning slowly, but still progressing two to four years after their arrival in this country. Individuals' relative positions within the group with regard to proficiency level remained much the same over time.

Both the experiences individuals have prior to coming to this country and their current activities are highly correlated with their English proficiency. Due to the ongoing nature of current activities (such as attending school, having American friends, speaking English at the store, etc.), it is difficult to isolate their mutual influences on one another. The causal relationship of background variables with English acquisition can be analyzed, however. Multivariate analyses indicate that certain background characteristics--especially proficiency in reading Hmong, age and education in Laos--are powerful predictors of English proficiency. Further data may identify the reason why some variables seem to influence acquisition, whereas others do not. As noted, many other measures not considered in this paper were gathered during the study. As the additional data are analyzed, particular attention will be paid to the apparently strong role played by literacy in Hmong and to the pervasive interaction between literacy and language acquisition.

ACKNOWLEDGEMENTS

There are numerous people whose help made this study possible. Our colleagues, Michael P. Sweeney and Mary L. Cohn, contributed thoughtfully to the study design and labored tirelessly in the field. We are equally grateful to Dan X. Mua, our research assistant, and the many Hmong interpreters who arranged and facilitated interviews and accompanied us throughout the fieldwork. Thanks also to our colleague, Nancy Faires Conklin, for her comments on the manuscript. And finally, we would especially like to express our appreciation to the twenty Hmong families who welcomed us into their lives and tolerated seemingly endless hours of questions and discussions. Their good will and hospitality formed the basis for this research.

This work was funded by a contract from the National Institute of Education (No. 400-83-0005). The opinions expressed in this publication do not necessarily reflect the position of the National Institute of Education, and no official endorsement by the Institute should be inferred.

NOTES

[1] These figures were compiled for the longitudinal study population from the proficiencies reported in the household survey. Ensuing visits with these individuals indicated that more literacy in Hmong exists than was previously reported. This discrepancy is due in part to continuing acquisition of Hmong literacy in this country. These more recent data have yet to be fully analyzed.

[2] The results of these background interviews have been presented in Reder, Green and Sweeney (1983) and in Reder, Green, Sweeney and Cohn (1983).

[3] Developed by Smith (1971).

[4] A Latin Square design was used to vary the order of administration randomly across subjects.

[5]Each of the six sets of noncore items consisted of ten items randomly selected from the pictured vocabulary item sets and fifteen items chosen from the literacy portfolio materials and other literacy artifacts in which these vocabulary items were more contextualized. The core words included five words from these last two sources and five easy words common in everyday life.

Pearson Correlations of Scores* by Personal Background Characteristics

Proficiency Measures	Age	Sex	Proficiency in Speaking Lao	Proficiency in Reading Hmong	Proficiency in Reading Lao	Education in Laos	Education in U.S.**	Time in U.S.
B.E.S.T.								
First Test Total	-.58	.50	.32	.67	.63	.68	.56	.04
Last Test Total	-.54	.52	.30	.63	.56	.59	.61	.06
Pictured Vocabulary								
Noncore Words – First	-.53	.04	.02	.46	.50	.44	.64	.17
Noncore Words – Last	-.67	.15	-.01	.40	.44	.34	.66	.24
Core Words – First	-.66	-.03	-.05	.38	.41	.41	.59	.14
Core Words – Last	-.64	.10	.01	.38	.33	.34	.57	.04
Written Vocabulary								
Noncore Words – First	-.41	.39	.23	.60	.70	.78	.43	.13
Noncore Words – Last	-.40	.31	.12	.65	.64	.69	.52	.28
Core Words – First	-.45	.34	.08	.60	.55	.56	.64	.35
Core Words – Last	-.59	.22	-.06	.54	.51	.54	.58	.20

Note: Unless otherwise indicated, data on background characteristics were gathered during the household survey conducted in April and May 1981.

*of individuals who took both first and last test

**by the time of Assessment 2 (July and August 1982)

Pearson Correlations of Scores* by Current Personal Activities

Proficiency Measures	Attending School Now or Within Last 2 Months	Have American Friends	Speak English With American Friends	Speak to Americans Daily	Speak English at the Store	Speak English to the Doctor
B.E.S.T.						
First Test Total	.55	.46	.49	.52	.63	.68
Last Test Total	.67	.38	.41	.58	.62	.58
Pictured Vocabulary						
Noncore Words – First	.47	.29	.34	.52	.38	.49
Noncore Words – Last	.51	.26	.29	.55	.41	.37
Core Words – First	.47	.32	.37	.45	.44	.36
Core Words – Last	.56	.29	.33	.48	.46	.41
Written Vocabulary						
Noncore Words – First	.45	.44	.49	.44	.55	.72
Noncore Words – Last	.52	.29	.32	.54	.49	.60
Core Words – First	.63	.38	.33	.60	.52	.49
Core Words – Last	.60	.32	.27	.47	.56	.47

*of individuals who took both first and last test

REFERENCES

Bailey, Nathalie, Carolyn Madden, and Stephen Krashen. 1974. "Is There a 'Natural Sequence' in Adult Second Language Learning?" Language Learning 24(2): 235-243. Reprinted in Second Language Acquisition: A Book of Readings, edited by Evelyn Marcussen Hatch, pp. 362-370. Rowley, Mass.: Newbury House Publishers, Inc., 1978.

Chamot, Anna Uhl. 1981. "Applications of Second Language Acquisition Research to the Bilingual Classroom." Focus, No. 8, Sept. Rosslyn, Va.: National Clearinghouse for Bilingual Education.

Dulay, Heidi, and Marina Burt. 1974. "Natural Sequences in Child Second Language Acquisition." Language Learning 24(1):37-53. Reprinted in Second Language Acquisition: A Book of Readings, edited by Evelyn Marcussen Hatch, pp. 347-361. Rowley, Mass.: Newbury House Publishers, Inc., 1978.

Ervin-Tripp, Susan M. 1973. "Structured Language Acquisition." In Language Acquisition and Communicative Choice: Essays by Susan M. Ervin-Tripp, edited by Anwar S. Dil, pp. 92-129. Stanford: Stanford University Press.

Gardner, Robert C., and Wallace Lambert. 1972. Attitudes and Motivation in Second-Language Learning. Rowley, Mass.: Newbury House Publishers, Inc.

Krahnke, Karl J., and Mary Ann Christison. 1983. "Recent Language Research and Some Language Teaching Principles." TESOL Quarterly 17(4):625-649.

Krashen, Stephen D., Michael A. Long, and Robin C. Scarcella. 1979. "Age, Rate and Eventual Attainment in Second Language Acquisition." TESOL Quarterly 13(4):573-582.

Lambert, Wallace E.   1981.   "Bilingualism and Language Acquisition."   Paper presented at Conference on Native Language and Foreign Language Acquisition, at New York Academy of Sciences, January.

Reder, Stephen.   1982.   "A Hmong Community's Acquisition of English."   In The Hmong in the West: Observations and Reports, Papers of the 1981 Hmong Research Conference, edited by Bruce T. Downing and Douglas P. Olney, pp. 268-303.   Minneapolis: Center for Urban Regional Affairs, University of Minnesota.

Reder, Stephen, Karen Reed Green, and Michael P. Sweeney. 1983.   Acquisition and Use of Literacy in the Hmong Community of Newton: 1981 Annual Report of the Functional Literacy Project.   Portland, Ore.: Northwest Regional Educational Laboratory.

PART FOUR

HEALTH CARE ISSUES

INTRODUCTION

Amos S. Deinard

In an effort to provide high quality medical care for Indochinese refugees, medical clinics in the United States trained and hired bilingual interpreters. It soon became apparent, however, that language was not the only barrier to be hurdled. Health care providers must make other modifications to win the confidence of groups of people unaccustomed to the Western approach to medical care.

Medical personnel at first did not appreciate how overwhelming it was to be confronted with so much that was new. Indochinese groups resisted pressure to accept quickly and on faith new methods of curing. This was especially true for the Hmong, who had the least experience with Western-influenced medicine. The health care professionals did not know how the different refugee groups conceptualized causes and cures of disease. The rush to do good before adequate background information could be gathered resulted in conflicts that prejudiced consumers against some specific medical treatments.

For human service organizations to survive and to remain credible, they must continually consider how they can best meet the needs, both objective and subjective, of those who use their services. Neither the health care providers nor the consumers alone can define these needs. Rather, there must be a constant determination that what a health service organization offers and what the consumer desires are matched to their mutual satisfaction. This requires an ongoing dialogue between the provider and the consumer. Without such considerations, instead of developing a harmonious relationship with the consumer, the health care system may be faced with angry, suspicious and uncooperative parents and patients. A fragmented rather than a unified health care program may emerge as parents and patients, terrified at the thought of certain procedures, shop around for noninvasive or nonsurgical alternatives. Both the consumer and the provider must acknowledge the notion that good health care requires compromises between their different cultural perspectives.

The following papers touch on some of these considerations. The first three help us to understand Hmong perception of illness. They suggest the possibility that Western medical practitioners might incorporate some Hmong ideas or at minimum utilize them in some manner complementary to their own.

Lemoine points out that "Hmong shamanism is not a religion but a way of healing." Illness is seen as an integral part of the individual's whole being. Causation is ascribed to the activities of the unseen or "spirit" aspect of life which only the shaman is able to access. He sees particular benefit in utilizing shamanistic activities in the treatment of psychophysiological diseases.

Bliatout also believes that many Hmong who have resettled in Western societies and who suffer from mental health problems would benefit from using one or more of the wide variety of Hmong traditional healing arts. His paper provides a solid review of the types of traditional Hmong healers and of traditional beliefs about mental health problems. He discusses which factors should be considered when deciding whether it is appropriate to refer a Hmong client to traditional healers. He points out, quite astutely, that "since Hmong treatments never hurt anyone, but could possibly help a patient," it should be considered as part. of a patient's course of treatment, to be offered in conjunction with Western regimens.

Thao's paper considers the Hmong's perceptions of illness and traditional ways of healing more from a medical standpoint than from the mental health standpoint. The paper contains a good discussion of the concept of soul loss, of ways of recalling the soul, and of natural and organic causes of illness. He explains the Hmong belief in "a mandate of life," i.e., the idea that every person is given a mandate to be a human being, with illness ocurring because the mandate of life predetermines illness and death occurring, should if ensue, because death is due. Thao points out that "the Hmong have evolved many different methods to deal with each causal element and to counteract illness as a whole. By learning more about Hmong attitudes about health and illness, Western health care providers can do much to improve the quality and appropriateness of care for this special group of new immigrants."

Munger reports on field work conducted in the Ban Vinai refugee camp on the problem of sleep disturbances and sudden unexpected nocturnal death syndrome (SUNDS) in Hmong refugees. His paper reviews the work of other investigators who have studied this puzzling, complex phenomenon. Several reports of SUNDS cases in Ban Vinai erode the popular conception that SUNDS only affects Hmong who have resettled in the United States. Reacting to the sensitivity of the subject matter and to the attitudes of the Hmong toward medical research in general, Munger urges that a survey of sleep disorders not be attempted until a clinical response can be offered to individuals identified as having a sleep disorder. This position appears to run contrary to the scientific process practiced in the Western world, wherein research is often conducted even though no treatment is available. Munger addresses the need to involve scientists from both the medical and social science areas as this issue is studied, and he correctly points out the importance of teaching Hmong refugees cardiopulmonary resuscitation and how to use emergency medical services.

Oberg, Muret-Wagstaff, Moore and Cumming conducted a cross-cultural assessment of maternal and child interaction. The findings of their well-designed study, reported here, are provocative. On an assessment of parent-child interactions, Hmong mothers were shown to obtain higher ratings on parenting skills than a mixed Caucasian sample did. The Hmong mothers were rated as more attentive, expressive, sensitive, responsive, and patient in child-rearing. The quality of the mother-child relationship throughout infancy has clear implications for the subsequent development of the child. Contrary to observations linking isolation, stress and lack of social support in economically disadvantaged groups to negative parent-child interaction patterns, Hmong mothers demonstrate that the ability of a mother to be sensitive and responsive to her toddler is not entirely dependent on the absence of stress or on higher socioeconomic status. The authors concluded that "the sensitivity shown by these Hmong mothers seems related to a cultural priority for attentive child-rearing and the availability and use of a strong extended family network."

Chun and Deinard, in their paper on undue lead absorption in Hmong children, address an issue that has been of primary importance to those providing health care to Southeast Asian refugees--particularly Hmong children, in Minneapolis, Minnesota--since the first years of their immigration. Basic descriptive information of Hmong children shown to have undue lead absorption draws attention to several features that distinguish them from American children who in the past were identified as having the same problem. The Hmong tended to be younger, with several being only six months of age at the time their undue lead absorption was detected. The problem, however, appears to be fleeting, for the peak of Hmong cases occurred in 1981. Since 1983, the Hmong incidence is more akin to that of the American population. Of specific interest in many of the Hmong cases is the failure to find a source of lead in the homes. The authors concluded that the etiology of undue lead absorption detected in Hmong children is far from delineated. However, in view of the Hmong's documented tendency to use herbal medicines and other cultural kinds of medicines, a consideration must be given to the possibility that, at least in some cases, the etiology of undue lead absorption is related to the covert use of such medications.

The final paper, by Hurlich et al., describes the attitudes of Hmong towards medical research projects. The authors, in conjunction with other investigators, wished to pursue a study of the sudden unexpected nocturnal death syndrome and associated electrolyte abnormalities both in Ban Vinai and in several locations in the United States. The authors summarize related projects and describe in detail the frustrations they encountered in attempting to initiate the project, which included blood drawing, in Ban Vinai. Questions raised by the Hmong in the camp and in the United States reflect the frustrations that they have had with Western medical practices and suggest reasons why the Hmong ultimately became unwilling to participate in the study. On the basis of their collective experience in working with Hmong communities in the United States and Thailand, the authors describe several important lessons that they learned about undertaking research, particularly regarding the responsibility of researchers toward refugee communities.

SHAMANISM IN THE CONTEXT OF HMONG RESETTLEMENT

Jacques Lemoine

INTRODUCTION

You may wonder why I chose the subject of shamanism in a meeting mainly concerned with the problems facing Hmong refugees in a Western cultural environment. This very morning, different orators have been debating Hmong culture, Hmong history and Hmong ethnicity from the perspective of change. To summarize my own experience, I would like to say that the present ethnic consciousness of the Hmong—whether they are in the United States or in France or (I suppose) in Australia—is a strong feeling that they all belong to a unique people who are not only different from other peoples but who are positively resolved to avoid any kind of assimilation.

In this respect, Hmong refugees are faithful to their ethnic past. Since the dawn of their history, as part of the Miao group of peoples in China, they managed to escape this fate of assimilation. This is the key to explain their political attitudes in Indochina since they fled and settled there in the mid-nineteenth century. Their involvement in the two Indochina wars, their early upsurge against the French colonial system in the 1920s, as well as their latest resistance to Vietnamese and Communist Laotians who wanted to drag them into a bureaucratic slavery: all their choices, even their political mistakes, have been dictated by the same collective urge to preserve Hmong ethnicity. We have to keep this in mind if we really want to help them in their resettlement problems. For they did not come to our countries only to save their lives, they rather came to save their selves, that is, their Hmong ethnicity. It would be an egregious misunderstanding to advise them to forget it all and become another sheep in the flock, even if we can allow them more freedom than they could expect in the country they fled. I don't need to elaborate on this. Obviously, this meeting would not take place if we were not all conscious of this fact.

Let us now consider for a while the meaning of Hmong ethnic consciousness among the refugee population. Be-

sides being born a Hmong, it means using (at least) one
dialect of the Hmong language.   Through the language, all
the Hmong share a measure of Hmong traditional culture.
As it is not the same amount for all, I avoid speaking of
"one people, one culture."   This would misrepresent the
facts.   Hmong culture is still very alive, but in the past
sixty years, with the opening of the ethnic group to contacts with other people and other cultures, Hmong culture
has lost its overall command of Hmong thoughts.   The Hmong
indeed have experienced what has happened to most peoples
on earth; they have been influenced by foreign traditions.
Some of them have converted to Christianity (with all the
transformation of thinking that this entails).   Some others have given up all religious practices, whether Christian or traditional.   Finally, part of these two groups
and a certain number of more conservative individuals have
tried to pattern their social and political activities on
a more sophisticated neighbor, namely the Lao plain-dwel-
lers who also were the rulers of the Hmong people's adopted country, Laos.   From the mixing of these diverse currents, new trends have emerged among the younger generations.   The results range from dancing Lamvong to rock
dancing, playing country music and singing with a guitar
in a band, to free matching and marriage, to divorce and
sexual liberation, and so forth.

    In time of adversity and persecution, Hmong culture
has always conjured up a messianic gathering of Hmong people in order to oppose what was thought of as alien oppression.   This was the case with Pachai, who dared to
rebel against French colonial agents from 1918 to 1921.
This was also the case of Ya Shong Leu, who in 1967 challenged a Hmong authority in Western guise: General Vang
Pao, the administrator of Military Region No. 2.   The reason I mention this latest messianic reaction to the growing anxiety of the Hmong who were facing more and more destructive warfare, is that Ya Shong Leu's ideas did not
die with him in the early seventies.   They must have
spread widely among the people, for they surfaced again
after the great flight to Thailand in 1975.   These ideas
have produced a new Hmong church, whose influence is now
swiftly spreading among the refugees of the younger generation.   The establishment of a church instead of the gathering of an army is in itself a remarkable adaptation to
the circumstances.   In the seclusion of a refugee camp,

those who established the new faith could observe (and probably regret) the growing impact of Catholic and Christian churches on their fellow tribesmen.

Thus, when we now speak of Hmong culture, we must keep in mind not only a perennial Hmong tradition, but also that of the followers of Christian and Catholic Churches, the neo-traditional standards of the new faith, and finally a materialistic current. I must apologize for having expended so much on the religious situation. I found it necessary to locate the cultural setting of the refugees before introducing Hmong shamanism. Whatever historical influences it may still carry, Hmong shamanism remains a central part of Hmong traditional culture. And it is that part which is now facing the conflicting trends of Christianity and neo-Hmong cults.

SHAMANISM: A HMONG WAY OF PSYCHOTHERAPY

Hmong shamanism is not a religion but a way of healing. Hmong traditional beliefs form a religion of souls and spirits, gods and devils. It also answers man's most agonizing questions about the genesis of life, death and disease, and the perpetuation of life through reincarnation. All these Hmong metaphysics are well explained in an initiatory song to the dead: the Qhua Ke ("Showing the Way") (see Lemoine 1983). Shamanism deals only with prophylaxis from disease and death. Contrary to some reports, a shaman never performs religious rites as such, like the funeral, the releasing of a dead person's soul or the commemorative buffalo sacrifice to dead parents. If a shaman is seen taking part in a ritual, it is never as a shaman but in his capacity as a ritualist after he has secured a further qualification. All qualifications—from playing and singing musical parts in weddings and funerals, to dealing with a corpse and, later on, with his returning soul—are learned orally from a renowned specialist. An initiation fee is usually paid to the master. Shamanism is also a tradition transmitted from master to disciple. But it differs from all other kinds of learning. Besides being taught, it has to be inherited.

The shaman's activity differs from that of the ritualist. One may say that it consists of a shaman exploring the unseen part of reality in order to chase devils and restore somebody's health.   The total reality that everyone experiences in this world includes what you see and what you do not see.   For an ordinary Hmong person, it does not follow that unseen reality does not exist.   The unseen--namely the souls of the people, the spirits of the departed, tutelary gods, wild spirits and evil influ- ences--is strongly perceived as existing even when ordi- nary human eyes cannot catch a glimpse of it.   The main difference between a Hmong shaman and an ordinary fellow is that the shaman can enter the unseen part of reality and deal with it.   For that he needs to put himself in what Michael Harner (1980) rightly called "a shamanic state of consciousness."   It means that he must leave this side of reality and enter the unseen.   Two of his acces- sories symbolize this transition.   The first is the veil with which he covers his head, meaning that he is absent from this side of reality, blind to us.   The other one is the lamp that must be alight on his altar, shedding light on the unseen.

To enter the unseen, a Hmong shaman, as most shamans in other cultures, has to reach this state of shamanic consciousness.   He attains this goal through a trance. Trance is a distinctive feature of the Hmong shaman.   One cannot be a shaman without a predisposition to go into a trance.   But trance is not only achieved through physical training.   It is an inherited ability that one cannot have at will.   It must be provoked by spirit helpers.   The sounds of the gong, the rattle and the finger bell cer- tainly give the tempo and help the shaman to alter his own consciousness.   But they accompany rather than precede the shaman's singing.   The trance always starts first, for it is, as the shamans themselves explain, provoked by spirit helpers.

SPIRIT HELPERS AND SHAMAN'S VOCATION

Where do the spirit helpers come from?   When a Hmong shaman dies, his altar is undone and thrown away in the jungle.   But his tools are carefully kept by his sons.   In fact when he feels himself about to die, he summons all his sons to come to his bedside and gives them the con- tents of his bowl of magic water to drink.   This bowl is also known as "the dragon pond" (lub paas zaaj).   It is the place where the dragon who rules lightning and thunder comes to rest when invited by the shaman. To most East Asian peoples, thunder and lightning, in their capacity to kill suddenly, are the paragon of magic arts. And several traditions, including Chinese Taoism, claim to derive their magic from thunder power. A Hmong shaman also enjoys a special relationship with the Thunder-Dragon. Properly invited, it will become another spirit helper Drinking the Dragon-Water (dtej zaag) means that the children will absorb the essence of magic in their bones and flesh in order to keep it in the descent line. "I shall give them my bowl to drink because I want them to keep my spirit helpers. If they are incapable of shamanizing themselves, then I shall be reborn as one of their sons, I shall be able to be a shaman again...," says Chu Yao, a proficient master.

As a matter of fact, the spirit helpers of a deceased shaman will not exactly set themselves up in the bodies of his sons. What will stay with them after drinking the magic water is a mark, a token of the former alliance. The spirit helpers themselves will return to their base: the Cave of Nya Yi on a high cliff in the third layer of heaven. This is the original abode and the common base for all the Hmong shamans' spirit helpers, Nya Yi (or Shi Yi) being the first shaman who initiated the practice. Shamans of this world are but the heirs of his talents.

The dead shaman himself will join his troop as a head spirit (thawj neeb). After a while, when he thinks that the time has come, he sends two of his troops, the Inspiring Spirit (Leej Nkaub) and the Spirit of the Trance (Tsheej Xeeb), to "importune" one of his sons. These two spirits are essential to the vocation of the shaman. They will make him sick in a strange way, with fever, attacks, shivering and pain, until he calls for a shaman who will diagnose his illness as the vocation. This shaman will summon his patient's spirit helpers and the veracity of his diagnosis will be proven by the subsequent relief experienced by his patient. So it becomes plain that his problem is the vocation imposed on him by these spirit helpers, who will not leave him alone until he starts calling them regularly, following the instruction of the consultant shaman. The latter thus becomes his first master. (It should be noted here that women as well as men can become shamans, although female shamans are much less common.   The Hmong would explain that a male soul has been reincarnated in a female body.)

Then follows a training period which may last two or three years, maybe more, during which the disciple learns from his master not only how to call his spirits, but also the ways of the world beyond: the important souls, i.e., the different parts of the self; the way to restore the integrity of a soul once it has been captured by another power or become a runaway that needs to be fetched back; and last, but not least, the different wild and evil spirits that he will have to fight.   His spirit helpers come to him already structured as a task force with scout spirits, engineer spirits, horsemen and foot soldiers.   The Inspiring Spirit and the Spirit of the Trance, who never part from him, act as staff and liaison officers.

Other spirits who have a specific function will be described as animals or insects whose features correspond to that function.   For example, the vanguard of the engineer spirit will be the spider who can stretch a thread of "copper and iron" for the troops to settle on.   Other engineers will throw a suspension bridge of "copper and iron" to let the foot soldiers and the horsemen cross space from one point to the other.   This thread and this bridge appear in the shaman's house where one can see a thread of cotton following a specific course between his altar and the main door, and on certain occasions, a cloth bridge also stretched between the altar and the main door. Another insect is a type of fly, the Sphex, whose property is to anesthetize its prey (other insects) in order to carry them alive to its nest.   This peculiar hunting habit is used by the Sphex spirit of the Hmong shaman when it is told to get hold of a very volatile soul: the protruding shadow.   Another of these functional spirit helpers is the woodpecker, who can pull worms and caterpillars from the growing bamboo soul.   Other animals like the bear or the elephant will be used for their strength.[1]   The hawk and the eagle will be sent to catch a shadow soul in flight, and so on.   However, the large number of spirit helpers remain anonymous: horsemen or soldiers, or a Chinese detachment to remind us of the Chinese sources of the shaman's tradition.

THE SHAMAN AT WORK

Once a shaman is established as a full-fledged practitioner, he erects in his house a two-storied altar. His master comes to summon once more his spirit helpers and invite them to settle there as soldiers in their barracks. Training is not yet completed and each year the master will come and help his disciple to send his spirits on holiday to Nya Yi's Cave. But the people will start coming to consult him in his house. More likely, unable to move, they will send someone of their family to invite him to their house. He will go there with minimal equipment: gong, rattle, finger-bell, divination blocks and veil. All these are carried in a bag by the emissary of the sick person. The patient's kin will erect a makeshift altar for summoning the shaman's spirits. A bench of the house or of a neighboring house will be prepared for the shaman to sit on, because the shaman in most of the trance is riding his "dragon charger," his "speedy steed," his "ship of wind and clouds." This fantastic Pegasus is of course represented by the bench on which he is rocking backwards and forwards, impersonating a very suggestive horse-riding.

His first intervention, as he calls it: "ua neeb sai",[2] will be an exploration of the sickness in order to identify its causes. If his diagnosis proves right, the sick person will feel great relief within a few days. Then he will decide to call the shaman back to perform the second part of his intervention, namely the "healing" (ua neeb khu).[3] What need is there, will you ask me, to have a healing follow when the patient is already better? This is indeed the great challenge of the Hmong shaman. Psychoanalysts say that a patient is cured when he does not want to come and pay his analyst anymore. The Hmong situation is the reverse. When a patient feels better he wants to pay his healer who did not charge him anything yet. If a patient feels no better after a few days or a few weeks, he only calls another shaman to try his talent. But if he feels relief, it means that the shaman's intervention was appropriate. Then, in order to fulfill his previous agreement with wild spirits or gods, or to enforce his analysis of the disease, the shaman must perform a healing ceremony with the participation of his patients.

It is a dramatic re-enactment of his findings in the unseen, a show of the various causes of the previous illness. For example, supposing that the illness has been provoked by the running away of the running bull soul; he will summon his spirit helpers to go with him to the place where he found that soul and bring it back home. In the first session (ua neeb sai) when he was still searching, his patient would not participate at all. But this time, he is invited to stay in the middle of the room and as soon as the shaman has brought back his running bull soul, an assistant will sacrifice a piglet in order to build a magic corral around the patient's running bull soul. The shaman will eventually seal the fence around the running bull by stamping blood from the sacrificed pig on the back of his patient. Another pig's life could be used to make an umbrella over the patient to hide him from evil spirits, and so on. In that case life is considered as a material object. So a pig's life may be used to repair human life.

The sacrifice of one or several pigs is usually a central part of this performance. And it is not (as one may guess) in order to provide food to spirits but to mend or to strengthen a collapsing soul. For that he needs to use a similar substance, spirit to back spirit, life to strengthen life. What he does in a pig sacrifice is to take hold of the pig's soul and use it to support or protect his patient's soul. Both human and animal souls are thought to be made of the same substance and man can reincarnate in a domestic animal. In respect to the spirit, the shaman will always burn a small amount of joss money to provide him with money for the journey in the world beyond. But this animal soul will be kept prisoner as an assignment given by the shaman until the end of the year. Meanwhile the shaman keeps the lower jaws of the sacrificed pigs in a basket close to his permanent altar. He will burn all of them when sending his spirits on holiday, meaning then that they are freed and can leave their duty.

The Hmong shaman has two main obligations. One is restoring the self, which he divides up into five different souls: the protruding shadow (ntsuj dluab ntsuj hlauv), the reindeer soul (nyuj caab nyuj kaub), the running bull (nyuj raag nyuj rhi), the chicken soul (ntsuj qab ntsuj noo), and the growing bamboo soul (ntsuj xyooj ntsuj ntoo).   This division could be paralleled with the Freudian analysis of the Ego.   It has the same purpose, namely to come closer to the complexity of man's psyche. By finding and bringing back the runaway, he helps his patient to recover his psychic balance.   But there remains an obligation: to take over his patient's fight for life. Like antibiotics in a weak body, his fierce troops supply resistance to the evil miasmas and spirits.   Exorcism is the most thrilling part of his performance.   Cleansing or purification by magic water blown on the patient is also very common.   All these actions are very theatrical and contribute to prop up the patient's morale.   Certainly, a good Hmong shaman has a decisive influence in this respect and I have been surprised to see that this technique was successful not only with Hmong fellow tribesmen sharing the same culture, but also with Westerners, provided that the shaman's analysis is explained to them.   Some shamans now in Western countries have remarked that their treatment of hysteria is far more efficient than the drugs of the psychiatrist.

It does not mean that shamans are opposing the use of drugs or any other therapy.   They are often themselves distinguished herbalists and they always welcome the use of Western drugs in conjunction with their own magic.   It is not that they doubt their own power, but that they acknowledge their healing as essentially psychosomatic.   Diseases and infections may remain out of reach of their spirit fighters.   From my own observations I would conclude that, in spite of a wild appearance, Hmong shamanism is generally a positive therapy to counteract anxiety and other psychic and psychosomatic disorders.

SHAMANISM AND THE PSYCHOMENTAL COMPLEX OF THE HMONG REFUGEES

After this brief description, I hope that you now enjoy a clearer idea of the part played by the Hmong shamans in Hmong traditional society.   This part is obviously to relieve anxiety and to cure psychophysiological diseases. In a traditional context, back in Laos and far from any Western medicine, all the diseases will be put into the shaman's hands.   But he himself will possibly use herbal medicine instead of spirit helpers.   If no local medicine works, he will then try magic and spirit helpers. As soon as a more sophisticated medicine is introduced in the village, it will be used jointly or separately for the patient's sake, with the shaman's approval.

The people who worked in refugee camps must have noticed a large number of shamans at work, making an almost continuous musical background all the day long. This may be indicative of a high degree of anxiety and psychic vulnerability for the Hmong in the refugee camps. But I must stress that it was already the case in the context of a traditional village. I remember counting no less than 30 shamans in a cluster of 90 households.

In third countries, the number of shamans has decreased for various reasons. Some did not want to leave Thailand, where they lived in an exclusively Hmong environment, which they enjoyed very much in spite of the difficulties of being in a refugee camp. Others were excluded from the resettlement list as useless religious practitioners.

The fact is that when Hmong refugees are free in their religious attitudes, they keep calling in shamans to help, even when they have to cover long distances to bring them. The situation in the refugee camp and the situation in a Western country during the adaptation stage seem to me to be broadly parallel, generating an increased anxiety about the present and the future. It would take too long to enumerate here all the different sources of stress ending up in more-or-less deep depression. I refer you here to studies by Westermeyer and Vang (1983a, b).

The causes for anxiety range from unemployment and the shame of living on welfare, to the religious pressure of a fundamentalist sponsor. It is not in my capacity to judge the different efforts--successes and failures--that have happened in the resettlement of the Hmong in the United States. Broadly speaking, they parallel what I have observed in France. But when thinking of helping the Hmong to preserve their selves, one should pay more attention to the delicate workings of their psychic balance. I must say that I was shocked to hear in St. Paul last year that the religious sponsors of some of my Hmong friends would allow them to practice recalling the souls, but not shamanism. This seemed to me a gross misunderstanding of the shaman's role. He is not competing with a medical doctor, nor with a priest nor a minister, but with Dr. J. Westermeyer and his like: the psychiatrist and the psychologist.   I know Dr. Westermeyer well and I doubt that he would advise any of his Hmong patients not to see a shaman.

Last year, together with British anthropologist, Christine Mougne, I conducted an inquiry on the problem of sudden death during sleep among Southeast Asian refugees.   To make a long story short, our findings have shed light on the possible triggers of sudden death among subjects physically predisposed to cardiac arrest.   Among the triggers we found were dreams and night terrors and the modern substitute for dreams: TV shows.   But the strangest thing is that many of the cases we investigated were people who had already adapted or were adapting themselves.   They had given up their traditional protection and were highly motivated to competition and success in Western societies.   This very motivation drew them into "the fast lane" of American society, with all the resulting stress and anxiety.   The young intellectuals who died were almost exclusively either Christian or atheist.   They had no resources yet in the Western context to ease their stress or anxiety.   And they had abandoned their traditional protection and help.   May I venture to say that perhaps the comfort of a shaman before the stress had become too high would have prevented their heart failure?

But I must also add that there are instances in which the shaman did not succeed.   Whatever his insight, the shaman--like the psychoanalyst--never gets total control of his patient's mental health, and even when the treatment has been successful, it may not necessarily be permanent.

In any case, at the time of the seizure the shaman and the psychiatrist are powerless.   Only a resuscitation team that arrives within five minutes of the seizure has any chance to save the patient, as has been demonstrated in Seattle and Santa Ana, California.

I shall conclude by a thought which came to me while watching a Hmong shaman curing a young, educated German student from a deep and long-lasting melancholy.   Comparing his work to psychiatric procedure, I noticed that while the analyst tries to provoke self-analysis by scratching the wounded part of the self, a Hmong shaman will provide an explanation which avoids all self-involvement of the patient. He is always represented as a victim of an assault from outside powers or of an accidental separation from one part of his self. When this situation has been identified and overcome by the shaman, health is recovered. At no point has there been a feeling of guilt associated with suffering.[4] Maybe in the healing power of the Hmong shaman's art there is a lesson which the psychotherapist could learn.

NOTES

[1]For instance, to raise up a fallen soul.

[2]Va "to do, to manage," neeb "spirit helpers", sai "to see". The shaman is himself a txiv neeb "father (or master) of spirit."

[3]Va "make", neeb "spirit helpers", khu "heal (or cure)".

[4]Even when illness is provoked by angry ancestors to whom the patient did not offer proper rituals, he is not made to feel that he is "bad," only that he made a mistake that can be corrected.

REFERENCES

Lemoine, Jacques. 1983. L'Initiation du mort chez les Hmong, Bangkok, Thailand.

_____. Le chamane Hmong sur les Chemins de l'Au-dela (in press).

Westermeyer, Joseph; Tou Fu Vang, and John Neider. 1983a. "Migration and Mental Health Among Hmong Refugees," Association of Pre- and Postmigration Factors with Self-Rating Scales." The Journal of Nervous and Mental Disease, vol. 171, no. 2, pp. 92-96.

_____. 1983b. "Refugees Who Do and Do Not Seek Psychiatric Care, An Analysis of Premigratory and Postmigratory Characteristics." The Journal of Nervous and Mental Disease, vol. 171, no. 2, pp. 86-91.

GUIDELINES FOR MENTAL HEALTH PROFESSIONALS TO HELP HMONG CLIENTS SEEK TRADITIONAL HEALING TREATMENT

Bruce Thowpaou Bliatout

Many mental health professionals are beginning to understand and accept that some members of minority groups who suffer from mental health problems may be helped by using cultural support systems and/or traditional healing practices. It is probable that a great majority of the Hmong resettled in Western societies who suffer from mental health problems would benefit from using one or more of the wide variety of Hmong traditional healing arts.

Some mental health professionals may wish to facilitate their Hmong clients' needs to seek traditional healing arts, but lack the background knowledge about what is considered acceptable to Hmong individuals or what is available in the Hmong community for patient use. The purpose of this paper is first to familiarize readers with Hmong traditional beliefs about mental health. The second purpose is to introduce the various Hmong traditional healing arts and explain how they can help certain Hmong mental health clients. Third and lastly, this paper will suggest how to identify those Hmong clients most likely to benefit from dual (Western and Hmong) treatments versus those who may progress better by using only one type of treatment.

HMONG TRADITIONAL BELIEFS ABOUT MENTAL HEALTH PROBLEMS

The Hmong society has long recognized that some Hmong individuals suffer from mental health problems. In fact, they have their own terminology for those who suffer from such illnesses. The Hmong associate the liver as the organ which governs a person's emotions, in contrast to the Western association of the heart. For the Hmong, it is the liver which is thought to most directly affect individuals' personalities and mental stability. In the Hmong language, the liver is often used to describe a person's character. For example, a person who is "pure-hearted" is considered to have a "white liver" or siab dawb.

Hmong Terminology of Mental Health Problems

When the Hmong refer to a person as having mental health problems, they usually use one of a variety of "liver" terms. These "liver" terms do not in any way imply a physiological problem with the liver. Rather, the terms are idiomatic and refer only to emotional problems. These are some examples:

"Siab Phem" or Ugly Liver. When a Hmong person is said to have siab phem, it usually means the person has suddenly become destructive and abusive.

"Nyuab Siab" or Difficult Liver. This usually indicates a patient who is suffering from excessive worry. Patients often become confused and cry. Many suffer from loss of sleep.

"Tu Siab" or Broken Liver. This term refers to individuals suffering feelings of guilt or grief.

"Siab Luv" or Short Liver. Patients with this problem often are those with suddenly appearing aggressive behavior, and a change from normal to extreme bad temper.

"Kho Siab" or Murmuring Liver. Those suffering from kho siab usually exhibit the development of certain nervous habits. Commonly seen are constant coughing, humming, whistling or shaking of the head. Patients often begin to talk of death and suicide.

"Lwj Siab" or Rotten Liver. Some clients who are unable to accomplish their goals or are unhappy with their present lives often develop lwj siab. Clients such as these usually exhibit symptoms of loss of memory and delusions.

Relationship Between Mental Health Problems and Traditional Hmong Religion

The Western mental health practitioner should recognize that a Hmong person's belief about his or her health and mental health status is firmly tied in with some tra-

ditional Hmong religious beliefs.   Those Hmong who have
not yet converted to a Western religion are usually ancestor worshipers.   This is not to be confused with the
type of Buddhist religion found in Southeast Asia, which
many of the Lao ethnic group follow.   Unfortunately, no
Hmong literature on their form of ancestor worship exists.   The Hmong have handed down their religious practices and rituals from father to son over the generations
without any written text.   Although this has led to some
regional, clannal and family differences in some ritual
details, most unconverted Hmong continue to follow the
same general broad outlines of ancestor worship.

Hmong families who follow traditional Hmong ancestor
worship practices usually believe that the majority of
mental health cases are caused by certain religious problems.   The most common situations thought to cause these
problems to individuals are either the loss of one's soul
or souls, or problems with spirit entities.

Hmong Beliefs About Soul(s) and Mental Health.   The
Hmong believe that each person has three major souls.
One soul lives in the head area, one in the torso area
and one in the legs area. It is believed that upon death,
one comes back to live with the descendants, one remains
at the grave site, and one goes back to heaven and may
eventually be reborn (either as a human or something
else).   That is how the Hmong believe in both ancestor
workship and reincarnation.

All souls must be united with the body for a person
to have good health--and particularly good mental health.
Loss of one or more souls is thought to cause a wide variety of mental health problems.   The more souls that are
lost, the more serious the symptoms of illness usually
are.   In addition, the longer one has been separated from
one's soul or souls, the more severe the symptoms of illness become.

Whatever the reason for the loss of soul or souls,
the mental health symptoms are usually one or more of the
following: depression, disorientation, delusions, .loss of
appetite, nightmares, aggressive behavior, change in personality and inability to sleep.   Very often victims suc-
cumb to a "liver" disease.   It is the family's responsibility to seek a cure for the person who is sick from
loss of soul.

Hmong Beliefs About Spirits and Mental Health. The Hmong ancestor worshipers believe that the world is coinhabited by a variety of spirit entities. These spirits are thought to affect a person's health and mental health status sometimes. A brief review of the Hmong types of spirits which are thought to commonly affect the mental health status of individuals follows below.

1. Ancestor spirits: Ancestor spirits are the spirits of ancestors who have died. As stated earlier, one of the souls of each ancestor comes back to live with his or her descendants. Ancestor spirits must be kept satisfied to insure the good health and prosperity of the family. Proper burial procedures and the carrying out of certain rituals to strictest detail are considered necessary to keep ancestor spirits content after death. In addition, certain annual ceremonies must be carried out correctly. If these duties are not performed, or are performed incorrectly, the offended ancestor spirit may cause illness or mental health problems to the erring descendant or to a member of the descendant's family. The causing of illness is considered a form of communication rather than a malicious act. The family of the ill person then becomes responsible to find out which ancestor is unhappy or needs something and to perform the necessary conciliatory ceremony.

2. Nature spirits: The Hmong believe that almost all things occurring in nature are governed by a nature spirit. Ponds, streams, rivers, hills, valleys, trees, rocks and even wind currents are believed to have a spirit. Some nature spirits are thought to be very powerful, especially those which have a post serving "god," while others are lesser, localized deities. The localized nature spirits are the ones which sometimes cause illness or mental health problems to some Hmong persons.
   Although nature spirits are usually uninterested in human beings' affairs, if offended, they may cause health or mental health problems to the offending person or to a member of that person's family. Unfortunately, it is difficult to know how to avoid offending nature spirits.

3. Evil spirits: Many Hmong believe that in addition to nature spirits, there are innumerable evil spirits that also coinhabit the earth. Most evil spirits are thought to live in areas not populated by mankind. This is why most Hmong persons prefer not to travel in uninhabited spots alone.   However, evil spirits can also follow humans to their villages and homes and cause all sorts of illness, mental health problems and even some disasters such as a accidents, financial ruin and so forth.   Evil spirits have no known reason for their choice of victim.   The spirits need not have been offended.   Being a victim of an evil spirit is just bad luck.

It is a little more difficult to deal with illness or mental health problems caused by evil spirits.   This is because only sometimes can the evil spirit be bribed into accepting an animal sacrifice in return for allowing the victim to regain good health.   Sometimes the evil spirit is not willing to relinquish the victim and a Hmong person skilled in a certain healing art must then be called in to fight the evil spirit away.

4. House spirits: The last of the spirit entities the Hmong believe to cause health or mental health problems commonly are the house spirits.   Every Hmong house is thought to be inhabited with a set of house spirits.   These include two door spirits, one for the front door and one for the back or side door; two fireplace spirits, as the traditional Hmong home usually has two fireplaces; and four corner spirits, one for each corner of the house.   Usually house spirits help foster the well-being of the family.   However, if offended, the house spirit may then cause illness or mental health problems in the family.

Usually it is relatively easy to help patients with house spirit problems.   House spirits are always benevolent and usually minor sacrifices and the appropriate ceremonies will restore the patient to good health.

Other Hmong Beliefs About Mental Health.   There are two less common causes for Hmong mental health problems. Although these two causes of mental health problems may appear to be less believable or acceptable than the a-forementioned reasons, for some Hmong persons, these causes are very real. Several cases of Hmong mental health problems have been linked to these two causes and a large majority of Hmong still believe in these forces.

1. Curses: The Hmong believe in the power of righteous curses. These curses are not like voodoo or other "black magic" curses. Rather, Hmong curses only have power if the person cursing is morally right to curse.

    If one's mental health problems are caused by a curse, it becomes necessary to locate the cursing person and convince the person to take back the curse. If the cursing person is already dead, it becomes necessary to contact the spirit of that person. Since the cursing person is always morally right, the victim or the victim's family will usually have to make some sort of conciliatory act and/or pay a fee, as well as to conduct a series of ceremonies.

2. Tame evil spirits: Certain persons are thought to know "magic spells" which, when spoken, take the form of an evil spirit. This is not a wild evil spirit like the ones previously mentioned, but an evil spirit tamed by a person. Most Hmong claim that the origins of these tame evil spirits lies with other ethnic groups found in Laos. It is said that some Hmong persons paid a fee to learn this power from these other ethnic groups and, in turn, passed the power on to other Hmong individuals.

    Tame evil spirits are thought to have one of two possible powers. One is the power to magically implant foreign objects such as bones, nails or rocks into victims. The victims then become ill or crazed, and death can follow quickly. The other power is the power to symbolically suck the blood and therefore the life of victims away.

    Only tame evil spirits with the ability to implant foreign objects in a person can take them out. And only tame evil spirits able to suck blood can fight other tame evil spirits of that type. Relatives of victims of tame evil spirits must seek other owners of tame evil spirits and pay them to fight for

the life of the victim. Alternately, they may find
the owner of the tame evil spirit attacking their
relative and bribe him or her to call off the attack.

TYPES OF TRADITIONAL HMONG HEALERS

Just as the Hmong believe there is a wide variety of
causes for mental health problems, they have a wide variety of healing arts that can help cure Hmong mental
health patients. It must be remembered that any one person can know more than one healing art. Since most of
these arts are learned, many Hmong health practitioners
know a variety of traditional healing skills.

Hmong Diagnosticians

Some Hmong health practitioners are only diagnosti-
cians. They provide patients with the probable cause for
their mental health problem or illness, and advise them
on what type or which healer they should contact. The
patient or the patient's family can then proceed on this
advice to obtain a cure. This is considered an important
health care function because each Hmong health praction-
er, even among those following the same discipline, is
thought to have a different level of power. Sometimes
only a certain person will have the power to cure a patient.

Hmong Fortuneteller. This art is thought to have
been originally learned from the Chinese. The Hmong fortuneteller uses a series of charts, reads various omens
and consults with certain gods, and is then able to tell
clients various types of information. Clients who have
mental health problems or who are ill can find out what
the cause of their problem is because the Hmong fortuneteller is able to tell whether the cause is due to spirit
entities, loss of soul, a curse or whatever. In addition,
he can sometimes tell the patient what type of healing
practitioner is most likely to succeed in curing the victim. Of course, Hmong fortunetellers are often consulted
for reasons other than health.

Egg Readers. Many Hmong ask an egg reader for advice at times. Persons who have learned the skill can
talk to a freshly laid raw chicken egg. They will per-

form the right ceremony, then ask the egg the necessary questions.   Most times the egg will be asked which health practitioner can best cure a patient.

Bean Readers.   Bean readers are also usually consulted when a patient does not know which health practitioner to approach.   Three dry soy beans are placed in a bucket of water and are questioned as to whether a certain health practitioner is the right one for a patient. If the beans form a certain configuration, then the answer to the question is affirmative.

Rice Grain Readers.   Rice grain readers perform the same function as Bean Readers except that they use three grains of rice in a cup of water as their tools.

Ear Readers.   Ear readers can tell clients how many and which souls have been lost.   Clients are taken out into bright sunlight.   The ear reader gently holds the client's ear out and looks at it while sunlight streams through it. The fine lines of the ear tell the ear reader what has happened to that person's souls.

Basket Talkers.   Certain people are able to talk to spirits using a large basket.   The spirits are sometimes able to tell why certain patients have become ill.

When evening comes, a basket is dressed up to look like a person.   A "head" is attached and a long stick stuck through to represent arms.   The basket is taken to the door and a spirit is invited to inhabit the basket.

The basket talker can then ask the spirit in the basket questions about almost any subject.   If there is a sick person, the basket spirit can give information as to why that person is sick.

Spoon Talkers.   Some persons are thought to be able to visit the spirit world by using a spoon spirit.   The spoon talker waves a spoon over the fire three times, and then places it down by the fireplace.   The spoon spirit then leads the spirit of the spoon talker to the spirit world.   While in the spirit world, the spoon talker can talk to spirits and ask them questions.

This skill is looked upon skeptically in some Hmong circles while others believe in it.   In Laos, spoon talkers were often asked to talk to spirits simply to entertain or pass time during the village evenings; the practice was only occasionally done to diagnose a patient. In the United States and probably other Western societies, the Hmong do not practice this as much, probably because it is not as easy to build a big fire in the evening.

    Person with a "Neng." A person whose body hosts a "neng," or healing spirit, is probably considered the Hmong diagnostician with the greatest abilities. He or she is also a healer. All of the other Hmong diagnostic techniques and healing arts can be learned. But a person with a neng must inherit his skill and his neng from another member of his clan.

    Each neng has its own level of power and ability. However, almost all of them can diagnose most medical and mental health problems. The host of the neng must have a special altar and certain tools which he uses to help patients. Persons with a neng use their skills exclusively to help ill people, in contrast to other diagnosticians, who sometimes find out information on other subjects.

Hmong Traditional Healers

    After a Hmong patient has been diagnosed, a cure must be found. Over the centuries, the Hmong have developed a variety of healing skills. Sometimes more than one skill must be used to cure a patient. This is usually not a problem because there is little or no professional jealousy among conventional Hmong healing practitioners. Each practitioner is bound by custom not to be competitive and is secure in his or her own ability.

    Herbalist. Almost every Hmong family has a portion of its garden devoted to herbs. In most Hmong families, herbs are quite commonly used for a variety of health problems. However, there are certain persons who are especially skilled in using a larger variety of herbs.

    Masseuse. The Hmong use massage as a technique to cure a variety of body aches. The most skilled masseuses are able to bring relief to head, muscle and even some forms of stomachaches. They are able to massage without irritating or hurting the skin.

    At times, masseuses rub herbs into the skin of the patient while massaging. At other times, hard boiled chicken eggs and silver bars are used in the massage technique.

Needle Users.   The Hmong have not developed the art
of acupuncture.   However, they do on occasion use needles
for "blood pressure" problems.   Most commonly used are
regular sewing needles.

Soul Callers.   When a person's soul is lost or
thought to be lost, often the family of that person will
perform a soul calling ceremony.   There are three variations of the ceremony.   However, whatever the variation,
at least a pair of chickens (one rooster and one hen,
each about two to three months old) and one egg must be
sacrificed.

The first variation is the least complicated.   Usually most Hmong elders and heads of household know how to
do it.   The positions of the claws, the jaws, the eyes
and the skulls of the chickens all say whether the soul
has returned or not.   If the soul has not returned in a
few days, additional chickens must again be sacrificed.

The second variation of soul calling is usually performed for those who suspect they know where their soul
was lost.   For example, if the patient was suddenly
frightened at the riverside, the soul caller will go to
the riverside.   He or she will then perform the necessary
ceremonies and say the correct words and lead the soul
back to the village and the house of the patient.   Again,
at least two chickens and an egg must be prepared in the
same manner described earlier.

The third variation involves a time period of a day.
Three soul-calling ceremonies are performed in the home:
one at sunrise, one at midday, and one at dusk.   However,
chickens need be sacrificed only at dusk.

Person with a "Neng."   A person with a neng is
thought to be the most skilled of the Hmong healing practitioners.   He or she is most commonly asked to assist
only in relatively serious medical or mental health
cases.   While in a trance, the person with a neng can not
only find out if the patient is suffering from problems
with spirits, but also if the patient needs assistance
from other health practitioners in case it is not a spiritual problem, or if another person with a neng would
better be able to help the patient.

When dealing with illnesses caused by ancestor, nature or house spirits, the person with a neng usually
makes a deal with the offended spirit.

When dealing with evil spirits, the person with a neng must sometimes literally fight with the spirit. He or she will pick up the neng sword and tambourine and jump about the room fighting the spirit.

At times, when the person with the neng finds out that the patient is simply suffering from old age and that it is time for the patient to die, the person with a neng may even visit heaven and ask the god in charge of human beings' "visas" on earth if the patient's life can be extended in return for a sacrifice.

Persons with a neng are also skilled in finding people's lost souls. While in a trance, friendly spirits can help the neng locate a lost soul and entice it back to the patient.

Persons with a neng are thought always to be ethically moral people. This is because the neng which selects them are supposed to select goodhearted people and keep their hosts from doing any medical evil. They are greatly respected in the Hmong community and a very rigid protocol must be followed when requesting a person with a neng to take a medical or mental health case.

FACTORS TO CONSIDER WHEN REFERRING A HMONG CLIENT TO TRADITIONAL HEALERS

Having reviewed Hmong attitudes on mental health problems and how the Hmong community traditionally treats mental health problems, I will now consider which Hmong clients of Western mental health professionals would most likely benefit from referral to traditional healers. The Western practitioner should make several considerations before arriving at his or her decision.

Consideration of Cross-cultural Differences in Initial Assessment of Client

Some Hmong clients may give unsuspecting Western mental health practitioners the firm impression that the client is suffering from delusions and/or a wandering mind. This is because a Hmong person's description of his or her symptoms may sound very unusual to the Western ear. What Hmong society often feels is a straightforward description of a disease may cause a Westerner to be convinced that the client needs mental health care. For example, clients who complain about their blood being unable to flow, or bugs eating away their flesh, or rocks in their stomach are often thought to be suffering from delusion. In addition to complaints about strange symptoms, the Hmong client may give an unbalanced appearance because he or she may not seem to be able to answer questions in an appropriate manner. It is normal for a Hmong client, especially an elder one, to ramble as he or she recounts his or her health or mental health history. Accounts of dreams or encounters with spirit entities may even be included.

The Western mental health practitioner must consider that these mannerisms and accounts are within the norms of Hmong society in relation to mental health problems. While deciding the course of Western treatment, professionals should also consider referring the client to traditional healers. Perhaps some clients may not even need Western mental health counseling, while others may be suited for Western health care and not traditional care.

Hmong clients who complain of being depressed, being forgetful, having loss of appetite and so forth have in the past often been treated successfully by traditional means. It is almost safe to say that most Hmong clients above the age of twenty-five years would receive some form of emotional support if he or she received a form of traditional treatment, either in conjunction with Western treatment, or alone. It must be remembered that Hmong healing treatment does not prohibit use of other medical systems, so dual (Western/Hmong) treatments can readily be accomplished if the client desires. For those younger than twenty-five years of age, particularly teenagers, referral to traditional treatments may not be as necessary unless the teenager belongs to an extended family which places great value on Hmong healing arts.

Availability of Hmong Health Practitioners in the Community

It is the custom that a Hmong health practitioner not advertise his or her skill. Thus, it is often hard for Westerners to obtain a list of who and what skills are available in the local Hmong community. Usually the Hmong grapevine is quite adequate in providing this information, but on occasion, certain clients may not have access to this information either.

Most large Hmong communities have quite a large variety of healing persons with different skills available. Unfortunately, some of the smaller Hmong communities may not. However, when traditional treatment is desired but not available, Hmong patients sometimes are willing to travel to another town to seek cures. At times, family members in another city can ask a person with a neng to perform a ceremony without the patient being physically present.

Western mental health practitioners who deal largely with Hmong clients should be encouraged to become familiar with the social organization of their local Hmong community. Usually there will be one or more community leaders who can supply information regarding availability of traditional healers. It must be remembered, though, when discussing traditional healing arts, that young Hmong community leaders may not know as much as Hmong elders and clan leaders.

Clan or Family Preferences

It is the custom of Hmong families to seek cures for sick family members, rather than the sick person seeking a cure for himself or herself. Thus it is difficult for younger Hmong persons without an extended family to seek traditional health treatments. It must also be remembered that when utilizing traditional health practitioners, some fees may be involved. Depending on what is involved, fees can be nothing, part of the animal sacrifice or as high as in the hundreds of dollars. In addition, it must be remembered that if one utilizes certain types of Hmong health practitioners, one must be prepared to sacrifice chickens and/or a pig. Families who cannot afford, or do not know how to obtain, or do not have the

transportation to obtain these items, may hesitate to
seek traditional treatments. In Laos, each Hmong family
kept at least a few live chickens and pigs around their
farm. So obtaining live sacrifice was not the problem it
has become in Western societies.

Some Hmong persons may prefer to utilize only Hmong
health practitioners who are of the same clan, or who are
relatives. This may be in the hope that the fees will be
less, or the sacrifice for the spirits less expensive.
It may also be due to less friendly relations between
some clans. Therefore, it is sometimes difficult for an
outsider to recommend with confidence any particular
Hmong health practitioner without considering interclan-
nal as well as personal relations. It may be best to advise a client to seek preliminary counseling from his or
her clan leader.

Religious Background of Client

There are sizable numbers of Hmong in Western communities who have converted to some form of Christianity.
A large number of these belong to the Christian & Missionary Alliance group, while some are Catholic and others belong to miscellaneous Protestant groups. Almost all
Hmong Christians are reluctant to participate in soul-
calling ceremonies or to accept treatment from a person
with a neng. Some even go so far as to charge that
chickens or pigs sacrificed for these health practices
are "devil's meat." Thus, if the Western health practitioner encounters a Hmong Christian, it would be safest
to suggest that if the patient wishes traditional treatment, he or she should seek only the herbalists, mas-
seuses, and/or needle users.

Most Hmong ancestor worshipers are probably more re-
ceptive to using any variety of Hmong traditional healing
arts. It might be mentioned here that many Hmong clients
may not admit to being ancestor worshipers for fear that
the Western health practitioner may not understand this
religion. One must tactfully question a client as to his
or her true beliefs before deciding whether to recommend
traditional healing treatments.

CONCLUSION

There are many factors to consider before a Western mental health practitioner may decide that a client would benefit from traditional healing treatments. However, since Hmong health treatments never hurt anyone, but could possibly help a patient, it should be seriously considered as part of a client's course of treatment. Even if the traditional treatments may not appear to do any clinical good to the Western observer, the support the patient feels from his family as the family goes about performing the traditional ceremonies provides the patient with positive feelings. The sacrificed animals almost always lead to a small party of sorts to consume the meat, and this too can engender positive feelings.

The Hmong have been treating their own mental health problems for centuries and although many of their methodologies may sound very unusual to Westerners, many Hmong mental health patients have been successfully cured or helped using these methods. There is enough of a variety of different Hmong health disciplines that almost any Hmong client may find something that suits his or her case. Even if a Western health practitioner may not actually want to refer a client to a Hmong health practitioner, it is the intent of this paper to encourage him or her to foster an understanding environment in the counseling sessions and to accept a Hmong client's terminology of mental health problems, and perhaps even to suggest that the client may, on his own, seek traditional healing treatment without fear of ridicule.

HMONG PERCEPTION OF ILLNESS
AND TRADITIONAL WAYS OF HEALING

Xoua Thao

The Hmong have a traditional system of dealing with illness. This traditional system consists of shamanism, herbal medicines or a combination of the two. In leaving Laos, the Hmong knew that their traditional ways of healing would be challenged by Western medical practices in their countries of resettlement (Catanzaro and Moser 1982). In my experience as an interpreter at a large metropolitan hospital, I have observed that few Western health care providers have prior experience in caring for patients who do not share their scientific rationalism.

This paper attempts to provide Western health care workers with an introduction to the Hmong perception of illness and traditional methods of healing. Most of these traditional .practices are still carried on by the Hmong in their new countries. It remains for future research to discover what and how modifications have been instituted.

The draft of this paper was discussed with many Hmong experts who have knowledge of shamanism and herbal medicines. Many Hmong bilingual workers who have experience in Hmong medical practices also have read it.

The Hmong healing system shares many common elements of traditional folk medicines found in numerous rural village settings (Snow 1974). Incantations, rituals and herbs have been the traditional medicines for most of history (Balikci 1967). In the Hmong world, shamanism and herbal medicines come in a variety of forms and procedures. I will discuss some elements of Hmong shamanism and herbal medicines, the concept of soul loss, ways of calling back the soul, the mandate of life, the different causes of illness, the traditional use of herbal medicines and, finally, the highest and most complex ritual in Hmong shamanism, called Ua Neeb.

HMONG SHAMANISM

Hmong shamanism is a repository of many esoteric rituals and incantations. They constitute the main processes the Hmong use to cure and are substantially based upon oral texts which only a few individuals know. These few individuals could be males or females. They become experts through a period of training, and they are the only ones to practice. Hmong shamans keep an altar at home to convince the community of their skills.

The altar is the shaman's "diploma," announcing his or her expertise to individuals who seek help, much like the framed certificates that hang in a Western physician's office. The altar also symbolizes the shaman's devotion to the sick and suffering.

Shamans perform rituals at the altar and elsewhere, depending upon the type of ritual. However, for the rituals and incantations to work, every step in the procedure must be followed and everything done as prescribed. The individual must believe in the process and have confidence in the shaman. One often offers the shaman food, money or some words of thanks as a sign of trust and appreciation.

There are many rituals and incantations. Like drugs, each is good for a symptom or a specific illness. There are rituals and incantations for headache, vomiting, rash, eye and ear complications, soul loss, etc.

HERBAL MEDICINES

In the Hmong community, herbal medicines rally against illness along with shamanism. Herbal medicines are part of the women's world. As the women claim, "We are given the gift and knowledge. Only we can make herbal medicines effective. Men are much too careless."

Medicinal herbs are used on a trial-and-error basis. Not every woman has the knowledge of and access to these herbs. Gifted women pass on their knowledge informally to their daughters or grandaughters. In fact, experts in this area of healing rarely teach anyone unless the novice is a relative or a trusted friend.

The effectiveness of the herbs depends extensively on the attentiveness given to their preparations. Without care and proper use, they are futile. If the herbs fail to satisfy people's expectations, as a female herbalist says, "they curse the experts and condemn the medicines." Unlike shamanistic rituals, however, one herbal medicine can be used for more than one illness.

The Hmong perceive illness as a condition that renders an individual incapable of eating, drinking or getting out of bed. An individual who can still force himself or herself out of bed is hardly considered ill. Thus, a person is sick only when he or she cannot perform or fulfill his or her social tasks and responsibilities.

THE CONCEPT OF SOUL LOSS

Hmong believe there are many sources of illness. But the primary cause is the loss of soul. Illness can also be of natural causes, supernatural or spirit causes, magical causes or organic causes. Each of these causes has certain characteristics and is determined by the condition and history of the illness. Usually a mild illness is believed to be of natural or organic causes while the serious ones are ascribed to the supernatural, spirit or magical causes.

Though there are various beliefs, soul loss deserves first mention. To the Hmong, every person has a soul which lives in and governs the body. However, the soul may leave a person's body when the person is frightened or alone in a dark place, or when he or she feels depressed and lonely due to separation from family or loss of a loved one. In any highly emotional circumstances, there is a possibility that the soul will go away.

When a baby cries constantly at night, the Hmong would say that the baby might have lost its soul. Customarily, an adult family member takes a burning stick to the door and swings it back and forth. This shines the way for the lost soul to return. If that fails to pacify the baby, then the family member places some corn or rice in a tray and waves it in circular motion above the baby's head. While doing so, he or she pleads to the soul to come back.

Children or adults who have lost their souls ordinarily become thin, tired or pale. They sleep heavily and lose appetite. A shaman claims that behind the earlobes of these people, a tiny blister exists on top of a small capillary. When these symptoms appear, they should not be ignored because they indicate soul loss. If left unattended, the person will become sick. The soul, then, will be difficult to call back.

Normally, the wandering soul returns to its host. However the vagrant soul can also change into other forms of life. When the soul has transformed, as the Hmong believe, it does not recognize its owner. It cannot return. The Hmong say, "The soul cannot find its way home." If the transformed soul is accepted into a new form of being, then the owner becomes seriously ill. Death can result. If a ritual is not performed to call the soul back, the sick person will not get well.

However, if the soul transforms and is not accepted into a new form of being, it then wanders until it is hungry and exhausted. In this state, the soul would not survive long. It is willing to come back to its owner if the necessary measure is taken to get it back.

Because the Hmong believe the soul leaves the body easily, wherever they go, before returning home, they usually utter words that say it is time to go home, and the soul, wherever it is at that moment, must return, too. When the Hmong are at an unfamiliar place or even when they are out at a picnic, they rarely return quietly. Parents would call loudly to their children's souls. Individuals can also call their own souls. If the parents fail to summon the souls back, their imprudence dooms their children to eventual sickness. Out of this belief that the soul needs to know its owner and to be called into the body springs the practice of giving a newborn baby a name in a welcoming ceremony on the third day.

WAYS OF CALLING THE SOUL BACK

Traditionally there are many ways to call the soul back. If the person is sick because the soul cannot find its way home, then the family of the stricken individual prepares two small rectangular boards. The parents take them to the intersection of two pathways near the house

and place them in a criss-cross pattern. This placement
symbolically serves to guide the soul back home. If any
stranger happens to pass by at that occasion, the parents
would ask for a few words of blessing.

If the person is seriously ill because the soul either has gone too far or was transformed into another
form of life, then an animal has to be sacrificed. Before the animal is slaughtered, the shaman performs the
ritual by standing inside the door, chanting a lengthy
incantation. When the incantation is complete, the animal is killed. Its head is cooked and brought back to
the door. At this time, the shaman performs the second
and last round of the calling ritual. The Hmong believe
the animal's soul will replace the person's soul. The
type of animal depends on the shaman as well as the situation. For instance, if the child falls into a pond, then
a duck is needed. However, sometimes a dog is used; at
other times, a pig, chicken or cow is acceptable.

Although there are many methods, each with a different procedure, the use of an egg is most popular. Initially the shaman massages the sick with some ginger,
starting from the head, then the fingers and toes. The
massage gradually moves toward the center of the body,
and the shaman continually says he is gathering and calling the soul back. As he finishes, the ritual begins.

Normally, three poles and one of the sick person's
shirts are required. The first pole is staked outside
the door, the second at the threshold, and the third a
few feet into the house. A string is tied to them. The
shirt is placed on the ground at the third pole with its
front facing inward. As the shaman stands at the threshold calling, another person must sit at the third pole,
holding an egg upright on the palms of both hands which
are laid on top of the shirt. Whenever the egg falls
backward, as the shaman chants, that symbolizes the return of the soul. Immediately, the shaman cuts the
string. The egg and shirt are steamed together. Then
the egg is burnt to destroy the path which led the soul
astray. The shirt can be worn again. To further stabilize the soul, white strings are tied to the wrist of the
sick person.

THE MANDATE OF LIFE

In addition to soul loss, there is the belief of a "mandate of life." The Hmong believe that every person is given a mandate to be a human being. On it, the Superior Being foretells the length of the person's existence and his or her fate. An individual, therefore, becomes ill because the mandate of life predetermines illness and dies because death is due.

NATURAL CAUSES

Besides the soul and the mandate of life, nature can cause illness to men. Historically, the Hmong settle in the highlands and mountainous areas. They grow up adapting to nature, hills and jungles. This ecological relationship influences their perception of illness, which is strongly based upon the equilibrium of men and nature. Also, the locations of Hmong villages expose them to a constant range of weather. They are sensitive to its fluctuation and the seasonal changes.

Because men and nature must coexist in equilibrium, the Hmong consider illness a distortion of this relationship. Rheumatism is a good example. The pain of joints and the aching of the body are symptoms the Hmong associate with the coming of either warm or rainy weather. Fever, cold, runny nose and coughing are ascribed to the shifting of the man-nature relationship.

The Hmong are conscious of the impact of natural factors upon the health of an individual. They exercise preventive measures. A mother who has just given birth to a baby is discouraged from participating in the family's daily work for a month. They believe that her body is "unclean" and already in "disequilibrium" with nature. Forcing herself to work in such a condition will make her ill in later life. When the weather changes, she will become sick. Furthermore, such a mother should be very careful in using water and food. She must eat right. Hot is always preferred because, as a Hmong woman says, "cold water and food will make our blood congeal and give us sickness. Our skin will become wrinkled and very itchy in old age."

ORGANIC CAUSES

Although the Hmong place great credence in natural causes of illness, they also find organic explanations appropriate. Illnesses which exhibit physical evidence-- such as stomachache, chicken pox, nose bleeding, or leprosy—are always accepted to have some organic bases. A weak individual is thought to lack something in the body.

When this person eats well but gains no weight, the Hmong claim that there is not enough fat and blood to feed his or her body. To get more fat and blood (and thus strength), a chicken is killed and cooked with some herbal medicines which give the healing power. The chicken is needed because the herbs are not usually eaten directly. This procedure is repeated three or four times.

TRADITIONAL USE OF HERBS

The Hmong use herbal medicines to deal with some of the organic illnesses. Massage is often the initial step to treat a stomachache. Then certain herbal medicines are used. Sometimes some dry roots are sliced into tiny pieces and put in a glass of hot water for the person to drink. Other times the person eats the pieces. The procedure depends on the types of herbs and must be followed correctly. For example, if the herbal roots are given to a male, there should be nine slices. If given to a female, seven are required. The number has to be exact.

In addition to the utilization of herbs, the Hmong also believe that sometimes a person is sick because there is too much pressure inside the body due to stress. To relieve the internal tension, the yolk of a hard-boiled egg and a silver bar are wrapped together in a piece of cloth. The person either sits still or lies down, and someone rubs the pack over the person's back, arms and forehead.

Although herbal medicines help many symptoms, they are not used for every illness. The Hmong still turn to the rituals and incantations for many conditions which appear to have organic bases. When a baby or an adult has a rash in the mouth, a specific incantation remedies it. A hoe and some cotton are used. While the shaman is outside, another person sits inside the door with the individual who has the rash. This other person points the hoe's handle toward the sick person's mouth. The shaman lights the cotton and chants a three-verse incantation. The person holding the handle responds to each line respectively. Most Hmong prefer this method over herbal medicines or foreign medications.

There are also very specific incantations for ear and eye problems. The shaman points the socket of a hoe to the inflamed ear. A small paddle is used to strike the hoe gently while the shaman chants the incantation. The trouble is relieved by its words. For a person with repeated eye pain, the shaman points two or three burning incenses to the troubled eye and chants the incantation. When he finishes, he stakes those incenses beside the door. For conditions that lack appropriate incantations or herbal medicines, the sick person will be brought to medical attendants using Western practices as a last resort.

MAGICAL CAUSES

Magical sources can also cause illness. The Hmong believe words can cause illness when they are cursed upon others. Furthermore, there are magical people who can cast spells on someone to cause sickness. They can send an "egg stone" to the person.[1] When the person is hit by this inanimate object, unless it is discarded, the individual can die.

When someone is inflicted with this magical thing, it can be removed by an incantation. The shaman asks the victim for the place of pain and begins to suck out that area. He then spits the magical stone into a bowl of water. The stone is thrown away, and the person should feel fine. A Hmong shaman asserts that it is bad to learn to cast magical spells because one has to use the acquired skills. If not, the magical spells can turn harmful to the expert or members of the expert's family.

SUPERNATURAL OR SPIRIT CAUSES

Aside from natural, organic and magical causes, the belief in spirits makes up a large system encompassing virtually every serious illness. In addition to severity of the condition, an illness caused by the spirits must show certain consistent patterns. The person feels more pain or is disturbed more often at a certain period of time. When that time arrives the next day, the person experiences the same plight. Such a characteristic of the illness is readily attributed to the doings of spirits. Furthermore, if the sick person shows some kind of peculiar physical symptoms such as mumbling, trembling, convulsion or the deformation of facial expressions, the Hmong most often describe that as being hit by the spirits.

Spirits dislike being disturbed. If people are not careful and do not keep away, they can be hit and become sick. The individual catches illness by touching and destroying the spirits' places or by cursing and ignoring them. When a person sees a whirlwind, for example, the person should stay away at a distance. If such an individual ignores the phenomenon and is hit, the spirit of the whirlwind can make the person dizzy. A pregnant woman disturbing the spirit of a stream when she crosses it can expect a miscarriage.

The spirits and the people must live in harmony. Otherwise, the spirits can afflict them with illness, plague or natural catastrophe. An unhappy spirit might abduct the soul and threaten it to make the host severely ill. In that case, an animal is needed to get the soul back. Even if the spirit does not kidnap the soul, it can come to the individual and disturb the soul in the body. In such cases, the individual experiences excruciating pain when the spirit is present and alleviation when it goes away. The illness is expected to persist if nothing is done to chase away the spirit, to hide the soul of the sick person or to negotiate with the spirit.

WAYS OF DEALING WITH SPIRITS

There are several ways to encounter the spirits. All involve rituals and incantations. A person who has been hit by the spirit of the sun, for example, would have pain in the head in late morning and again in late afternoon. To get rid of this spirit, a small crossbow is made. An arrow, with an egg shell inserted into it, is shot over the person's head in the directions of north, south, east and west. The arrow, however, is shot only after the incantation has been chanted by the shaman. This ritual is done early in the morning when the sun just starts to rise and is repeated for several mornings. The Hmong believe that the arrow transfixes the sun and, as it sets, the spirit goes away as well. The arrow and the egg are posted outside the house.

There is also an incantation to drive away the spirit that causes vomiting. The sick person puts five coins into a glass of water. As the shaman begins chanting, he pokes the water slightly with the handle of a hammer. After the three verses, the person is given the glass of water for three sips. If the sick person is in bed, then the shaman turns the glass of water--however much of it is left--upside down beneath the bed. But if the sick person is brought to the shaman's house, then the shaman places the glass of water upside down where the sick person sits. A few days afterwards, the glass is removed, and the shaman keeps the coins. The water serves as the antidote for this condition.

Sickness can be caused by all kinds of spirits, and each incantation only works against one type. So, to be effective, the right one must be used. A certain ritual requires the use of knives. After it is performed, the knives are placed at the door to scare away the spirit. Another incantation is accompanied by the spitting into a fire around the sick person. The shaman holds an oil lamp and takes in some water into the mouth. The water is spit back over the oil lamp to cause a flash of fire. These are extreme cases for incantations, and the shaman must be paid some money. After these rituals, a tree branch is always put up in front of the house to keep outsiders from entering. It is feared that outsiders might make way for the spirit to return.

In addition to chasing the spirit away, a person's soul may be hidden so that the spirit cannot find it. Thus, it will go away. The shaman takes a few hairs from the person, puts them in a glass of water and chants the incantation. The glass is sealed very carefully with a piece of white cloth. It is placed underneath the bed where the sick person is.

Another method is to use charcoal instead of hairs. Three pieces of charcoal are put in the glass of water. In addition, five bamboo meshes are made. When the shaman completes the incantation, four bamboo meshes are put on poles in four different corners of the house. The fifth one is staked near where the sick person sleeps. The glass is also carefully sealed and placed underneath the bed. This ritual is traditionally called "sealing of water" and serves two functions. First, it camouflages the soul so that the spirit does not recognize and cannot bother it. Second, the ritual confines the soul so that it does not wander off to disturb the spirit.

THE RITUAL CALLED UA NEEB

When a person is sick and various incantations fail to help, the person resorts to a particular shaman who has the ability to travel to the spirit world to search for the lost or kidnapped soul. This ritual is called Ua Neeb. Through it the shaman comes in contact with the spirits and negotiates the price for getting the soul back to the owner. This process is the ultimate expression of Hmong shamanism.

These shamans must have some decent characteristics and appropriate qualities to be called or chosen to this vocation. The recurring sickness they experience convinces them that they have been called, even against their will, to learn this craft of healing. A Hmong shaman proclaims, "If I refused to obey the sign and did not start the craft, I would always be sick."

Some shamans perform Ua Neeb in half an hour while others may begin in the morning and end in the afternoon. Others may begin in the afternoon and end late in the evening. Still others may begin early in the morning and end the ritual the following morning. The length of time for the ritual varies from one individual shaman to another and certainly depends on the practice of the teacher shaman from whom one learned the procedure. Although the time length varies, a shaman who finishes the ritual in less than half an hour is suspected and might even lose credibility in the eyes of the sick person.

Before Ua Neeb, the shaman needs certain objects. Incenses and an egg in a bowl of rice are placed on the altar, which is found against the front wall of the house. The shaman covers his face with a black piece of cloth and begins. A gong is also played along by the shaman's helper. When the shaman is on the way to the spirit world, he communicates this fact to his helper who then silences the gong. As the shaman searches for the causes of the illness, he constantly sends back messages. The helper relays the messages to the family of the sick.

When the ritual stops, the shaman explains to the family what he has found. Sometimes the shaman discovered that the soul was lost and could not find its way home, but he has gathered it back to the body. In that case, no future ritual is needed. However, if the shaman discovered that the soul of the sick person has been kidnapped or transformed, then he asks the family to get an animal and sets another time for the next set of rituals. The type of animal--be it chicken, pig, dog or cow--is what the shaman negotiated with the spirit.

In the second ceremony, the family of the sick person prepares the animal for sacrifice. When the shaman gets to the spirit world, he starts negotiating with the spirits. When the concession is accepted, the shaman sends back the message. The helper lets the family know, and immediately the animal is slaughtered. Some ritual papers will be stained with the animal's blood and be burnt as a payment to the spirits. This is the most exhausting healing task.

A TURNING POINT

If illness persists after Ua Neeb, the family turns to the "position of an egg." In this traditional practice, an egg is stood up on a bottle that lies flat on a tray of rice. The positioning of an egg serves as an outlet to search for another shaman or mode of healing. When the egg suddenly stands up at the mention of a shaman's name or a new set of rituals the family goes to that shaman for help, or prepares the new set of rituals. A new process then begins.

CONCLUSION

Shamanism and herbal medicines make up the Hmong's traditional world of dealing with illness. Shamanism is elaborate, esoteric, and based on rituals and incantations. Herbal medicines, however, are solely in the women's world and also come in a variety of forms and procedures. Though the concept of soul loss is most strongly believed, illness can be caused by many other sources such as nature, physiology, mankind, magic and spirits. The Hmong have evolved many different methods to deal with each causal element and to counteract illness as a whole. By learning more about Hmong attitudes toward health and illness, Western health care providers can do much to improve the quality and appropriateness of care for this special group of new immigrants.

ACKNOWLEDGEMENTS

I would sincerely like to thank my parents, Mr. Chadang and Mrs. Xang Yang Thao, for their patience and sincerity in sharing with me the Hmong's traditional arts of healing. I extend my appreciation to Mrs. Youa Cha, Mr. Cher Ker Moua, Mr. Pakoua Vang, and Mr. Chong Lee Chue for their enthusiasm in teaching me our ways of doctoring. I wish to say <u>ua tsaug</u> to John Finck and Donna Dryer for their help in writing this paper.

NOTE

[1]An egg stone is a tiny piece of stone that the shaman sucks out from an area where the victim feels a shocking pain.

REFERENCES

Balikci, Asen. 1967. "Shamanistic Behavior among the Netsilik Eskimo." In <u>Magic Witchcraft and Curing,</u> edited by J. Middleton. Austin: University of Texas Press.

Catanzaro, A. and R.J. Moser. 1982. "Health Status of Refugees from Vietnam, Laos, and Cambodia." JAMA 247(9): 1303-1307.

Snow, L. 1974. "Folk Medical Beliefs and Their Implications for Care of Patients." Annals of Internal Medicine 81: 82-96.

SLEEP DISTURBANCES AND SUDDEN DEATH OF HMONG REFUGEES: A REPORT ON FIELDWORK CONDUCTED IN THE BAN VINAI REFUGEE CAMP

Ronald G. Munger

Sudden unexpected deaths during sleep continue to be a significant public health problem of Southeast Asian refugees in the United States. Sudden deaths in sleep of Hmong refugees in Thailand were reported by Hmong in interviews in the United States in 1981, shortly after sensational newspaper reports of sudden deaths appeared in this country (Munger 1982). These refugee accounts and an interest in studying the problem of sudden death as a phenomenon of migrant populations led the author to conduct field studies in Southeast Asia. A study of sudden death in sleep of Hmong refugees was conducted in the Ban Vinai refugee camp, in northeastern Thailand, from October 1982 to June 1983.

One goal of this fieldwork was to document whether or not sudden unexpected deaths during sleep occurred among Hmong refugees in Thailand. The next step was to study the characteristics of sudden death victims (cases) as compared to randomly selected individuals in Ban Vinai of the same ethnicity, age and sex (controls). The study design thus used a "case-control" method (Schlesselman 1982). The purpose of this report is to describe cases of sleep disorders which may be related to the sudden deaths in sleep. Presented here are case reports of four sudden death victims with a history of previous nonfatal sleep disturbances and reports of similar nonfatal sleep disturbances occurring to individuals who are still living at the time of this writing. Such cases of nonfatal sleep disturbances are consistent with the hypothesis that disorders of the control of respiration during sleep--the sleep apnea syndromes--may be related to the Southeast Asian sudden deaths in sleep (Munger 1982). Nonfatal sleep disturbances may identify a group of individuals who are at a high risk of dying suddenly during sleep.

Sudden death of adult Southeast Asian refugees in the United States during sleep has been recognized as a syndrome. The distinction must be made between a syndrome, a collection of signs and symptoms, and a disease, defined by specific abnormalities of bodily structure or function. The disease process that is the underlying cause of the Southeast Asian sudden death syndrome is unknown; further clinical studies are necessary. The distinction between disease and illness is also important. Illness refers to an individual's perception of disease and disability, which may be quite different from the physician's perception of the disease involved. Interview studies of Hmong refugees cannot precisely define the underlying disease process of the sudden death syndrome, but the observations and explanations offered by Hmong refugees can provide clues to the chain of events responsible for this malady.

The pattern of sudden deaths in sleep among Southeast Asian refugees has stimulated research in several disciplines, including the social sciences, medicine and epidemiology. The history and methods of some of these studies and some reactions of the Hmong community to these studies are reviewed in this volume by Hurlich, Holtan and Munger (p. 427). The initial results of studies summarized below serve to guide the course of future research and public health programs.

SUDDEN DEATHS OF SOUTHEAST ASIAN REFUGEES IN THE UNITED STATES

The United States Centers for Disease Control (CDC) has reviewed at least seventy-nine cases of sudden, unexpected death of Southeast Asian refugees in the United States occurring between 15 July 1977 and 30 April 1983 (Baron et. al. 1983). The first cases of these sudden deaths were recognized by Larry Lewman, M.D., of the Multnomah County, Oregon, Medical Examiner's Office. Of the seventy-nine cases reported to the CDC, thirty-nine were Laotian Hmong, twenty-one were ethnic Lao, ten were Kampuchean and nine were Vietnamese. Only one of the victims was female. All of the deaths occurred during sleep and none of the victims had a significant illness prior to death. Witnesses to the deaths often described moaning, groaning or choking respiratory sounds, and several victims had seizure-like activity at the time of death. Routine autopsies and toxicological analyses did not indicate a cause of death (U.S. Centers for Disease Control 1981; Baron et al. 1983).

The suddenness of the deaths and the lack of specific pathologic changes are consistent with death due to cardiac dysrhythmia. The CDC received three reports of documented abnormal cardiac electrical activity in the victims; ventricular fibrillation was confirmed in each case. Three other Asian men have been successfully resuscitated from episodes of ventricular fibrillation in sleep (Tauxe et al. 1982; Tauxe, personal communication). All three patients recovered from the initial episode and showed no evidence of coronary artery disease. One patient was found to have self-limiting polymorphic ventricular tachycardia which was easily induced by electrophysiologic stimulation. Quinidine therapy successfully abolished this response; procainamide had no effect. Tauxe and his colleagues concluded that the sudden death syndrome is the result of a primary cardiac abnormality predisposing certain individuals to lethal cardiac arrhythmias.

Detailed studies of the cardiac conduction system of Southeast Asian sudden death victims are being conducted by Robert Kirschner, M.D., Deputy Medical Examiner, Cook County, Illinois, and Friedrich A. O. Eckner of the University of Illinois School of Medicine. Conduction system abnormalities which may predispose individuals to sudden death have been observed by these investigators (Eckner et al. 1983).

The review of pathology reports and the case-control study conducted by the CDC have ruled out infectious agents, unusual physical illness, pharmacologically active substances and agents of chemical or biological warfare as causes of the Southeast Asian sudden deaths (Baron et al. 1983). The CDC study also did not find any significant emotional experiences or stressful events that characterized cases as compared to controls; this investigation was not designed to be an in-depth study of cultural or psychological factors contributing to the deaths. The CDC investigation found no evidence that the sudden death victims under study were related, although

it was reported that one relative of a sudden death victim died under similar circumstances in Laos.

A study of cultural, socioeconomic and familial factors possibly related to the sudden deaths of Hmong in
the United States was conducted by Dr. Bruce Thowpaou
Bliatout (1983). Bliatout conducted case investigations
from his unique position as a native-Hmong researcher.
Of the forty-five cases investigated by Bliatout, eight
of the victims had at least one other relative who died
under similar circumstances. Bliatout presents this evidence to support the hypothesis that a genetic factor may
predispose some individuals to sudden death. Bliatout
suggested two triggering mechanisms that he thought might
act upon a background of genetic susceptibility to sudden
death. The first triggering factor he suggested is
stress due to the inability to continue certain religious
practices in Western countries, inability to find traditional healers or difficulty in adapting to a new lifestyle. The second triggering mechanism suggested by
Bliatout is an acquired weakness due to exposure to
agents of chemical warfare in Laos.

A clustering of sudden deaths within families does
not necessarily mean that a genetic factor is responsible
for the deaths. Family clusters may also result from an
environment the family shares from psychological or social factors they share, or from chance alone.
Bliatout's study, conducted at his own expense, would be
strengthened by further support which would allow the
addition of a control group with which the cases could be
compared.

Professor Jacques Lemoine and Ms. Christine Mougne
interviewed twenty-nine families of Hmong, Lao and Mien-
Yao sudden death victims in the United States (Lemoine
and Mougne 1983). In four of the twenty-nine families of
sudden death victims, evidence was found of similar
deaths occurring among close male relatives. Lemoine and
Mougne speculated that night terror may lead to sudden
death in sleep. The sudden death cases were classified
into two categories: victims of "culture shock" whose
deaths occurred within days or weeks after arrival in the
United States and victims who died after a longer period
of time in this country. Members of this latter group
were thought not to exhibit acute psychological trauma,
but perhaps were exhausted, had family quarrels or were

provoked by terrifying images from television. Lemoine and Mougne concluded that the Southeast Asian sudden deaths are a result of the interaction of psychological, cultural and physical factors. A case-control comparison would be more convincing than a presentation of selected cases and should be incorporated in future research on the sudden death syndrome. Lemoine and Mougne also do not provide statistical data to support their hypothesis that two distinct categories of sudden death exist. Based on their experiences in Southeast Asia and on the reaction of refugees interviewed in the United States, Lemoine and Mougne responded with a "qualified no" when asked whether sudden deaths in sleep occur in the refugees' own homeland, noting that "mainland Southeast Asian populations have never had a sophisticated medical surveillance system such as found in the United States (Lemoine and Mougne 1983, p. 10).

The sudden deaths of Southeast Asian refugees are strikingly similar to sudden deaths of Filipino men, known in Tagolo as bangungut. On the basis of the circumstances of the deaths, the distribution of the time of death, and the distribution of the rates of death by age, Munger (1982) concluded that the Southeast Asian and Filipino sudden deaths are part of the same syndrome, which is perhaps a regional phenomenon in Southeast Asia.

The studies of the Southeast Asian sudden deaths have not yet identified a factor that is alone responsible for the deaths. The cause of the syndrome of sudden deaths is most likely a complex interaction of genetic, environmental and behavioral factors; the author's research on sudden deaths of Hmong in the Ban Vinai refugee camp supports the hypothesis that each of these three factors is involved. The evaluation of genetic, environmental and behavioral hypotheses is in progress and will be presented elsewhere. Evidence linking the sudden deaths of Hmong with sleep disorders is presented in this report. Sleep disorders may be more prevalent in Southeast Asian populations than currently recognized.

THE BAN VINAI REFUGEE CAMP

The Ban Vinai refugee camp is located in northeastern Thailand, near the Mekong river bordering Laos.

The camp population in November 1982 was 33,117, including 32,935 Hmong, 143 ethnic Lao, 20 Khamu, 10 Mien-Yao and 9 Thai Dam (UNHCR 1983). The case-control study was limited to the Hmong refugee population. The problem of sudden death in sleep could not be studied in Ban Vinai as it had been in the United States. Death certificates were rarely completed in Ban Vinai; most deaths occurred outside of the hospital. Even in the relatively rare event of a death in the hospital, a death certificate was not likely to be completed. Reverence for the spirits of the deceased was not overpowered by laws requiring post-mortem examinations; autopsies were unthinkable in Ban Vinai.

A United States State Department physician, upon a return trip to Ban Vinai, remarked that he previously was unable to turn up any evidence of sudden death in sleep. The expatriate health workers were aware of only one victim of sudden death in sleep, a twenty-six-year-old Hmong man who worked in the public health program. These initial reports were less than encouraging; where were the sudden death victims, if they existed at all? It soon became apparent that most relief workers had little contact with what was now the largest Hmong community in the world. The largest number of expatriate volunteers were workers who arrived each morning, worked within the hospital compound, then left the camp in the evening. The health workers had contact with a small proportion of the Hmong refugees who were ill. The bamboo fence around the hospital was symbolic of a wide cultural gap between the Western medical workers and the Hmong community. Even if this gap did not exist, sudden death cases would still be more likely to occur in residences than in the hospital and go unreported. Thus the hospital was not a useful setting for locating sudden death cases, although the staff was very supportive of the author's research project.

Soon after the author's arrival in Ban Vinai a meeting was arranged with Mr. Vang Neng, the chief leader of the Hmong in Ban Vinai. The purpose of this meeting was to outline what was known of the sudden death syndrome of Southeast Asian refugees in the United States and to seek Vang Neng's advice and assistance for a study of similar deaths in Ban Vinai. Vang Neng was well aware of the sudden deaths of Hmong in the United States and thought similar deaths occurred in Ban Vinai; he said that a letter was sent to the United Nations High Commissioner for Refugees (UNHCR) field office in Ban Vinai which described several unexpected sudden deaths that had occurred recently.

RESEARCH METHODS

An effective surveillance network that would report cases of sudden death had to be organized. Information was sought on any death that was sudden, unexpected or unexplained. Sudden death cases were defined as any death occurring within twenty-four hours of the onset of acute illness; thus this study was not limited to sudden deaths in sleep. Discussions with Vang Neng included how to use best the existing social structure in Ban Vinai to locate cases. Vang Neng arranged a meeting with the Hmong Advisory Council at which the study proposal was presented. The Hmong Advisory Council includes center chiefs, clan leaders and elders. The center chiefs, leaders of the eight districts in Ban Vinai, mediate disputes and oversee the distribution of food, supplies and mail within each district. Seventeen clans are represented in Ban Vinai, each having an appointed leader. The clan leaders, usually older and more influential than the center chiefs, are the most important negotiators on matters concerning clan members. After the introductory meeting, individual interviews were held at the offices of center chiefs and in the homes of clan leaders. The leaders were overlapping components of a surveillance network; the center chiefs searched for cases within their districts, which included many clans, and clan leaders searched for cases within their clan, including cases of members who may have lived in different centers. Once cases were reported, interviews with the victims' relatives were sought. The interviews were conducted with the assistance of Mr. Vang Lia, a Hmong interpreter appointed by Vang Neng. Vang Lia was selected on the basis of his exceptional linguistic talents and stature in the community.

Interviews were conducted with relatives or spouses who lived with the victim and either witnessed the death or discovered the body of the deceased. Notes were taken

on second-hand reports of sudden deaths, but formal interviews were conducted only with actual witnesses.
Interviews were conducted at the home of the informant
after permission had been granted by the center chief or
clan leader.   The interview was initially "open-ended"
with the informant describing how the death occurred and
any events considered to be related to the death.   An
interview form was then used to record demographic data,
the circumstance of death, migration history, medical
history, sleep habits, occupational history, military
experience, personal habits and dietary history.   A gene-
alogy was constructed of all relatives who could be remembered by household members; it included information on
residence and age of living relatives and the age, date,
location and cause of death for deceased relatives.   Case
reports of sudden death in sleep were crosschecked by Ms.
Elizabeth A. Booton, C.R.N., and a female Hmong interpreter, Ms.   Mai Lee Lor, both unaware of the results of
the initial interview.   Comparison interviews of individuals randomly selected from the UNHCR's list of camp
residents (controls) were conducted and were matched to
cases by age, sex and ethnicity.   The case interviews
included information on the characteristics of the deceased as reported by a relative.   Rather than interviewing the control subject directly, a relative of the
control was interviewed, so that the information on cases
and controls was more comparable.   Further, the relationship of the informant to the control subject was matched
to that of the informant and the deceased in the case
interview with which the control was compared.

CASE REPORTS

Twenty-seven formal interviews were conducted in Ban
Vinai with relatives of sudden death victims.   Sixteen of
these were cases of sudden unexpected death during sleep
in which the victim was not previously ill.   Data on
these cases and controls are being analyzed at the time
of this writing and will be reported elsewhere.   Four
case reports were collected in which victims of sudden
death in sleep had experienced previous nonfatal sleep
disturbances,   including   abnormal   respiratory   sounds,
breathing difficulties or transient loss of conscious-

ness.   None of the controls experienced such sleep disturbances.   Several personal accounts of similar sleep
disturbances were also obtained from Hmong refugees in
Ban Vinai who were still alive at the time of this
writing.

Case 1

    In October, 1981, a thirty-nine-year-old Hmong male
died during sleep in the Nong Khai refugee camp, also in
northeastern Thailand.   The wife of this man, interviewed
in Ban Vinai, reported that at midnight her husband made
a noise during sleep that sounded like an obstruction in
his throat.   The abnormal respiratory sounds were made
for several minutes.   The wife called to her husband; he
did not respond and his body was flaccid.   The subject's
breathing while unconscious was reported to be very slow.
The wife massaged the husband and he regained consciousness in four to five minutes.   The wife asked her husband
what was wrong and he replied that something had caught
in his throat.   No physical object was known to have
caused the obstruction.   The subject went back to sleep
until 7:00 A.M.
    At 7:00 A.M. the subject held his infant while
seated on the bed and his wife went into the kitchen to
cook.   A relative came to the kitchen soon after and
reported that the woman's husband was regaining consciousness and the infant was on the floor, having either
been dropped or set down.   Her husband complained of a
pain in his chest; he had never complained of this before.   The wife gave her husband a massage, and while
doing so noticed that his eyes had rolled back.   She
called to him, but he was unconscious again.   The husband's arms and legs flexed and his entire body became
rigid.   The woman noticed that her husband was not
breathing and tried to administer mouth-to-mouth resuscitation.   The man was taken to the camp hospital, but was
dead on arrival.

Case 2

    A forty-year-old Hmong man was found dead in his bed
in Ban Vinai on 6 June 1981.   At 6:00 that morning, the
wife of this man got up to make a fire for cooking.   The

woman heard the children crying and called to her husband
to take care of them. Her husband did not answer and she
returned to the bedroom to see what was wrong. The woman
found her husband dead on their sleeping platform; his
body was lying undisturbed on the bed with his head still
on the pillow. The wife remarked that her husband
appeared to be sleeping, with no signs of a struggle or
distress.

This victim's wife described dreams her husband had
in Laos in which a ghost, called a poj ntxoog,[1] would
appear. The poj ntxoog is a female spirit, which is believed to live in the jungle and is greatly feared.
Heimbach reported (1979, p. 28) that poj ntxoog refers to
a spirit that rides a tiger and whose father is a tiger.
Interviews with Hmong in Ban Vinai generally confirmed
Heimbach's characterization; the poj ntxoog may take away
the spirits of the living, thus causing illness and
death, and shamanistic ceremonies may be performed to
protect against poj ntxoog. The subject told his wife
that the poj ntxoog would sometimes visit during sleep
and sit on his chest. Breathing during these episodes
was very difficult; the subject would make a sound in
sleep, either a moan or a cry, and then his wife would be
awakened. At other times, the subject would awaken
first, then wake his wife to tell her what had happened.
Such sleep disturbances were first noted by the subject's
wife in 1979 in the Laotian highlands, and were estimated
to occur once every two or three months. The subject had
been in Thailand less than a year at the time of his
death. The sleep disturbances had not yet occurred in
Thailand; the last one was in 1980, when the family was
still in Laos.

Case 3

Near midnight on 12 June 1981, a Hmong man heard his
twenty-five-year-old son moaning and groaning in his
sleep in the Nong Khai refugee camp. The man called to
his son and asked what was wrong. The subject was awakened without great difficulty and reported that his legs
hurt. He described the pain as a tingling sensation, as
if needles were sticking him in both thighs, and said
that his legs felt very weak. The subject returned to
sleep. In the morning the subject's legs were numb, so

his wife gave him a massage. Concerned about the sleep disturbance that occurred the night before and the numbness of his son's legs, the father then took him to the camp hospital which was just across the road.

At 7:00 A.M. the camp physician examined the subject but could not find any abnormalities. The physician requested that the patient return later in the day so that a chest x-ray could be obtained. The family returned home shortly after 8:00 A.M. and family members stayed home all day. At 2:00 P.M. the subject said that he felt tired, asked his wife for a blanket, and went to bed. Shortly after the subject fell asleep, the family noticed that his right arm jerked and rested perpendicular to his body. The parents called to their son to ask him what was wrong, but there was no answer. The subject's body was motionless on the bed and he could not be awakened. The relatives carried the unconscious man across the road to the camp hospital. The physician ordered that the patient be rushed to the Thai hospital in Nong Khai. The subject was dead upon arrival at the Thai hospital and a death certificate was issued in English and in Thai. The physician gave a copy to the family and instructed them to present the certificate if anyone inquired about the death. The cause of death was listed as "unknown."

Case 4

At about 10:00 P.M. on 23 August 1978, in Ban Vinai, the mother and father of an eighteen-year-old Hmong girl heard their daughter making abnormal respiratory sounds during sleep. Unable to awaken their daughter, the parents immediately responded by giving her a massage and sticking needles into the inside of her arm. The mother of the subject knew of similar cases of sleep disturbances and had learned the massage and acupuncture treatment from other Hmong refugees in Ban Vinai. At the onset of this treatment the subject was breathing with difficulty, as if something was obstructing her throat; the abnormal breathing sounds lasted several minutes. The subject then awakened and asked why her parents were massaging her and sticking her with needles. The parents replied that she was making noises in her sleep and could not be awakened. The subject could not explain what happened, and went back to bed, sleeping normally for the rest of the night. The next morning, the subject felt normal.

On 11 April 1981, the subject was sleeping in the same bed as her eighteen-year-old female cousin; the subject's mother and father were also sleeping in this room. At 3:30 A.M., the subject's arm moved while she was sleeping, hitting and awakening her cousin. The cousin and the parents then heard abnormal respiratory sounds that were said to be the same as in the episode of 23 August 1978. The parents again responded by massaging their daughter immediately after hearing the sounds she made during sleep. The sounds lasted two to three minutes, then gradually subsided. The subject was unresponsive and having seizures, with her body moving side to side and her legs kicking. The family tried without success to detect a pulse on the subject's chest. When the respiratory sounds ceased, the subject's body was flaccid. Perspiration was noted over the entire surface of her body. The girl was dead within minutes after the sounds ceased, although the family continued the massage in vain for one hour.

Other Sleep Disturbances Noted in Ban Vinai

For the purposes of the case-control study, a case had to be narrowly defined; sudden death during sleep was a prerequisite. Soon after the fieldwork in Ban Vinai began, several Hmong people reported that they had sleep disturbances similar to those already presented. Leaders were asked about problems in sleep, but because a non-fatal sleep disturbance is much less dramatic than a death, it is more likely to remain unnoticed outside of the household. A systematic survey of households for people with sleep problems was not feasible due to a shortage of time and funds. We located five Hmong people--three women, twenty, twenty-five and thirty-two years of age, and two men, thirty-two and fifty-five years old--with histories of sleep disturbances in which the relatives were alerted by moaning, choking or groaning sounds and seizure-like activity, and the subjects were unresponsive to attempts to awaken them for some time. Hmong refugees who were well aquainted with the study of sudden death in progress brought these five cases to the author's attention, thinking that these nonfatal episodes might be caused by the same factors leading to death in others. Four of these cases had multiple episodes, some as often as two to three times a month. All of these people were anxious about their condition and feared dying in sleep.

A sixth individual, a thirty-five-year-old Hmong woman, was observed having sleep disturbances by the medical staff in the Ban Vinai hospital, and is the best documented case of a nonfatal sleep disturbance in Ban Vinai. This patient was admitted to the Ban Vinai hospital on 10 May 1983, with complaints of diarrhea, numbness of the extremities for one month and tightness of the chest. The admitting physician suspected that vitamin B deficiency and intestinal parasites were the basis of her illness. Over the next three days, while receiving vitamin supplements and antiparasite medication, the numbness and pain in her extremities gradually decreased; general weakness and chest pain persisted.

At 12:30 A.M. on 17 May 1983, an elderly Hmong man staying in the hospital noticed that the woman was having a seizure in her sleep, with her fists clenched and arms shaking. A Hmong nurse on duty was notified immediately; he could not detect any heart sounds with a stethoscope. The patient was not breathing and artificial respiration was given. Breathing was restored in five minutes. The attending physician, Dr. Bibba Holland, arrived soon after and noted that no reason could be found for the cardiorespiratory arrest and seizure in sleep. The next day the patient complained of numbness in the hands and lower legs, as well as general weakness. Headache and chest pains, described as a squeezing sensation, were intermittent. Walking did not increase the chest pain but rather eased it somewhat.

On 18 May 1983, at noon, the patient experienced another episode of cardiopulmonary arrest accompanied with a seizure. A Hmong nurse heard a brief groan and noticed that the patient was unconscious on her bed. The patient's face was described as blue; the hands were said to be white. The patient began having a seizure and became incontinent of urine; cardiopulmonary resuscitation (CPR) was initiated by the Hmong nurse. Dr. Holland arrived and confirmed that heart sounds were not audible with a stethoscope and that the patient was not breathing and cyanotic; he then continued CPR. The seizure stopped in less than five minutes and the patient regained regular cardiac rhythm and breathing. Within a half-hour the patient, while very drowsy, was able to answer some questions and recalled having a severe headache before the episode. The patient requested a massage, with acupuncture. The hospital staff did not respond to this request, but the patient's family did. Bruises were left on the patient's arm by the vigorous massaging and pinching.

Over the next three days, the headaches, chest pain and numbness subsided, although the patient continued to feel tired and weak, with a poor appetite and abdominal pain. A chest x-ray showed no evidence of tuberculosis or cardiac enlargement. No abnormalities were noted in the physical examination or in the routine blood, urine and stool tests. The patient was discharged on 25 May 1983 with a tentative diagnosis of hypovitaminosis and seizures of unknown origin.

The patient and her family were interviewed several times in the hospital and at home after discharge. The patient had experienced a seizure during daytime sleep on 8 May 1983, two days before her admission to the Ban Vinai hospital. After the subject was found to be having a seizure and to be nonresponsive, a vigorous massage was given by her family, during which she regained conciousness. Further interviews revealed that a similar episode had occurred six months earlier; shortly after midnight the woman made abnormal respiratory sounds during sleep, alerting her husband. The woman's limbs were rigid and she was incontinent of urine. Her husband called other relatives to assist in giving a massage. The woman did not fully regain consciousness until about three hours later.

One more episode that occurred in early 1982 was recalled. The woman collapsed one morning in the market where she made and sold textile goods, which was next to the camp hospital. Her teenage daughter witnessed this episode and reported that two American nurses were nearby and began CPR because the woman was not breathing. After the woman's breathing was restored, she was taken, still unconscious, to the camp hospital. The woman remained as a patient for three or four days. Hospital records are not kept longer than three months, so no documentation was available.

DISCUSSION AND CONCLUSIONS

Of the sixteen cases of sudden, unexplained death during sleep studied in Ban Vinai, four included a history of nonfatal sleep disturbances. Two of the four cases had sleep disturbances in which relatives were alerted by abnormal respiratory sounds, described as moaning, choking or groaning, accompanied by seizure-like activity, and the subjects were unresponsive to attempts to awaken them. The third case experienced repeated episodes of difficult breathing during sleep. The fourth case was found groaning in sleep with later complaints of weakness and numbness in his legs; the next day he died suddenly during daytime sleep. None of the sixteen control subjects experienced any of these sleep disturbances.

Six Hmong refugees in Ban Vinai, all alive at the time of this writing, also reported episodes of seizure-like activity and unresponsiveness in sleep. The relatives of each of the six subjects, all alerted by abnormal respiratory sounds, responded with a vigorous massage, pinching and acupuncture treatment. The purpose of this treatment was to release the "bad blood" from the body, which is perceived as a small amount of dark, thick blood, believed to be "cool." If the "bad" or "cool" blood is allowed to circulate, it is thought to "cool" the limbs and eventually the heart, causing death. Massage is a common treatment used when a Hmong person becomes ill. Vigorous massage, which may include slapping, hard pinching, even hitting with a shoe, and acupuncture in special sites are a specific response to loss of consciousness. The knowledge and practice of this treatment seemed to be spreading quickly in Ban Vinai.

The reports of sleep disturbances presented here are an indication that sleep disorders may be related to the sudden deaths of Hmong refugees during sleep, and may be more common than previously recognized. Lemoine and Mougne (1983, p. 18) described the case of a Hmong man who had been successfully resuscitated from a nearly fatal episode of ventricular fibrillation. The subject described a sleep disturbance that had occurred in Laos five years before. The subject described being under the attack of a spirit called a dab coj which rests on the chest of a sleeping person:

> You want to listen, you can't hear; you want to
> speak, you are dumb; you want to call out, you
> cannot; you feel you are dying; you want to run
> away. You piss with fear in your sleep.

Tobin and Friedman (1983) also described a case of repeated sleep disturbances of a twenty-two-year-old Hmong man in the United States. After three nights of disturbed sleep, the subject described his problem to a Hmong resettlement worker. Tobin and Friedman wrote:

> The first night he woke suddenly, short of
> breath, from a dream in which a cat was sitting
> on his chest. The second night, the room grew
> darker, and a figure like a black dog came to his
> bed and sat on his chest. He could not push the
> dog off and grew quickly and dangerously short of
> breath. The third night, a tall, white-skinned
> female spirit came into his bedroom from the
> kitchen and lay on top of him. Her weight made it
> increasingly difficult for him to breathe, and as
> he grew frantic and tried to call out he could
> manage but a whisper. He attempted to turn onto
> his side, but found he was pinned down. After 15
> minutes, the spirit left him, and he awoke,
> screaming (Marshall Hurlich, this volume, p. 440).

The breathing difficulties were interpreted by the subject and other Hmong people as a spirit problem and a shamanistic ceremony was performed to protect the subject from further spirit visits.

The accounts described in this paper and published previously support the hypothesis that the broad group of disorders of respiration during sleep, known as the sleep apnea syndromes, may be related to the Southeast Asian sudden death syndrome (Munger 1982). This is not an explanation of the deaths, but rather a plausible mechanism in which genetic, environmental and behavioral factors may increase the risk of sudden death. Sleep apnea was discounted as a factor contributing to these sudden deaths in a CDC report which stated (1981, p. 582), "According to their families, none of the victims manifested clinical signs of the sleep apnea syndrome, such as obesity, snoring, frequent nocturnal awakening or hypersomnolence."   A later report by Baron et al. (1983, p. 2950) stated that "refugee victims did not manifest symptoms of sleep apnea."   As stated previously, sleep apnea is a broad group of disorders of respiration during sleep, not a single syndrome.   Obesity, snoring, frequent nocturnal awakening and hypersomnolence characterize one of the earliest described sleep apnea syndromes, the Pickwickian syndrome (Jung and Kuhlo 1965), but do not represent necessary symptoms for all sleep apnea problems.   Sleep apnea has been found to be more prevalent in males, may be asymptomatic and may give rise to fatal cardiac arrhythmias (Block et al. 1979; Cherniak 1981; Phillipson 1978).   Only sleep studies will determine with certainty whether or not one or more syndromes of sleep apnea are prevalent in Southeast Asian refugee populations, and whether or not these disorders are related to sudden death in sleep.   Sleep disorders do not alone easily explain why the deaths occur during sleep.   Sudden deaths in sleep of Southeast Asian refugees may be related to both sleep apnea and cardiac abnormalities.

Clinical and cultural studies of sleep disorders of Southeast Asian refugees are warranted.   A survey of sleep disorders should not be attempted until a clinical response can be offered to individuals identified as having a sleep disorder.   Investigators from the clinical and social sciences must work closely with Southeast Asian community leaders, family leaders and researchers. Although the mechanism of sudden death and factors which increase the risk of sudden death are unclear, it is known that quick intervention has already prevented some deaths.   Training in CPR and the use of emergency medical services should be a high priority for health education programs serving Southeast Asian refugees.

ACKNOWLEDGEMENTS

The support and assistance of my wife, Elizabeth A. Booton, through often difficult situations, has contributed greatly to all phases of my dissertation research. The Royal Thai Government, especially the National Research Council and the Ministry of the Interior, kindly granted approval for the extended research in Ban Vinai. Dr. A.G. Rangaraj, Ms. Ailsa Holloway, Mr. Daniel Bellamy and Ms. Wadtanee Phiktakpao of the United Nations High Commission for Refugees provided generous assistance in Ban Vinai and Bangkok. I am also grateful for the assistance of The Christian Medical Team-Christian and Missionary Alliance of Thailand, The International Rescue Committee, The American Refugee Committee, World Vision of Thailand, and Mr. Hang Sao, Dr. Bruce Thowpaou Bliatout, Mr. Vang Neng, Mr. Vue Mai, Mr. Chong Moua Lee, Mr. Chong Koua Vang, Mr. Hang Doua, Mr. Vang Lia, Ms. Mai Lee Lor, Dr. Amara Pongsapich, Dr. Bibba Holland, Dr. Marshall G. Hurlich, Dr. Neal Holtan, Dr. Robert Tauxe, Dr. Tom Prendergast, Ms. Nampet Panichpant-M., Dr. Steve Helgerson, Mr. Bob Johnson, Mr. Doug Hulcher and Ms. Andrea Crossland. All errors of fact or interpretation are my own. Financial support was provided in part by the Intergovernmental Committee for Migration and the Graduate Student Research and Travel Fund of the University of Washington, Seattle, Washington. Finally, I offer my deepest sympathy to the Hmong families who have suffered great losses, and my appreciation for their cooperation and patience during this research.

NOTES

[1] The orthography used for Hmong terms in this paper is that of G. Linwood Barney and William A. Smalley, as used by Ernest Heimbach in his White Hmong-English Dictionary (1979).

REFERENCES

Baron, R., S. Thacker, L. Gorelkin, A. Vernon, W. Taylor, and K. Choi. 1983. "Sudden Death Among Southeast Asian Refugees." Journal of the American Medical Association 250 (21):2947-51.

Bliatout, B.T. 1983. Hmong Sudden Unexpected Nocturnal Death Syndrome: A Cultural Study. Portland, Oregon: Sparkle Publishing Enterprises, Inc.

Block, A.J., et al. 1979. "Sleep Apnea, Hypopnea and Oxygen Desaturation in Normal Subjects: A Strong Male Predominance." New England Journal of Medicine 300(10):513-517.

Cherniak, N.S. 1981. "Respiratory Dysrhythmias During Sleep." New England Journal of Medicine 305(6): 325-330.

Eckner, F., R.H. Kirschner, and R. Baron. 1983. "Sudden Nocturnal Death in Southeast Asian Refugees: A Progress Report." Proceedings of the 1983 Meeting of the American Academy of Forensic Science. Abstract G-32.

Heimbach, Ernest E. 1979. White Hmong-English Dictionary. Ithaca, New York: Linguistic Series IV, Southeast Asia Program, Cornell University.

Jung, R., and W. Kuhlo. 1965. "Neurophysiological Studies of Abnormal Night Sleep and the Pickwickian Syndrome." Progress in Brain Research: Sleep Mechanisms 18, p. 140. Amsterdam: Elsevier.

Lemoine, J., and C. Mougne. 1983. "Why Has Death Stalked the Refugees?" Natural History, November: 6-19.

Munger, R.G. 1982. "Sudden Death in Asian Populations: The Case of the Hmong." Hmong in the West: Observations and Reports. Papers of the 1981 Hmong Research Conference, edited by Bruce T. Downing and Douglas P. Olney. Minneapolis: Center for Urban and Regional Affairs, University of Minnesota.

Phillipson, E.A. 1978. "Control of Breathing During Sleep." American Review of Respiratory Disease 118:909-939.

Schlesselman, J.J. 1982. Case-Control Studies: Design, Conduct and Analysis. New York: Oxford Press.

Tauxe, R.V., et al. 1983. "Sudden Nocturnal Death in Laotian Refugees." First International Symposium on Public Health in Asia and the Pacific Basin. Honolulu: School of Public Health, University of Hawaii.

Tobin, J.J., and J. Friedman. 1983. "Spirits, Shamans, and Nightmare Death: Survivor Stress in a Hmong Refugee." American Journal of Orthopsychiatry 53(3): 439-448.

United Nations High Commissioner for Refugees (UNHCR). "Population Statistics of the Ban Vinai Refugee Camp." Unpublished. Bangkok, Thailand.

United States Centers for Disease Control. 1981. "Sudden, Unexpected Nocturnal Deaths Among Southeast Asian Refugees." Morbidity and Mortality Weekly Reports 30:581-89.

A CROSS-CULTURAL ASSESSMENT
OF MATERNAL-CHILD INTERACTION:
LINKS TO HEALTH AND DEVELOPMENT

Charles N. Oberg, Sharon Muret-Wagstaff,
Shirley G. Moore and Brenda Cumming

Over two hundred years ago the Hmong people migrated from China to the mountaintops of Laos (LeBar and Suddard 1960). In the last decade, as a result of war, thousands have come to the United States and to the Twin Cities metropolitan area. Their arrival here has given us the opportunity to explore from a cross-cultural perspective the differences in the perception of health and disease and the utilization of the health care system. In addition, we have attempted to compare and contrast Hmong and Caucasian toddler development, parenting techniques and maternal-child interaction, all of which are so important for subsequent growth and development.

METHOD

The present study was conducted in the Pediatric Clinic at Hennepin County Medical Center from November 1982 through March 1983. The subjects consisted of twenty-four mother-child dyads, twelve each from the Caucasian and Hmong communities of the Twin Cities. The average ages at the time of the study for Hmong and Caucasian children were 20 months (range: 18.0 to 21.5) and 19 months (range: 18.0 to 20.3), respectively. All families were of low socioeconomic status. In addition, all children were born at Hennepin County Medical Center and were part of a larger longitudinal study (Muret-Wagstaff and Moore 1983) which was begun in the newborn period.

During a one-hour pediatric clinic visit for each child and parent, a pediatrician (Charles N. Oberg) who was unaware of the results of the earlier newborn study and was trained in the use of the cited instruments, collected data in the areas of health, development and parent-child interaction. First, sociodemographic data and a medical history were obtained by interview. Next, a developmental assessment was conducted, using the Denver Developmental Screening Test (Frankenburg, Goldstein and Camp 1971), followed by a complete physical examination. Throughout the clinic visit, mother-child dyads were observed and rated on several scales of mother-child interaction. These were (1) items from the Mother-Child Rating Scales (Egeland, Deinard, Brunnquell and Taraldson 1975); (2) Ainsworth's System for Rating Maternal-Care Behavior (1976); and (3) interaction items from the Home Observation for Measurement of the Environment (HOME) (Caldwell and Bradley 1978). The maternal-child interaction instruments are described below.

Mother-Child Rating Scales

Fourteen items from the Mother-Child Rating Scales were chosen from those used by Egeland, Deinard, Brunnquell and Taraldson when they observed feeding, play and clinic waiting room behavior of mothers and infants from the same urban population from which the present Caucasian sample was drawn. Eight of the fourteen items were among ten which were weighted significantly toward Mother's Caretaking Skills and Mother's Affective Behavior factors in the original authors' analysis--factors which strongly contributed to differentiation between subsequent adequate and inadequate parental care groups (Egeland, Deinard, Brunnquell, Phipps-Yonas and Crichton 1979; Vaughn, Taraldson, Crichton and Egeland 1980). Selection of the fourteen items was directed by their relevancy to the toddler period and the likelihood of their expression during a typical pediatric visit, confirmed by pilot testing. The items focus on the specific quality and variability of the mother's handling of the child and responsiveness to fussing and crying, as well as her general patience, attentiveness and expressiveness toward the child. Each item is scored on a nine-point scale, with scale points defined for individual items, high scores indicating optimal performance.

Ainsworth's System for Rating Maternal-Care Behavior

Ainsworth's nine-point rating scales represent a more global assessment of the parent-child relationship

in four areas: Sensitivity vs. Insensitivity to the
Baby's Communications, Cooperation vs. Interference, Acceptance vs. Rejection, and Accessibility vs. Ignoring
and Neglecting. The Sensitivity vs. Insensitivity to the
Baby's Communication scale, which distinguished between
the consistently high-scoring Hmong and more variable
Caucasian mothers in the newborn period, has been most
widely used in other research (Vaughn, Taraldson,
Crichton and Egeland 1980; Whitt and Casey 1982) and is
described here in greater detail.

1. <u>Sensitivity vs. Insensitivity to Baby's Communication.</u>
   This scale reflects the mother's ability to perceive
   accurately the signals and cues implicit in her infant's behavior. A mother rated as highly sensitive,
   or 9, is one who is exquisitely attuned to her child's
   signals. She responds promptly and appropriately to
   the child's subtle cues. She is empathic and respects
   the child's point of view. Her interactions with the
   child seem complete and well-rounded, and she monitors
   the child and the environment closely, anticipating
   problems. A rating of 7 is considered a sensitive response. The mother generally interprets the child's
   signals accurately and is never seriously out-of-tune
   with the baby's state. However, she may be less sensitive to more subtle cues. For example, she may feed
   him when he fusses and sucks his fist, but she might
   miss the message in his uncomfortable squirming. A
   A mother rated 5, or inconsistently sensitive, is vis-
   ibly more ambivalent. She may be sensitive on occasion, but is inconsistent and at times may be unaware
   of her baby's whereabouts or needs. An insensitive
   mother is scored 3. She fails to respond promptly or
   appropriately. However, the capacity for sensitivity
   may be seen on some occasions. Finally, a highly insensitive response, or 1, is characterized by a mother
   who is geared almost exclusively to her own wishes,
   moods and activities. She responds to the baby's signals only if repeated, prolonged and intense, and only
   if they are in keeping with her own needs.

2. <u>Cooperative vs. Interference.</u> The central issue addressed by this scale is whether the mother's initia-
   tions of interaction are geared to the baby's state or

whether she interrupts and fragments the child's on-going activity.   A highly cooperative mother capital-izes on spontaneity and sees her baby as a separate person whose activities have a validity of their own. A highly interfering mother fails to acknowledge this autonomy and is arbitrary in her interference.

3. <u>Acceptance vs. Rejection.</u>   This scale deals with the mother's behavior that indicates the extent to which she integrates the positive and negative feelings that come with parenthood.   The highly accepting mother re-spects the fact that the baby has a will of his own, even when it opposes hers.   Her periods of irritation and frustration are brief, and she accepts responsi-bility for his care without resentment.   At the other end of the continuum, highly rejecting behavior in-cludes pervasive irritation and scolding, rough hand-ling and ill-concealed anger, and maternal escalation of conflict in power struggles.

4. <u>Accessibility vs. Ignoring and Neglecting.</u>   This scale deals with the mother's awareness of and responsive-ness to child.   A highly accessible mother is aware of the baby consistently; she actively acknowledges and responds to him or her.   An inaccessible mother ig-nores her baby and in this sense she neglects her baby.   It is the simple acknowledgment of the baby's real presence that is important to this scale--not the quality of her response to him tapped by the Sensitiv-ity-Insensitivity scale.

HOME

Finally, a subset of ten parent-child interaction items from the HOME was used to assess (1) the emotional and verbal responsiveness of the mother, (2) the avoid-ance of restriction and punishment, and (3) maternal in-volvement with the child.

This instrument uses a Yes/No dichotomous scoring. The rating is such that the higher the total score, the more optimal the environment for the child.   Such scores derived from the use of the complete instrument have been related to later evidence of positive cognitive develop-ment (Elarao, Bradley and Caldwell 1975).

The examiner was trained in the use of the observational instruments, and pilot testing was conducted over a three-week period during medical visits in the pediatric clinic in which this study was to take place. In pilot testing it was noted that both parent and child behavior became more stilted with two observers present rather than one. Therefore, in an attempt to maintain high validity of study observations, we decided to conduct five reliability observations on Hmong and Caucasian children who were from the same clinic population but who were not participants in the project sample. Interscorer reliability between the study examiner and a second simultaneous independent observer, defined as within 1-point agreements for 9-point scales and exact agreement for yes/no dichotomous ratings, was .83 and 1.0 for the two parent-child dyads tested immediately prior to the study, 1.0 for the two tested while the study was in progress, and .87 for a mother-child pair tested at the conclusion of the study. Interobserver reliabilities for the Mother-Child Rating Scales, Ainsworth's System for Rating Maternal-Care Behavior, and the HOME, respectively, were .94, .95, and .93.

Statistical analyses of the sociodemographic and medical data and scores from the mother-child interaction scales were carried out with two-tailed t tests and Fisher's exact test. Denver Development Screening Tests were scored and compared according to the manual (Frankenburg, Dodds and Fandal 1973). Thorough physical examinations followed a standard format (McKay 1975) and are reported descriptively.

RESULTS

Sociodemographic Data

While in early infancy each child in the study lived in a household with the mother and at least one other adult, interviews with parents during the toddler period revealed that the make-up of the family network and the integration of family roles was much different for the two groups, as might be expected. The family size was larger for Hmong than for Caucasian families with a significantly greater number of adults (t = 2.06, p <.05) and children (t = 3.73, p <.01) in Hmong households. However, the ratio of adults to children was not different between groups. Most striking was the availability of family support for the Hmong people. They come from a tradition of extended patrilinear families, while their Caucasian counterparts live in more nuclear and isolated families. This family support is shown by the significantly greater reported involvement of the Hmong grandmother (t = 2.49, p <.05) in the child-rearing experience. The Hmong mothers also reported involvement of the father in childrearing more often than the Caucasians, but the difference did not reach statistical significance. This pattern of care appears to have been carried forward from the Hmong tradition in Laos.

There were also important family differences involving marriage and pregnancy. Twenty-five percent of the Caucasian mothers had experienced disruption within the nuclear family during the baby's first year, as indicated by a separation or divorce, compared to none for the Hmong families. On the other hand, only 17 percent of the Caucasians had another new baby at the time that their toddlers were examined, compared to 67 percent of the Hmong mothers (Fisher's exact p <.05).

Both groups were highly mobile. Seventeen of the twenty-one families in each of the original two groups had moved at least once since the birth of the study child; that is, over 80 percent for both groups.

Medical History

The Caucasian children were more likely than the Hmong to be up-to-date on their immunizations by twenty-four months of age and to be weaned from the bottle (Fisher's exact p <.05). However, in spite of later weaning, the Hmong toddlers' diets were more nutritionally balanced than those of the Caucasian toddlers according to servings per day of the basic four food groups (Fisher's exact p <.01). Middle ear disease was relatively common, and there was no significant difference in rates between the two groups.

Figure 1 shows a graphic display of significant medical events reported by the two groups and confirmed by medical records. There was a significant difference (Fisher's exact p <.01) between cultural groups in utili-

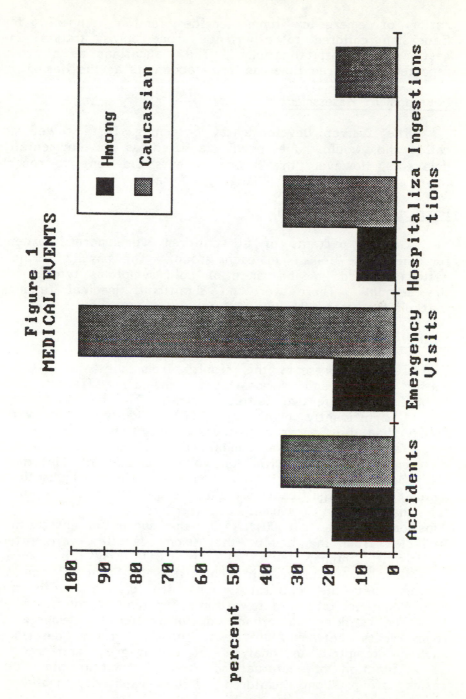

Figure 1
MEDICAL EVENTS

zation of emergency room services, and a tendency for
Caucasian children to experience more burns, trauma, ingestions and hospitalizations. The Caucasians as a group
reported over three times as many accidents as the Hmong.

Development Assessment

The Denver Developmental Screening Test showed no
child who would have been classified as developmentally
delayed. However, the Hmong parents did tend to report
fewer items passed in the language domain.

Physical Examination

Growth patterns of all children were normal except
for one obese female in each group. The physical examinations showed an abundance of cold symptoms typical for
the season. There were no significant medical findings
that differentiated the two groups.

Mother-Child Interaction Measures

Table 1 presents the results from the Mother-Child
Rating Scales and demonstrates markedly different patterns between the two cultural groups. The Hmong mothers
scored significantly higher (p <.001) and with less variability than the Caucasian mothers on all items.
Table 2 shows a similar pattern of cross-cultural
differences observed with Ainsworth's Scales of Maternal-
Care Behavior and the HOME inventory. The Hmong mothers
again scored significantly higher and with less variability than their Caucasian counterparts on each of the
Ainsworth scales (p <.001). On the subset of interaction
variables from the HOME, the Hmong families were rated
significantly higher (t = 3.17, p <.01) than the Caucasian families. The graphic comparison in Figure 2 demonstrates that the cultural groups are distinct, with the
Hmong mothers clustered toward the high end of the scale.
The striking difference in utilization of emergency
room visits between the two cultural groups described
earlier prompted an analysis of within-group differences
as a function of maternal sensitivity. Within the Caucasian group alone, children of low-sensitivity mothers

Table I

Comparison of Hmong and Caucasian Dyads
on Mother-Child Rating Scales*

		Hmong		Caucasian	
		X	SD	X	SD
1.	Attentiveness	8.58	0.52	6.17	1.64
2.	Quality of Physical Contact	8.92	0.29	5.42	1.31
3.	Facility in Caretaking	8.58	0.79	6.12	1.75
4.	Speed of Responsiveness to fussing and crying	8.67	0.65	6.42	1.68
5.	Effectiveness of mother's response to crying	8.58	0.90	5.83	1.80
6.	Variability of mother's behavior	8.08	0.90	4.92	1.67
7.	General expressiveness of mother towards child	8.50	0.52	5.17	1.70
8.	Frequency of expression of positive regard	8.17	0.58	4.92	1.88
9.	Frequency of expression of negative regard	9.00	0.00	7.67	1.16
10.	Mother's alertness	8.08	0.79	5.25	1.36
11.	Appropriateness of mother's interaction	8.50	0.80	5.33	0.78
12.	Delight	8.67	0.65	4.42	1.56

	Hmong		Caucasian	
	X	SD	X	SD
13. Quality of mother's verbalizations	8.92	0.29	6.08	1.44
14. Mother's patience	8.92	0.29	5.83	1.27

(X = mean; SD = Standard Deviation)

*Every item shows significant group difference, 2-tailed t test, p < .001

Table 2

Comparison of Hmong and Caucasian Dyads on Ainsworth's Scales of Maternal-Care Behavior and the HOME

	Hmong		Caucasian	
	X	SD	X	SD
Cooperation vs. Interference*	8.58	0.52	5.67	1.30
Acceptance vs. Rejection*	9.00	0.00	6.50	1.17
Accessibility vs. Ignoring*	8.83	0.39	5.50	1.68
Sensitivity vs. Insensitivity*	8.58	0.67	5.17	1.27
HOME†	10.00	0.00	8.40	1.73

(X = mean; SD = standard Deviation)
†2-tailed t test, p <.01
*2-tailed t test, p <.001

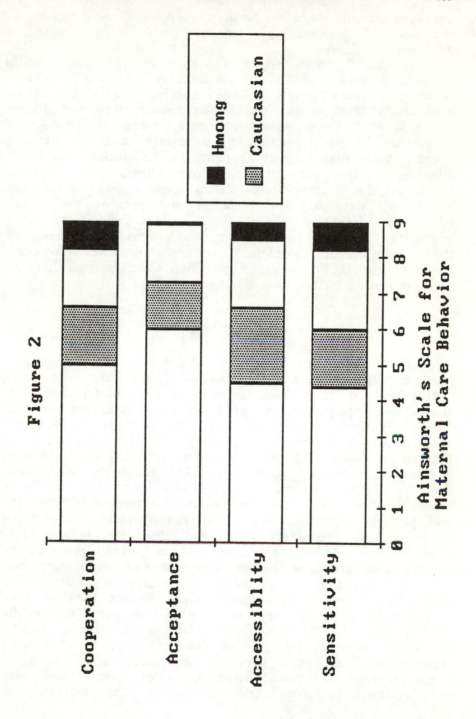

Figure 2

Ainsworth's Scale for Maternal Care Behavior

Hmong
Caucasian

averaged three times as many emergency room visits as children of moderately sensitive to highly sensitive mothers.

It should be noted that items on the mother-child interaction measures in all probability are highly correlated with each other. Consequently, t-tests on individual items tend to inflate the magnitude of group differences found. Nevertheless, the data comparing Hmong and Caucasian mothers' parenting behaviors are so striking overall that they clearly appear to be reliable and replicable. The decision to apply t-tests to individual items of the Mother-Child Rating Scales and Ainsworth's Scales of Maternal-Care Behavior did present the possibility of detecting items (or clusters of items) that might fail to differentiate the two groups of mothers, or that might favor Caucasian mothers. In fact, however, there appear to be no areas in which Caucasian mothers as a group scored better than Hmong mothers.

DISCUSSION

The Hmong sample in this study obtained higher ratings on parenting skills on each of the four Ainsworth scales and on the HOME assessment instrument, indicating that these mothers were rated as more attentive, expressive, sensitive, responsive and patient in child-rearing than Caucasian mothers. Hmong mothers also were more effective in protecting their children from harm, evidenced by fewer emergency room visits for accidents and ingestions, and they reported a more nutritious diet for their toddlers than did Caucasian mothers, despite similar incomes. In contrast, the Caucasian children were more likely to be adequately immunized than the Hmong children. This difference strikes at a major dissimilarity in the perception of health and disease. The American Caucasian families have come to accept the preventive approach to health as routine, while Hmong families generally have had no experience with this particular medical approach. The conflict of having the child receive an injection when he or she appears well, coupled with reports of significant nerve injury secondary to injections received in Laotian villages, makes some Hmong parents reticent to accept immunization as an important aspect of health care.

Although the ratio of adults to children in the two populations was approximately the same (with Hmong households having larger numbers of both), Hmong families appeared to support the mother in her responsibilities to a greater extent than Caucasian families. There were significantly fewer disruptions from separation and divorce in the Hmong population and more sharing of child care among the adults in the families--particularly by the grandmothers present in the home.

Anecdotally, during clinic visits with the Hmong, the observer was particularly impressed with the effectiveness of the infant's use of the mother as a secure base for exploration, the fluidity of interaction, subtle adjustments made by the mother specifically to accommodate the child, and obvious parental pride in the child's smallest accomplishments. While some Caucasian dyads demonstrated similar patterns, the group differed in that a number of parents responded to the child in rigid, stereotyped ways, were sometimes unaware of the child's whereabouts in the exam room, demanded performance, spoke in irritated tones and showed clear disappointment in the toddler's failure to meet parental expectations.

Despite the high degree of reliability Oberg attained in the administration of all instruments, a single observer conducting all assessments and making all mother-child ratings is an important potential source of bias. Three kinds of findings from this and other reports support the validity of the current results. First, a high degree of consistency is apparent across other measures, including such indicators of maternal care as nutrition, accidents and emergency room visits for toddlers. Differences in these factors were observed between cultural groups and, in the last case, between high- and low-sensitivity Caucasian mothers. Second, the patterns of associations between variables which distinguish cultural groups in this study have been noted in other research. For example, strong social networks seem to support positive mother-baby interaction patterns (Crockenburg and Smith 1982), and family stress, disruption, and tense or distant interaction patterns have been linked to childhood ingestions and emergency room visits (Sibert 1975; Sobel and Margolis, 1965). Third, although reports of Hmong mother-infant relations are sparse, they are quite consistent with the present findings. Bernatzik (1963) notes that, in the traditional Hmong community, the child is regarded as "the most treasured possession a person can have" (p. 77) and describes the baby's life as rich in physical contact and social inter- action with the active participation of mothers, grand- mothers and older siblings. Newlin-Haus (1982) compared ten-to-twelve-month-old infants of immigrated Hmong in Portland with those of white middle class American fami- lies and found that Hmong mothers held and touched their infants more frequently and were more extensively com- forting and consoling, while American Caucasian mothers, although attentive, playful and vocal, were often in- clined to interrupt the baby's activities and lived in object-filled rather than people-filled environments.

The quality of the mother-child relationship throughout infancy has clear implications for the subse- quent development of the child. Ainsworth, Blehar, Waters and Wall (1978) demonstrated that early patterns of care are significantly related to subsequent patterns of at- tachment. The child raised in a caring, consistent and sensitive manner is likely to develop a secure attachment with the care-giver and to utilize the care-giver as a base from which to investigate the environment. The child cared for in a fragmented and insensitive manner is more likely to develop an attachment pattern character- ized as anxious and insecure. Later, the two-year-old child previously assessed as securely attached is more likely than the insecurely attached child to show greater cooperation, persistence at task, and enthusiasm during problem-solving (Matas, Arend and Sroufe 1978). In ad- dition, Sroufe (1983) found that children who were se- curely as opposed to insecurely attached as toddlers showed greater ego resiliency at four years of age.

Isolation, stress and lack of social support in eco- nomically disadvantaged groups have been implicated as factors in negative parent-child interaction patterns (Vaughn, Egeland and Sroufe 1979; Yarrow, Rubenstein and Pedersen 1975; Zegiob and Forehand 1975). Within a low socioeconomic group, mothers of maltreated children are more likely to have shown insensitivity to the child's needs in the infancy period than those of children who subsequently are not maltreated. Additionally, anxious and/or avoidant rather than secure relationship patterns are more common in the early toddler period for the previously insensitive group (Egeland and Sroufe 1981).

In the present study, the children in both of these populations appear to be healthy and within the normal range for their ages developmentally. Nevertheless, the marked differences between the two groups in the adequacy of parenting place the Caucasian children at greater risk for subsequent adaptational problems if there is not improvement in the quality of mothering many are receiving, in the general state of the parent-child relations, and in the circumstances which perpetuate these difficulties. Hmong mothers, on the other hand, demonstrate that the ability of a mother to be sensitive and responsive to her toddler is not entirely dependent upon the absence of stress or on socioeconomic status, as is commonly construed. The factors related to their particular strengths in providing uniformly responsive caregiving deserve further study. The sensitivity shown by these Hmong mothers seems related to a cultural priority for attentive child-rearing and the availability and use of a strong extended family network. The payoffs are not necessarily seen in growth parameters or in general developmental testing, but possibly in fewer home accidents and in positive parent-child relationships which bode well for the child's future. The data invite our attention to the importance of the maternal-child relationship and how it is influenced by cultural factors. Such understanding and awareness is essential when providing pediatric care and counseling.

REFERENCES

Ainsworth, M. 1976. System for Rating Maternal-care Behavior (Test #008053). Princeton, New Jersey: Educational Testing Service.

Ainsworth, M., M. Blehar, E. Waters, and S. Wall. 1978. Patterns of Attachment. Hillside, New Jersey: Erlbaum.

Bernatzik, H.A. 1963. "Akha and Miao: Problems of Applied Ethnography in Farther India." Translated by A. Nagler. Human Relations Area Files.

Caldwell, B.M., and R.H. Bradley. 1978. Home Observation for Measurement of the Environment. Little Rock: University of Arkansas.

Crockenberg, S.B., and P. Smith. 1982. "Antecedents of Mother-infant Interaction and Infant Irritability in the First Three Months of Life." Infant Behavior and Development 5: 105-119.

Egeland, B., A. Deinard, D. Brunnquell, S. Phipps-Yonas, and L. Crichton. 1979. "Final report: A prospective study of the antecedents of child abuse." Unpublished manuscript. (Available from Byron Egeland, University of Minnesota, Minneapolis).

Egeland, B., A. Deinard, D. Brunnquell, and B. Taraldson. 1975. "Three-month Observations of Feeding Situations, Six-month Observations of Feeding and Play Situations, waiting room observation scales." Unpublished manuscripts. (Available from Byron Egeland, University of Minnesota, Minneapolis).

Egeland, B., and L.A. Sroufe. 1981. "Attachment and Early Maltreatment." Child Development 46:71-76.

Elarao, R., R. Bradley, and B. Caldwell. 1975. "The Relationship of Infants' Home Environment to Mental Test Performance from Six- to Thirty-six Months: A Longitudinal Analysis." Child Development 46:71-76.

Frankenburg, W.K., J.B. Dodds, and A.W. Fandal. 1973. Denver Developmental Screening Test Manual/Workbook for Nursing and Paramedical Personnel. Boulder: University of Colorado Medical Center.

Frankenburg, W.K., A.D. Goldstein, and B.W. Camp. 1971. "The Revised Denver Developmental Screening Test: Its Accuracy as a Screening Instrument." The Journal of Pediatrics 79:988-995.

LeBar, F.M., and A. Suddard. 1960. Laos: Its People, Its Society, Its Culture. New Haven, Connecticut: New Haven Human Relations Area Files Press.

Matas, L., R.A. Arend, and L.A. Sroufe. 1973. "Continuity of Adaptation in the Second Year: The Relationship Between Quality of Attachment and Later Competence." Child Development 49:547-556.

McKay, R.J. 1975. "General Considerations in the Care of Sick Children: Clinical Evaluation of Infants and Children." Nelson Textbook of Pediatrics (10th ed.), edited by V.C. Vaughn, R.J. McKay and W.E. Nelson Philadelphia: W.B. Saunders.

Muret-Wagstaff, S., and S.G. Moore. 1983. "Hmong vs. American Caucasian Newborn Behavior and Rearing Practices." Paper presented at the biennial meeting of the Society for Research in Child Development, Detroit, April 1983.

Newlin-Haus, E.M. 1983. "A Comparison of Proxemic and Selected Communication Behavior of Anglo-American and Hmong Refugee Mother-Infant Pairs." Doctoral dissertation, Indiana University, 1982. Disserta- tation Abstracts International 43(8):2724B-2725B. (University Microfilms No. DA8300862.)

Sibert, J.R. 1975. "Stress in Families of Children Who Have Ingested Poisons." British Medical Journal 3: 641-651.

Sobel, R., and J.A. Margolis. 1965. "Repetitive Poisoning in Children: A Psychosocial Study." Pediatrics 35: 641-651.

Sroufe, L.A. 1983. "Infant-Caregiver Attachment and Patterns of Attachment in Preschool: The Roots of Maladaptation and Competence." In Development and Policy Concerning Children With Special Needs. The Minnesota Symposium on Child Psychology (Vol. 16), edited by M. Perlmutter. Hillsdale, New Jersey: Erlbaum.

Vaughn, B.E., B. Egeland, and L.A. Sroufe. 1979. "Indi- vidual Differences in Infant-Mother Attachment at 12 and 18 Months: Stability and Change in Families Un- der Stress." Child Development 50:971-975.

Vaughn, B.E., B. Taraldson, L. Crichton, and B. Egeland. 1980. "Relationships Between Neonatal Behavioral Organization and Infant Behavior During the First Year of Life." Infant Behavior and Development 3: 47-66.

Whitt, J.K., and P.H. Casey. 1982. "The Mother-Infant Relationship and Infant Development: The Effect of Pediatric Intervention." Child Development 53:948-956.

Yarrow, L., J. Rubenstein, and F. Pedersen. 1975. Infant and Environment: Early Cognitive and Motivational Development." New York: Wiley.

Zegiob, L., and R. Forehand. 1975. "Maternal Interactive Behavior as a Function of Race, Socioeconomic Status, and Sex of the Child." Child Development 46: 564-568.

UNDUE LEAD ABSORPTION IN HMONG CHILDREN

Karl Chun and Amos S. Deinard

INTRODUCTION

In the spring of 1981, the Bureau of Maternal and Child Health at the Minneapolis Health Department, along with other institutions in Minneapolis and St. Paul, became aware of an extraordinary number of Hmong children identified with undue lead absorption. In retrospect, the screening data for lead were present as far back as the fall of 1980, but had been lost in the mass of other refugee health problems at the time. As time became available to investigate this "epidemic" of lead poisoning, however, the incidence melted away so that it is no greater today than the incidence of undue lead absorption normally found in Minneapolis. The finding of lead in a folk remedy during the summer of 1983 in St. Paul offered some insight into the seemingly unexplainable high lead levels found in some very young children, but leaves unanswered the question of why Hmong children in general have had such high lead levels.

This report describes the experience of the Minneapolis Health Department, one of the major health care providers for the Hmong in Minneapolis, and does not include the experience in St. Paul. To put the problem in perspective, the Minneapolis Bureau of Housing Inspections is the sole agency that receives reports of undue lead absorption from the entire city. In 1980 they received the usual number of case reports, twenty to thirty. In 1981 the Hmong alone accounted for twenty-four cases, over half the total. The number of case reports has declined since that year.

BACKGROUND

Lead poisoning, which has been recognized at least since the Roman Empire, is a clinical entity with numerous manifestations. Lead colic in children is generally recognized by irritability, lessening of play activity,

417

headaches, poor appetite, abdominal pain, vomiting and constipation. In its most severe form, lead encephalopathy is characterized by vomiting, stumbling, falling level of consciousness, coma and seizures, with subsequent mental retardation, blindness and paralysis.

Fortunately, these frank features of lead poisoning have become less common since efforts to reduce lead in the environment first began in this country in the 1950s. In Minneapolis, clinical lead poisoning is rarely encountered. The subject of this paper is an entity known as undue lead absorption which refers to excessive absorption and retention of lead without overt clinical symptoms. At these levels children are primarily at risk for developing behaviors that result in impaired learning abilities: more distractable, not persistent at tasks, dependent, impulsive, easily frustrated, tendency to daydream, inability to follow simple directions or sequences of directions, and lower overall function (Needleman et al. 1979). In population studies IQ scores proved to be measurably lower, in the range of four to ten points, depending on the level of lead exposure (Rutter 1980). Unfortunately, these findings have been demonstrated in children whose blood lead levels have been well below the thirty mcg/dl (micrograms per deciliter) level currently defined by the Centers for Disease Control in Atlanta, Georgia, as representing undue lead absorption. Biochemical evidence of lead toxicity (including some of the lead screening tests) has also been shown to occur in the range of ten to twenty mcg/dl.

Exposure to lead is a by-product of industrial society. Industries that use lead represent an occupational source. In the urban environment leaded paint once accounted for a large proportion of identifiable sources; however, since the ban on leaded indoor paint in 1957, paint has become less of a problem. Leaded gasoline probably produces much of today's urban lead, which is available to children to children in high concentrations in dust and especially in inner city neighborhoods.

Children are at a greater risk of lead's toxic effects for a number of reasons: (1) Children absorb a greater proportion of a given load of ingested lead than adults. Adults absorb approximately five to ten percent of ingested lead, whereas children absorb in the range of thirty to fifty percent (Ziegler et al. 1978). (2) The brain is rapidly growing and acquiring skills at an ear-lier age, so that the greater amount of lead that crosses into the brain has a devastating effect on development (Rutter 1980). (3) diets deficient in protein or calcium enhance the absorption of lead. Because of the rapid growth in a young child, nutritional deficiencies are quite common.

METHODS

The data to follow come from two sources: the South-east Asians who have been through the screening program for iron deficiency and undue lead absorption at the Min-neapolis Health Department (hereafter referred to as the Health Department) and a few additional cases detected through Hennepin County Medical Center. Comparisons will be made with two earlier reports on the same screening program at the Health Department from 1978 to 1980 (Yip, Schwartz and Deinard 1983) and a similar program at Min-neapolis Children's Health Center, a private hospital and clinic, from 1979 to 1980 (Yip, Norris and Anderson 1981).

The Health Department clinics routinely screen all children for lead with a screening test called the ery-throcyte protoporphyrin (EP) test. Children from one to six years of age are tested yearly. Those children whose EP exceeds fifty mcg/dl are further tested to determine their lead level. In accordance with the Centers for Disease Control's guidelines, an elevated blood lead lev-el is defined as thirty or more mcg/dl. Children with elevated blood leads are classified into risk groups by the degree of elevation of the EP and blood lead level. Risk class II is low risk, class III moderate risk and class IV high risk. All children with blood lead levels of thirty or more are reported to the Minneapolis Housing Inspections Division, which inspects the housing for sources of lead and makes and enforces recommendations for removing identifiable sources. Children in class II are followed without medical intervention other than re-moval of the source, and education on avoiding lead. Those in risk class III are generally further analyzed by a lead mobilization test to quantitate the total body lead burden and in this way to determine the necessity of

therapy.   Those in class IV are hospitalized for a three-
to five-day course of chelation therapy to remove lead
from the body.   Follow-up continues until lead levels
fall into and remain in a normal range.

RESULTS

Of 870 screenings of Hmong children up to six years
of age at the Health Department from 1980 to March 1983,
the incidence of undue lead absorption was 4.3 percent.
If only the highest at-risk age group is considered
(children up to thirty-six months of age), the incidence
of undue lead absorption increases to 5.5 percent.   In
comparison to a survey of the same clinic's population
before the arrival of the Southest Asians, the incidence
was 1.3 percent, demonstrating a three-fold increase in
the Hmong (2-tail t-test: $p < .0001$) (Yip, Schwartz and
Deinard 1983).   The Minneapolis Children's Health Center, from 1979 to 1980, reported an incidence of 2 percent, a two-fold increase in the Hmong (2-tail t-test:
$p<.01$) (Yip, Norris and Anderson 1981).

The incidence of undue lead absorption in Hmong at
the Health Department has been changing over the years
(see Table 1).   For children less than six years of age,
the incidence has gone from 3.9 percent in 1980 to a high
of 7.8 percent in 1981 to much lower levels of 2.5 percent and 2.1 percent in 1982 and the first quarter of
1983, respectively.   There is a significant downward
trend over the years 1981 to 1983 (Mantel-Haenszel test
for trend: $p=.02$).   Quite notably, the incidence in 1983
is no different from that for other children in the two
previously mentioned studies.

Table 1

YEARLY INCIDENCE OF UNDUE LEAD ABSORPTION IN HMONG CHILDREN, RECORDED BY DATE OF FIRST ELEVATED ERYTHROCYTE PROTOPORPHYRIN.

	1980	1981	1982	1983	Total
Children under 6 years					
Cases	5	20	9	2	36
Screenings	127	258	366	95	846
Proportion	.039	.078	.025	.021	.043
Children under 3 years					
Cases	5	18	8	2	33
Screenings	84	179	259	76	598
Proportion	.060	.101	.031	.026	.055

Of the forty-six Southeast Asian children identified with undue lead absorption by the Health Department and Hennepin County Medical Center through August 1983, forty-two were Hmong and four were Laotian. The mean age was twenty-four months at the time of discovery; however, a more accurate reflection of the age groups was the median age of nineteen months. All but four children were less than four years old, and the older children were identified by blood-testing the entire family for lead after the discovery of a younger sibling index case. By adjusting this group to include the Minneapolis Children's Health Center, the mean age was twenty months, eleven months less than the mean of thirty-one months at the Children's Hospital (Yip 1981). Fifty-nine percent were male and 41 percent were female, in keeping with the general notion that males are affected somewhat more often than females. The majority (65 percent) fell into the lowest risk classification, which is no different from that observed in the Minneapolis Children's Health Center group (Yip, Norris and Anderson 1981).

The medical work-up of children with undue lead absorption usually includes studies of radiographs of the abdomen to determine recent ingestion of paint chips, and radiographs of the knees, where deposition of lead in the growing portion of bones will indicate long-term exposure. No child has had radiographic evidence either of recent paint chip ingestion or of long-term exposure. A further measure of total body lead burden is obtained by a mobilization test. The child is given an injection of EDTA (ethylenediaminetetraacetic acid), which then forms a soluble complex with lead in the soft tissues of the body. This soluble complex is carried to the kidneys and excreted in the urine, where the excreted lead can be measured. None of the moderate risk children in class III has shown a high total body lead burden by this test. The high risk children in class IV are usually hospitalized and treated immediately, so that a mobilization test is not routinely performed.

Housing inspections are routinely conducted to identify leaded paint on interior surfaces. For ten instances in which a completed inspection report is available, eight houses had interior leaded paint and two did not. However, most of the housing units with leaded paint had no easily ingestible peeling paint; thus a causal link between paint and body lead burden is difficult to establish. Anecdotally, one apartment complex has produced six of the cases. The only apartment with lead in the interior had no children in it; the other apartments were all free of lead. Mielke (in press) has established that the Hmong live in areas of high soil lead, as do all inner city residents, which may serve as another source of ingestible lead, but this does not explain why Hmong children in particular absorb lead and other residents in the same area do not.

SUMMARY

The basic descriptive information on Hmong children with undue lead absorption shows several features that distinguish them from other American children with undue lead absorption. They tend to be of a lesser age, with three only six months of age at the time of detection. A noticeable trend in the incidence of undue lead absorption has occurred between 1980 and 1983, with the peak incidence in 1981 and an incidence more akin to that of the general American population in 1983.

One of the more intriguing aspects is the failure to find a source of lead in the homes. Certainly leaded indoor paint can be found, but most of the paint has been considered a poor source since it was not peeling or peelable. The etiology of undue lead absorption in Hmong children is far from clear, both for the general population and in individual cases.

DISCUSSION

The usual investigation of children with undue lead absorption has failed to uncover the common sources: peeling leaded paint, plaster, lead in jewelry or other household items, lead in pottery, industrial exposure or pica (the excessive mouthing of objects). We have routinely asked about the use of herbal medicines, knowing that Chinese herbal medicines and Mexican folk medicines have been identified as a cause of lead poisoning. Indeed, in St. Paul doctors identified one six-month-old child who had been given a lead-contaminated folk medicine, pay-loo-ah, an earthen mixture whose source is not clear to us. We have been unsuccessful in obtaining a history of pay-loo-ah use in all subsequent new cases.

Radiographic studies have failed to implicate paint chips as a possible source. Mobilization tests have shown low total body lead burdens, and radiographic evidence of long-term exposure by lead lines in the long bones is lacking. One would not expect long-term exposure because of the intermittent screening for lead in children since their arrival in the United States and the low likelihood of lead exposure in the Thai camps. Although the refugees in the Thai camps have never been tested for lead, the EP screening tests done on arrival in Minneapolis do not indicate that lead exposure could have occurred before arrival in this country.

Do the Hmong absorb, retain and excrete lead in a different manner from others? Age and diet determine the amount of lead absorbed through the gut. Younger children absorb more of a given load of lead--approximately 30 to 50 percent in contrast to 5 to 10 percent by adults. Diets deficient in calcium or protein enhance lead absorption. Conceivably, the high incidence in 1981 could have been from a poorer nutritional status in regard to calcium and protein, and perhaps an improved intake of calcium and protein over time has corrected these deficiencies.

Further investigation of hypotheses on the uniqueness of the Hmong experience with lead has become less possible in Minneapolis, as the "epidemic" proportions reached in 1981 have disappeared. St. Paul, with a larger Hmong population, does not report a diminishing number of cases. The Health Department's approach to all children with undue lead absorption concentrates on attention to the usual environmental sources, mouthing activities, nutrition and childhood development. Additionally, we can offer to test for the possibility of lead contamination in household folk medicines, a phenomenon also seen in some Chinese and Mexican folk medicines.

Because undue lead absorption is a silent affliction, efforts to communicate its harmful effects on a child's development have been difficult, especially since lead is one of many newly encountered problems in the United States. Until society develops a policy directed at further efforts to eliminate lead and its sources from the urban environment, public education on lead and identification of cases must suffice to avoid lead's deleterious effects.

ACKNOWLEDGEMENTS

The authors wish to acknowledge Ms. Brenda Grabenstein for the analysis of the blood samples and Ms. Virginia Miller for tabulating the data. The computerized storage and analysis of the data was possible through a grant from the University of Minnesota Computer Center. Mr. Gerald Takumi and Dr. Lydia Caros provided the data on housing inspections.

REFERENCES

Mielke, Howard. In press. On soil lead levels in Minneapolis-St. Paul and with specific reference to Hmong neighborhoods.

Needleman, H.L., C.E. Gunnoe, A. Levition, R. Reed, H. Peresie, C. Maher, and P. Barrett. 1979. "Deficits in Psychologic and Classroom Performance of Children with Elevated Dentine Lead Levels." New England Journal of Medicine 300: 689-695.

Rutter, Michael. 1980. "Raised Lead Levels and Impaired Cognitive/Behavioural Functioning: A Review of the Evidence." Supplement to Developmental Medicine and Child Neurology 22:1-26.

Yip, R., T.N. Norris, and A.S. Anderson. 1981. "Iron Status of Children with Elevated Blood Lead Concentrations." Journal of Pediatrics 98:922-925.

Yip, Ray, Samuel Schwartz, and Amos S. Deinard. 1983. "Screening for Iron Deficiency with the Erythrocyte Protoporphyrin Test." Pediatrics 72:214-219.

Ziegler, E.E., B.B. Edwards, R.L. Jensen, K.R. Mahaffey, and S.J. Fomon. 1978. "Absorption and retention of lead by infants." Pediatric Research 12:29-34.

ATTITUDES OF HMONG TOWARD
A MEDICAL RESEARCH PROJECT

Marshall Hurlich, Neal R. Holtan
and Ronald G. Munger

INTRODUCTION

Migrant populations are always of interest to epidemiologists (Kasl and Berkman 1981) and biological anthropologists (Baker 1981). Besides carrying certain infectious diseases from place to place, migrating groups provide observers with large-scale "natural experiments" by removing themselves from one set of environmental factors and substituting a new set. Migrant studies have aided in the understanding of health conditions such as cancer, in which diet and environmental agents are thought to play a role (Haenszel and Kurihara 1968; Modan 1980; Knudson 1977).

However, the response which the migrant population itself has to a biomedical research effort usually goes unreported. This report deals with the responses which a refugee migrant population from Laos has had to the various attempts made to investigate an unexplained, sudden unexpected nocturnal death (SUND) syndrome reported since its arrival in the United States (United States Centers for Diesease Control 1981; Munger 1982; Baron et al. 1983). Attention is given to how these studies have been received by a specific refugee community in the United States and in a refugee camp in Thailand, and how the studies have created problems preventing the successful completion of physiological research in a refugee camp in Thailand. It is not our intention to review biological and medical results of the research efforts made; rather, we wish to focus on certain research and data-gathering procedures and on responses of the refugee community.

BACKGROUND

Over one hundred thousand Hmong people have moved as political refugees from their native country of Laos to Thailand, and then to the United States and other countries for permanent resettlement (Office of Refugee Resettlement 1984). The complex health system in the United States has allowed close scrutiny of the Hmong's health status, leading to the first reports of SUND syndrome among them (CDC 1981). One of us, Ronald Munger, spent nine months in the Ban Vinai Refugee Camp in Loei Province of northeastern Thailand in 1982 and 1983 collecting data on sudden deaths there (Ronald G. Munger, this volume, p. 379).

Meanwhile, in Minnesota, several physicians at St. Paul-Ramsey Medical Center were noticing occasional Hmong patients with unexplained abnormalities in their serum electrolytes, including low levels of potassium and magnesium (Holtan et al. 1983). Considering the role that serum electrolytes play in the regulation of the heartbeat, they began to speculate on the possibility, thus far unproven, that these abnormalities were related to the SUND syndrome.

In December 1982, a party of five health workers dealing full-time with refugee health at St. Paul-Ramsey took a pleasure and fact-finding trip to Thailand. Two of them, a nurse and a doctor, had been medical volunteers at Ban Vinai in 1980, and a third was a Hmong-American whose family still resided in the camp. After meeting by chance at Ban Vinai, the St. Paul team and Munger shared information about the SUND syndrome and the electrolyte abnormalities which had been observed in the Hmong patients in the United States. It was thought that blood and urine samples collected at Ban Vinai could be sent to St. Paul for analysis in order to determine whether or not there were electrolyte abnormalities in any part of the Hmong population in Ban Vinai.

Shortly thereafter, several researchers at St. Paul-Ramsey Medical Center began communicating with other researchers at the University of Washington about hypotheses, study design, logistics and cooperative arrangements. A comprehensive proposal to study Hmong in Ban Vinai and in several locations in the United States was written and submitted for funding consideration. Two small research proposals, pilot studies for the larger proposal, were approved for funding by the St. Paul-Ramsey Medical Education and Research Foundation.

One of the proposals, entitled "Electrolyte and hormonal regulation in clinically healthy Hmong subjects," entails the investigation of fifty apparently healthy Hmong, twenty-five of each sex. Both sexes are included in order to determine base-line data for a wide segment of the Hmong population which is at apparent risk for SUND (CDC 1981; Baron et al. 1983). Each of the subjects would have blood tests and urine tests over a twenty-four-hour span of time. Subjects would also have a formal diet history, a brief medical history, a short medical examination, and a genealogical listing of direct ancestors. In addition, they would wear a Holter heart monitor for a day to look for abnormal cardiac rhythms. Criteria for subject selection included apparent good health, absence of thyroid disease, age between twenty-five and forty-four years, and absence of vomiting or diarrhea. This study is now in progress in St. Paul (January 1984), but is not sufficiently advanced to judge its eventual success.

In the same proposal, funding was also approved to analyze blood and urine samples from a comparable group of Hmong subjects in Ban Vinai. For the St. Paul pilot study, the fifty subjects are adequate to define the normal circadian pattern of hormone and electrolyte levels for the Hmong population. The St. Paul subjects could therefore serve as the standard against which to compare the Ban Vinai subjects. Therefore, the subjects in Thailand needed to be sampled only twice each, once at the eight A.M. circadian peak of serum electrolytes and once at the midnight circadian trough. Subject selection criteria were: (a) residence in the camp of at least two weeks, (b) male, and (c) the same medical criteria applied to the subjects in St. Paul. For this Hmong population, we decided to test only males, because most SUND cases among refugees in the United States are males, and because we didn't want to complicate what we anticipated would already be a delicate investigation. The Ban Vinai subjects were also to have medical histories, physical examinations, diet histories and genealogical interviews taken. Holter monitors were not proposed for use in Ban Vinai. Research funds for the project in Thailand were provided by the St. Paul-Ramsey Medical Center.

The coordinator of the research project in the United States, Dr. Neal Holtan, and Munger, the coordinator of the work in Ban Vinai, spent time with many persons and organizations to obtain cooperation for com-

pletion of the Thailand phase of the project. In spite of
all efforts, the researchers did not succeed in obtaining
the blood and urine samples in Ban Vinai. They did, however, gain experience in conducting research in Thailand
and in interacting with the Hmong people to achieve a
goal. We believe it is useful to share in detail the
problems they encountered so others can avoid them in the
future, as well as learn from them.

First Reports to the Centers for Disease Control

Larry Lewman, chief medical examiner in Portland,
Oregon, was the first to report cases of sudden unexpected nocturnal deaths among Southeast Asian refugees
to the Centers for Disease Control (CDC) in Atlanta,
Georgia, in February, 1981. Between February and December, 1981, the CDC had been notified of thirty-eight SUND
cases throughout the United States. Of these, twenty-five
were Hmong, eight were among other Laotian ethnic groups,
four were Vietnamese and one was Kampuchean. The deaths
reported had occurred between 15 July 1977 and 28 October
1981 (CDC 1981). In response to these deaths, the CDC
initially planned to establish a SUND surveillance network, to review the various causes of deaths among Indochinese refugee populations in the United States between
1975 and 1980, to investigate individual SUND cases, to
conduct genealogical investigations of cases, to review
refugee electrocardiographic status and to investigate
the question of prior exposure to toxic chemicals in
Southeast Asia (Vernon and Baron 1981). It was assumed
at the time that chemical warfare had been conducted
against Hmong people in Laos, and that such exposure
could constitute a risk factor for the SUND syndrome.
To achieve these goals, an investigator from the
CDC, using a case-control study design, interviewed members from the families of twenty-six Hmong and ethnic Lao
SUND victims and interviewed three groups of matched controls using the same questionnaire (Schlesselman 1982).
The questions from the prepared form covered birthplace,
migratory history, occupational history, military history, the reported exposure to toxic chemical weapons,
foods eaten, marital and reproductive history, health
status, drug use and other topics. No significant differences were reported between cases and controls (Baron

et al. 1983).

Many Hmong leaders were not initially aware of the CDC investigation. Unfortunately, some individuals in the Hmong community said that they believed that the CDC study would determine the biological cause of the SUND syndrome. Some said they believed that CDC investigators thought the SUND cases were related to episodes of presumed chemical warfare in Laos. The lack of findings did nothing to clarify this point for the Hmong or to put suspicions to rest.

Cultural Studies of Sudden Death

The first completed investigation into the cultural aspects of the SUND syndrome among the Hmong was conducted by Bliatout (1982). He initially presented his study to the Hmong community as a research effort which might reduce the psychological fear associated with the sudden death syndrome, and also as an investigation of five hypotheses which had been proposed as potentially explanatory. Bliatout, himself a Hmong, emphasized in his interviews that his study could not guarantee an answer, but was instead part of a long-term effort needed to uncover the causes of sudden deaths among Hmong refugees.[1]

Bliatout interviewed surviving family members of forty-five Hmong SUND victims who died between 1973 and 1982. His sample, however, does not exactly overlap that obtained by the CDC. Of his forty-five cases, thirty-eight occurred in the United States, three in Laos, two in Thailand, and one each in Canada and France. Twenty-six occurred between 1977 and 1981 (compared to twenty-five Hmong cases reported to the CDC during approximately the same period), and thirty-seven occurred since 1978.

A second investigation of the cultural associations of the SUND syndrome was conducted by Lemoine, who interviewed relatives of SUND victims in the United States and France, gaining access to the Hmong, Mien and Lao communities through the network of his former students from Laos (Lemoine and Mougne 1983).

Neither Bliatout nor Lemoine limited their interviews to prepared questionnaires, and, as both are intimately familiar with Hmong culture, they were able to design their studies to be sensitive to the cultural attitudes of the individuals they wished to interview.

Reactions to Studies Described

During and since these studies, we have interviewed Hmong in a variety of leadership positions. During the course of these interviews, it became apparent that many Hmong felt that the CDC was withholding information from them.[2] They asked the following questions: Several investigations of the SUND cases had been made. Why wasn't the answer available? Did CDC "know" the cause, but refuse to reveal its knowledge? Was it because the primary "cause" was in fact chemical warfare, and the CDC did not wish to contribute to the developing debate about the use of toxic chemicals in Southeast Asia? Was it because CDC did not wish to provide fuel for arguments made by some individuals that Hmong should be eligible for U.S. war veterans' benefits? Was it because the CDC felt that Hmong were not sophisticated enough to understand the cause of the sudden deaths? Or was it because the CDC did not care about refugees?

Additional Biological Studies

A fourth set of studies of the SUND cases were undertaken by pathologists, quite removed from the view of the refugee community. Post-mortem studies were performed on tissues from the victims to determine if there were traces of drugs or poisons, or if the victims had anatomical abnormalities which were the cause of death (Eckner, Kirschner and Baron 1983).

The law in every state provides that in cases of unexpected and unexplained deaths, autopsies must be performed. Consequently, tissue samples—including in many cases the entire heart—were removed from a number of SUND victims under the direction of local medical examiners. Studies of cardiac pathology are in progress, focusing on the conduction system and the aortic root. Although some anomalous structures have been suggested, the physiological significance of the findings is not clear (Eckner and Kirschner 1983).

In most cases where autopsies were performed on SUND victims, the Hmong victims' families did not understand the procedures and results. The families' permission was not routinely requested; the autopsy protocols were not uniformly described; the need for tissue samples was not always discussed. Some Hmong families, upon receiving the corpse of their dead family member, noticed that the body had been cut open. The relatives then proceeded to open the body and found, to their horror, that some organs had been removed and that sometimes the organs had not been properly repositioned in the body.

EFFECTS OF PREVIOUS RESEARCH EXPERIENCE ON CURRENT PROJECTS

The background of sudden-death studies is important because it very likely conditioned the responses of the Hmong in Ban Vinai during the recent attempt to obtain blood and urine samples.

Let us start with the fact-finding trip made by five health workers from St. Paul to refugee camps in Thailand in November and December, 1982. During their stay in Ban Vinai, Mao Thao, a Hmong-American woman living in St. Paul, and the first Hmong-American to visit Ban Vinai, agreed to answer questions about life in the United States at a public meeting. Over ten thousand people formed the unexpectedly large crowd. These were among the questions Mao Thao was asked: (St. Paul Pioneer Press, 1983).

"When Hmong people die in the United States, is it true that they are cut into pieces and put in tin cans and sold as food?"

"After you die, why do American doctors try to open up your head and take out your brains?"

"Why do some Hmong in Minnesota go to sleep and never wake up again?"

"Do American doctors eat the liver, kidney, and brain of Hmong patients?"

"Why do American doctors draw so much blood from patients?"

These questions suggest some of the concerns, misunderstandings and fears in the Hmong community (not only

in Ban Vinai but also in the United States) concerning
the health care practice in this country. These problems
stem in part from the following factors:

1. Leadership. Misunderstandings have arisen from fail-
    ure of American medical researchers to approach the
    Hmong community through the structure of its true
    leadership. Part of this problem results from the
    fact that most Americans do not know who the "true
    leaders" are in the Hmong community and why it is im-
    portant to consult with them. The Hmong community
    structure includes exogamous clans and their former
    military leaders. The lack of communication between
    researchers and community leaders allows for consid-
    erable speculation on the part of Hmong leaders and
    community members about the true intentions of medi-
    cal and social science researchers.
        A related problem is that, although clan members
    rely on clan leaders for advice, clan leaders fre-
    quently are not in a position to give advice in an
    area where they themselves are uncertain about the
    long-range consequences of advice they might give,
    such as the participation of clan members in re-
    search. If clan leaders fear loss of esteem within
    the clan when their advice "fails," they might refuse
    to accept the responsibility of potential failure.[3]

2. Explanations of medical procedures. Misunderstandings
    have arisen from the failure to explain the justifi-
    cation for normal medical laboratory procedures. The
    relationship between a person feeling ill, his going
    to a medical clinic, having a sample of tissue (usu-
    ally blood) removed, laboratory analysis of the
    blood, diagnosis of the finding, determination of
    medication and administration of medication is un-
    clear to many Hmong. The rationale behind this chain
    of events has not in general been explained to Hmong
    patients in research projects or in health clinics in
    a manner which the Hmong understand. This lack of
    successful communication leaves much room for specu-
    lation by Hmong about medical researchers' and prac-
    titioners' motives. For example, it raises the types
    of questions asked at Ban Vinai: Why do doctors take
    so much blood? Why do they remove organs?

3. Are researchers hiding something? Some difficulties stem from the perception by some Hmong that, since several studies have already been done into the problem of sudden deaths, American doctors already know what causes the deaths, but they are not telling. We speculate that at least three factors contribute to this difficulty. First, most Hmong who are subjects in research projects do not understand the conceptual basis for undertaking research, nor the relationship between research efforts and the treatment of medical conditions. Consequently, when a Hmong subject is seen by a doctor during the course of a research effort, the Hmong individual may expect either to be checked for a medical condition or to receive medication for it at the end of the "visit." While this does not apply to all Hmong individuals, it does seem to characterize the majority of Hmong, who only since their arrival in the United States are beginning to receive Western education and literacy skills (Office of Refugee Resettlement 1984).

    Second, problems result when researchers, in efforts to "sell" research effort to the subject community, promise greater returns for the research than can in fact be expected. A researcher may be tempted to tell the Hmong interpreter that this research "will" contribute to an effort that "might" determine the causes of sudden death which can then "help lead" to a cure or at least preventive action. The Hmong interpreter most likely does not or even cannot translate the subtleties of the English words "may" and "might" to the Hmong subject, who is then left with expectations that participation will lead to a cure. Thus, difficulties arise when Hmong subjects, perceiving American medicine as powerful, believe that the answer can be quickly learned.

4. Methods. A fourth set of problems derives from the methods of investigation used. The unexplained removal of organs at the autopsy, if not adequately explained, generates a response which is based on Hmong beliefs about the relationship between organs of the body and the body's souls. For example, some Hmong say the body has seven souls, one of which resides in the heart. As Chindarsi notes:

When a man dies the souls of the ears, nose and mouth remain in the grave, but the souls of the eyes and heart go to the afterworld, from which they will return in due course to be reincarnated. Some Hmong say that after the body rots away, the souls of the ears, nose and mouth leave the grave to rejoin the souls of eyes and heart in the afterworld. It is the souls of the eyes and heart which wander at night and cause their owners to dream (The Religion of the Hmong Njua, 1976).

The practice of removing organs at autopsy possibly led to the sort of questions raised publicly in Ban Vinai, when some individuals asked, "Do American doctors eat the organs of dead Hmong people?"

5. Additional problems exist which are beyond the scope of this report. For example, the popular media have tended to portray the problem of the sudden deaths in a light which makes the deaths seem bizarre, and by implication, the Hmong are made to seem bizarre or at least unintelligible (Monagan 1982).

This background affected Munger's attempt to secure blood and urine samples in Ban Vinai, and influenced the design of the long-term study proposed for St. Paul and Seattle.

THE BAN VINAI EXPERIENCE

Munger and Elizabeth Booton, a nurse practitioner, spent ten months in Ban Vinai Refugee Camp, Thailand, during 1982 and 1983. Between 5 February and 3 June, 1983, they attempted to organize a collection of urine and blood specimens from a sample of Hmong in the camp. Aided by project directors in the United States (Holtan and others), this effort required the cooperation of several Thai ministries, including the National Research Council, the Ministry of thè Interior, the Secretary General of the Thai Medical Council, and the Thai Military Commander of Ban Vinai. Due to the political volatility created by refugee populations in Thailand, securing approval proved difficult and time-consuming. Our experience suggests that negotiations are best facilitated by personal meetings with the proper official and that important correspondence should, when possible, be hand-delivered. In one case several months were spent waiting for approval because key officials did not receive important correspondence.

Logistical and personnel support were requested from several American agencies, such as the American Refugee Committee in Minneapolis and in Bangkok, and the International Rescue Committee in the United States and Bangkok. The Christian Medical Team and World Vision International also provided support. Assistance was also requested from the office of the United Nations High Commissioner for Refugees, Bangkok.

During these four months, many letters and telephone calls crossed between the United States and Thailand; many meetings were held; many expected and unexpected obstacles were overcome. (Among the obstacles were the need to figure out how to ship dry ice from Bangkok to Ban Vinai, and how to prepare and preserve and ship blood specimens). Some individuals in the American agencies mentioned in the preceding paragraph acted as couriers for letters and for telephone messages, and some were on site in Ban Vinai and offered their services during the study. The usefulness of their support proved that good relations with voluntary agencies holding influence in Ban Vinai are essential.

The most important meetings, however, were those between American investigators and the Hmong leadership in the United States and in Thailand. The relationship between these parties is the single most important factor in carrying out this kind of research project. A great deal of time was spent in negotiations before the project and during the sampling procedures. The following discussion focuses mainly on this aspect of the project, due to the importance of these interactions.

After clearance with the Thai ministries, Munger met with the Hmong Advisory Council (HAC) in Ban Vinai on 7 May 1983, because the HAC had previously requested that the Thai government approve all work done. The council consists of clan leaders, center chiefs and Hmong elders. The purpose of the meeting was to consider the blood study project, at the same time discussing sudden deaths of Hmong in the United States, Thailand and Laos, and the laboratory work completed in St. Paul on serum electrolyte levels of Hmong. The leaders said they approved of a blood study being done in Ban Vinai as part of the investigation into the cause of sudden death, but that they wanted to pick the sample of individuals who donated blood for the study. The Hmong leaders suggested that they pick twenty-five subjects whom they classified as "rich" and twenty-five they classified as "poor," because they thought that living conditions and marginal nutrition of the poor might be contributing to the problems of sudden deaths. Further, they approved the idea that the subjects could be compensated with food and drink.

A second meeting with the HAC, the Thai Military Commander of Ban Vinai and Munger was held on 30 May to discuss the specifics of the protocol for obtaining blood samples. An immediate topic of discussion was the amount of blood to be drawn from each subject. Munger initially requested a sample of 20 cc at two separate times for each subject. The council, while it had initially agreed, was now not so willing. Members made a counter-proposal that 2 cc of blood be drawn at the midnight sampling, and 3 cc of blood drawn at the morning sampling. Their main concern seemed to be about the amount of blood drawn, and they consequently negotiated for the smallest amount possible. With less blood, fewer diagnostic tests could be performed; Munger, however, agreed to the reduction in blood volume drawn, since one major goal of the effort was to work out all procedures for obtaining specimens.

Munger met next with Vue Mai, president of the HAC. Vue Mai related the reasons that Hmong were reluctant to give blood, including fears that giving blood would make an individual weak and susceptible to illness, and fear over what would be done with the blood. For example, he indicated that many Hmong believe that if blood is transfused into another person and if the recipient becomes ill, then the donor may become ill as well.

On 2 June 1983, a third meeting with the HAC included vigorous debate between Hmong leaders about whether or not to allow the blood sampling project. The central issues were fear of illness because of giving blood and the amount of blood requested. Not all leaders agreed to the study being done.

The leaders did reach a consensus acknowledging the importance of studies of blood samples as part of the research efforts on the SUND syndrome. However, most people in the Hmong community were unwilling to give blood samples, stating that they already felt ill or weak, and that giving blood would make them feel worse. Another concern expressed was that medical assistance should be made available after the blood sampling, to treat any complications that might arise. Many of the leaders were willing to donate their own blood, but only if there was a health assessment beforehand and if the total amount of blood collected was 5 cc or less. The leaders agreed to reconvene the next day with volunteers from their own clans to have their blood pressure, pulse and general health conditions assessed. Those found in good health would then give blood samples that night.

Unfortunately, time was running out. Booton examined thirty-one males on 3 June. Ten volunteers did not meet the screening criteria because of high blood pressure, report of illness, enlarged thyroid gland or obvious fear of the procedures. Fourteen of the seventeen clans in Ban Vinai were represented.

The effort to collect blood samples was canceled soon after this initial screening. The main reason for the cancellation was that a medically qualified person who was part of the research team could not stay in Ban Vinai for a significant time after the sampling. An attempt to obtain blood samples over a short period of time might have been successful, but the fact that the research team had to leave soon after would have endangered the prospect for a more complete study at a later time.

DISCUSSION

The authors of this paper by now have had a fair amount of collective experience in working with the Hmong communities in the United States and in Thailand. We feel we have learned several important lessons from the review of studies of the SUND phenomenon, and our participation in some of the investigations.[4] These lessons, discussed below, deal with undertaking research in Thailand, with conducting research within the Hmong community and with the responsibility of researchers toward refugee communities.

A. Undertaking research in Thailand.

1. Frequent and personal communication between research-
    ers and Thai officials is essential. Similarly, good
    relations with   voluntary agencies in Bangkok, in
    refugee camps and in the United States are also es-
    sential.   All agencies have limited resources and
    cannot be expected to provide much assistance or per-
    sonnel.

2. Thai researchers and assistants should be included in
    studies conducted in Thailand, whenever possible. We
    feel that this is an obligation of foreign research-
    ers for several reasons.   First, foreign researchers
    are guests in Thailand and should act to bolster and
    utilize Thai research capabilities.   Second, engaging
    Thai researchers may make both them and the foreign
    researchers more cognizant of research opportunities
    and public health problems. As Hmong individuals be-
    come increasingly educated and sophisticated in con-
    ducting research, and as some become interested in
    investigations into SUND, they should also be invited
    to participate in investigations.

B. Conducting biomedical and biosocial research with the
    Hmong community.

1. Hmong interpreters must be carefully selected. The
    selection should be based not only on language abil-
    ity, but also on the status this individual has in
    the community. After discussing our research and the
    language requirements needed for interpretation, it
    proved most productive for us to follow the recommen-
    dations of Hmong leaders in our choice of interpret-
    ers. We suspect research procedures and rationale
    could be better explained if interpreters first went
    through the research protocol as subjects.

2. The most crucial aspect, as already indicated, is the
    relationship between the research group and the Hmong
    community. Research efforts must proceed initially
    through the network of Hmong leaders, requiring that
    researchers go to the effort needed to identify the
    appropriate leaders. Time must be provided for full

discussion of all research goals, methods and ratio-
nales. Careful attention must be paid to community
concerns, such as (in this case) fears attendant upon
the removal of samples of blood. Suggestions by Hmong
of additional factors which the research group ought
to consider—such as the possible role of nutrition
and poverty as risk factors for SUND—should be fully
evaluated and discussed.

3. Researchers should schedule sufficient time for negotiations and remain available for a period of time
after completion of data collection to respond to any
physical conditions claimed to be the result of sampling or testing procedures.

C. General considerations.

1. Some of the problems discussed above may be avoided
by careful negotiations between researchers and the
subject group. This exchange gives subjects additional opportunity to provide clues and suggestions
of potential interest to researchers, and it enables
researchers to determine if their approach to the
community is effective or possibly if their research
is threatened by local political developments which
do not deal with the perceived quality of the research, but with such issues as differential access
to resources resulting from, for example, medical
screening and payment of subjects.

2. It is necessary to describe exactly what a specific
research effort is designed to learn, as well as how.
Often, this proves to be a difficult task, especially
when it is necessary to minimize use of culturally-
specific code words such as "research," "experiment,"
"test" and "risk factor." Explanations of the ration-
ale underlying a research activity in layman's terminology can lead to increased clarity for the researcher as well.

Finally, as should be obvious from this case study, one research effort is related to other research efforts dealing with the same problem, especially in the minds of the subject populations. We now approach a Hmong community that is already sensitized by its experiences with previous research efforts. For the continued success of studies attempting to uncover the cause and prevention of the SUND phenomenon, researchers must develop methods to deal with the numerous complicating factors discussed here.

ACKNOWLEDGEMENTS

We wish to thank those members of the Hmong community who gave their time to discuss research dealing with SUND. Valuable comments on an earlier draft of this report were made by Dr. Robert Tauxe, CDC; Dr. Amos Deinard, University of Minnesota Medical School; Mr. John Finck, Office of Refugee Resettlement, State of Rhode Island; Ms. Toyo Biddle, Office of Refugee Resettlement, Social Security Administration; Ms. Sherry Muret-Wagstaff, Pediatrics, Hennepin County Medical Center, Minneapolis. The authors are solely responsible for the views expressed in this report.

NOTES

[1] Personal communication to M.G. Hurlich. Bliatout did not interview any controls in his study, so his results are not comparable to those from the CDC. The five hypotheses he examined to explain SUND syndrome in the Hmong were: (1) The possibility that maintenance of traditional animistic religious beliefs was associated with the likelihood of suffering SUND--not supported. (2) The possibility that use of traditional health practices was associated with SUND. (3) The possibility that SUND cases clustered in certain clans or lineages. (4) The possibility that the regions of geographic origins were not randomly distributed among the SUND victims. (5) The possibility that SUND victims differed from the average Hmong individual with respect to socioeconomic factors.

[2]We wish to emphasize that these statements reflect opinions of Hmong people interviewed about work conducted by the CDC, and that their opinions are no doubt influenced by many of the factors outlined in this report.

[3]Dr. Amos Deinard alerted us to this problem.

[4]For example, both Hurlich and Munger assisted the CDC investigator, Dr. Roy Baron, in his epidemiological investigation in part of Washington State; Hurlich assisted Lemoine in his interviews in western Washington State; Holtan is involved in studies of serum electrolytes of Hmong in St. Paul; Munger has conducted an epidemiological and cultural investigation of the SUND phenomenon as it occurs in Ban Vanai, Thailand; all three authors have interviewed various Hmong individuals about investigations into the problem of SUND.

REFERENCES

Baker, P.T. 1981. "Migration and Human Adaptation." In Migration, Adaptation and Health in the Pacific, edited by C. Fleming and I. Prior. Wellington, New Zealand: Wellington Hospital.

Baron, R., S. Thacker, L. Gorelkin, A. Vernon, W. Taylor, and K. Choi. 1983. "Sudden Death Among Southeast Asian Refugees." Journal of the American Medical Association 250(21):2947-51.

Bliatout, B.T. 1982. Hmong Sudden Unexpected Nocturnal Death Syndrome: A Cultural Study. Portland, Oregon: Sparkle Publishing Enterprises, Inc.

Brataas, Anne. 1983. "Hmong Medical Interpreter Fields Questions from Curious." St. Paul Pioneer Press, 20 March 1983, p. 10A.

Chindarsi, N. 1976. The Religion of the Hmong Njua. Bangkok: The Siam Society.

Eckner, F., R.H. Kirschner, and R. Baron. 1983. "Sudden Nocturnal Death in Southeast Asian Refugees: A Progress Report." Proceedings of the 1983 Meeting of American Academy of Forensic Science. Abstract G-32.

Eckner, F., and R. Kirschner. 1983. Letter. See also: Baron, R., and Kirschner, R. 1983. "Sudden Night-time Death Among Southeast Asians too." Letter. The Lancet 8327:764.

Haenszel, W., and M. Kurihara. 1968. "Studies of Japanese Migrants. I. Mortality from Cancer and Other Diseases Among Japanese in the United States." Journal of the National Cancer Institute 40:43-69.

Holtan, N.R., F.E. Kaiser, T. Davin, and E. Haus. 1983. Unpublished Observations. St. Paul-Ramsey Medical Center, Departments of Medicine and Pathology.

Kasl, S.V., and L. Berkman. 1981. "Health Consequences of the Experience of Migration." Annual Review of Public Health 4:69-90.

Knudson, A.G. 1977. "Genetic and Environmental Interactions in the Origin of Human Cancer." In Genetics of Human Cancer, edited by J.J. Mulvihill, R.W. Miller and J.F. Fraumeni, Jr. New York: Raven Press.

Lemoine, J., and C. Mougne. 1983. "Why has death stalked the Refugees?" Natural History, November 1983:6-19.

Modan, B. 1980. "Role of Migrant Studies in Understanding the Etiology of Cancer." American Journal of Epidemiology 112(2):289-95.

Monagan, D. 1982. "Curse of the Sleeping Death." Science Digest, April 1982: 36-7.

Munger, R.G. 1982. "Sudden Adult Death in Asian Populations: The Case of the Hmong. In The Hmong in the West: Observations and Reports, Papers from the 1981 Hmong Research Conference, edited by Bruce T. Downing and Douglas P. Olney. Minneapolis: Center for Urban and Regional Affairs, University of Minnesota.

Office of Refugee Resettlement, Social Security Administration. 1984. "The Hmong Resettlement Study." Prepared by Literacy and Language Program, Northwest Regional Educational Laboratory. Portland, Oregon.

Schlesselman, J.J. 1982. Case-Control Studies: Design, Conduct, Analysis. New York: Oxford Press.

United States Centers for Disease Control. 1981. "Sudden, Unexpected, Nocturnal Deaths among Southeast Asian Refugees." Morbidity and Mortality Weekly Report 30:581-89.

Vernon, A., and R.C. Baron. 1981. Discussion on Hmong sudden deaths. Held at the Centers for Disease Control, 20 April 1981. Review notes and cassette tape.

CONTRIBUTORS

Bruce T. Bliatout: Refugee Coordinator, City of Portland; B.A. (Sociology), University of Hawaii; M.P.H. (International Health & Health Services Administration), School of Public Health, University of Hawaii; M.S. Hygiene (Tropical Diseases), School of Public Health & Tropical Medicine, Tulane University; Dr. P.H.C.-A.B.D. (Tropical Diseases), School of Public Health & Tropical Medicine, Tulane University; Ph.D. (Health Services Management), Century University.

Karl H. Chun: Fellow, Ambulatory Pediatrics, University of Minnesota; M.D., University of Hawaii; Two years experience in medical clinics in Minneapolis with Hmong pediatric patients.

Mary L. Cohn: Research Specialist, Northwest Regional Educational Laboratory, Portland, Oregon; Instructor, English as a Second Language, Mt. Hood Community College, Portland, Oregon.

Robert Cooper: Resettlement Officer (Indochinese) UNHCR, Geneva; Deputy Representative, UNHCR, Lao Peoples Democratic Republic; Lecturer in Southeast Asian Anthropology, University of Singapore; Ph.D. Social Anthropology, University of Hull; many publications on Asians include the book Resource Scarcity and the Hmong Response.

Brenda J. Cumming: School Psychologist; Doctoral candidate (Educational Psychology) University of Minnesota; B.A. (Psychology) San Diego State University.

Amos S. Deinard: Associate Professor of Pediatrics, University of Minnesota; M.D., University of Minnesota; Five years experience providing primary health care to Southeast Asian Refugees; Bureau of Maternal and Child Health, Minneapolis Health Department, Minneapolis, Minnesota.

Nancy D. Donnelly:	Ph.D. Candidate, University of Washington (Anthropology); B.A., University of Wisconsin; M.A. (English Literature), New Mexico State University; currently Principal Investigator, "Research on Hmong Women", funded by Social Science Research Council, Department of Anthropology, University of Washington, Seattle, Washington.

Bruce T. Downing:	Associate Professor of Linguistics, University of Minnesota; Ph.D., University of Texas; Research and publications on language contact, bilingualism and language learning in Vietnamese and Hmong refugee communities.

Timothy Dunnigan:	Associate Professor of Anthropology, University of Minnesota; Ph.D., Scholarly interests include socioeconomic change, linguistic acculturation, and ethnicity in Native American and Southeast Asian cultures.	Publications on the Pima, Ojibwe, Dakota Sioux, and Hmong.

Simon M. Fass:	Assistant Professor of Planning and Public Affairs, Hubert. H. Humphrey Institute of Public Affairs, University of Minnesota; Ph.D. (Planning), University of California at Los Angeles; Ten years of economic development experience in Asia, Africa, Carribbean and North America.

Judith W. Fuller:	Ph.D. candidate, University of Minnesota (Linguistics); B.A. (Psychology) DePauw University; M.A. (Linguistics) University of Minnesota.

Beth L. Goldstein:	Ph.D. candidate, University of Wisconsin-Madison (Educational Policy Studies); Thailand Refugee Instruction Project, Ban Vinai, Thailand; Instructor, Chinese University of Hong Kong.

Karen R. Green: Research Associate, Literacy and Language Program, Northwest Regional Educational Laboratory; B.A. (Spanish), Lewis and Clark College; M.A. (Latin American Studies), The University of California, Los Angeles; specialist in cultural change efforts and literacy and language development among selected ethnic groups; four years of field research with Hmong refugees in the United States.

Catherine S. Gross: Coordinator and Trainer, Intercultural Relations Institute, Palo Alto; Special Curriculum Director, Language Pacifica Institute; B.A. (Anthropology and Sociology), University of California Santa Barbara; TESL Certificate, University of California; ESL Instructor, Indochinese Language and Literacy Project; eleven years overseas experience with Department of State.

Glenn L. Hendricks: Associate Professor of Anthropology; Coordinator, Southeast Asian Refugee Studies Project; University of Minnesota International Student Adviser; research and publications in area of migration and resettlement from Caribbean and Southeast Asia.

Neal R. Holtan: Staff Physician, Department of Medicine, St. Paul-Ramsey Medical Center; Assistant Professor of Medicine, University of Minnesota Medical School; B.A. (Biology), Saint Olaf College; M.D., The University of Iowa; M.P.H. (Epidemiology), The University of Minnesota; American Refugee Committee, Thailand.

Marshall G. Hurlich: Assistant Professor of Anthropology, Department of Anthropology, University of Washington, Seattle; Ph.D. (Physical Anthropology), SUNY-Buffalo; Extensive research with Hmong refugees in the United States, dealing with nutrition, growth and development, demography, resettlement history, secondary migration, sudden unexpected night-time deaths.

Annie C. Jaisser: Graduate student in Linguistics, San Diego State University; B.A. (English and Linguistics), University of Strasbourg, France; M.A. Thesis on Hmong Syntax, San Diego State University, San Diego, California; E.S.L. Instructor, San Diego Community College District.

Gary Y. Lee: Coordinator, Lao Community Advancement Cooperative, Sydney, Australia; Public Relations Officer, Hmong-Australia Society; Youth Development Worker for Indochinese Refugees, Ethnic Communities Council of New

South Wales; Teacher in Social Welfare, Sydney Techni-
cal College; M.A. (Social Work), University of New
South Wales; Ph.D. (social anthropology), University of
Sydney; specialist in Hmong and refugee resettlement.

Jacques Lemoine: Charge de recherche, Centre nationale
de recherche scientifique, Paris; Coordinator of the
Thai and Miao-Yao Projects of CEDRASEMI (School of Advanced Studies in the Social Sciences, Paris).

Sarah R. Mason: Historian, Researcher, Southeast Asian
Refugee Studies Project, University of Minnesota; B.A.
(History) College of Wooster; M.A. and Ph.D. (Asian
History, United States History, United States-Asian Relations) Northern Illinois University; Research Associate, Minnesota Historical Society; specialist in history of Asian and Asian American women; extensive experience in Asia.

William H. Meredith: Assistant Professor, University of
Nebraska-Lincoln; Ph.D. (Community and Human Resources), University of Nebraska-Lincoln.

Shirley G. Moore: Professor of Child Psychology, Institute of Child Development, University of Minnesota; Co-
Director of the Center for Early Education and Development; M.A. (Child Development and Early Childhood Education), University of Iowa, Iowa City; Ph.D. (Child
Psychology), University of Iowa, Iowa City.

Ronald G. Munger: Ph.D. candidate, Department of Anthropology; M.P.H. candidate, Department of Epidemiology,
University of Washington.   Fieldwork on sudden death in
sleep in the U.S., the Philippines, and Thailand.

Sherry Muret-Wagstaff: Director, Southeast Asian Children's Clinic, Hennepin County Medical Center; M.S.
(Public Health), University of Minnesota; Ph.D. student, Institute of Child Development, University of
Minnesota.

Charles N. Oberg: Congressional Science Fellow in Child
Development, Society for Research in Child Development,
Washington Liaison Office, Washington, D.C.; B.A.

(Child Psychology) University of Minnesota; M.D. (Pediatrics) University of Minnesota Medical School and Hospitals; M.P.H. (Maternal and Child Health) University of Minnesota School of Public Health.

Douglas P. Olney: Ph.D. Candidate (Anthropology), University of Minnesota.

Laurel A. Owensby: Graduate student (Linguistics), San Diego State University; Instructor, ESL, San Diego Community College District.

Martha S. Ratliff: Ph.D. candidate (Linguistics), The University of Chicago; Senior Research Associate, The Linguistic Atlas of the Middle and South Atlantic States; B.A. (English), Carleton College; M.A.T. (English Education), The University of Chicago; five years experience teaching ESL to Indochinese.

Stephen Reder: Director, Literacy and Language Program, Northwest Regional Educational Laboratory; B.A. (Psychology), Stanford University; Ph.D. (Cross-cultural Psychology), The Rockefeller University; specialist in literacy and language development among selected ethnic groups; director of research on adult literacy development Southeast Asian refugee English language training, Hmong resettlement and American Samoan adaptation in the United States.

George P. Rowe: Associate Professor, Department of Human Development and the Family, University of Nebraska, Lincoln; Ph.D., Florida State University; has taught at the University of Missouri and North Dakota State University; current teaching and research interests include: families in crises, long-term marriages, and kin relationships in the retirement years.

Louisa Schein: Graduate student (Anthropology), University of California at Berkeley; B.A., Brown University; 1982, Arnold Fellow, Research in Thailand and the People's Republic of China; 1980-81, refugee resettlement work in Providence, Rhode Island; production of documentary "The Best Place to Live" on Hmong resettlement.

William A. Smalley: Professor of Linguistics, Bethel College, St. Paul, Minnesota; Ph.D. (Anthropological Linguistics), Columbia University; researcher and translation consultant in Laos, Thailand and Vietnam; participant in the development of the current romanized Hmong writing system.

Nicholas C. Tapp: Research student, School of Oriental and African Studies, London University; M.A. Hons. Cantab. (English Literature); M.A. (Southeast Asian Studies), London; four years in Thailand, and eighteen months fieldwork with White Hmong for Ph.D. in Social Anthropology.

Xoua Thoa: Student, Dartmouth Medical School, Hanover, New Hampshire; B.A. (Biology), Brown University.

Shur Vang Vangyi: Indochinese Refugee Economic Development Consultant, LTG Associates, San Francisco, California; MBA, United States International University; currently working toward a DBA degree in General Management at the United States International University; four years of experience as Trade Director, Internal and External, for the Laotian Government, Ministry of National Economy; six years experience as Executive Director of Lao Family Community, a nonprofit organization assisting the Indochinese refugees adjusting to their new life in America.

Gail Weinstein: Adult Educator; B.A. (Anthropology); M.S. (TESOL); Ph.D. Candidate (Sociolinguistics), University of Pennsylvania; teaching/travels in China and Thailand; admirer of Hmong people and culture.

INDEX